The Self in Early Modern Literature

Medieval & Renaissance Literary Studies

The

Self in Early Modern Literature

For the Common Good

Terry G. Sherwood

DUQUESNE UNIVERSITY PRESS
Pittsburgh, Pennsylvania

To Nancy

Published in the United States of America by
Duquesne University Press
600 Forbes Avenue
Pittsburgh, Pennsylvania 15282

Library of Congress Cataloging in Publication Data

Sherwood, Terry G. (Terry Grey), 1936–
     The self in early modern literature : for the common good / Terry G.
Sherwood.
          p. cm. — (Medieval & Renaissance Literary Studies)
     Summary: "Responding to the debate stimulated by cultural materialist
     and new historicist claims that the early modern self was fragmented by
     forces in Elizabethan England, Sherwood argues that the self was capable
     of unified subjectivity, demonstrating that the intersection of Protestant
     vocation and Christian civic humanism was a stabilizing factor in the early
     modern construction of self" — Provided by publisher.
     Includes bibliographical references (p.) and index.
     ISBN-13: 978–0–8207–0395–4 (acid-free paper)
     ISBN-10: 0–8207–0395–8 (acid-free paper)
     1. English literature — Early modern, 1500–1700 — History and criticism.
2. Self in literature. 3. Common good. 4. Renaissance — England. 5. England —
Intellectual life — 16th century. 6. England — Intellectual life — 17th century.
I. Title. II. Medieval & Renaissance Literary Studies.
     PR428.S45S54 2007
     820'.9384 — dc22

                                                              2006039055

Contents

Acknowledgments

This book's progress was generously supported by others. A fellowship at the University of Toronto's Centre for Reformation and Renaissance Studies provided a study leave retreat aided by the center's staff. In Victoria, two fellowships at the Centre for Studies in Religion and Society contributed an encouraging research haven within my own university. The staff at several libraries furthered my progress: the Robarts Library and its Toronto affiliates, the Huntington Library, the British Library, and the indispensable McPherson Library at the University of Victoria. To Marnie Swanson, university librarian, I give special thanks for providing carrel space at various times.

Victoria colleagues Edward Berry and Patrick Grant assessed the completed manuscript with characteristic grace and insight. Edward Pechter recommended welcome improvements in the introduction while buoying my sinking spirits. To Thomas Cleary and Joseph Kess I am indebted for moral support. Persons elsewhere include Duquesne University Press's anonymous reader for helpful suggestions, Director Susan Wadsworth-Booth for continuing support, and Stephen Fallon for assessing an early version of the Milton chapter. I thank the editors of *John Donne Journal* for permission to publish from the original version of the Donne chapter.

On previous occasions I have dedicated studies to Nancy, and to Graham and Megan, our son and daughter. They remain in those places deepest in the heart, where Eduardo, Mateo, and Lucas now join them. It is to Nancy, in whom we find our center, that this book is dedicated.

Obeying Time

Shakespeare's King Lear finds his grasp failing in a changed world. Reduced, hedged in and scolded by an unsympathetic daughter, he asks in confusion: "Who is it that can tell me who I am?"[1] The play itself poses this double question: who is he and who can tell him? Precipitous action and self-indulgence have collapsed the frame where he has presided as a king of subjects, a father of children and a master of servants. He no longer knows who and what he is, only that his former self is crumbling and that his identity depends upon others. Further deterioration of mind and body amid the chaos of civil war dramatically inhibits whatever formation of self and identity may be possible in a world of thoroughgoing personal, political and natural disruption.

For many recent critics, *King Lear* supports an influential critique of early modern subjectivity. Lear's disintegration is offered as evidence of a contingent self decentered by dislocations in Elizabethan and Jacobean culture. For Jonathan Dollimore such disintegration as Lear's invalidates any received critical position based upon "essentialist humanism" and its assumption of a centered, unified self.[2] Dollimore was an early and formative voice in a varied chorus including cultural materialist, new historicist, and postmodernist critics, who despite their differences tended

1

to reinforce each other in setting the terms of a continuing debate about early modern subjectivity. Other influential voices included Catherine Belsey, Alan Sinfield, Francis Barker, Stephen Greenblatt, and Louis Montrose. They envisioned a decentered, provisional, contingent self incapable of a unified subjectivity. This is a self constructed by contending historical forces, especially discursive ideologies and power formations.

Claiming a decentered self is not just a theoretical weapon against an allegedly outdated "essentialist humanist" critical position. It expresses a secularized belief about human subjectivity allegedly expressed in early modern works and clarified by late twentieth century assumptions. The success of this secularized claim, by concentrating attention on historically specific cultural discourses said to construct human subjectivity and its representation in literary works, owed much to the kinship between British cultural materialism and American new historicism. Both were indebted to influential French poststructuralist thought, in particular the early works of Michel Foucault.

This secularized orientation, when brought to bear on early modern religious culture, stimulated two related objections in the debate about self that followed. One is the status of inwardness in early modern subjectivity; the other, the necessary religious context for considering the self. Katharine Maus's search for inwardness in Renaissance drama addressed the problematical "claim that a conception of personal inwardness hardly existed at all in Renaissance England."[3] A secular critic herself, she confronted the blinders on modern literary criticism when faced with "Renaissance religious culture that nurtures habits of mind that encourage conceiving of human inwardness."[4] Maus's stance brought her in line with broadening awareness and emphasis in English studies, captured in Debora Shuger's explicit reminders, that we are dealing with a religious culture: "Religion during this period supplies the primary language of analysis. It is the cultural matrix for explorations of virtually every topic: kingship, selfhood, rationality, language, marriage, ethics, and so forth. Such subjects are, again, not masked by religious discourse but articulated in it; they are considered *in relation to* God and the human soul.

That is what it means to say that the English Renaissance was a religious culture, not simply a culture whose members generally were religious."[5] It is in this spirit that we need to engage the lingering presumption of a decentered self in early modern subjectivity.

The current study, which argues that the intersection of Protestant vocation and Christian civic humanism as a stabilizing factor in early modern construction of self in support of the common good, enters a continuing debate by interrogating claims of radical discontinuity in a "contingent" and "fragmented" self. To ignore this source of stability is to ignore a crucial element in what Judy Kronenfeld has aptly called the "sheer magnitude and weight of Christianity in the Renaissance."[6] She rightly argues that a pervasive cultural discourse allowed rigorously opposing and often-divisive perspectives on crucial cultural issues while nonetheless preserving a common ground of Christian values. On that common ground we can find the answer to Lear's question about the source of his identity, and not in a poststructuralist argument about cultural dislocations.[7] But before looking in detail at the stabilizing combination of Protestant vocation and Christian humanism as a necessary perspective on Lear's plight, there are some related issues in the debate about the self that deserve our attention.

A slippery problem of terminology is implicated in these issues. Two influential, early titles highlight the problem: one, *The Subject of Tragedy* by Catherine Belsey; the other, *Renaissance Self-Fashioning* by Stephen Greenblatt. John Lee has complained that when discussing subjectivity, Belsey, Dollimore, and Greenblatt "collapse terms such as 'the self,' the 'human subject,' and 'identity' into one another."[8] Admittedly, some slurring of categories is unavoidable given the absence of an explicit, developed notion of "self" in the early modern period and a need for comprehensible terminology in our time. More significant is that Belsey and Dollimore, in settling for "subject," and Greenblatt for "self" and "identity," pursue different ends. For Belsey the "subject" is the site of contending social and cultural discourses, a "destination of meaning," a fragmented participant in a "range of subject-positions defined by the discourses."[9] Her depersonalized language, while stressing the overriding role of social and cultural construction, assumes subjection to external forces. However, her preference for "subject" ignores factors usually taken for granted in our informal considerations of "self" and individual identity. At the same time she ignores inwardness, agency and individuality conceived as givens in unitary consciousness of the later bourgeois culture's misguided conception of self. In contrast, Greenblatt's humanized "self" reflects his original project to "analyse" how "major English writers of the sixteenth century created their own performances, to analyze the choices they made in representing themselves and in fashioning characters, to understand the role of human autonomy in the construction of identity." Ironically, his project led to an unexpected conviction that the human self was a contradictory, disunified "cultural artifact" produced by "relations of power" and lacking in autonomy, free agency, and unified consciousness.[10] Like Belsey in discovering, in general, a decentered construct, he is sensitively attuned to the individualized self-fashionings of persons he discusses, whether real or literary. He appreciates the contradictory humanity of early modern writers and their literary representations. Greenblatt does not dehumanize his portrait of "self," though he denies a unified self-constituting consciousness. Greenblatt's "self," however decentered and constituted by external factors, is not dehumanized and is even allowed inwardness, as in his characterizations of More and Wyatt.

This juxtaposition of Belsey and Greenblatt points to factors, both absent and present, that distinguish debate about "self" or "subject" as it developed. Conspicuously absent in discussion of both Belsey's depersonalized "subject" and Greenblatt's more fully conceived "self" is a common and everywhere-present early modern terminology of "person." Oddly, this vocabulary is also excluded from later debate despite its centrality in important texts like Spenser's *The Fairie Queene,* discussed at length in chapter one, and in Donne's sermons as we will see later in this introductory chapter. The *OED* illustrates one meaning of "person" — "an individual human being" — with a King James Bible reference to "ninety and nine just persons" (Luke 15.7) in the lost sheep parable. The absence of "person" as a working term alongside "self" and sometimes "subject" and "identity" is particularly conspicuous in Greenblatt's case, given his theatrical notion of self-fashioning. Alternatively, "person" was a "character sustained or assumed in a drama or the like, or in active life" (*OED*); to "personate" is "to act or play a part of any person" (*OED*). It is fair to say that self-fashioning includes "personation." No less fair to say is that the contemporary "person," as discussed later in commentary on Spenser and Donne, contributes much to debate about early modern "self." The "individual human being," the "person," was conceived as having outward physical identity informed by an inward intellectual and spiritual presence.

Attempts to define inwardness became an important stage in debate about the early modern subjectivity. Greenblatt avoided a general tendency in new historicism and cultural materialism to downplay the importance of inwardness. The cultural materialist, Alan Sinfield, was another exception by narrowly focusing on "Puritan" self-scrutiny as a product of aggressively ideological Calvinism with its emphasis on the "intense and immediate relationship" between a sinful believer and a predestining god.[11] Despite such exceptions, the general tendency to overlook inwardness expressed a strongly secular orientation encouraged by residual Marxist materialism later tutored by a poststructuralist conviction that individuals are constructed by social ideologies. Katharine Maus, in her search to find inwardness expressed in the popular drama, usefully reminded readers that early modern religious belief provided cultural grounds that created pervasive inwardness as a contemporary mode of being that must be understood on its own terms: "Renaissance religious culture thus nurtures habits of mind that encourage conceiving of human inwardness, like other truths, as at once privileged and elusive, an absent presence 'interpreted' to observers by ambiguous inklings and tokens."[12] Despite her useful injunction to understand inwardness as a cultural habit necessary for understanding the early modern "self," she surrenders to other secularist shortcomings. Just as she does not recognize in the contemporary "person" another appropriate context for understanding inwardness, she ultimately contributes to the misconception of a radically disunified self, a profound "discrepancy between 'inward disposition' and 'outward appearance.'"[13] For her, the "absent presence" of inwardness, interior self, is a safe place to hide from external pressures, the outward world. Signals of hidden inwardness in dramatic representations reveal a broader cultural habit formed by enforced religious conformity inviting equivocation, unadmitted Machiavellian subversion, sexual secrecy, and forms of false pretense and hypocrisy, to name a few. What the drama represents is ways by which this inner self is revealed only by "ambiguous inklings and tokens." Outward belies inward; what you see is not what you get; the self is divided. Like those before her in the debate, her concentration on theatrical examples emphasizes cultural dislocation and not continuity, the concealment that separates inward from outward self.

But if we go beyond the theater with its tragic representations and look for continuities elsewhere, both inward and outward, a different kind of debate emerges. Robert Ellrodt finds an "unchanging self" manifest in metaphysical poetry that confronts the postmodernist "'Lacan/Barthes/Derrida line'"[14] and its denial of essential authorial identity. Ellrodt arms his strong objections to "postmodernist cognitive relativism"[15] not only with modern psychological theory but, more important, with patient comparative reading of this group of poets. He finds in each poet what he finds in Donne, "permanent modes of imagination and sensibility of their unique creator."[16] Such permanency suggests at least a stable working center in the self. Ellrodt's stubborn opposition to postmodern cognitive relativism reinforces a common sense reaction that an individual self is more than an anonymous, provisional construction of social and cultural forces. However, his selective support from modern psychology is vulnerable to a cultural materialist reaction that such support is produced by a contending ideology with no just claim to essential objectivity. Notably, however, Ellrodt's concentration on the lyric, a form devoted to "self-consciousness," sidesteps drama's attention to the social self and related allegations that the "subject" is a frag-mented construct lacking in stable continuities.

Taken together, Ellrodt's "unchanging self" on one side and cul-tural materialism's decentered "subject" on the other should not be seen to illustrate an intransigent polarity. Instead, this appar-ent polarity cautions us against restricting the boundaries of debate on early modern subjectivity too narrowly. Salutary com-mentaries by Maus and Ellrodt on early modern subjectivity are governed by their limitations. While underlining the importance of inwardness, Maus largely bypasses lyric as a primary measure of early modern self-consciousness and self-reflexiveness; and Ellrodt filters out consciousness of social participation that per-vades even religious inwardness. Maus's conception of humans as beings bifurcated between inward and outward life bypasses the unifying subjectivity of those who think and act in concert with dominant cultural values. For his part, Ellrodt removes from the "unchanging self" those habits of shared cultural participa-tion that inform self-awareness and, in various ways, ensure con-tinuities and resist change.

Continuities inherent in cultural participation that infuse inward life must be included in further debate about early mod-ern subjectivity. These continuities are the subject of the current study. The notion of a "decentered self," schooled as it is by late twentieth century postmodernist relativism, political skepti-cism, and suspicion sustained by the abuses of power, underesti-mates the force of these continuities that stabilize the self. Support for this notion of decentering also tends to ignore how these con-tinuities inform representations of self in major literary texts of the period. Ellrodt's salutary reaction against decentering applies primarily to literary *genera* representing continuities of human consciousness. But, as I shall argue in the chapters that follow, claims of a decentered or fragmented self are no less vulnerable in the context of major literary works that represent participat-ing members of society.

Assumptions of Christian humanism and Protestant vocation, both separate and together, left indelible marks on the modern self. The following study of five major early modern writers, while sympathizing with Ellrodt's strong resistance to claims of a radically decentered self, shifts the grounds of debate to responsibilities binding the self to others for common good. However much they differ in some assumptions, particularly the limits of human capacity and the reach of divine intervention, both Christian civic humanism and Protestant vocation stress the importance of responsibly serving common good. This widely held cultural assumption withstood dislocations that opposed moderate Catholic Reform to Reformed Protestantism, "Anglican" to "Puritan," new science to old, monarchical absolutism to parliamentary republicanism. Responsible contribution to common good stabilized and sustained the self.

To be sure, a cultural materialist might view contending notions of social responsibility as further evidence of a worldview coming unglued. Service in an absolute monarchy versus service in a constitutional republic is a possible case in point. The ardent divide distancing Edward Coke's defense of common law and judicial courts from Francis Bacon's argument for civil law and royalist prerogative was widened further by personal animosity and contending ambitions. That divide, nonetheless, cannot obscure a shared dedication to stabilizing English law and justice.[17] The unifying commitment to common good, which emerges in representations of self variously stamped by elements of Christian civic humanism and Protestant vocation, links the works of major writers examined in chapters that follow. Included are Spenser's "gentleman or noble person," Shakespeare's characterization of Hal/Henry, the vocational Donne, the center of "truth" in Jonson, and self-defense in Milton. Claims that the "self" or "person" or "subject" became unstuck in early modern literature are strongly opposed by adhesive bonds of responsibility to common good.

An Intersection of Values

Philip Sidney's passing reference to poetry as his "unelected vocation"[18] points to that often uneasy marriage of assumptions from Christian civic humanism and Protestant vocation that strengthened the self's participation in common good. However fleeting, Sidney's reference in *The Defence of Poetry* carries the burden of his own personal history. A gentleman with close family ties to an aggressively Protestant circle surrounding the Duke of Leicester, Sidney was born on a vocational pathway set out by his father, Henry Sidney, a high level public servant to the Elizabethan crown. This pathway leading to important public service included a Christian humanist education presided over by Reformed Protestants,[19] followed by three years studying and traveling on the continent while mentored by a much-respected Huegenot diplomat and humanist, Herbert Languet. This carefully designed pathway was ultimately blocked by unresolved differences between Sidney and Queen Elizabeth. "Unelected" poetry was not his first choice.

The ambiguous "unelected" alludes to the divine role in his vocational experience. Its more immediate meaning is that public service was his first choice, not poetry. However, it also plays on the central Reformed tenet of divine election, God's active hand in particular human experience. Even though Sidney had envisioned public service as his vocation, God may have chosen for him a different pathway, however winding. Vocation as defined by William Perkins, the most significant English Calvinist theologian of Elizabethan times, gives a useful perspective on this ambiguity: "A vocation or calling, is a certaine kinde of life, ordained and imposed on man by God, for the common good."[20] It is God who determines what vocation is fit for the believer. God's call may delay the believer's first choice or not lead to it at all. Like the Duke of Leicester and, later, the Earl of Essex, Sidney favored a militant pursuit of the Protestant cause against continental Catholicism. Outspoken opposition to Elizabeth's cautious restraint compromised his opportunity to fulfil his elected vocational goals. Ironically, his "unelected" vocation included a humanist defense of poetry encouraging virtue necessary for active life. We are left to assume that, for Sidney, the constant in both vocations, elected and unelected, was active life serving common good, both in word and deed.

Like Spenser, Sidney was variously informed by the Reformation and by Christian humanism, the two most significant cultural influences in sixteenth century England. Focused and encouraged by Erasmus, Catholic humanism of early sixteenth century was less pushed aside then overtaken by Reformed thought, first Lutheran, then Calvinistic. Ascendancy of more radical reform, in which debate on free will between Erasmus and Luther is an early benchmark, led ultimately to an encroaching Calvinism much later in Elizabethan and early Stuart England. The temperate, rational pietism of Erasmus's widely influential *Enchiridion militis christiani* yielded to a more strenuous Reformed emphasis on justification by faith, dependence on Grace, and divine election that was strengthened, not weakened, by Marian oppression. But the reproduction of Erasmian texts throughout the sixteenth century reflects both Erasmus' lengthened shadow and the continuity of humanist ideas stretching well into the seventeenth century.[21] In general, humanistic endorsement of pagan moral and political thought, as well as intimacy with original texts, indelibly marked the education of early modern Protestant English ruling classes. Such markings can be found later even in the "hotter" Protestantism of the Calvinistic "Puritans," or whom Alan Sinfield calls "Puritan humanists."[22] Much earlier, the humanistic piety of Erasmus's *Enchiridion* had been embraced by many within Henry's court, including Catherine Parr, whose broad educational influence stretched as far as the young Princess Elizabeth. The longevity of *Enchiridion* in the century and after[23] bears witness to its influential humanistic emphasis on moral philosophy; virtuous, active commitment to common good; and a lay person's direct access to sacred texts. Such Christian humanist principles continued to inform Reformed culture, especially social thought. Long before Sidney's citations in the *Defence,* the *Enchiridion* endorsed the virtuous example of Aeneas.[24] A look in more detail at the *Enchiridion's* relationship to texts by Cicero further reveals the deep roots in the cultural heritage, which reach into the seventeenth century and the authors we will examine.

The *Enchiridion* resembles Stoic moral handbooks such as Cicero's *De Officiis* or Epictetus's *Enchiridion* as well as

Augustine's spiritual handbook *Enchiridion*.[25] Erasmus's work is a handbook of Christian piety that respects pagan moral philosophy. Its *philosophia Christi* assumes an individual believer's unmediated access to sacred scripture while guided by reason and supplemented by pagan thought. Its spirituality, its prayerful inwardness, is compatible with active moral life in the world and opposes monastic retreat. Prayer and learning, the two independent major "weapons" of Christ's active soldiers, arm a Christian piety in the world exercised by reason: "Devout prayer raises our desires to heaven, a stronghold inaccessible to the enemy, and the knowledge in turn fortifies the intellect with salutary opinions that one will not be lacking to the other. 'Each asks the other's aid / and makes with a friendly pact' [Horace, *Ars Poetica*, 409–10]. One makes prayerful entreaty; the other suggests what should be prayed for. Faith and hope ensure that you pray ardently and, as St. James says, 'free of doubt' [James 1:6]. Knowledge teaches you to pray in the name of Jesus, that is, to ask for things that will lead to your salvation" (*Enchiridion*, 30–31). Scripture is the primary source of knowledge. But a ready validation of pagan literature advances a Christian spirituality inwardly sustained by prayer and outwardly by humanistic learning: "the good precepts of a pagan author should not be rejected, since not even Moses spurned the advice of his father-in-law Jethro." Erasmus extends the boundary further: "it would be profitable to have a taste of all pagan literature" (*Enchiridion*, 33). Reason tastes in order to know, guiding the search for knowledge centered in scripture and strengthening the Christian soldier against ignorance. And, more, reason as "king" through virtue controls passions and conquers the self. The goal for virtuous life is Christ, in whose Father lies essential virtue; to have faith in Christ is to have a moral life. In pursuit of that goal, reason enables the sound learning that gives knowledge; it also presides over the virtuous self-control that incorporates morality in active life according to Christ. Reason's kingship defines a temperate piety that incorporates morality in the inward life of the spirit and grants much to human capacity.

Spirituality imitating Christ includes a social vision serving common good. Scriptural accounts of Christ's words and deeds, imitated by believers, include virtuous action. Designed as a portable handbook, the *Enchiridion* is half-filled with rules to inform both inward devotional practice and outward right action. A primary virtue is charitable service to others in the Body of Christ and in the large social community: "no Christian should think that he was born for himself or should wish to live for himself . . . all that he has or is he should not attribute to himself but accredit to God, its author, and should regard all his goods as common to all . . . No one should pursue merely his own interests, but should contribute to the best of his ability to the common good" (*Enchiridion*, 93, 95). Imitation of Christ central to Erasmian piety necessarily leads to political life, by necessity applying with special force to public officials: "There is no separate Lord for bishops and another for civil magistrates. . . . If you aspire after public office, not to benefit the common good, but to fill your own coffers . . . your office is an act of brigandage in the eyes of God . . . The truth is that you must consider Christ Jesus the Lord of all men and you must resemble him as much as possible, since you take his place" (*Enchiridion*, 98–99). Imitating Christ requires mutual service: public servants, including kings, serve and are served by the people: "the essence of princely power" is to serve "the greatest number possible," to "think only of the public good" (*Enchiridion*, 100). Like all virtuous humans whose desire is raised by prayer and guided by reason to seek knowledge of Christ, princes are responsible to serve others in accordance with virtue. In short, Erasmian piety includes virtue; virtues inform moral action; right actions serve the common good.

His emphasis on an individual's responsibility for the common good, based upon textual authority and virtuous action mediated by reason, placed the writings of Erasmus in the mainstream of English humanist culture. Personal affection for pagan texts warmed his humanist embrace of classical culture, which distinguishes sixteenth century English education. Erasmus edited *De Officiis*, as he had Seneca's moral letters earlier. Cicero's moral handbook along with other texts by Cicero, including *De Oratore*,[26] were standard within the mainstream educational tradition that fashioned English public servants and writers like Sidney and

Spenser. Like *Enchiridion*, this handbook tells us much about humanistic assumptions.

Closely allied with Christian humanism, these two handbooks stand on the same ground in endorsing participation in common good, for Erasmus through likeness to Christ, for Cicero by following Nature. Citing the Stoics, Cicero affirms that all earthly products are "created for man's use"; so, too, "men . . . are born for the sake of men, that they may be able mutually to help one another." It is Nature that guides humans "to contribute to the general good" through mutual benefit (*De Officiis*, 1.22).[27] By nature social, humans exist for others through commitment to common good. All social life, private and public, including public service, is guided by virtue that is encouraged by this moral handbook. Private and public share the same moral foundation. Humans are mutually bonded through *officia*, variously translated as mutual "responsibilities," "duties," "dutiful services," and "kind services" to each other emerging from their respective roles in the social scheme.[28] Cicero assumes the Stoic notion of "appropriate action" for a given role.[29] Dutiful service to other humans by pursuing what is commonly good for others is necessary to an active life within the community. For Erasmus, to serve common good is to follow Christ's example; for Cicero, it is to realize an essentially social human nature.[30] In both cases pursuit of active, virtuous lives serving common good confirms the self.

Like the *Enchiridion* of Erasmus, Cicero's moral handbook includes an anatomy of virtues. Along with Aristotle's discussion of virtue in *Nicomachean Ethics*, Cicero's anatomy of four fundamental, interwoven virtues was a staple in humanist discussions of moral philosophy throughout the early modern period. These four virtues assuring moral rectitude or goodness are "sources" of responsibilities or duties (*officia*) to common good. Wisdom distinguishes truth; temperance subdues passion and preserves propriety [*decorum*] (*De Officiis* 1. 93), fortitude ensures the self's greatness. Justice, the most "extensive," is the "principle by which society and what we may call its 'common bonds' are maintained." It is that source of goodness associated with beneficence and liberality (*De Officiis* 1. 20). In short, these four virtues — wisdom, temperance, fortitude, justice — discipline the human self in concert with others in the community.

Intended ruling class readers of Cicero's handbook included his son, in particular, to whom it was addressed, with the expectation that he would play an active, virtuous role in Roman life; more generally, Cicero had in mind other aristocratic readers encouraged to serve common good. Conceived as a living text, like *Enchiridion*, to be incorporated in actual lives, *De Officiis* is also a book of moral philosophy that centers virtue in the *vita activa* while assuming that learning guided by reason informs the pursuit of virtue. Cicero's conception of *studia humanitatis*,[31] learning necessary for dutiful civic life serving the common good, contributed to an educational model developed by early modern English humanists. Appropriately, then, *De Officiis* became a fundamental text in English humanism. Political implications of the common good are rooted in an assumption that human beings are by nature sociable, linguistic beings. One side of the coin is personal virtue; the other side is dutiful public service that sustains community. Neither side can exist without the other. Similarly, the power of speech, which along with reason forms "common bonds" in human "fellowship and society" (1.50), is exercised privately in conversation and publicly in oratory according to rules established by rhetoricians (l. 132). Cicero's *De Oratore*, which like *De Officiis* became a standard text in English early modern humanism, falls into this category. Through acts of reason and speech, "teaching and learning, communicating, discussing and reasoning associate men together and unite them in a sort of natural fraternity" (*De Officiis*, 1.50). The private and the public are distinct, but not separate dimensions; the same virtues prevail in both, and Cicero in *De Officiis* sees private and public life as necessary parts of a natural whole. Dutiful political life is merely the virtuous, communicative, private self acting in the public domain.

Cicero's concept of the private as merely a related expression of the naturally social human self distinguishes him from the

Christian Erasmus, for whom the "private" includes inner spirituality as well as the social. Ultimately, *philosophia Christi* leads in one direction toward political involvement and, in the opposite direction, toward the inner life of Christian prayer. Cicero and Erasmus intersect, but they also differ. And that difference provides a useful foil, in turn, for differences distinguishing Erasmus from Reformed Protestants, for whom vocation bonds the individual to common good. These significant differences, however, cannot obscure a shared sense that individual selves are both identified and stabilized by integration in the community.

Here, we need to look in some detail at vocation's role in commitment to the common good. In England, Reformed "vocation" developed on the heels of Erasmian Christian humanism and stabilized early modern subjectivity. While sharing a humanist emphasis on the individual's participation in the common good, the Reformed notion accentuates the divine role in "calling" believers to perform specific work in the world as a fulfillment of a worshipful relationship to God. Reformed thought carried humanist emphases further while, on one hand, emphasizing God's more active intervention in individual lives and, on the other hand, aiming more broadly at all human beings, not just a ruling elite. Such notions, which developed in the lengthened shadow of Luther and Calvin, emphasized a more direct relationship to God consistent with Reformed anticlericalism and the priesthood of all believers. But it left more in God's hands and granted less to powers of human initiative inherent in Erasmian *philosphia Christi* and sustained by classical humanism. Debate between Erasmus and Luther is thus an important benchmark in the differing notions of human capacity in relation to God.

Humanist thought, having been entrenched increasingly in English culture generally and in elitist education particularly, was gradually overtaken by Reformed thought in Edward VI's time. Until then, William Marshall notes, discussions of Reformed vocation were scattered and tightly enclosed by medieval assumptions of fixed, hierarchical estates resistant to the Reformed emphasis on believers called individually by God and sanctified through work. In fact, the first full-scale English treatment awaited the Calvinist William Perkins's *The Treatise of the Vocations*, written in the 1590s, but not published until 1603. Nonetheless, vocation had already been addressed in the first edition of the official Elizabethan homilies published in 1547.[32] Marshall locates a midcentury watershed: "It was in the 'Commonwealth Party' that the idea of calling flowered in English. It formed the core of the party adherents' views on social duty, and then became widespread throughout the country.[33] Commonwealth men were largely, though not exclusively, "radical Protestants" who, as Quentin Skinner puts it, "tended to be strongly humanist in their education and allegiance — a further proof of close spiritual connections between humanism and the Puritan movement."[34] A. N. McLaren provides a variation on this theme: "the commonwealth ideology exemplified the mixed ideals of Protestant refor-mation in linking theological with social reform in a new framework of national election."[35] Ardent social critics like the early Catholic humanists targeted social injustice and disruptive pursuit of personal wealth; their views remained central in Elizabeth's reign. Skinner notes that the "basic aim of these moralists" was to "identify and denounce the various social groups for undermining this traditional concept of the public good."[36] Their numbers included important Protestants like Hugh Latimer, Thomas Becon, Thomas Lever, Robert Crowley, John Hales, and Thomas Smith.

Smith is the presumed author of *A Discourse of the Commonweal of This Realm of England*, regarded as the most significant work to emerge from this group.[37] Written in 1549, though not published until 1581, and even then anonymously, "it offers one of the most sophisticated surveys of the political as well as economic philosophy associated with the Commonwealth group."[38] Impressively learned, Smith was a moderate Protestant, distinguished humanist, and experienced civil servant. And he was a product and one-time vice chancellor of Cambridge University, at that time a primary incubator of both Ciceronian *studia human-*

itatis and Reformed thought. Later, he served as principal secretary to Edward VI's Lord Protector, the Duke of Somerset, then several times as a member of Parliament and as a frequent ambassador to France. In late career he served on Elizabeth's Privy Council. Written by an important public servant, *Discourse* was a diagnostic response, in dialogue form, to a contemporary economic and political malaise afflicting England. Symptoms included selfish enclosure of public lands, nagging inflation, corrupted currency, and a punishing "dearth" of usable goods. The same nagging problems were present in 1581 at the time of the book's posthumous publication. The dialogue features a knight/gentleman, a husbandman, a merchant, a capper [capmaker], and Smith's spokesperson, the learned Doctor Pandotheus, a legal expert. A festive dinner follows a troublesome day during which the knight and other justices of the peace of the King's High Commission have conducted hearings on the disruptive enclosure problem. Though wearied by these hearings, the Knight allows that "the King must be served and the Commonweal. For God and the King have not sent us the poor living we have but to do service broad among our neighbors" (*Discourse*, 16). The doctor's response, a strategic keynote at the dialogue's outset, establishes the philosophical basis of all service. Mary Dewar points to Smith's reliance here on both Plato and Cicero[39] in establishing a foundation for his detailed diagnosis of contemporary economical problems and their moral, social, and political implications: "It is well if you take it so; for nature has grafted that persuasion in you and all others that follow the clear light of nature. As learned men have remembered, saying, we be not born only to ourselves but partly to the use of our country, of our parents, and of our kinfolk, and partly of our friends and neighbors. And therefore all good virtues are grafted in us naturally, whose effects be to do good to others, wherein shows forth the image of God in man whose property is ever to do good to others and to distribute his goodness abroad, like no niggard nor envious thing" (*Discourse*, 16). For Smith this broad, multiple commitment to the common good separates humans from animals. Undergirding his searching social criticism

of contemporary shortcomings is a notion of an ideal commonwealth.

The aggressive social criticism of the more radical commonwealth man and reformer, Robert Crowley, likewise assumes
an idealized notion. Crowley's *The voyce of the Laste Trumpet . . .
callyng al estats of men to the ryght path of theyr vocacions*
(1549) is reductively schematized according to responsibilities of
different vocations. Twelve separate, doggerel "lessons" that comprise the work express the trumpet's "voyce," modeled after
John's "seventh Angel (as mentioned in the elleuenth of the
Apocalips) callyung all estats of men to the ryght path of theyr
vocation."[40] Respective vocations will hear their respective
"fautes" so that they "myght them emende" ("The Boke to the
Readar," 13). Crowley's stair-stepping vocational roster rises from
beggar, servant, yeoman to priest, scholar, learned man to physician, lawyer, merchant to gentleman, magistrate. In a different
register his "call" concludes with inclusive "woman." Crowley's
apocalyptic trumpet in "calling" to each vocation in the commonwealth recapitulates God's unifying call to all vocations.

His book itself "calls" sinners to fulfil their duties, spelled out
negatively according to "fautes" of individual callings. Unfulfilled
vocations threaten social order within the commonweal that is
necessarily sustained by prescribed vocational duties in each
degree of each estate. Stewardship of land itself is pivotal. Crowley
shares Smith's social concern with selfishly ambitious merchants
who prepare to vault their offspring into gentility by accumulating money to buy property. He no less targets pleasure seeking,
landed gentles whose excessive rental fees sap lower classes.
A shared "faute" is selfish misuse of property. More specifically,
the merchant's buying and selling must be guided by "loue and
charity," reaching "Unto all the Lordes creatures" (1151–52) while
following fair, just practices. The "lesson" taught to merchants
applies to all: "Apply thy trade therfore, I sai,/ To profit thy coun-
trey with al" (1029–30). Gentlemen must pursue the same end,
the common good, according to their place in a hereditary class
"borne to lande and rente" (1177). Selfish pleasures — "To dice,

to carde, or to reuell" (1202) — are a "faute" endemic to that class that violates "vseyng thyne owne callyng well" (1204). Property requires attentive stewardship, duties to do right by those that rent and work the land. As with a king and his subjects, fair treatment is obligatory. Expensive pleasures infect the dutiful management of land and the fairness to tenants inherent in a gentleman's vocation.

Ideally, vocations stand in harmony. Those related to proper land use should be coordinated with those preserving communal order through law, justice, and power. Similarly, learning that trains and maintains wise thought and action should encourage harmony. Priestly ignorance is a violation to "walke forth in thy callynge" (516): an injunction to teach ignorant parishioners how to read confirms the Reformed endorsement of the vernacular Bible and individual believers' private access to divine truth. Reinforcing the humanist conviction of learning's importance is a lesson for a young "scholar" to work harder at his studies so that he not "rob the commone wealth / Of one that would be a treasur" (585–86). A "Learned Man" in the making, a scholar is a person appropriate for many roles, whether to teach the young or to counsel the King. And scholarly habits of learning must inform all those with the duty of ensuring order through law. Lawyer and judge work together to protect others in the commonwealth. The lawyer must bear in mind the purpose of the law:

> Fyrst call vnto thy memorye
> For what cause the laws wer fyrst made;
> And then apply the busily
> To the same ende to vse thy trade.

> (901–04)

Greed diverts a lawyer from his duty; bribes divert a judge. But those vocations when "grounded on good lawes" (952), that is, upon knowledge of traditional "commune lawes" (994), protect the commonwealth and those in it. Power to enforce law, "To beare the swerd of punishment" (1338), lies with the magistrate to "se that all good statues be / Executed before al thynge" (1395–96).

Such power requires learning, and it is in the crown that law, justice, learning, and power merge. The chief magistrate, sensitive to learned counsel, exerts power according to law and justice. The magistrate's evaluation of evidence, assessment of witnesses, judgments rendered and enforced are all informed by "workes of writers olde" (1378). Such learned action, "the chief dutie" of his "state and vocation" (1387–88), supports the vocational duties of others in the commonwealth. Appropriately, Crowley's Pauline refrain unifying the *Trumpet* requires each person, magistrates not least of all, to "walke in thy vocacion" (1492).[41]

The coalescence of civic humanism and Reformed thought in Philip Sidney noted earlier also distinguishes the mid-sixteenth century works of Crowley and Smith. Sharp differences in temperament and audience do not obscure their shared emphasis upon social responsibility. Doggerel simplicity, moral bluntness, and programmatic structure in Crowley's 12-part *Trumpet* suit a social criticism aimed at a broad audience and expressed a stormy, insubordinate nature driven by vocational sense of duty to correct "fautes" and, on occasion, to defy ecclesiastical authority. In contrast, skillful dialogic nuances in Smith's *Discourse* speak to a less popular, more reflective audience from a philosophically tempered, courageous public servant and diplomat. But both have in mind the active work of individual selves within the commonwealth, however varied their vocational roles and personal temperaments.

Behind Crowley's detailed roster of vocations lies notions of Martin Luther and John Calvin. With Luther, vocation included all roles played by humans when called by God, not just the priestly class; and with Calvin "vocation" more pointedly included all legitimate occupations that contributed economically to common good. A revised relationship between the individual and God resulting from direct access to sacred scripture, effected through Erasmus, Tyndale, and others, was thus revised further by Reformed theology of the indwelling spirit and doctrine of vocation that revalued all forms of work. All believers walking in their vocations served both God and common good. Put differently, working in one's vocation was a form of worshipping God, and all persons walking in their vocations were equal in God's eyes.

The value of work was not a uniquely Protestant emphasis. Reforming Catholic humanists of the early sixteenth century no more privileged the clerical calling than did Protestants later, and they also regarded idleness and greed as both personal and social evils. As Margot Todd puts it, with Erasmus as one example, idleness particularly offended the commonwealth: "They clearly saw idleness as more than an individual failing: it is rather an offense against the commonwealth — in Erasmus' opinion, the source of most evil in the state. Erasmus compared idleness to a contagious disease, which infects the whole society with poverty, exploitation and inequity."[42] Leisure class pleasures of nobles and self-indulgent idleness of priests were both targets in the humanists' respect for labor. Another direct line can be traced from the charitable concern for the poor expressed by Crowley and Smith to Catholic humanists earlier. Employment of the willing poor claimed a high priority in humanist thinking and social planning. The uneasy marriage later between civic humanism and the Reformed theology of vocation included a respect for labor as well as a commitment to the commonwealth. Humanist commitment to a specified *vita activa* helped make that match. Cicero's *"genus vitae" (De Officiis,* 1.117,120), sometimes translated as "vocation" (wrongly, except in our loosened modern sense), nonetheless strikes a chord similar to William Perkins's definition of calling as "a certaine kinde of life, ordained and imposed on man by God, for the common go[o]d." Differences between the two notions need to be spelled out, but even more we need to underline the shared commitment to common good linking them together.

God's active role in human life, "imposed" through election and stressed by the Reformed conviction of divine intervention in human affairs, brings us to the late-century influence of William Perkins. His widely shared distinction between the general and particular calling descended from Calvin.[43] This double action as conceived by Perkins includes a call to salvation within the church, then a personal call to individuals to take up a defined action: "The generall calling is the calling of Christianity, which is common to all that liue in the Church of God. The particular, is that special calling that belongs to some particular men: as the calling of a Magistrate, the calling of a Minister, the calling of a Master, of a father, of a childe, of a seruant, of a subiect, or any other calling that is common to all" (*Vocations,* 752). God is "author" of every calling. Paul's injunction, recycled as Crowley's refrain, also serves Perkins as a frequent reminder enunciating the expected human response: "As God hath called every man, let him Walke."[44] God's authorship carries a necessary caveat that the calling must be a "lawfull" response to God's will, not a *sub rosa* activity like usury, dicing, or gaming (750).

For Perkins, "imposition" of a calling occurs when God "doth particularly set apart any man, to any particular calling; and this must be understood of all callings in the world" (751). There are two ways: God may speak directly to a believer as when calling Adam to dress the garden, or indirectly through human and angelic intermediaries, including preestablished roles in both church and commonwealth. The troublesome "imposed" is partially mollified by noting God's establishment of human social frames: "God in his word hath ordained the societie of man with man, partly in Common-wealth, partly in the Church, and partly in the family; it is not the will of God that man should liue and conuerse alone by himselfe" (755). God also ordains that various persons will be distinguished by different functions within these frames hierarchically. Perkins has in mind various estates and degrees within which humans are born with varyingly appropriate gifts. By inference, humans come with a disposition for a specific role within a given place. At first glance "imposed" erodes the will's latitude consistent with Perkins's Calvinistic sense of divine election but paradoxically allows choice. "Every man must choose a fit calling to walke in; that is, every calling must be fitted to the man, and every man be fitted to his calling" (758).[45] Yet the ambiguity of Sidney's "unelected" calling reminds us that divine pressures of Reformed thought do constrict this choice. Life "imposed" seems no less ambiguous in recalling both hands laid on in blessing and the authority of office bestowed as a burden (*OED*).

This imposed way of life categorically situates believers within both church and commonwealth, serving God by serving others through vocational labors. Perkins, when pinpointing the "finall cause or ende or euery calling," circles back on his own definition: "I note in the last words of the description; *For the common good:* that is, for the benefite and good estate of mankinde. In mans body there bee sundrie parts and members, and euery one hath his seuerall use and office, which it performeth not for it selfe, but for the good of the whole bodie" (751). To follow Paul, and Crowley, and walk in a vocation is to perform those "works" or "labours" that contribute to common good. All vocations exist reciprocally within collective Bodies of family, church, and commonwealth in mutual service to God. Each person walks and works within the "compasse" (751) of a calling that includes specific duties consistent with the general calling of all Christians that "common is to all that liue in the Church of God." For Perkins "common good" clearly articulates with the "generall" vocation, which contains the "particular."

Here, I have been arguing for the common good as a cultural ideal dispersed very broadly among sixteenth century commentators. Crowley and Smith join together against selfishness corrupting that idea. Subordination of church to crown in official Elizabethan policy is reversed in Perkins's thought, thereby placing him on the opposite side of the divide from Richard Hooker, the other most important Protestant theologian of late Tudor England. Nonetheless, they shared a cultural commitment to common good that remained a defining continuity in the early modern self. Such continuity needs to be understood in light of the ways of obedience and patterns of service in hierarchical society. However contradictory, as we will see next, obedience in particular is a constant in early modern subjectivity that positions us for viewing much at issue in King Lear's plight.

Frames of Obedience

Perkins viewed vocation as a life of obedience. Obedient response to both general and particular callings defines a believer's relationship to God and others. A pastoral exhortation puts it in a nutshell: "Exercise thyself to eschew every sin and to obey God in every one of his commandments that pertain either to the general calling of a Christian, or to thy particular calling."[46] In both callings the believer "is bound" by the general calling to obey God's commandments "in all good conscience" (*Vocations*, 776). In each particular calling, works contributing to common good are made holy when "done in faith and obedience" serving "Gods glory" (778). Here is a resilient cultural disposition to obedience and service that shaped the early modern self and stood against dislocating historical crosscurrents. Contributions to selfhood from Christian humanism and Protestant vocation cannot be understood without reference to this continuing disposition. Crosscurrents threatening this disposition will eventually bring us back to *King Lear* in terms of ironies of obedience and service distinguishing early modern history and thought.

Obedience was a given in the early modern self, but not without a sense of the ironic complexities that reveal its profundities as a cultural habit. A direct thematic line leads from the state-sanctioned homilies of the Elizabethan church, which required obedience to the Crown, to Donne's *Pseudo Martyr*. The personal history leading Donne to this text was tortuous. Here, in his first text written for a public audience, this one-time Catholic urged English Catholics to take the Oath of Allegiance to the Protestant Stuart Crown: "the first roote and parent of all propositions in this matter of Obedience" is "*That we must obay such a power, as can preserve us in Peace and Religion.*"[47] Papal authority in England was spiritual, not civil, and Donne urged obedience to James, in disobedience to the Pope's order, thereby avoiding specious suffering. Donne enlisted well-worn biblical support from Paul's command: "*Let every Soule be subject unto the higher powers*" (Rom. 13:11). For an English Catholic taking Donne's advice while continuing in Roman spiritual practices, resulting conflicts would be virtually palpable: this believer would be simultaneously obedient to James, disobedient to the Pope, and obedient to aspects of Catholic doctrine. Paul's universally exploited command was one cultural norm ready at hand; the Son's obedience to the father was another. For George Herbert's suffering Jesus in "The Sacrifice," the multiplying ironies invade each other:

> *Herod* in judgment sits, while I do stand;
> Examines me with a censorious hand;
> I him obey, who all else command
>   Was ever grief & etc.
>
>   (81–84)[48]

The sacrificial son juggles more than one authority: "I him obey." He is submissively obedient to established but murderous civil authority while obediently serving an all-powerful Creator's spiritual authority that he himself shares.

Such ironies, based on clashes between conflicting powers and captured by Donne and Herbert, have a long history. Approximately a century earlier in *The Obedience of a Christian Man*, William Tyndale yoked together two assumptions that progressively pulled apart from each other in radical Reformed thought. Tyndale forcefully argued for hierarchical order necessitating obedience to monarchical authority but, contradictorily, his pervasive Biblical support assumed the individual believer's right of direct access to sacred scripture. Then, Reformed thought, as it evolved from Tyndale to the Puritan revolution much later, had armed the literate conscience with Biblical truth in rejecting obedient submission to monarchical authority. John Milton, working toward a holy commonwealth, had participated in ultimate political disobedience by endorsing regicide. Yet a subjectivity of obedience no less centers his thought than it does Tyndale, Hooker, Donne, and Herbert before him, whatever their differences. Paradise, lost through "Man's First disobedience" (*Paradise Lost* 1.1),[49] is regained by "one man's firm obedience fully tried" (*Paradise Regained* 1.4). The Jesus of *Paradise Regained* faultlessly obeys his father's will while patiently interpreting terms of his divine calling. He deliberately rejects the temptation of political power that would subject others to his monarchical will. His spiritual example will ultimately unsettle existing political realms through obedience to God. Milton's own role in the "Puritan" rebellion against the Stuart monarchy was overt, but his patient Jesus, in submitting to the divine monarchical will, ironically demonstrates a vocational obedience to God that was common in the early modern self, whatever Milton's disobedience to hierarchical earthly power.

A related late-sixteenth century irony shadowed a widening divide separating "Puritan" from "Anglican," the "hotter" sort of Protestant from conforming members of the established church. Both sides incorporated a culturally profound tenet embodied in Milton's great epics. Disobedience against God was primal sin; Christ's obedience was the necessary antidote. David Little shows that the two sides were divided: both sides agreed that obedience was necessary; they disagreed on the object of obedience.[50] We need to pause here for just a moment to underline this necessary point in understanding the early modern self. Like commitment to the common good, obedience was a given. On that point even committed opponents could agree.

A similar opposition came to a head in the heated 1590s debate between the ecclesiastical reformer, Thomas Cartwright, and Elizabeth's Archbishop, William Whitgift. Like Perkins, Cartwright was a willing descendant of Calvin, for whom human disobedience destroyed order, requiring a new system of order to be established through a holy community obedient to God. Believers need look for repair not to the state, which embodies the habits of disobedience, but to a reconstructed, consensual church community. Within that new system of order, believers must obediently submit their wills to God following Christ's command. Although Whitgift owed some theological debts of his own to Calvin, he faced Cartwright from across the divide, defending a traditional hierarchical system of order fundamentally at risk from Cartwright's notion of the church: "Whitgift stands sharply over against the Calvinist Puritan position. Whereas for Calvin,

Cartwright, and Perkins, God's command breaks through the structures of worldly order and calls for a new order with a new kind of obedience, for Whitgift God's command emerges from the structure of things as it already exists. The command of God can in no way be discontinuous with the ways things are, nor can the reverse be true. On the contrary, the divine command issues in the existing order and the existing order gives form and content to the command."[51] Whitgift spoke for the crown as Elizabeth's archbishop, and protector of traditional Christian order. That office must be obeyed: "The rule of obedience, that is betwixt the magistrate and the subject, holdeth twixt the husband the wife, the father and his child, the master and the servant. Therefore measure thou the obedience to the magistrate, as though wouldest they should perform it unto thee."[52] On Whitgift's side of the divide stood Richard Hooker and his *Laws of Ecclesiastical Polity*, the primary theoretical statement defending Whitgift's position. For Hooker, church and commonwealth participated together in one society following divine laws perceived and obeyed by believers. Hooker and Whitgift spoke together in defending obedience to Tudor order. In comparison to Perkins, they endorsed but soft-pedaled the importance of personal vocation, viewed not as edification of the holy community, but as another buttress for the general social order with its established hierarchical places.[53] Whitgift's case against Cartwright follows a steady Tudor course to sustain established order through political obedience.

That course included the official Tudor homilies commanded for universal public reading in English churches, at least one each Sunday. Obedience to this command ensured consistent influence and a continuity of shared public truths. Their universal use in England, extending well into the seventeenth century, cannot be underestimated for they provided a seedbed of widely shared truths expressed in a commonplace vocabulary. These homilies initially served the Tudor monarchy's urgent desire to solidify a Protestant order threatened by competitive Catholic influences. Unvarnished political and Protestant religious motivations led to their publication and obligatory use, the first book under

Edward in 1547, the second under Elizabeth in 1563, to which was added *An Homelie against Disobedience and Wylfull Rebellion* in 1570. A bold claim that the "Holy Word" teaches "delight in obedience as the beginning and foundation of al goodness" clearly intends to arm a monarchical regime against civil unrest (*Homilies*, 236). More broadly, it encourages the disposition to obedience pervasive in sixteenth and seventeenth century English political life.

Among the official homilies, "An Homelie against Disobedience and Wylfull Rebellion" and "An Exhortacion concerning Good Order and Obedience to Rulers and Magistrates" used the basic terms in this disposition that influenced the Tudor notion of self. A traditional set of assumptions is clearly at work in these two homilies. Hierarchical order descends from God downward through princes and magistrates to subjects; through masters, husbands, and fathers respectively to their servants, wives, and offspring. Superiors command inferiors, whose obedience deserves the blessings of order. The fall through disobedience disrupted created order, and by divine command Christ obediently suffered to provide a restoring pattern through his teachings and actions. Scripture commands obedience to that pattern, to necessary laws, and to civil authorities appointed by God to maintain order: "Let us considre the Scriptures of the Holy Ghost, whiche perswade and commaunde us all obediently to be subject: first and chiefly, to the Kynges majestie, supreme hed over all, and next, to his honorable counsail, and to all other noble men, magistrates and officers, which by gods goodnes be placed and ordered" (*Homilies*, 162). Obedience to God requires obedience to civil authority; spiritual and political obedience merge.

Two biblical texts receive the closest attention. These "two special places out of the New Tastament," in Paul and in Peter, "stand in steade of all other." Paul commanded the Romans (13:1), as we have already noted in Donne's *Pseudo Martyr*, "to be subject unto the higher powers, for there is no power but of God, and the powers that be are ordayned of God" (211). To resist these civil powers is to resist God; and to resist God invites damnation, a fearsome punishment. A magistrate is a "minister of God, to take vengeaunce upon hym that doth evill" (163); and "if thou do evyl, feare" (211). The Pauline gist, as the homily on obedience tells its audience, is "bounden duetie . . . in conscience, obedience, submission and subjection to the high powers" (163). In turn, Peter's command (1 Pet. 2:13) to "Submit yourselves unto al maner ordinaunce of man for the Lordes sake" (211) is applied to both kings and their agents. Superiors are to be honored, feared, and obeyed, even when in error. The homilies represent Paul and Peter as God's agents who, in commanding fearful submission, subjection, and obedience to civil powers, served God's order. Their message is that even bad kings, as inadvertent servants of God, must be obeyed. The emphasis on fear is noticeably consistent with Whitgift, as noted earlier.

Fear that drives submission, subjection, and obedience to civil authority counters a rebellion against established order. The ultimate negative example, the rebel Lucifer, kindled God's wrath; his fearsome punishment, damnation, awaits other rebels as well. Much to be feared as provoking divine wrath, rebellion's main causes are ambition and ignorance. A partisan Protestantism in the homilies compulsively targets papal ambition as the main cause of rebellion and exploits widespread anxiety about disorder. Protestant knowledge of God through Scriptural study is enjoined to combat papal manipulation of ignorance. Just beneath the surface lies the implied threat of divine wrath for ignoring the Protestant truths offered in the homilies. The northern uprising, which inspired a homily against rebellion, galvanized widespread disorder that excites fear of God's vengeance; fear, not love drives this spirituality of obedience. Religion guarantees social order, and fearful obedience guarantees authority.

Fear is not exclusive, although prevalent, in this spirituality. Sanctioned homilies risk overstatement by stoutly presupposing fear in preservation of civil order. But love and, more pointedly, conscience are not crowded out entirely by historical and political exigency. The homily on obedience stakes out early claims for love by reminding its audience that civil "high power and aucthoritie of kynges," as God's agencies, demonstrate his love: "Here is also well to be considered and remembred that this good ordre is appoynted of Gods wisedom, favor and love, specially for them that love God, and therfore he saith, I love them that love me" (*Homilies*, 162). Civil obedience is love's answer to God's love and, we are soon told, conscience plays its part in obedience to civil rulers: "Wherefore ye must nedes obey, not onely for fear of vengeaunce, but also because of conscience, and even for this cause paie ye tribute, for they are Gods ministers, servyng for the same purpose" (163). Conscience walks a razor's edge between blind obedience and right choice. But the fear of disorder that so unifies Tudor thought increasingly rings the alarum fear of punishment for disruption and disobedience. Love and conscience are not ignored so much as circumvented when faced with the prospect of disruption. Even a parade of tyrants, great criminals of absolutist rule, including Nebuchadnezzar, Caligula, and Nero, cannot shake the fearful conviction that submission to established authority, however abusive, is better than the disruption of chaos. The high price of civil order is submission charged by fear of divine wrath.

In sum, the authorized homilies provided a standard set of truths intended to be applicable in every corner of the realm. In particular, the homilies on obedience and disobedience, which were intently political in their orientation, skew the spirituality of obedience toward hard-edged worldly applications. Viewed broadly, these two homilies can be more fully understood as members of a family of texts written both before and after their initial publication that suggest a continuing debate about the dimensions of obedience. This debate reveals both broader and softer dimensions in the spirituality of obedience that are far less rigid politically and less intimidating psychologically.

Tyndale's *The Obedience of a Christian Man, and how Christian rulers ought to govern* (1528) is the first important English vernacular text in the debate. Tyndale has attracted modern scholars as an early sixteenth century Protestant political thinker, and this work is political, but in the broad sense of political life as a frame for human existence in relation to God. The first half of the split title makes clear that the treatise is primarily addressing duties of all classes in society, including reciprocal duties of those having political authority over those below them in the hierarchy. Published before Henry VIII's categorical break with Rome, it advances with unwitting prescience Henry's ultimate position, and hence was initially regarded with great favor by the early Tudor court. Tyndale attacks the Pope as the Antichrist, while arguing for active submission to a secular monarch.

Here Tyndale's text occupies common ground with the homilies, but with differences that reverberate throughout the early modern period. Extreme anti-papalism, biblical justification for nonresistance to civil authority, and a hierarchy maintained by obedience to commands of higher powers lay foundations of much early English obedience literature. But differences between Tyndale's treatise and the official homilies likewise identify a tension within that literature that eventually contributed to its demise and redefined obedience much later in the spirituality of Milton and other more humanistic Christians. The nub of the matter is what Tyndale calls the "law of love," a reciprocal relationship between those who command and those who obey, what we might call a hierarchically connected "power relationship" mollified by two-way love. Fear yields to love as the primary source of reciprocal duties that frame identity. As we will see later, these issues necessarily inform our understanding of *King Lear.*

Tyndale's prologue, in sniping against papal structures which are blamed as the cause of disobedience, establishes a destructive counterpoint to the proper system of order. This counterpoint informs the structure of opposites in Tyndale's treatise. Like the homily on obedience, Tyndale's treatise initially sets out a frame of obedience determining earthly life: children to parents, wives to husbands, servants to masters, and subjects to kings. Extended treatment of the subjects' obedient submission to kings is accompanied by an attack on the papal "False Power"[54] that undermines legitimate power and enforces idolatrous obedience to a false God. The succeeding section, in examining the legitimate duties of superiors to inferiors, supplies the other side of the legitimate power arrangement; then, in a section entitled "Antichrist" (88), Tyndale trains his sights on papal influence that perverts the true system of order. Thereafter, the treatise programmatically sets out the true and false elements of religion necessary for legitimate belief. Thus, the negative example of false belief and dangerous practices of papal servitude define true subjection through counterpoint.

True subjection for Tyndale concurs with Luther's allied emphases on nonresistance to secular authority and on love's central place in obedience. Like the Tudor homily, Tyndale acknowledges all three motives, fear of vengeance, conscience, and love; but his ultimate emphasis is on loving conformity to Christ as a basis for obedience to both God's command and to secular authority. He also justifies other motivations besides love: "ye must needs obey, not for fear of vengeance only: but also because of conscience" (50). But the prevailing motivation is love of God, which leads, in turn, to love of his commandments: "If we keep the commandments of love, then are we sure that we fulfil the law in the sight of God and that our blessing shall be everlasting life. Now when we obey patiently and without grudging evil princes that oppress us and persecute us and be kind and merciful to them that are merciless to us and do the worst they can to us and so take all fortune patiently and kiss whatsoever cross God layeth on our backs: then are we sure that we keep the commandment of love" (181). Love of others subsumes all commandments of the law: "all are comprehended in this saying: love thine neighbour as thyself. Love hurteth not his neighbour: therefore is love the fulfilling of the law" (37). Shifting emphasis from negative fear to positive love neither weakens the command to obey nor shakes the frame of subordination. Quite the contrary. The vocabulary of subjection and submission permits no doubt about the unabashed system of strict order throughout the social degrees. But love is the ultimate binding tie.

Obedience requires subjection and submission. Obedience to parents is sacrosanct, and pleasure in their children's obedience is God's pleasure, just as their anger is God's anger; and until a disobedient child has "submitted . . . unto thy mother and father," God's favor is withdrawn (31). Tyndale enlists both Peter and Paul to speak for a wife's contributing obedience: "Peter (1 Peter 3) exhorteth wives to be in subjection unto their husbands"; then "Paul (Eph. 5) saith: women submit yourselves unto your own husbands, as unto the Lord." Pauline relationships of husband to wife, of Christ to church, are tightly cinched together in service and subjection: "For the husband is the wife's head even as Christ is the head of the congregation. Therefore as the congregation is in subjection to Christ, likewise let wives be in subjection unto husbands in all things" (34). About submission of servants, we hear once again the ventriloquized voices of Paul and Peter. Paul commands that a "carnal" master must be obeyed as if he were Christ; in turn, Peter commands that servants obey their masters even when grieved, after Christ's model (35).

Not surprisingly, Paul's familiar command that "every soul submit himself unto the authority of the higher powers" emerges in support of political subjection, the outer frame of Tyndale's structure of orderly subjection. No one is exempted: "all souls must obey." All "higher powers," glossed as the "temporal kings and princes" (40), come from God and must be feared by lawbreakers. These "powers," even tyrants, arm God's wrath and vengeance against wrongdoing, and every soul must submit. Tyndale is unequivocal about the scope of an earthly "power," its acts of vengeance, its punishing force, its absolute strength. But the law of love remains active. Believers with God's law written in their hearts know that earthly law and the governing "powers" are established by God's love. Obedient submission returns love to God.

Love's law works reciprocally, up and down the hierarchical steps. Tyndale's title tells us that he will first ascend, then descend these steps; first, duties of inferiors toward superiors, then *vice versa*. Duties of children, wives, servants, and subjects reciprocate duties of parents, husbands, masters, and princes. Mutual duties create mutual identities, with Christ as a two-way unifying pattern, both commanding lord of love's law and lovingly obedient servant.

An omnibus command to "Seek Christ in your children, in your wives, servants and subjects" melds all persons together as servants (60), "one thing" together in Christ. Those looking down the hierarchical steps must discover that authority, paradoxically, involves submission: "In Christ we are all one thing, none better than another, all brethren and all must seek Christ and our brothers' profit in Christ. And he that hath the knowledge whether he be lord or king, is bound to submit himself and serve his brethren and to give himself for them, to win them to Christ" (60). The duty to command obedience is to serve lovingly, even when authority necessarily exhorts, rebukes, corrects, and punishes. Parents who are "wayward, hasty and churlish, ever brawling and chiding" (59), instead of living the "knowledge" of Christ, only demean and dishearten their children. Paul's ready-made formula governs the ruling of wives, just as the head loves its own body and Christ loves the church. In turn, servants are to be exhorted "kindly to do their duty" (61). And kings should remember that "the people are God's and not theirs"; they are "Christ's inheritance and possession bought with his blood" (63). A king's duties are those of lord and of servant; so, too, are those duties of parent, husband, or master. Such reciprocal duties framed by love's law according to Christ's pattern can mollify inherent problems of obedient submission in a hierarchical state.

But corrupt civil authority remained a problem to be solved. The initial Reformed solution of ceding spiritual priority to the holy community over the state not only threatened to divide loyalty, but also left civil problems unsolved. Believers living under a tyrannical or corrupt magistrate faced the dilemma of obeying a sinful regime politically while obeying God spiritually through Christ's pattern in the church. The dilemma stimulated various responses leading down different pathways, ranging from passive obedience, to disobedience, to resistance, each with its own problems. Calvin's initial response was like Tyndale's: passive obedience and nonresistance to flawed secular authority on behalf of social order. Later, Calvin equivocally allowed resistance, but only by inferior magistrates standing for the people. A more radical position that would advocate direct resistance by the people, whether violent or nonviolent, was unacceptable to Calvin as a threat to order. A point I would underline is that neither disobedience nor resistance necessarily denies the principle of obedience. Instead, obedience to divine authority and the need for legitimate earthly authority together motivate disobedience and resistance to insupportable, aberrant magistrates. Principled disobedience or resistance is a corollary of obedience to higher authority.

English resistance theory stimulated by Mary's reign illustrates this corollary. Reformation thought ascendant in Edward's brief reign was summarily rejected by Mary's single-minded Catholicism. The fearful exodus to the Continent stimulated by Marian persecutions included the Reformed clerics, John Ponet and Christopher Goodman. Both contributed to what earlier I called an English family of texts concerned with obedience and its proper boundaries. And both contributed to a doctrine of obedience that included resistance. Ponet's "A Shorte Treatise of Politike Power" contained a doctrine of political obedience illustrated by a corporate metaphor: "As the body of man is knit and kept together in due proporcion by the sinowes, so is euery commun wealthe kept and maintened in good ordre by Obedience. But as if the sinowes be to muche racked and stretched out, or to muched shrinked together, it briedeth wonderfull paines and deformitie in mannes body: so if Obedience be to muche or to litell in a common wealthe, it causeth muche euil and disordre."[55] Obedience is not absolute. Commandments of earthly magistrates, who should act as God's ministers, must not contravene his powers and commandments: "What so ever God commaundeth man to doo, he ought not to considre the mater, but straight to obeie the commaunder" (52). A magistrate's political power must be consistent with God's power, and only true human obedience within the political realm, that is, "sinowes" appropriately tight, follows accordingly. As a mere human, a magistrate cannot command more than is consistent with God's law: "For all men what so euer mynisterie or vocation they exercice, are but men, and so maye erre. We see councelles against councelles, parliamentes against parliamentes, commaundement against commaundment, this daye one thing to morow an other." Responsibility to assess appropriate tightness in the sinew of obedience lies with the individual conscience. Earthly magistrates must not command obedience "contrarie or repugnaunt to Goddes commaundementes and iustice." In that assertion lies responsibility to resist; such an earthly commandment "ought not to be obeyed" (53). Ponet thus goes beyond Calvin's reluctant authorization of resistance by legitimate lesser magistrates only. True obedience to God requires a conscientious individual to disobey evil counsel and commands. Nonetheless, as Quentin Skinner notes,[56] Ponet and Goodman after him both argue that people should be led by lesser magistrates.

Goodman persistently clarifies the blurred boundaries between "obedience" and "disobedience." Conformity to divine commands and justice constitutes "true obedience." But believers "bewitched with Satan's false illusions" are unable "to put difference betwyxte obedience & disobedience."[57] Obedience to false earthly commands turns out to be disobedience to God's commands. Goodman's discussion points out a double failure, respectively by magistrates and servants. Selfish magistrates violate their own necessary obedience to God's command and justice by commanding unlawful obedience from their subjects. In turn, the subjects fail to distinguish false obedience from true by obeying the magistrate's false command, thus disobeying God's higher command. Accordingly, both magistrate and subject disobey God. In addition, the deluded subject is practicing only a false obedience to the magistrate: a subject practicing "true obedience" to God would "disobey" or "resist" such a magistrate. All persons, of whatever vocation and degree, are duty-bound to disobey or resist unlawful magistrates who issue false commands. By collapsing false "obedience" and "disobedience" into one another, Goodman repeatedly reminds his readers that unlawful earthly values encroach on true obedience to divine values. Modern readers are reminded that, for Goodman, what we call "political" obedience is, more broadly, an element in Christian spirituality that imposes the divine on the earthly. We find here further evidence that a disposition to obedience, even when misguided, is indelible in the early modern self.

Obedience and disobedience, conceived as the same voluntary disposition pursuing different allegiances, emerge within hierarchical structures buttressed by codes of mutual service. Habitual "sinowes" of obedience, to borrow Ponet's metaphor, strengthen duty and responsibility that center the early modern self, but not without developing ambiguities. The ambiguous boundaries of obedience, disobedience, and resistance lead us back to where we began, to questions about self posed in *King Lear.* Extreme dislocations represented in *King Lear* test the self and its constituents. The answer to Lear's question — "Who is it that can tell me who I am?" — lies in reconsidering his residual vocation as a king, a father, and a master responsible for common good. He would need to help reconstitute the sinews of true obedience that strengthen common good. His failure to heed the full answer, despite experiencing anew the truth of love's law, contributes to his tragedy.

Edgar's Choice

In *King Lear* Shakespeare represents human life at the extremes. For Shakespeare's early Jacobean audience, aftershocks of succession fears, which had unsettled Elizabethan England with a possibility of cataclysmic civil war, could still be felt despite James I's orderly succession.[58] The aged King Lear nearing the end of his natural life without a male heir has the vocational duty to provide responsibly for the future of his endangered kingdom. A preconceived plan to subdivide the kingdom and preempt disagreement and civil dislocation is scuttled by his own impromptu staging of a public love contest between his daughters. An old man's need for reassurance is understandable, but irresponsible self-indulgence in extreme circumstances violates his vocational responsibility to preserve order. Both he and the kingdom's systems of order disintegrate. He becomes disoriented, naked, and vulnerable to the extremes of nature while the kingdom suffers murderous sibling rivalry, usurpation, and civil war. His own cry of lost identity is one early effect of his intemperate actions. His behavior has invited extremes he cannot welcome as the hierarchical order held together by principles of service, obedience, and vocational responsibility breaks down.

The answer to Lear's anguished question is to be found within these principles. Jonas Barish and Marshall Waingrow single out the master/servant relationship, which with interrelated king/subject and father/child relationships comprises the play's traditionally hierarchical frame. The play's "ideal of service," against which true and false servants are judged, assumes reciprocal obligations binding master to servant, as it does king to subject and parent to child. Reciprocal bonding can remain "dynamic and vital" only through mutual love and responsibility.[59] The ideal, which has much in common with Tyndale's law of love, assumes that a king is both a master and servant of the state; loyalty and love are incumbent on him in both roles, just as obedience, loyalty, and love are incumbent on those who serve. Lear violates this loving reciprocity between master and servant, just as he violates a reciprocal relationship of responsibility and loyalty in service that must apply between king and subject, father and child. His treatment of Cordelia, a true daughter and subject, in turn stimulates Kent, an equally true subject and servant, to perform an act of disobedience leading to his banishment.

Distinctions between true and false servants mirror true and false obedience within its hierarchical frame. The "superserviceable" Oswald (2.2.16) slavishly obeys Goneril at all moral costs. In sharp contrast, Kent disobeys wayward Lear, but continues loyally to serve him even when exiled. His disobedience of Lear is, in ultimate terms, both true service and true obedience that condemns Lear's wrongdoing in terms of his own true responsibility. Kent thus exemplifies the ambiguous nature of disobedience addressed in the resistance theory of Ponet and Goodman. Kent's disobedience to unjust earthly authority is obedience to true value; in contrast, Oswald's obedience to unjust authority is disobedience to true value. For Richard Strier the "distinction between virtuous disobedience and improper loyalty" in *King Lear* later becomes "axiomatic in the romances."[60] Citing Ponet, he notes that Kent, like Saul's subordinates who refused his unlawful command to kill Ahimelech, proved themselves "'yet the kinges true servauntes and subjectes.'"[61] However, Strier's constructive emphasis on the "strictly *political* context"[62] of *King Lear* leads away from a broader assumption in Ponet and Goodman that variations of obedience, true and false, express a disposition of self in the early modern hierarchical context. Also, by delimiting obedience to the "political," Strier ignores the vocational implications of obedience in *King Lear*. Lear's disruptive actions violate several dimensions of his vocational responsibility as a king, a father, and a master. Preserving a loving reciprocity within the frame of obedience is a king's vocational responsibility. The disruption of this frame leaves him as an individual asking who can tell him who he is.

One answer lies in his reciprocal bonds with others. We never see him alone. Even when assaulted by tempest, denuded by his own hand, raging in and out of madness, he is served by others. The Fool's acerbic questioning drives Lear to self-knowledge; the hovering Kent remains a loyal servant; so, too, Gloucester despite his own plight. An inadvertent servant, Edgar disguised as Tom O'Bedlam ironically mirrors Lear's condition. His destitution and pretended madness protect him from discovery while expressing the unreason of his experience. Lear projects his own sense of injury on Tom: "What, has his daughters brought him to this pass? / Couldst thou save nothing? Didst thou give them all?" (3.4.61–62). Stripping away his own clothing is a complex act of human sympathy and identification that seeks an answer to another painful question: "Is man no more than this?" His own embodied realization that "unaccommodated man is no more but such a poor, bare, forked animal as thou art" (3.4.95–100) lies in his sympathy for another suffering human whom the former king invites to share protection from the rain in a hovel. Disguised Edgar, however inadvertently, serves Lear's growing understanding of essential humanity; Lear finds in his own sympathy the basis of who he is. By nature social, the human is naturally "accommodated" through connection to others. This essential human bond constitutes a basis for all those formalized vocational responsibilities defining various degrees in society.

A complete answer to his question is always latent in those who serve him. But reawakening in Kent and Cordelia's nurturing presence provides the explicit answer. It is she who can tell him most fully but, tragically, he comprehends only by half. Kent has led the unhinged Lear away from pursuers to Cordelia, returned as Queen of France to save him and his kingdom. His guilt has impeded meeting with her earlier. Her address awakens him: "How does my royal Lord? How fares your majesty" (4.6.36). Her refusal that he kneel to her, rather she to him, assures him of her love and his place as king. His self-abnegating "I am a very foolish fond old man" (4.6.53) admits his remaining confusion without blurring the certainty of his parental affirmation: "Do not laugh at me; / For, as I am a man, I think this lady / To be my child Cordelia" (4.7.69–71). Now wisely chastened, Lear can tell himself that he is a human, and a father. But he rejects his vocational status as king even when Cordelia tells him where he is: "In your own kingdom, Sir." Though surrounded by Kent, several gentlemen, and a daughter who think themselves his subjects, he recoils, "Do not abuse me" (4.7.78). Though newly awakened, he cannot or will not consider himself a substantial presence who, at least in spirit, can bolster others attempting to restore public order.

A measure of his tragedy is that he no longer accepts his vocational responsibility to his own kingdom although his subjects continue to do so. Later, Edmund's forces capture Lear and Cordelia. She is depressed, "cast down," for the sake of "thee, oppressed king"; in contrast, buoying her, he lyrically welcomes the privacy of prison where they two alone "will sing like birds i'the cage" and playfully enjoy "Talk of court news" (5.3.5–14). To Kent he is ever "my king" and "my master." After Edmund's mortal defeat, Albany, with Edgar and Kent, stands to share power, but he also defers to Lear:

> You lords and noble friends, know our intent.
> What comfort to this great decay may come
> Shall be applied; For us, we will resign
> During the life of this old majesty,
> To him our absolute power.
>
> (5.3.295–99)

Lear's death soon after keeps open the question of the kingly vocation rejected by Lear. Not just temperamental reticence leads Albany to suggest that Kent and Edgar take on the heavy vocational burden. This call is inappropriate for Kent, whose vocation remains as servant to Lear: "My master calls me; I must not say no" (5.3.321). First Lear, then Albany, then Kent have refused the call to the kingship. In Edgar's elusive response the ambiguity of the kingly vocation remains open:

> The weight of this sad time we must obey;
> Speak what we feel, not what we ought to say.
> The oldest hath borne most; we that are young
> Shall never see so much, nor live so long.
>
> (5.3.322–25)

Edgar addresses the extremity of Lear's and the blinded Gloucester's experience. Both old men have suffered more than their irresponsibility seems to deserve, although Lear's refusal to serve as "royal lord" does reflect with tragic irony the destructiveness of his earlier actions. The "weight of this sad time" looks backward at what has been lost and forward to the responsibility that the younger generation must shoulder.

The obligation to obey requires both consideration and action. The obligation applies particularly to Edgar and more generally to all persons with responsibilities within the hierarchy. Like Ponet and Goodman, the play defines necessary disobedience as true obedience according to a higher frame of value necessary for the common good. Consistently loyal to his master, Lear, whom he technically has disobeyed, Kent conforms to a higher standard ambiguously suggested by his Master's "call." Whether or not the play is "secular," as Strier suggests, it shares with Ponet's and Goodman's explicitly Christian arguments the idea that there is a higher order of value to be obeyed by both kings and subjects. It is also helpful to bear in mind Perkins's notion that a believer's obedience to a particular calling serves the common good. Translated in secular terms, obedience to a calling fulfills duties within a given estate. Obeying the time includes an assessment of historical circumstances before accepting one's responsibilities to serve common good; to assess damage, grieve for loss, and confront grueling renewal. Such obedience is common to the early modern self. Kent demurs, naming a higher duty, leaving Edgar to answer the call that Lear's advanced years and self-indulgence had first destroyed, then refused. Events in Lear have demonstrated the damage possible in extreme circumstances when the sinews of obedience and vocational duty tear loose. A responsibility falls on those who are called to learn from loss and then work toward restoration. Though daunted by extremes, a remaining vocational thrust is tenacious. Lear's radical suffering taxes him more than he can manage, but Kent, the Fool, Gloucester, and Cordelia remain faithful to the best in the king; and even Edgar, abused and ambivalent, remains obedient to his father's goodness. Their vocational loyalty stands against Lear's ultimate failure. They represent the power of restoration inherent in vocational responsibility, though faced with profound loss.

The play's last word belongs to Edgar [Folio text]. A foil to Lear, the innocent younger man does not cause his own excessive suffering. He pretends madness and bodily destitution to protect himself from others. Events pull Lear apart, then put him back together, leaving the final step to him; but he shies away from publicly serving the kingdom, preferring a private retreat. In contrast, the ambivalent and still disguised Edgar stabilizes his suicidal, despairing father and fights to restore the kingdom on behalf of common good; his disguises protect him while expressing his reluctance and sense of injury. His indirect response when Albany surrenders rule to him and to Kent maintains that reluctance. Yet his imperative "to obey" the time, along with his wise assessment that his generation will not face such extreme circumstances, reveals his yet unspoken but emerging vocational intentions.

To obey a calling is to make a choice. Lear's failure to choose does not disclose a self decentered by historical dislocations. Rather, he is the negative, tragic foil to other characters who choose to work for common good against profound dislocation. Our humane sympathy for his painful extremity does not release him from the responsibility of choice. The willing struggles of Edgar, Cordelia, and Kent represent the importance of vocational duty as one source of coherence in the early modern self. Even if the play provides a secular version of that necessity, as many have argued, it represents a continuing disposition that resists history's dislocations.

Problems in Defining "Self"

Finding a disposition that resists fragmentation, in even a deeply troubling narrative like *King Lear*, underlines its important contribution toward stability, coherence, and continuity internalized in the early modern self. However, defining "self" in this period is problematic in two regards. The first is the relation between the "inward" and "outward" dimensions of experience said to work against the unified self. The second is the early modern idiom of "person," largely absent in debate about the "self," but pervasive in early modern English writing while assuming the conscious interdependence of inward and outward dimensions. These closely linked issues deserve our further attention.

Debora Shuger addresses the first of these issues in stressing the importance of inwardness in the dominant English religious culture. The self she conceives within the dominant religious culture is not decentered and fragmented, but bifurcated by largely discrete compartments of being, spiritual and social, inner and outer. Here we recall Katharine Maus's secularized version of a bifurcated early modern self. But Shuger locates the root of this division in Luther's "two regiments" in which believers live. William Perkins allegedly expands this bifurcation: every believer is a double "person" residing within both regiments.[63] The public person has a social office (husband, father, mother, daughter, wife, lord, and subject) in the public regiment; the private "person" lives in the spiritual regiment in relation to Christ. Shuger's salutary argument keeps the spiritual domain (or the "inward" as Maus has it) within the debate about the early modern self. But she is less successful in solving the problem she identifies of not "overschematizing" the "tendency to isolate inwardness" in the dominant culture.[64]

A solution lies in seeing the importance of vocation as a bridge between the inner and the outer. Cristina Malcolmson underscores the importance of this bridge in both William Perkins and George Herbert, two of Shuger's primary examples of the bifurcated self. Malcolmson points to Perkins's insistence on the interdependence between the general call to believe in Christ and the particular call to each individual to serve in a vocational role.[65] Malcolmson's theoretical point can be teased out further if, in addition to recalling that the vocational office serves the common good in obedient service to God, we note that obedient prayerfulness pervades vocational as well as devotional life. Perkins notes that the "offices and works of our callings . . . must be done in obedience to God, that is with a mind to please and obey God." That motivation is sustained only through the individual's "prayer and thanksgiving in the name of Christ."[66] The prayerful relationship with Christ in answer to the general calling likewise pervades obedience to a particular calling in all its various stations. Vocational activity necessarily participates in the prayerful, worshipful relationship with Christ that works against schematized bifurcation and compartmentalization in the self.

George Herbert builds the same vocational bridge between private and social. Elsewhere I have discussed the unifying prayerfulness of his poetry and life.[67] Herbert's attention to the priestly vocation is a staple in Herbert scholarship, especially in relation to his prose vocational handbook, *The Country Parson,* and to individual lyrics in "The Church," the long devotional middle of

The Temple. This vocational bridge emerges much more broadly if we assume that Herbert, like Sidney and Milton, regarded his poetic gift as vocational. The duality seen by Shuger fades if his poetic representation of prayerful experience in "The Church" not only satisfies a personal spiritual need, but also simultaneously fulfils a poetic vocation. Isaac Walton reports that Herbert said that "The Church" incorporated his own prayerful "conflicts" with God. Walton also reported that when, dying, Herbert had *The Temple* delivered to Nicholas Ferrar for assessment of its value for "any dejected poor soul."[68] This artifact representing his own prayerful communion with God invites the participation of other believers. Like Perkins, Herbert assumes a constant, prayerfulness that pervades inner and outer life.

Mapping boundaries in early modern selfhood between inner and outer experience is made more difficult by the limitations of generic forms and by our own categories for understanding. Debora Shuger recognizes in the "dominant" Protestant culture both inner and outer domains, yet her sense of a bifurcated self-hood is closely related to her tendency to exclude popular drama from her conception of the dominant culture. But boundaries between inner and outer self are far more permeable than our set categories allow. Donne's Trinitarian theology, which turns on conformity between the tripartite God and the tripartite human soul. is a case in point.[69]

For Donne, both disciplined devotional practice and vocational life, the inward and the outward, work in tandem to repair that created likeness damaged by sin. Meditative practices prayerfully exercise reason, memory, and will. Likewise, vocational duties enlivened by the indwelling Spirit fulfil the sufferings of the incarnate Son, obedient to the Father on behalf of the communal Body. The boundaries between inner and outer experience become even more permeable by likeness to the communal nature of God enhanced by meditation and prayer.[70] The three divine persons communicate with each other just as human creatures fulfil their social natures through vocations serving the Body of Christ. The lingering conviction of Donne's singularity inherited from an older critical generation is thus strongly contested by the spiritualized vocational stance represented in his religious prose. What the mature Donne shares with the other writers discussed in the following chapters is a notion of selfhood that includes personal responsibility to common good, all the more compelling in a Catholic convert.

The nature of personal engagement brings us to the second issue, the general absence of "person" in debate about early modern subjectivity initiated by cultural materialist and new historical voices. Vocabularies of "subject," "self," and "identity" have been played through each other in attempts to establish nuanced representations of subjectivity while the category of "person," for the most part, lies dormant in critical discussion. In a different context, Anthony Dawson describes how early modern theater audiences identified with fictive "persons" embodied in natural "persons," the actors. He points to the Protestant belief that Christ's body and blood were spiritually present in eucharistic elements. Just as believers subjectively "participate" in Christ through the Eucharist, audiences "participate" in the fictive "person" enacted through the body of the natural "person," the actor. An analogous transformation thus emerges through religious spirituality habitually practiced in a profoundly Christian culture. Further, viewers and eucharistic communicants respectively "participate" together as embodied, natural, individual physical "persons" visible to each other.[71] Several early modern aspects of "person" recorded in the *OED* come together here. An individual actor, as a natural "person" or self, puts on a "masque" or "persona"; in his body, viewed by others, the actor "personates" a character or fictive "person." As we will see in Spenser's *The Faerie Queene*, that bodily presence visibly interacting with other bodies is essential to "person."

Reid Barbour, in discussing Caroline England's "fascination with the status of personhood and with the nature of impersonation,"[72] cites John Donne's vocational conception of "person" as an illustration. Church ceremony was part of broad patterns of social behavior, relationships, and responsibilities. Parallel to the theater, the pulpit occupied a central cultural space; pulpit orators like Donne played central cultural roles in the "theater of preach-ing."[73] Barbour concentrates specifically on Caroline culture in his examination of practices inherent in the priestly vocation, but his choice of the largely Jacobean Donne as a primary example assumes that the emphasis on the "person" in relation to voca-tional responsibility extends through both regimes. Vocation enhances a natural "person" socially, culturally, and spiritually.

Barbour appropriately links Donne's conception of "person" and "vocation" to his Trinitarian God. "Like Andrewes, Donne advo-cates a plural and sociable template for the Christian person, its model a Trinity of divine persons at once variously employed and fundamentally conformable."[74] As I have indicated earlier,[75] and will again in chapter 3 below, Donne's tripartite human soul, first created in divine likeness, then damaged by sin, takes part in its own repair by coordinating with motions of the Holy Spirit in fulfilling vocational duties. Barbour quotes a 1628 Donne sermon on vocation specifically addressing aspects of this change: "'In nature the body makes the place, but in grace the place makes the body; The person must actuate it self, dilate, extend and prop-agate it self according to the dimensions of the place, by filling it in the execution of the duties of it.'"[76] The bodily "person" is progressively enhanced through various vocational actions, broadly and influentially serving others on behalf of the tripartite God. Each person choosing a vocation must select, follow, and person-ate a vocational "exemplar" (*Sermons* 8.180), in turn imprinting his own enhanced example on others. For the theatricalized pul-pit orator, fulfillment comes in influencing others through voca-tional personation of a Paul or a Stephen.

Dawson's claim that the early modern actor transforms from a natural to fictive "person" in whom audiences "participate" is even more persuasive in light of vocational impersonation. Dawson points to a cultural disposition informing contempo-rary theatrical performances within a pervasively religious cul-ture. This disposition is inherent in early modern "subjectivity," although the vocabulary of "spirituality" and "person" is more nuanced in this instance. This is a "person" moved by the Holy

Spirit, prayerfully imitating an "exemplar" while actuated, dilated, extended, and propagated by vocational duties and participating in common good. We need to keep this resonating vocational "person" alive in debate about the early modern self. Here, along with exemplars of virtue trained in principles of civic humanism and serving common good, we find a disposition that resists decentering and discontinuity.

The related vocabulary of "person" adds further complexity to debate about the early modern "self," especially given the absence of a developed contemporary notion. More than one authoritative voice has struggled with the difficulty of "self." Anne Ferry prefaced her study of sonnets by Wyatt, Sidney, Shakespeare, and Donne with a caveat: her study examined "the language of poets writing about inward experience before the term *the self* meant more than what we mean by *itself* or *the same*."[77] Robert Ellrodt's argument for an "unchanging self" in seven metaphysical poets draws on empirical evidence from the poetry itself. He finds in these poets an emergent "self-consciousness" or "self-reflexivity which turns the very activity of the subject into an object."[78] He is unflinching in his attempt to fit words to the phenomenon: "'Self-awareness' is the more comprehensive term, devoid of implication. 'Subjectivity' is also used in a general way. But there is a particular kind of self-awareness I called 'self-consciousness' rather than coin a special word. It is not the philosophic consciousness of our individuality, but the self-awareness which comes spontaneously into play whenever I perceive an action, a thought, or an emotion as *mine* in the very moment of experience, whenever the experience and the experiencing self are apprehended in the same instant. I can then watch myself act, feel, and think.[79] Ellrodt assumes that we know informally what "self" means, while not defining it or noting its absence in the early modern period. The terminology devised by others, ranging from the "decentered self" to "self-fashioning" to "self-presentation'"[80] works within the same limitation.

And so does my discussion in the following chapters. Most of us can agree informally that a human "self" is a rational agent imbedded in society and culture, capable of volitional thought and action in relation to other beings, and deepened by personal inwardness. Our informal agreement permits us to debate, employing a mixed critical vocabulary, whether the early modern "self" has continuities and how much history can alter its design. My conviction is that sustaining continuities in the early modern religious culture, including a sense of duty to the common good, define that early self. These continuities have a resilience that resists fragmentation. And they also resist arguments that a centrifugal, radical decentering is a necessary condition of the early modern self.

Despite their obvious differences from each other, dutiful commitment to the common good shared by major writers discussed in the following chapters illustrates this claim. The reasons they differ are many. The sometimes-uneasy mix of influences from Protestant vocation and civic humanism was made more complex by tendencies to secularization. Donne and Jonson were almost exact contemporaries and friends; both were deeply learned. But the mature Donne became increasingly theological, whereas the humanist Jonson, trained in commercial theater, had little taste for writing about theology or formal religious subjects. The commercial dramatist, Shakespeare, less committed to fixed intellectual categories than given to borrowing for dramatic purposes, draws on both Protestant vocation and Ciceronian virtue in representing the development of Hal/Henry. The variable mix of vocation and humanism is perhaps most obvious in Protestant writers of epic, Spenser and Milton, both humanists educated at Protestant Cambridge. Milton's strenuous republican spirit is a far cry from Spenser's service to the crown. But Milton's admiration for his predecessor as a moral teacher marks a humanistic intersection in two Protestants for whom poetry was a vocation.[81] It is, perhaps, not too opportunistic to suggest that the very differences distinguishing these five writers from each other demonstrate the strength of their shared cultural continuities, which oppose a decentered and fragmented self.

ONE

Spenser

Persons Serving Gloriana

Edmund Spenser's *The Faerie Queene* begins *in medias res*. A "Gentle Knight" (1.1.1.1)[1] on a "great adventure" given by Gloriana, the "greatest Glorious Queene of *Faerie* lond," is silhouetted against a plain. The occasion for his "adventure" rides beside him, a "louely Lady" (1.i.4.1) grieving for royal parents in "subiection" to an "infernall fiend" (1.1.4.6–7). Contemporary readers would recognize in this chivalric silhouette the commitment to common good shared by Christian civic humanism and Protestant vocation. Readers would view the poet's epic intention to "sing of Knights and Ladies gentle deeds" (Proem 1.5) in the same light. Spenser's letter to Walter Raleigh accompanying publication of the poem's first three books throws further direct light on his vocational "intention": "The generall end therefore of all the booke is to fashion a gentleman or noble person in vertuous and gentle discipline" ("Letter," 737). In fashioning fictional heroes as "ensamples" and, through them, virtuous citizens,

Spenser's poetic discipline subsumes the humanistic emphasis on active virtue serving common good within a Protestant vocational imperative. Each "person" — reader, fictional hero, poet — fulfilled by obeying this imperative is strengthened against threatening cultural discontinuities. To follow Spenser's development of this notion, a thread running throughout *The Faerie Queene*, is to discover the self or the person in his thought.

The Letter to Raleigh

Basic vocabulary expressing elements of "person" can be found in Spenser's letter to Raleigh.[2] Nagging critical problems resulting from the letter[3] do not diminish the importance of this vocabulary everywhere in the poem itself. Published with books 1–3 (1590), the problematical letter disappeared in the expanded 1596 edition, which included the books 4–6 and the mutability cantos (1596), reappearing in print only after Spenser's death. Even in 1590 it enjoyed no pride of place, tagged to the poetic text just before tail-end dedicatory letters. Nonetheless, the working vocabulary of this text, pointedly "expounding his whole intention" to a friendly, respected patron, clarifies important dimensions in the poem.

A case in point is Spenser's interest in "intention," which, as the poem itself demonstrates, emerges as a distinguishing mark of "person," not just the poet himself, but the virtuous "ensamples" of human behavior which comprise his narrative poem and fashion his readers as "persons." We can usefully begin with connections between "persons," "intentions," and "ensamples." Spenser's intention in the poem, as he tells Raleigh, includes an object, an action, and a method. His ambiguous object is "a gentleman or noble person"; the action, "to fashion"; and the method, a "vertuous and gentle discipline." Spenser's ambiguity allows "gentleman" and "noble person" to be taken either as synonyms for the same category or as optional categories. The flexible "gentleman" in Spenser's time could include not just hereditary members of the landed gentry, but recent nonhereditary landholders, university graduates, lawyers, educated civil servants, and wealthy merchants.[4] A "noble person," while alluding specifically to persons of noble birth, thereby honoring class differences, more generally includes any virtuous person of high moral ideals, including gentlemen (*OED*).[5] This inclusiveness also makes way for Spenser's women readers. The poem offers several literary models, most notably Britomart representing the marital love so important to a Protestant audience. Spenser has in mind not only Queen Elizabeth and the high-born women honored in his dedicatory sonnets to the poem, but also the readership of learned Protestant women who distinguished his era. In short, Spenser's ambiguity multiplies categories of readers and, paradoxically, collapses them together in "noble person," including "gentlemen" and their literate wives. Spenser is keeping one pivoting foot stationed on "person." That is, the most "generall" object to be fashioned in a "vertuous and gentle discipline" is a "person" or, as we might say, a "self."

Widely assumed is that the "person" to be fashioned refers both to the fictional character as the virtuous "ensample," and ultimately to the reader who imitates that "ensample." But the fictional "ensamples" come first. Chosen as "most fitte for the excellency of his person," Spenser's primary fictional "ensample," Arthur, is a layered model, himself imitative of previous epic heroes: "I have followed all the antique Poets historicall, first Homere, who in the Persons of Agamemnon and Vlysses hath ensampled a good gouernour and a vertuous man . . . then Virgil, whose like intention was to doe in the person of Aeneas; after him Ariosto comprised them both in his Orlando: and lately Tasso disseuered them againe, and formed both parts in two persons, namely that part which they in Philosophy call Ethice, or vertues of a priuate man, coloured in his Rinaldo: The other named Politice in his Godfredo." Arthur includes additional layers as well, by incorporating other exemplary heroes of his poem: "So in person of Prince Arthur I sette forth magnificence in particular, which virtue . . . is the perfection of all the rest" ("Letter," 737). The conception of "person" also rules his rendering of Gloriana, the Fairy Queen. In his "generall intention" she is glory; in his "particular" intention she "beareth two persons" of Queen Elizabeth, "one of a most royall Queene or Empresse, the other a most vertuous and beautifull Lady." Gloriana and Arthur are both conceived as fictional persons with historical roots. As "persons" they are clearly related to the living reader, the ultimate object to be fashioned by "vertuous and gentle discipline."

By emphasizing necessary "ensamples" of virtue in fashioning "persons," Spenser's letter to Raleigh pointedly confirms his method of "discipline."[6] Unequivocally didactic, his "intention" to train or to teach moral doctrine employs a poetic mode relying on example: "So much more profitable and gratious is doctrine by ensample, then by rule. So haue I laboured to doe in the person of Arthure" ("Letter," 737). Spenser cites his own precedents: "In the Persons of Agamemnon and Vlysses," Homer "hath ensampled a good gouernour and a vertuous man"; likewise Virgil in Aeneas, Ariosto in Orlando, and Tasso in Rinaldo and Godfredo. Arthur, the example of "magnificence," the "perfection" of all other virtues, incorporates and perfects the virtues of which the poem's other major heroic persons are examples: Redcrosse Knight, Guyon, and Britomart. Spenser's "vertuous and gentle discipline" can thus be understood only in terms of "ensample" as a mode of knowing in which Spenser himself participates. Examples incorporate examples to beget other examples. Arthur, "ensample" of magnificence, assimilates previous epic heroes; so Spenser, "antique Poets historicall": "By ensample of which excellent Poets, I labour to pourtraict in Arthur, before he was king, the image of a braue knight perfected in the twelve priuate vertues" ("Letter," 738). In sum, the author is promising a "vertuous and gentle discipline" by "ensample" that will fashion both fictive and real "persons" in virtue. Much coalesces here. The poet's virtuous "ensamples" fashion "persons," real and fictive; as does a poet in vocationally serving his readers, so do his virtuous knights in "aduentures" that serve others. Such intentional actions complete persons.

Here we return to the poem's opening silhouette. The "great aduenture" on which Redcrosse is "bond" (1.1.3.1) suggests at the outset that a notion of intentional chivalric action on behalf of others rules *The Faerie Queene*. Vocabulary employed in the "Letter" is consistent on this point. A never-written twelfth book was to represent Gloriana's "Annuall feaste xii dayes" when "xii seuerall aduentures hapned, which being vndertaken by xii. seuerall knights." On day one, a raw Redcrosse came seeking "atchieuement of any aduenture"; on day two a Palmer "craued of the Faery Queene, to appoint him some knight, to performe that aduenture" of destroying the enchantress, Acrasia; on day three Scudamour "tooke on him that aduenture" of freeing his love, "a most faire Lady called Amoretta" from the "vile Enchaunter Busirane." Spenser's sorting of chivalric "aduentures" into "intendments" and "accidents" points to his nuanced definition of "aduentures" as intentional actions serving others. Whereas "intendments" are purposeful duties commissioned by the faery queen, "accidents" are unexpected, emergent narrative lines "intermedled" with "intendments" in the narrative. The nuanced vocabulary of "aduenture" extracts from chivalric "intendment" the intentional virtue of "persons" completed by serving others.

Spenser's narrative economy of "intendment" and "accident," while categorizing narrative action, links intentionality to the "vertuous and gentle discipline" fashioning a person. The brief proem to Raleigh's letter is pointed: "A letter of the Authors expounding his whole intention in the course of this worke: which for that it giueth great light to the Reader, for the better vnderstanding is hereunto annexed" (737). Vocational intentionality plays a necessary cognitive role in virtuous discipline completing the lives of "persons." Spenser's complete argument sits under this umbrella, including the supporting "generall" and "particular" intentions that inform his fashioning of the fairy queen herself. Cognitive roles played by purposive thought and understanding in the synonyms, intention or intendment, include the causally related activity of conception. Moved by the general intention to fashion a person, Spenser conceived that a discipline "coloured" by "historicall fiction" would be "more plausible and pleasing." He was led further to conceive the person of Arthur "after his long education by Timon" (737). Spenser cinches the causal logic between intention and conception in his concluding paragraph to Raleigh: "Thus much Sir, I haue briefly ouerronne to direct your vnderstanding to the wel-head of the History, that from thence gathering the whole intention of the conceit, yet may as in a hand-full gripe al the discourse, which otherwise may happily seeme tedious and confused" (738). That final intentional conceit recalls the proem and his intention to explain to Raleigh "the contin-ued allegory, or darke conceit" (737) of his chivalric poem. To Raleigh, Spenser speaks person-to-person about the "vertuous discipline" of persons necessary for common good.

Here we have a triangulation of author, character, and reader as intentional persons. To "fashion" a literary character and a reader hinges on a "discipline" of "ensamples" conceived as chivalric "aduentures" in an allegorical romance. The usefulness of this vocabulary in understanding Spenser's conception and fashion-ing of "person" does not solve nagging problems in the "Letter of the Author" that have perplexed its readers: how the complex of virtues can be conceived as Aristotelian; how the distinction between "private" and "politike" virtues actually work in the prob-ably incomplete poem that Spenser left us; and why Arthur seems to appear far less in the poem than the letter seems to promise. Nonetheless, Spenser's vocabulary in the "Letter" leads intention-ally to essential elements in *The Faerie Queene*. In following this lead, remaining discussion in this chapter includes his conceit of the person, the discipline of ensamples in fashioning persons, the place of gender in the Elizabethan gentleman or noble person, and exemplary chivalric "aduentures" in a vision of virtuous voca-tional wholeness shared by the poet.

Intentional Persons

Like our own informal notion of "self," the early modern notion of "person" comprised several overlapping dimensions. In chapter one we have already noted some: in particular, the indi-vidual human being, the bodily presence of the live human being, the individual actor physically "personating" another human being in whom theater audiences participate,[7] and the pulpit orator personally dilated through personating an exemplary vocational model. Additional meanings include a corporate agent like the queen or someone of importance (or personage); the related personage can also denote personal appearance or image, as well as individual identity (*OED*). Spenser draws on these several meanings in *The Faerie Queene,* but a dominant thread in his conception of person is an active, embodied presence in relation to other persons and informed by intention and attitude. Intention includes responsible, conscious thought, though not exclusively. And bodily presence, a primary medium of intention and attitude, can be said to function like a language. That conception of person informs Spenser's choice of literary form, since the chivalric romance, with its interplay of plot lines and clash of competing bodies, emphasizes the embodied presence as the medium of experience in relation to others. The key is the silhouetted "gentle Knight" intently "pricking on the plaine," accompanied by a lovely lady and a dwarf, on an assigned "aduenture" against a besetting dragon. That chivalric mission suggests an embodied vocational responsibility.

Spenser's allegory plays on our sense of an individual person's distinguishing bodily presence. Outline of figure, extension in space, beauty or ugliness of feature, the pressures of weight — all these features actively invade and capture our attention as a language to be read for truths, deceptions, and ironies. The introduction of Arthur speaks to our sense of concurrent physical and moral power:

> A goodly person, and could menage faire
> His stubborne steed with curbed canon bit,
> Who vnder him did trample as the aire,
> And chauft, that any on his backe should sit;
> The yron rowels into frothy fome he bit.
>
> (1.7.37.5–9)

Spenser's characterization balances on an edge between the traditional representation of passion as a horse and a powerful animal naturally resisting human governance. We are kept on that edge by our sense of a powerful human governing a horse just as he governs himself. Just as "stubborne" captures a powerful animal's muscular resistance, the ambiguous "goodly" speaks to Arthur's impressive bodily size and handsome figure. Also, "goodly" prepares us for his immediately gracious and kindly treatment of the grievously abandoned Una. But the characterization of his person centers on his imposing physical presence.

Britomart's relationship to Artegall pivots on a palpable sense of his physical person. We are introduced to Artegall before actually meeting him, first by Redcrosse's response to Britomart's sly interrogation, then the narrator's revelation that she had viewed his person earlier in Merlin's remarkable "mirrhour." Not too lovesick to take Artegall merely at face value, she traps Redcrosse into defending him against her trumped up accusations of shameful actions. Concurrently, her lovesickness demands a reinforced image of his physical person:

> Tell me some markes, by which he may appeare,
> If chaunce I him encounter parauaunt;
> For perdie one shall other slay, or daunt:
> What shape, what shield, what armes, what steed, what sted,
> And what so else his person most may vaunt?
> All which the *Redcrosse* knight to point ared,
> And him in euery part before her fashioned.
>
> (3.2.16.3–9)

Britomart's ploy makes Redcrosse an ironically unaware but reliable means of reinforcement since, unbeknownst to him, she had seen Artegall in Merlin's glass "in euery part before she knew" (3.2.17.1). Redcrosse's reliable account, along with the narrator's, confirms the same physical truth. Spenser's narrative strategy thus emphasizes Artegall's physical person as well as a need to verify what our eyes tell us. Artegall's image "in euery part before her fashioned," like that in Merlin's glass, is just that, an image like each character fashioned by Spenser. But it is an image understood through our sense of a physical person, a "shape" extended bodily in space with distinguishing "markes" seen and remembered. Spenser's narrative strategy confirms the truth of Artegall's physical person. In contrast, as we will later see, the dubiety of disguised "persons," if not subjected to verification, erodes the certainty of truth.

Spenser provides a necessarily close look at Artegall's physical person. Merlin's glass shows Britomart that the "comely knight, all arm'd in complete wize" (3.2.24.2) is a "Portly . . . person" (24.8) equipped in armor "wondrous massie and assured sound" (25.3), a "personage" that Britomart "liked well" (26.1–2). The solidity and integrity of "massie" and "sound" armor inflect the stately dignity and bearing of "portly" with a sense of true weight, as "comely" (24.2) underscores in "portly" the sense of handsome physical presence. The "personage" that pleases Britomart alludes simultaneously to the important presence and appearance of the embodied form, at first only seen as an image in the "mirrhour" (17.4) or glass. While stressing the physicality of person that attracts the nubile Britomart, herself physically ready for marital love, Spenser also reminds us that his "dark conceit" gives literary images of an important embodied "person," a heroic "personage" appropriate for Britomart.

Spenser never underestimates the power of physical beauty as an aspect of a body's presence. The sexuality of Artegall's "comely" attractiveness is restrained by his "portly" dignity. No such restraint governs the Squire of Dames, a "comely personage" with a "louely face" that fitted him to "deceive / Fraile Ladies hart with loues consuming rage" (3.7.46.2–4). He is the willing agent of perverted *frauendienst*. To prove his love after "weary seruicis" to the "gentle Lady, whom I loue and serue" (53.6–7), he must for 12 months "do seruice vnto gentle Dames" (54.6). A tally of sexual conquests, of "seruicis," is the required measure of willingness to pass his lady's perverted test of love. Spenser parodies social practices that pervert sexuality to demonstrate dominance; beauty as a sexual lure unrestrained by moral governance invites entrapment. The Squire is subdued and "Fast bounden hand and foote with cords of wire" (3.7.37.8) by the bestial Argante, whose unslaked lust feeds on multiple male partners, including her own brother, and animals. The squire's degrading bondage reflects his participation in a perverse and entangling social practice demanding sexual prowess. The sexual appeal of his "comely personage," a lovely figure without moral substance, may seduce morally "fraile ladies," but also leaves him immobilized in lust.

In contrast, the sexually charged beauty of Amoret's embodied "person" is guided by virtue and moral intention. Spenser's use of "comely personage" in characterizing Argante shifts the emphasis to superficial beauty, not the more substantial beauty embodied in the "person" of Amoret. Like Britomart, she is palpably ready for marital love, but her beauty and natural sexuality, however virtuous, unintentionally draw lustful male attention. Her potential for virtuous sexual union leading to motherhood stimulates her fear of others. Imprisonment and torture by Busyrene, later her incarceration with Emylia by the giant, Lust, dramatically justify her fear of sexual abuse triggered by her sexual beauty. In contrast, her embrace with Scuddamour concluding the poem's 1590 edition demonstrates a proper end of her chastely sexual "person":

> Lightly he clipt her twixt his armes twaine,
>   And streightly did embrace her body bright,
>   Her body, late the prison of sad paine,
>   Now the sweet lodge of loue and dere delight:
>   But she faire Lady ouercommen quight
>   Of huge affection, did in pleasure melt,
>   And in sweete rauishment pourd out her spright:
>   No word they spake, nor earthly thing they felt,
> But like two senceles stocks in long embracement dwelt.
>
>   (3.12.45.1–9)

Fear of male sexual domination, perhaps even in the marital state, is represented in Busyrene's hold on her. But the threat to her "person" is not just sexual, as we see in her experience of Arthur's guardianship. She and Amylia are freed from the giant captor, Lust, then eventually shielded by Arthur from physical assault. Unattached women, they remain vulnerable to besetting attack by Sclaunder. Alone and unprotected, Amoret becomes even more vulnerable after Amylia finds her appropriate place with

Placidas. Arthur's true virtuous nature is yet unclear to her, and "Her person late in perill" faces new dangers. Renewed "feare of shame" recalls both Lust and Sclaunder, violation of both body and reputation (4.9.18.3.5). Her fear extends beyond her physical safety to the social dimension of her person. Her body is a physical medium through which the full "person" as a moral and social being is perceived and understood. Reference to Amoret's embodied "person" follows her allegorical introduction in both the Garden of Adonis and the Temple of Venus. She is brought to the Garden of Adonis by Venus, there reared by Psyche:

> In which when she to perfect ripenesse grew,
>> Of grace and beautie noble Paragone,
>> She brought her forth into the worldes vew,
>> To be th'ensample of true loue alone,
>> And Lodestarre of all chaste affectione,
>> To all faire Ladies, that doe liue on ground.
>
> (3.6.52.1–6)

Her exemplary "chaste affection" embraces not just physical love, but also moral attributes represented more fully in Venus's Temple by the surrounding womanly presence of Womanhood, Shamefastnesse, Cherefulnesse, Modestie, Curtesie, Silence, and Obedience (4.10.49–51). Her person embodies these virtues, and her active bodily presence or "personage" conveys these qualities through her actions. Thus, Amoret's "person," imperiled prior to Arthur's guardianship, is an embodied presence inhabited by moral habits and intentions.

Our shopworn notion of "body language" offers a homely perspective here. That notion generally holds that what we call personality or temperament is expressed by posture, gesture, and disposition of physical presence in response to immediate social occasions. Not mere flesh and bone, our bodies are dramatic texts expressing general features of individual identity, specific attitudes, moral values, and intentions. Britomart's humiliating defeat of Radigund makes her a "proud person low prostrated on the plaine" (5.7.33.9). This ironic flattening evokes her self-presentation in preparation for successful battle against Artegall. In "stately port

and proud magnificence," her self-exalting person is surrounded
by Amazonian defenders playing musical instruments sounding
"vnto the heauens hight" (5.5.4.2–6). In contrast, we recall Belphoebe, however authoritative her governance, casually unbraced
and seated after the hunt, some followers bathing, others lying
shaded from the heat, only the "rest vpon her gaue attendance
great" (3.6.17.9). Radigund's self-exalting stance articulates a
prideful thrust for power and dominance in her nature. Belphoebe's
more generous and relaxed authority is reflected in her followers' varied but respectful stances.

Predictably, Spenser's embodied concept of person cannot
escape the ironies of misperception exacted by deception, false
likeness, pretense, and disguise. Archimago, Duessa, and Brag-
gadochio fraudulently masque as persons they are not, either to
destroy or pervert or counter the good. They are like actors who
personate others, but only to manipulate false truths. Protean
Archimago plots to separate Redcrosse from Una, first masquing
as a hermit ("Sober he seemde, and very sagely sad" — 1.1.29.5),
successfully deceiving both knight and lady. Later, it "seemde best,
the person to put on / Of that good knight, his late beguiled
guest" (1.2.ll.1–2). In theatrical terms, by putting on Redcrosse,
he "personates" him: he puts on his person, becoming a fraudu-
lent "persona." In the same canto, the imprisoned Fradubio
recounts to Redcrosse how Duessa personates a "comely person" (1.2.36.9), deceitfully competing with his own lady Fraelissa:
"Th'one seeming such, the other such indeede" (1.2.37.2). Her trick-
ery thwarted, Duessa is stripped of her disguises by Redcrosse and
Arthur, thereby revealing her appalling deformity, ugliness and
"secret filth good manners biddeth not be told" (1.8.46.9). Later,
she conspires with Archimago, and both fraudulently assume
new disguises, new personations:

> Her purpose was not such, as she did faine,
>   Ne yet her person such, as it was seene,
>   But vnder simple shew and semblant plaine
>   Lurckt false *Duessa* secretly vnseene,
>   As a chast Virgin, that had wronged beene:

So had false *Archimago* her disguisd,
To cloke her guile with sorrow and sad teene;
And also himselfe had craftily deuisd
To be her Squire, and do her seruice well aguisd.

(2.1.21.1–9)

Theatrical notions of "person" or "persona" or "personation" inform Spenser's characterization of Archimago and Duessa as false persons. Their believable personations, by complicating perception and truth, speak to the slipperiness of literary representations of truth and, more significantly, to the manipulation of embodied performance by real persons that distorts social realities and relationships. These performances are kinetic artifacts thematically related to false Florimell, whose false appearance of truth is universally successful. Like most things in Spenser's fictive world, the truth of persons is clouded by problems with perceiving the body. Persons are much more than just bodies, but bodily presence and physical actions are essential means through which full persons are expressed. The "darke conceit" of Spenser's narrative turns on this truth.

Here we need to return to an assumption in Spenser's letter to Raleigh, that a full person includes a physical presence identified by expressed intentions or, alternatively, intents or intendments. Essential intention tells us how we are to understand the gentleman or noble person to be fashioned by the poem.[8] The importance of personal intention is established early in characterization of Una, Redcrosse, and Arthur in book 1. Each person is defined by an overriding "intent." The narrator's preparation for the one-on-one battle between Redcrosse and the Saracen, Sans Foy, with Duessa as the winner's trophy, ironically balances Redcrosse's general motivation for his "aduenture" commissioned by Gloriana against his compromised, particular desire to defeat Sans Foy:

The noble hart, that harbours vertuous thought,
And is with child of glorious great intent,
Can neuer rest, vntill it forth haue brought
Th'eternall brood of glorie excellent:

> Such restlesse passion did all night torment
> The flaming corage of that Faery knight,
> Deuizing, how that doughtie turnament
> With greatest honour he atchieuen might;
> Still did he wake, and still did watch for dawning light.
>
> (1.5.1.1–9)

On a downward slide after separation from Una, Redcrosse suffers from inexperience competing with high chivalric aspiration, his "glorious great intent." The narrator's twisting irony lies in the particular application of a general truth. A "noble hart" necessarily has virtuous thoughts that conceive high intentions leading to praiseworthy actions. The reward is glorious fame. This general truth applied in particular to the deluded Redcrosse ironically reminds us that his ennobling "glorious great intent" remains despite his delusional slide downward. With an irony no less twisted, Archimago had shocked the virtuous Redcrosse with a sexually charged facsimile of Una. The knight's high-minded desertion strips away her virtuous presence from his "glorious great intent."

As for Una and her guiding intention to free her parents, her need for substitute protection subjects her to a series of incidents stressing the irony of Redcrosse's shortcoming. His impatient failure to interrogate unprecedented sexual forwardness contrasts sharply with the lion's touching protection of her. This inarticulate dumb beast nonetheless comprehends her "chast person": "From her faire eyes he tooke commaundement, / And euer by her lookes conceiued her intent" (1.3.9.8–9). Also, Satyrene's natural civility and grasp of truth are another implicit judgment of Redcrosse's defection. Una's containment by the community of idolatrous satyrs cannot obscure her intentions from Satyrene, however untrained his natural courtesy and grasp of truth. Aggrieved, but still committed to Redcrosse, she "shewed her intent" (1.6.32.7) that Satyrene should aid her escape. Una's mission to free her parents focuses her desire to find the absent, but necessary Redcrosse. She recognizes in Arthur an intentional nature similarly concentrated:

But what aduenture, or what high intent
Hath brought you hither into Fairy land,
Aread Prince *ARTHUR*, crowne of Martiall band?

(1.9.6.3–5)

Arthur's history, like Una's, guides his intentions. Cupid had sharply curtailed the youthful Arthur's avoidance of love, his misguided and doomed "intent" to freely roam the woods (1.9.12.9). Cupid fashions a dream in which he is visited by the "royall Maid" (1.9.13.7), Gloriana, the Queen of Fairies:

From that day forth I lou'd that face diuine;
From that day forth I cast in carefull mind,
To seeke her out with labour, and long tyne,
And neuer vow to rest, till her I find,
Nine monethes I seeke in vaine yet ni'll that vow vnbind.

(1.9.15.5–9)

Like Una's quest to reclaim Redcrosse and save her parents, Arthur's life is ruled by his intention to find Gloriana.

In Britomart we find Spenser's most engaging hero and, most important, a primary example of an intentional person. Like Arthur's parallel search for Gloriana, her search for Artegall contributes substantially to the poem's architectural frame. Britomart's amiable deception of Redcrosse, which stages his validating defense of Artegall, contains some of Spenser's subtlest and most appealing compound ironies. Unlike Duessa's and Archimago's duplicities, her virtuous personations seek the good. Whereas Archimago's personation of Redcrosse defies any moral likeness or chivalric ability, Britomart's self-defensive personation of an errant knight represents a genuine androgynous capacity to function in a male world. That personation is compounded by her pretended quest to take just revenge on Artegall for a previous violation. She is a pretend knight pretending revenge while enacting a justifiable duplicity:

All my delight on deedes of armes is set,
    To hunt out perils and aduentures hard,
    By sea, by land, where so they may be met,

Onely for honour and for high regard,
Without respect of richesse or reward.
For such intent into these parts I came,
Without encompasse, or withouten card,
Far fro my natiue soyle, that is by name
The greater *Britaine*, here to seeke for prayse and fame.

(3.2.7.1–9)

This doubled personation has a compelling half truth as does her unrelenting intent to find Artegall. Just as the person she claims to seek is not the person she hopes exists, she is and is not the person she appears to be. Her intention is and is not what she says, but intent she is. Her maternal companion, Glauce, recognizes the normalcy of her love anguish, distinguishing it from other lovers' "filthy lust" (3.2.40.4). That distinction little salves her painful dissatisfaction:

For they, how euer shamefull and vnkind,
Yet did possesse their horrible intent:
Short end of sorrowes they thereby did find;
So was their fortune good, though wicked were their mind.

(3.2.43.6–9)

Such short-term gratification opposes her virtuous intention; she is necessarily frustrated by an arduous and trying search to find her destined marriage partner. Frustrating deferral highly charges her anguish and prayerful longing that her "ship" reach "the gladsome port of her intent" (3.4.10.4–5). Spenser keeps reminding us that this strength of intention undergirds her adventures. Her unexpected duty to free Amoret when Scuddamour proves unable is strengthened by her intentional nature. On her own and unguided within the House of Busyrene while patiently interpreting the surroundings, she characteristically remains committed to her "first intent," not diverted by the uncertain meaning of the graphics.

Appropriately, Artegall as her destined mate mirrors her own intent nature. She first encounters his rough-cut self as the "Salwage knight," who challenges her supremacy at the tourney,

fiercely attacking her with "felonous intent" (4.6.11.6). Her abrupt
dispatch rejects his raw energy, "With fell intent" (4.6.23.3) taking command until both are eventually mollified by mutual recognition. The fierceness of this confrontation represents the
competitive accord necessary between two strong natures guided
by clear intentions. Whereas Britomart's intentionality is defined
by likeness to Arthur's search for a destined mate, Artegall's, like
that of Redcrosse, Guyon, and Caledore, is defined by serving a
royal mandate, even though Britomart and Artegall, both personally and allegorically, are a proper match. Following the wedding
ceremony that justly combines Florimell and Marinell, Artegall
leaves with Talus, his "gard and gouernment" (5.4.3.9) to follow
his "aduentures first intent / Which long agoe he taken had in
hond" (6–7). Later, his painful departure from Britomart, after she
releases him from Radigund's domination, emphasizes his intentionality by reiterating the same vocabulary. Accompanied only
by Talus, the "true guide of his way and vertuous gouernment"
(5.8.3.9), he resumes his "first intent" (6). Britomart's enabling support, in contrast to the constricting dominance of Radigund,
works to fufill the intentionality of persons.

To say that Spenser's conception of the person stresses bodily
presence and intent is not to ignore the necessarily connected
importance of the mind, the seat of thought, or the overlapping
notions of spirit and soul. The contrary is true. The language of
mind is used flexibly by Spenser to incorporate the various dimensions of intellective consciousness such as thinking, reasoning,
plotting, meditating, perceiving, conceiving, knowing, remember-
ing, ruminating, considering, imagining, intending, et al. Concerned
about the missing Timias, Arthur "wondrous pensive grew in
mind" (3.5.12.5). Britomart seeing her adversary, Artegall, his
beaver raised, recalls the earlier mirror image of his face:

> She gan eftsoones it to her mind to call,
> To be the same which in her fathers hall
> Long since in that enchaunted glasse she saw.
>
> (4.6.26.4–6)

Calidore governs his grief at Pastourella's imprisonment by conceiving a rational plan to free her: "in his mind with better reason cast" (6.11.34.4). For Spenser, the mind is predominantly, though not exclusively, intellective; it also includes the affective and volitional, the spiritual, and at times even the unconscious. Most broadly, "mind" denotes rational consciousness with all its participating faculties stamped with an individual's distinguishing moral temperament. Examples include Britomart's "noble mind" (3.11.4.7), Belphoebe's "Heroick mind" (3.5.55.5), Malbecco's "donghill mind" (3.10.15.3), Turpine's "mind malitious and ingrate" (6.6.2.5), the "fickle mind" of Blandamour "full of inconstancie" (4.1.32.5).

Affirmation in book five that the "gentle minde by gentle deeds is knowne" (6.3.1.2) cuts to the marrow and the formal heart of Spenser's narrative. Virtue is not just a mental state of disposition, but also a habit of purposeful action necessarily affecting others. Calidore reasons sequentially to the intention, then to the action that saves Pastourella: "in his mind" he "had closely made/ A further purpose" (6.11.38.7). Intention or purpose or minding is the seedbed of action that completes the person, either for good or ill. And, more, this defining action is relational, necessarily involving others. Accordingly, the work of the poem is to fashion virtuous intentions and actions in its heroes and, through their example, in its gentle and noble readers. The bare bones notion is that a person is a bodily presence enacting intentional, virtuous actions in relation to other persons. As we see later, these bones remain bare if Spenser's person is extracted from an English cultural frame in which basic relationships reflect male/female interactions and assume vocational responsibilities. But, first, more needs to be said about the "vertuous and gentle discipline" that fashions a full person contributing to common good.

A "discipline" of "ensamples"

Not just the letter to Raleigh, but *The Faerie Queene* itself reflects on virtuous discipline. Arthur tells Una that Merlin, who "had charge my discipline to frame / And Tutours nouriture to oversee" (1.9.5.3–4), had placed him in the hands of Timon, who "trained me vp in vertuous lore" (4.9). That exchange, by pointedly recalling the "pure" and "innocent" Una's adherence to "euery vertuous lore" (1.1.5.2) and her "discipline of faith and veritie" (1.6.31.9) taught to the satyrs, prepares for her similar role, supported by Arthur, in placing Redcrosse at the House of Holiness for rehabilitation. There he learns "celestiall discipline" taught by Fidelia (1.10.18.8). In book 5, the poet invokes "the first blossome of faire vertue bare" (5.Proem.1.4) in forming his own "discipline / Of vertue and of ciuill vses lore" (3.1–2). Accordingly, Artegall's "discipline of iustice" (5.1.6.9) at the hands of Astraea, now fled to heaven though still reflected in Elizabeth, also applies that principle. Like Arthur, Redcrosse, Artegall, and, by implication, other exemplars of virtue in the poem who learn "vertuous lore" through the teaching of others, readers are intended to learn from the poem's "vertuous and gentle discipline."

But it is not enough to say that persons are fashioned by "vertuous lore" or that resident teachers are essential. Spenser also goes out of his way to stress that his doctrinal mode is teaching by ensample, not by rule or precept. What he means by "ensamples" that fashion a "person" reveals still more about the marrow of his poem and the inherited habit of mind necessary to grasp it. The "ensample" of "Poets historicall" informed his making of *The Faerie Queene* just as each of the poem's heroes provided an "ensample" of "moral vertue" both "private" and "polliticke" ("Letter," 737).

Spenser's general concept of epic poets, the "ensample" of "Poets Historicall" and their exemplary heroes, is hardly novel, as revealed by a side glance at Sidney's *A Defence of Poesy* and its Italian humanistic precedents. The extent of Spenser's association with the Leicester circle is no more clear than whether or not he was party to discussions there of principles advanced in Sidney's *Defence*. Spenser did spend time there in 1579, and the *Defence*, presumably composed in 1580–85, praises the literary achievement of *The Shepheardes Calender*, a work concerned with issues about poetry. But it is clear that Sidney's *Defence*, like the letter to Raleigh and *The Faerie Queene* itself, asserts poetry's power to teach virtue through heroic example. In particular, Sidney cites Ulysses and Diomedes as examples of wisdom and temperance, Achilles of valor, Nisus and Euryalus of friendship. Like earlier humanistic treatises on poetry, the *Defence* cites Aeneas as the "virtuous man in all fortunes."[9] Spenser's "doctrine," bisected alternatively into "rule" or "precept," *versus* the pleasing and affecting "ensample" created by the "Poets historicall" is akin to Sidney's "feigned example" (*Defence*, 89) of poetry that conflates the bare universal "precept" of moral philosophy with the experiential "example" of history (*Defence*, 85–86). Sidney defends poetry for morally elevating the experiential particular beyond what is to what ought to be. Baxter Hathaway notes, "The poet makes the world's dross metal golden, as Sidney suggested."[10] Spenser's Arthur is like Sidney's Aeneas: "So in the person of Prince Arthure I sette forth magnificence in particular, which vertue . . . is the perfection of all the rest." In Arthur is "doctrine by ensample" ("Letter," 737), the inclusive virtue of magnificence in his exemplary experience.

Sidney's formal defense gathers, incorporates, and clarifies much in previous humanistic poetic theory for English readers. A Renaissance humanistic assumption that history recorded what actually happened, but poetry what should have happened, reached all the way back to Aristotle's *Poetics*.[11] A vision of the Roman Aeneas as the perfected exemplar that for Spenser also "ensampled a good gouernour and a vertuous man" was widely shared by Italian Renaissance humanists, in particular, Tasso, whose imprint can be found in both Sidney and Spenser. Tasso's conception of the epic hero as a virtuous example to be imitated is a staple of Italian humanistic epic theory.[12]

But the pivotal importance of virtuous "ensample" in *The Faerie Queene* cannot be attributed solely to the search for poetic models. Teaching and learning by example supported a habit of mind deeply engrained in the disciplines of both secular and divine literatures. Arthur in his "long education by Timon . . . throughly instructed" ("Letter," 757; cf. 1.9.4.1–9) and in Artegall's tutelage by Astraea in the "discipline of iustice (5.1.6.9) speak directly to Renaissance educational practice of "vertuous lore" presided over by moral tutors. A primary divine example not unrelated to Fidelia's "celestiall discipline" (1.10.18.8) taught to Redcrosse can be found in Protestant Thomas Becon's *The Gouernaunce of Vertue*. This programmatic work was dedicated to "the right honourable and most vertuous young Lady Jane Semer, doughter to the hie and mighty Prince Edward, Duke of Somerset his grace."[13] Like Timon, who had "trained . . . vp" Arthur in "vertuous lore" (1.9.4.9), Becon had presided for a time as a tutor over the education of Jane Seymour, daughter of Lord Protector, Thomas Seymour, and his devoutly learned Protestant wife, Ann Seymour. Lady Seymour had employed Becon, later a Marian exile, in their household. His presence attested to her deep commitment to Protestant principles and to appropriate learning. Becon's preface aims at the parents as well as their daughter and her brothers in affirming the connection between virtue and learning: "There are no parents (most godly Lady) that deserue better of the Christian publique weal, then they which thorow Gods gift hauinge children, employ all their endeauors to train them up even from theyr very cradels in good letters & in the knowledge of Goddes most blessed wil, that they with theyr young yeres, learning, and Vertue and Godlinesse, may growe and encrease . . . This carefull study and studious care for the vertuous bringing up of youth God in past earnestly required of all fathers and Mothers in the common wele of his people the Israelites" (*Gouernaunce*, fol. ccxxv). The book's discipline thus contributes to training Lady Jane, her brothers and other Protestant readers as virtuous, godly citizens serving common good.

   Strict form imposes discipline, and form no less than content is essential here. Dominating the *Gouernaunce* is an insistent, reiterative structure of chapters programmatically stacking short biblical "sentences" and "examples" in a relentless frame, to use Spenser's terms, for this "discipline" or "lore." Each chapter contains (a) "Sentences out of the olde Testament," (b) "Examples out of the olde Testament," (c) "Sentences out of the new Testament," (d) "Examples out of the new Testament." Within this frame, individual chapters address different remedies for different temptations. The range includes idolatry, "infidelitie or misbeliefe" (*Gouernaunce,* fol. ccxxix), the "grosse and fantasticall opinion of the Papystes" on the Eucharist (fol. ccxxxix), and the Protestant stance on faith/works. The brief "sentence" can be a significant fact or truth, or an exhortation; the also brief, answering "example" has a narrative cast. This reiterative structure of biblical sentences and examples enforces a Protestant emphasis on the Word. The Procrustean sentence/example structure can also be seen as reflecting on thought/action and soul/body relationships. By distinguishing principle from illustrative event, Becon's structure shares a kinship with Spenser's distinction between precept and example. And the title in pointing to virtue's governance clearly ties its content to the habit of virtuous action. The narrative cast of these reiterative biblical examples is especially telling in this regard, an instructive Protestant parallel to Spenser's narrative discipline or lore in *The Faerie Queene.*

Thomas Elyot's somewhat earlier *The Boke Named the Gouernour* (1531), is a primary humanist text that likewise centers on virtuous action taught by example. The long-lived influence of Elyot's *Boke* attests to the favorable reception of its assumptions by like-minded readers. And like Becon's *The Gouernaunce of Vertue* and Spenser's *The Faerie Queene,* Elyot's text was written for literate members of the governing class. In all three cases, a discipline of virtuous lore determines predominant and compelling structural features intended to shape human behavior through necessary learning by example. Elyot's conception of example in *The Boke* tells us more about the intellectual context for Spenser's similar notion.

Unfinished, like Spenser's *The Faerie Queene,* Elyot's book stops far short of his original humanistic intention to make a two-part work dealing first with education and virtues and second with the office and duties of a governor or lower magistrate. Though only half a loaf, since part two was never written, the often republished *Boke* remained popular throughout the sixteenth century and virtually obligatory for "gentlemen" and others of Spenser's generation. Elyot advances a cooperative mode of governance between the "one soueraigne gouernour or prince," and his appointed "inferiour gouernours called Magistrates" charged with "aydyng hym in the distribution of iustice in sondry partes of a huge multitude" (*Boke* 1:23–25). A select number of "inferiour gouernours" would serve as a prince's counselors. A. N. McLaren usefully characterizes this select group: "Elyot defined counsellors as virtuous men whose goodness would be capable of restraining and finally educating the king's will. The conjunction of king and counselors would therefore institute virtue in the realm."[14]

Elyot intended to fashion the lesser governors by constructing an agenda for their education, then by anatomizing virtues to guide their actions as servants of the Crown. One mark of Elyot's programmatic agenda is a continuing presence of moral advisors who, like Arthur's mentor Timon, guide the growing person through incremental moral development. Initially, there is a mature wet nurse "of no seruile condition or vice notable," overseen by a governess of "approued vertue, discretion, and grauitie" (*Boke* 1:29) to monitor exemplary behavior around the child in "wordes . . . faictes and gesture" (*Boke* 1:30). Education through an exemplary moral presence continues when formal training begins around age seven with a tutor, "whiche shulde be an auncient and worshipfull man" grave, gentle, worthy of imitating and if "lerned . . . the more commendable" (*Boke* 1:36). Graded subjects suitable for the child's intellectual development are introduced in this benign environment. In time, a teacher of Latin and Greek guides reading progressively selected for moral content that makes a virtuous person eventually able to serve the "publike weale" as an "inferiour gouernour."

Graded readings with examples of virtuous actions are followed at age fourteen by oratorical and other texts. Such early, graded moral readings rising to greater complexity frame the child's behavior. A younger child might begin with Aesop and later, Homer. At age 14, the child is introduced to texts on oratory by predictable authors like Demosthenes and Cicero, including "commodious examples of all vertues and pollicie" (*Boke* 1:76). Such readings prepare a future governor for right behavior and right speaking in counsels and public places. Geography and history are likewise important during this period. Again, the historians are predictable, including Sallust, Livy, Tacitus; so, too, are the many preferred values of elegant style, moral development, and pragmatic governance skill. The "yonge gentilman" taught "to note and marke" (*Boke* 1:90) the values in histories, then steps upward at age 17 to moral philosophy.

A conviction that stability of the "publicke weale" rests on the governor's moral power is perhaps nowhere more obvious than in this segment of Elyot's virtuous lore. Here the "yonge gentilman" is placed under the influence of Aristotle, Cicero, Plato, Erasmus, and books of the Old Testament. For Elyot, moral philosophy is less a final stage in an educational agenda than a constructed center for a lifelong, studious habit whereby moral philosophy "instructeth men in vertue and politike gouernaunce" (*Boke* 1:131), the coin's two sides. Elyot's educational agenda stations an exemplary good man as the master who prescribes graded moral reading for the youth. In turn, the mature governor, practiced in continued reading of appropriate texts, governs through the "noble example" of his life (*Boke* 2:1). Public order assumes virtuous living for which the governors are examples. Their personal virtue depends on continued learning, especially in history and moral philosophy.

Elyot's anatomy of moral virtues assumes that "example" is a necessary working connection between virtue and learning. All three subsidiary parts of the *Boke* work this connection. The first part is the educational agenda; the other two anatomize the virtues through a commentary freely intermingling precept and example. A full array of virtues includes the standard Ciceronian foursome of justice, temperance, prudence, and fortitude. These are supplemented from predictable Christian humanist virtuous lore with friendship, benevolence, patience, faith, and mercy applied to the political life of the governor. At the outset Elyot leaves little room for doubt about the role of example in his method. In advancing his notion of the "publike weale," he will "proue, by example of those thynges that be within the compasse of mannes knowledge, of what estimation ordre is" (*Boke* 1:4). The reader becomes habituated to Elyot's method. The anatomy of virtues cites examples from wide-ranging humanistic texts in support of reasons and precepts. The first three parts of the *Boke* insistently introduce examples that reinforce virtues necessary for ideal governance. And in Elyot's notion of example we find a cultural imperative that Spenser is also obeying in *The Faerie Queene.*

Elyot's definition of example as "experience" surfaces in his final extant chapter that deals with the intellective virtues essential in governance of the perfect "publike weale." Appropriately in a work recommending cooperative governance by a prince willingly counseled by lesser governors, Elyot's book comes to rest in essential counsel. His final distillation speaks for much: "And this conclude I to write any more of consultation, whiche is the last part of morall Sapience, and the begynnyng of sapience politike" (*Boke* 2:447). Consultation brings wise intellection and good will together on the common ground of wisdom, and "good counsayle" is the "ende of all doctrine and studie," the goal of Elyot's discipline, his virtuous lore. Early in the *Boke,* Elyot promises his reader to follow "the thre noble maisters, reason lernynge, and experience" (*Boke* 1:24). By implication, those who submit to his book's discipline will follow his masters' lead to the same goal, to good counsel. To adopt his educational agenda is to listen to his book's wise counsel. Reason is the agent of the intellect, the human's highest faculty, to be trained through learning and informed by experience. "The knowledge of this Experience is called Example, and is expressed by historie, whiche of Tulli [Cicero] is called the life of memorie" (*Boke* 2:384). Wisdom comes from this knowledge of "experience," from "example."

Experience comes in two forms. The first is the actions of other persons, both good and bad; the second is "experience . . . in our propre persones" called "practice" (*Boke* 2:402). Interaction between these two kinds of experience everywhere informs Elyot's conception of the *Boke.* From the beginning, the very experience of the educational agenda hinges on the exemplary presence of moral persons, then increasingly on selected readings from humanistic texts embodying exemplary human actions.

Elyot's educational agenda intends to fashion a moral governor whose own actions become examples for others, while he continues to search out informing examples from history embodied in significant texts. For Elyot, "example" as knowledge of experience centers on the observable "actes" of other persons (*Boke* 2:383).

Such exemplary physical "actes" can inform our understanding of virtue and bodily presence in Spenser's "person" represented in *The Faerie Queene*. The centrality of "actes" in "example" explains Elyot's emphasis on recreational physical activities, especially dancing, too easily dismissed by some readers as mere digression. For Elyot, such activity embodies the principle that appropriate physical exercise expresses moral values, as well as training for "actes" later in life. For instance, riding that "importeth a maiestie and drede to inferiour persones" is appropriate for "euery noble persone" (*Boke* 1:181–82). Alexander fighting valiantly with a lion exemplifies valor, hence demonstrating the value embodied in the act of hunting. (*Boke* 1:190), and shooting with a longbow, while training in the necessary use of weapons, also teaches moderation more than any other activity. Elyot's elaborated disquisition on dancing as an inherently social and ritualized activity between the sexes endorses the principle shared with Spenser that physical presence and actions are essential elements in the person and that good governance is consciously enacted through the body. Actions of good governors are examples to others and, as such, essential fibers in the "publike weal."

Elyot's extended commentary on dancing provides an especially telling perspective on Spenser's notion of "person" that includes women in *The Faerie Queene*. Virtuous interaction between the sexes represents an essential component of the full person: "It is diligently to be noted that the associatinge of man and in daunsing, they bothe obseruinge one nombre and tyme in their meuynges, was nat begonne without a speciall consideration, as well for the necessarye coniunction of those two persones, as for the intimation of sondry vertues, whiche be by them represented" (*Boke* 1.233). Elyot's introductory defense works to clear away a previous burden of moral objections to dancing in order to occupy those grounds himself. Underlying his justification of dancing is a main-line argument in *Boke* that educating a governor is essentially a virtuous endeavor. He enlists a host of historical authorities to justify the value of dance. He notes that among "all honest passe times" he found "daunsinge to be of an excellent utilitie, com-prehendinge in it wonderfull figures, or, as the grekes do calle them, *Ideae,* of vertues and noble qualities." His anatomy of ritualized bodily movements in dance is essentially an anatomy of pru-dence, "the firste morall vertue" (*Boke* 1.238–39). The first move, "honour" (*Boke* 1:241), comprising three motions, signifies the beginning of all acts, the necessary honoring of God that includes fear, love, and reverence. Later ritualized motions represent "*Maturitie*" (*Boke* 1:243), a moral ripeness that includes moder-ation and fullness. Other motions enact "Prouidence" (*Boke,* 1:246), a consultative disposition that weighs advantages for the "publike weale." And other "braunches" embodied in different motions include industry, circumspection, election, and experi-ence. Admittedly, Elyot's extended anatomy of other "braunches" of prudence can erode our own virtue of patience. Nonetheless, to Elyot, the very detailed performance of dance ritual embodies the complex moral involvement in a "publike weale."

Anatomized virtues essential in the governor are, by implica-tion, appropriate for women of the ruling class, an aspect devel-oped more fully in *The Faerie Queene*. In regard to gender, the "publike weale" of Elyot and his Henrician readers differed markedly from that of Spenser and his audience. Elizabeth's extended reign and pervasive influence required an attention to gender only latent in Henry's time, and Elyot's inattention to women in *Boke* contrasts sharply with complex intentions in Spenser's fashioning of Belphoebe and Britomart, to say nothing of less obvious female creations. But that sharp contrast cannot blunt the complex importance of Elyot's emphasis on dancing. Formalized and ritualized concord between male and female in dancing occurs within a social/political community. Male and female dance partners willingly, and, however unwittingly, become mutual examples enacting the moral/political virtues necessary in an ideal "publike weale." In short, dancing contributes to common good.

For both Elyot and Spenser, virtue is performed by visible persons conscious of their physical presence in relation to others. No doubt Spenser had read the *Boke*. But we need not assume that he had done so while we note their shared conviction that virtue exists as exemplary, physical, personal "actes" viewed by others. Reading the *Boke*, therefore, provides a useful cultural perspective on the assumptions guiding Spenser's own virtuous lore. Virtuous actions in his chivalric narrative, whatever allegorical inflections he fashions, are visible examples that can benefit other persons. Virtue exists most fully when seen by others.

Gender in the English Person

Elyot's educational regimen included a lifetime of reading, especially in moral philosophy and history that kept examples central in the governor's virtuous life. Virtuous lore embodied in Spenser's fictive "historicall" poem is fashioned to do likewise. However, the intentionality that defines exemplary personal virtue in *The Faerie Queene* is rooted by Spenser in British national culture, relationships turning on gender, vocational responsibility, and civic duty. Spenser may follow the "antique Poets historicall" in fashioning virtuous examples, but the dutiful actions of his heroes embody distinctive gender-consciousness under Elizabethan rule. Marked differences between his persons and Elyot's are instructive in this regard. First, we will look at male instances of British persons before incorporating the issues of gender incorporated in his person.

Spenser's "vertuous lore" is comprised of British "ensamples." Most obvious are the Redcrosse Knight and Guyon; the kinsmen Arthur and Artegall; and the latter's destined mate, Britomart. Allusions linking Redcrosse to St. George, England's patron saint, come early in the poem,[15] explicit nomination much later. At the House of Holiness, Contemplation, while climactically revealing that the knight is "sprong out from English Race" (1.10.60.1),

promises him a heavenly life with other saints if he follows a path
of active virtue:

> For thou emongst those Saints, whom thou doest see,
> Shalt be a Saint, and thine owne nations frend
> And Patrone: thou Saint *George* shalt called bee,
> Saint *George* of mery England, the signe of victoree.

(1.10.61.6–9)

Redcrosse and Arthur mirror each other as British heroes enacting a Christly paradigm by slaying a reptilian monster on behalf
of others. Arthur's nomination by Una prevenes Redcrosse's by
Contemplation later. In Arthur's report of his "discipline" framed
by Merlin (1.9.5.3) and taught by Timon, Una recognizes Arthur's
personal history. Timon had taught him "Vnder the foot of
Rauran," the source of River Dee (1.9.4.6), the border between
England and Wales. Arthur is a British person. Only later in book
2, when Arthur and Guyon are entertained at the House of Alma,
does Spenser examine how that national culture functions as a
necessary aspect of the person. The key lies in personal memory,
the living residence of historical example.

In book 2 Spenser is constructing forthright, but qualified
structural parallels to book 1 in order to characterize the human
being's natural capacities. Arthur's previous rescue of Redcrosse
from Orgolio's dungeon leads to the depleted knight's spiritual ther-
apy at House of Holiness. Later, Arthur's rescue of the vulnerable Guyon, exhausted after his willing ascent from Mammon's
subterranean hold, leads to healing physical rest and recreation
for both Arthur and Guyon in Alma's house. A broad-brush claim
that books 1–2 respectively engage the domains of Grace and
Nature,[16] if not viewed as mutually exclusive compartments,
invites consideration of temperance as the habit of rational self-
control that assumes an underlying need for Grace. Alma, the
human soul, presides over her allegorical House, the human body,
her rationally temperate governance preserving order inside the
house, while commanding it as a fortress from outside attacks.
She and her House represent a fulfilled natural state, and readers

accompany her two visitors on an allegorical walking tour that is a programmed exercise in self-understanding.

Spenser's allegorical rendering of the natural body and soul assumes that the full natural person necessarily participates in national culture and history. The intentionality that guides bodily presence cannot be understood apart from the national history that informs virtuous lore. Alma leads Guyon and Arthur to the "stately Turret" (2.9.44.8) housing the allegorical presentations of the rational faculties, imagination, reason, and memory. In the library of old Eumestes (Good Memory), the two knights find the two books, *Briton Moniments* and *Antiquity of Faerie*, glossed respectively in Spenser's header beginning canto 10:

> A chronicle of Briton kings,
> > from Brute to Vthers rayne.
> And rolles of Elfin Emperours,
> > till time of Gloriane.

What the two knights see represented allegorically in the "turret" chamber of Eumestes is the way national history imprints their own persons, both in the real British world and in the imaginary, idealized world of Faerie. Spenser would agree with Elyot's Ciceronian notion that history is "the life of memorie" (*Boke* 2:384) and that both good and bad examples from history teach persons. Spenser's allegory offers a compelling sense of how historical examples residing in the memory inform personal understanding and identity. In the chronicle of British royalty in the *Briton moniments*, Arthur discovers the civilizing work by successors of the second Brute, by which Spenser is tracing the Tudors' Welsh roots. Brute left a heritage of "lasting peace" to be enriched by his city-building son, Leill, and grandson Bladud, who were learned in "sweet science" that "mollifide their [savage residents] stubborne harts" (2.10.25.2,9):

> Ensample of his wondrous faculty,
> > Behold the boyling Bathes at *Cairbadon*,
> Which seeth with secret fire eternally,

And in their entrails, full of quicke Brimston,
Nourish the flames, which they are warm'd vpon,
That to their people wealth they forth do well,
And health to euery forreine nation:

(26.1–7)

A living memory is a historical library of good and bad "ensamples" that inform understanding and the actions that follow. A principle of Spenser's own virtuous lore — to borrow a phrase from a different context in the poem — is that examples "deepe written" in the human heart "with an yron pen" (1.8.44.8) fashion personal intentionality.

The place of national history in shaping persons is more complex in Britomart. No less than Arthur, Guyon, and Artegall, her person is defined as British. Her name clearly identifies her British nature while paradoxically identifying this palpably nubile young woman more with Mars, than Venus. Her chivalric disguise points to Elizabeth's political androgyny and her own occasional appearances in chivalric costume. At the same time Britomart's intent search for her destined marriage partner, Artegall, ever reminds us just how nubile she is. She is the most human of Spenser's characters and the most likely to break through her allegorical constraints. At the same time she represents Spenser's attempt to characterize the androgyny of some persons. Issues of gender and national identity are intertwined in her.

The "discipline" of Spenser's narrative romance foregrounds actions of both men and women. The intentionality of his heroes is basically gendered. Male persons are defined by their relationship to women, and vice versa. Arthur's intentionality is defined by his love quest for Gloriana, as is Britomart's for Artegall. Guyon serves Gloriana, later to be yoked with Medina. Betrothed to Britomart, Artegall follows her authority, not that of her destructive feminine shadow, Radigund. Calidore's discovery of Pastourella postpones his personal duty to Gloriana and uncovers a parallel pattern of courtesy outside the Court. The collection of friendships established in book 4 hinges on heterosexual linkages, including the friendship of Britomart and Amoret, sympathetically bonded by separation from destined male lovers. Just as a "person" is identified by cultural history, so too by heterosexual links. Arthur's "person" fashioned in Spenser's poem seeks personal fulfillment in Gloriana. And the gentle and noble persons to be fashioned by the poem are variations of gendered consciousness. That essential point is qualified, not compromised, by anomalous Belphoebe, who unlike Gloriana is served only by women, not men, but must learn to allow the appropriate service of Timias. Allusion to Elizabeth's treatment of Raleigh merely underlines the qualification.

For Spenser, cultural identity and gendered relationships are part of the same essential truth of person. By contrast, Elyot's male "person" can be extracted easily from British soil. Like Virgil and his other epic masters, Spenser fixes his heroic examples in his own historical time. A "person" for his time lives, moves, and possesses being in a culture dominated pervasively by Queen Elizabeth represented in Gloriana, idealized Queen of Fairie Land and "shadowed" in Belphoebe, Britomart, and others. Spenser's own life from the age of four was lived entirely within the cultural shadow cast by Elizabeth. Like Arthur, the persons fashioned by the poem must negotiate a world ruled by a queen served by male governors,[17] no less than Roman readers of Virgil's *Aeneid* faced a world dominated by the emperor, Augustus. A failure to negotiate the reach of Elizabeth's presence and its imprint on the "person" is not to follow "all the antique Poets historicall," who address in the persons of their heroes the essential experience of their times.

Too easily forgotten is that the gentleman or noble person living in Elizabeth's world and taught by Spenser's virtuous and gentle discipline necessarily included female as well as male readers. Elizabeth was Spenser's primary reader. His dedicatory sonnets honored the Countess of Pembroke, Lady Carew and, expansively, "all the gratious and beautifull Ladies in the Court" (*Hamilton*, 743). Increasingly, scholarship has discovered the expanded roles of many of the wives of Elizabeth's important civil servants and counselors. The Cooke sisters are especially notable. Their education was supervised by their father, Arthur

Cooke, tutor to Edward IV and later a Member of Parliament under Elizabeth. The oldest daughter, Mildred, married to William Cecil, Elizabeth's primary secretary and most trusted counselor, was acclaimed by Roger Ascham, a humanist tutor of Elizabeth, as "one of the most learned women of England."[18] Her influence was likewise considerable. Mary Ellen Lamb points to a complaint by the Catholic ambassador of Spain that she was a "'tiresome blue-stocking' and a 'furious heretic' of great influence over her husband."[19] Mildred managed Cecil's important political household and aided his activities as master of the Court of Wards, in particular, the education of wards within the Cecil household. Younger sister Anne was wife to Nicholas Bacon, lord keeper of the great seal and, like Cecil, a member of the Privy Council. Lamb quotes Sidney Lee's observation that "'the Queen was content for many years following her accession to leave the ordering of the Church matters for the most part' in the hands of Bacon and Cecil, a privilege they used to further the interests of the reformed religion."[20] The Cooke sisters' learned interest in religion is especially suggestive in this Reformed context. Mildred's learned achievement, praised so highly by Ascham, included wide reading in the church fathers and a translation of Chrysostom no longer extant. For her part, Anne translated 14 sermons of Bernard Occhino, an Italian Calvinist, as well as the *Apologia Ecclesiae Anglicanae,* an official text authored primarily by John Jewel and, at least in part, by William Cecil. Both sisters were appropriate mates for governors serving the Elizabethan commonwealth at the highest level. A third sister, Elizabeth, married Thomas Hoby, Reformist Tudor diplomat and translator of a Martin Bucer text as well as Castiglioni's, *The Courtier.* Knighted in 1565, Hoby was a product of St. John's College, Cambridge, a primary source of Reformist governors who served both Edward and Elizabeth. A translator like her husband, Elizabeth Hoby translated *A Way of Reconciliation Touching the True Nature and Substance of the Blood and Body of Christ in the Sacrament.* Her literary skill, command of other languages including Latin, and familiarity with religious issues, plus evidence of a "sharp legal mind,"[21] confirm that, no less than her sisters, she was an appropriate mate for a governing class male espousing Reformed values.

The Cooke sisters suggest a historical pattern. Like Britomart, who embodies the principle of married love destined to serve the nation, they stand in a line of women preceding them with similar contributions. Anne Cooke's active sheltering of Reformed preachers at her own estate parallels actions much earlier of Anne Seymour, wife to the Lord Protector, Edward Seymour. John King notes that Lady Seymour "granted positions in her household to three reformist authors: Thomas Becon, Nicolas Denisot and William Samuel."[22] Thomas Becon's forward to *The Gouernaunce of Vertue* praises Lord and Lady Seymour for educating both sons and daughters to suggest intellectual parity. Along with Catherine Brandon and Mary Fitzroy, Anne Seymour was an associate of Catherine Paar, Henry VIII's last wife, a distinguished patroness of learning who influenced the education of Princess Elizabeth. As John King tells us, Anne Seymour effectively succeeded Catherine Parr: "Anne Seymour rivaled Catherine Parr as the leading lady in the land after Henry VIII's death because of her husband's rise to a position of authority at the court of a minor king. Accordingly Mildred Cecil's dedication of her manuscript translation of a sermon by Saint Basil acknowledges Lady Seymour's prominent position at court. . . . She and the two other Protestant duchesses, Mary Fitzroy and, especially, Catherine Brandon, were wholly committed to the new Protestant ascendancy. Although they followed Catherine Parr's lead in appointing distinguished humanists as tutors in their households, they went beyond her noncontroversial piety to encourage the radical activities of a tightly knit school of professional authors and translators."[23] Roles played by devout, learned, aristocratic women in shaping the education of highborn Protestant young, especially through the choice of tutors, are of major significance. Their influence is a function of both their Reformist activism and their placement through marriage near seats of governing power.

This line of learned, activist women extending from Catherine Parr through the Cooke sisters contributed to a Reformist drift in the English church. Anne Seymour's presence in this line demonstrates how such devoutly learned and activist women affected the cultural vocabulary: "Biblical paradigms such as the Woman Clothed with the Sun (Rev. 12), which were applied in praise of such reformist heroines as Anne Askew and Princess Elizabeth, contributed to the emergence of the Reformation iconographical tradition of the 'true Christian woman.'" Formulaic praise of Anne Seymour as an example of the Protestant Woman of Faith is, for example, a recurrent theme in the many dedications addressed to her during the reign of Edward VI. The archbishop of Canterbury's printer, Walter Lynne, in his *Briefe Collection* (1549) of scriptural readings for consoling the sick, praises her as "the most gracious patronesse & supportar both of good learnynge and also of godly men learned."[24] In this notion of the "true Christian woman" lies a suggestive background for Spenser's characterization of Una as a representation of the true church. She is pure and innocent "in life and euery vertuous lore" (1.1.5.2); unveiled, "the glorious light of her sunshyny face" illuminates her surroundings (1.12.23.2). An activist, she first seeks aid at Gloriana's court, then accompanies Redcrosse on his assigned mission, then searches for him after their separation. With Arthur she leads the depleted Redcrosse to rehabilitation and spiritual discipline at the House of Holiness, where he regains strength to perform his role sponsored by Gloriana. Una's allegorical scope as the true Church, representing both the Bride of Christ and Queen Elizabeth as the church's constitutional head, can thus widen to include the educated activism of Protestant women.

Spenser would have been familiar with the contributions to the English church of this line of highborn Protestant women. Though born of low status, he was educated at Cambridge,[25] an epicenter of educated Reformist thought, which had produced a variety of Reformist governors. These included Thomas Hoby, William Cecil, and Francis Walsingham, high level governors in Elizabeth's regime, as well as ecclesiastical leaders like the archbishop of Canterbury, Edward Grindal. Spenser's specific knowledge of church matters would have been encouraged by his early stint as secretary to Bishop John Young, represented as Roffy of *The Shepheardes Calender*. His detailed treatment of ecclesiastical issues in the *Calender*, including sympathy with the beleaguered Grindal, represented as Algrind, demonstrates a keen interest in ecclesiastical issues and church reform.[26] Brief association with the aggressively Protestant circle around Duke of Leicester, including Philip Sidney, would have reinforced his understanding of Reformist culture and its influence on governance issues. His fashioning of Una's activism suggests that the church cannot be understood apart from the important shaping influence of its women members.

Spenser's traditional personation of the English church as female betrothed to the British believer serves a more fundamental truth in *The Faerie Queene* about the role of gender in fashioning persons. That truth ties the active contribution of Protestant women in establishing the Elizabethan church to the central activism of Britomart in pursuing her marital alliance with Artegall. That is, the essential "person" fashioned by the poem, whether male or female, is defined in relation to the opposite gender, through whom British cultural values are also filtered and embraced in various ways. Ideally, the essential person will accommodate to the opposing gender through marriage that endorses British values. Like Una, Britomart shadows Elizabeth in her activist contribution to British culture. Together with Gloriana, the idealized marriage partner of Arthur, Britomart also reflects the marriage option for Elizabeth. If not, Belphoebe in accepting the appropriate service of Timias represents an alternative mode that subordinates the male, but is also defined by that gendered relationship.

Gendered pairings through courtship, betrothal, wedding, and marriage provide essential narrative arteries of the poem, variously anticipated, pursued, enacted or deferred. Structural interplay between male and female reminds readers that each person incorporates habits of response to the other gender. More broadly, the reader is reminded that the habits of virtue guiding these responses are relational. The connection between the genders undergirds almost all other relations in the full person in a culture pervaded and self-consciously influenced by a female monarch.

Here lies Britomart's central importance. The forceful presence of an intentional, activist woman on horseback, frequently dominating her surroundings, governs books 3 through 5. Her exemplary "adventures" involving others do much to explain Spenser's choice of narrative as a form for "vertuous and gentle discipline." Chivalric adventure, a connected series of events necessarily affecting other persons, represents virtue as a habit of acting toward others in a patterned way. Britomart's willingness to aid others, in particular Scuddamour and Amoret, cannot be separated from the sense of cultural responsibility that defines her personal intentions to seek her destined mate and father of her British descendants. Nor can the Protestant emphasis upon marriage be forgotten here. Her pursuit of a relationship with Artegall defines a habit of chastity that is a cultural birthright, given, then developed. That destined relationship guided by the habit of chastity is her British duty, just as her chivalric forcefulness recommends an androgynous role for the female "person" fashioned by the poem. The model is Elizabeth, the activist British virgin queen, who herself would adopt chivalric costume on occasion. Her failure to marry stops short of her full destiny. But, like Gloriana, her virtues in relation to her subjects define her governance.

The relational sense of a person's duty leads inevitably to the notion of virtue in *The Faerie Queene*. Spenser begins his narrative with the silhouetted Redcrosse in relation to Una. His quest, sanctioned by Gloriana, is to free Una's parents and her homeland from a besetting monster. This silhouette contains much that is paradigmatic in Spenser's poem: male and female together serve a higher order by performing earthly duty. Redcrosse's chivalric adventures develop virtue necessary for his defeat of the monster. Learned holiness prepares the believer for residence in the heavenly Jerusalem, anticipated in a vision at the House of Holiness, but only after dutiful service to the true church on earth. Adventures moved by loving the true church are conceived through the personal relationship of male and female. Together with others, a fulfilled person — intentional, bodily present, guided by virtuous habit, bonded through gender — serves both an earthly and a heavenly order, two sides of the same truth. Spenser's poetic task is to fashion that person by defining the constituent virtues contributing to an umbrella virtue, magnificence. Fashioning personal duty is a poetic goal that sometimes recedes into the background in discussion of this complex text. But the virtuous habits encouraged by the poem's complex narrative discipline are framed by assumptions of Protestant vocation and humanistic civic duty. These assumptions link hero, reader, and poet together as persons defined by duty. Spenser's relational sense of virtue necessarily binds the individual person together with other dutiful members of the national community. The silhouette of Redcrosse and Una thus remains the keynote.

This bond between the individual and the nation helps to clarify Spenser's vexing traditional distinction between a "priuate" person's "morall vertues" and a public governor's "polliticke vertues" ("Letter," 737). Critical assessments have endeavored to account for the gulf between the ambitious plan traced out for Raleigh and Spenser's actual poem. One plausible take is that Spenser changed course following the 1590 publication of books 1–3, and that books 4–6 situating the person respectively in social (friendship), political (justice), and civic (courtesy) contexts, pointedly lead outside the private realm. This kind of argument is bolstered by the political allegory in book 5 and Artegall's forceful adventures on behalf of "polliticke" order. For many readers, this argument is weakened by Spenser's alleged disenchantment, late emerging in book 6, when Calidore shifts his gendered loyalty from Gloriana to Pastorella. He temporarily abandons his "former quest" serving Gloriana for "Another quest" to live with Pastorella and other "rusticke sort" (6.10.2.2–5); put differently, he retreats from the public to the private. He resumes the earlier quest later, capturing the Blatant Beast; but, the argument goes, the beast's escape further signals Spenser's lost faith in earthly order, in any but private virtues. The force of this counterargument suffers from another reading that emphasizes the prophetic, apocalyptic dimensions of the poem: the allegory points to an ideal communal realm that reassures ultimate harmony in spite of earthly disruption. That argument is further supported by blaming the disenchantment on practices at the Court, not the possibility of earthly political order.

Whichever direction we might take, seeing only private virtues or a modulation to "polliticke" or more public virtues, we need to carry in mind that the anatomized virtues, even the most "private" virtues, holiness and temperance, dutifully serve other persons. Enlightened through a vision of the New Jerusalem, the recuperated Redcrosse is sent back down the Hill of Contemplation obliged to resume "that royall maides bequeathed care" (1.10.63.7). The Dragon defeated, he is rewarded with Una's "ioyous presence and sweet company" (1.12.41.1), but dutifully remembers his oath "Vnto his Farie Queene backe to returne" (41.8). The higher duty includes the lower, since Elizabeth in her monarchical role as head of the English church, is shadowed in Una. Individual belief, spiritualized by private devotional practice and contemplation, actively serves the true British church, an earthly institution authorized by the crown. Established in faith by grace, private temperance depends upon natural reason, embodied in Guyon's faithful Palmer, but without denying the priority of holiness. Like holiness, temperate self-control bears social responsibility circumscribed by service to the crown. On others' behalf, Guyon destroys Acrasia's subversion of necessary marital and familial bonds. Holiness and temperance discipline "private" self-mastery that is fulfilled by a person's dutiful participation in a shared community, imagined or otherwise.[27]

Virtuous adventures earn temporary rewards that defer final earthly closure for individuals. Redcrosse and Guyon complete their assigned quests, though afterwards Redcrosse returns to serve Gloriana and Guyon seeks further worthy "adventures." Britomart and Artegall unite only temporarily until he leaves to continue his quest. Calidore first delays his quest in pursuit of Pastorella, then resumes it to stifle the Blatant Beast. Arthur, whose magnificence subsumes all other virtues, serves other persons while seeking the fairy queen, present to him only in a vision. All virtue assumes responsibility committed to a long-range communal goal as well as moral support of others along the way. The virtuous habits expressed in both kinds of adventures, defined variously by relationships between the genders, are complete only when seen by others.

Persons "Seeing Virtue": Fictive Heroes, Poets, Readers

Just as Spenser's heroes must learn to see the full meaning of their chivalric adventures, the reader must learn to see the allegory's varied reach. Spenser's "darke conceit" plays the fairy world, ruled by an idealized queen, against the real world and its queen, who can mirror that ideal only in part. The failure of the real world, suggested in the escape of Duessa or the Blatant Beast, neither dims the possibility of the ideal nor blunts the poem's apocalyptic promise. Divine power through earthly action can prepare for ultimate reward. The exemplary linkage achieved by Britomart and Artegall, however deferred its closure through mortal uncertainties, fulfills a cultural responsibility, promising charitable justice endorsed by heaven, however deferred, compromised or short-changed by earthly limitations. The poem's prophetic and allegorical vision gives the reader, a full person grounded in historical time, access to expanded dimensions of personal existence.

The importance of vision, a staple in discussions of *The Faerie Queene*, serves the triangulation of fictive hero, poet, and reader. The hero fashioned by the poet is distinguished by a growing capacity to see, to understand, and to interpret the adventures in a developing chivalric experience. Virtuous habit increases vision. The vatic and prophetic poet can "conceiue" persons embodying specific virtues that he can "sette forth" or "picture" or "portraict" or provide an "image" in a "historicall fiction" ("Letter," 737). These embodied "ensamples," virtuous persons acting through "severall aduentures" (738), teach the reader allegorically to see various dimensions of existence. The person fashioned by the poem's virtuous lore is disciplined to see what the poet sees.

Spenser's virtuous lore includes "visual epistemology."[28] He first sets forth an eager, but erring young Redcrosse, who sees the look-alike Una constructed by Archimago. It is not Redcrosse's physical eyes that betray him, but his lack of faith in the chaste Una he knows. He sees, but he does not see. By contrast, the reader sees in Redcrosse's actions what the knight himself does not, that perceptions by the physical eyes must be interpreted by inner eyes, by understanding. But what the reader also sees pictured in the events of the narrative is the difficulty in distinguishing true from false understanding. The false Una, like the false Florimell in later books, could betray any viewer's eyes. It is the inner vision that must learn to see. And the virtuous lore of book 1 assumes that the Christian reader must be reminded to see more clearly what is already known. A true vision of holiness develops through repeated blindness and the recognition of incapacity, requiring the help of both grace and spiritual discipline. Redcrosse must become spiritually blinded before he can assimilate the religious discipline to see the New Jerusalem on the Hill of Contemplation. He must first learn to see in order to kill the dragon.

Virtuous lore that collapses poet, hero, and reader together pivots on mental vision. Spenser's rationally conscious "mynde" is comprised of powers necessarily coordinated together in intentional acts of seeing, of comprehension and knowing. The "mynde" sees "ensamples" of heroic behavior comprised of chivalric "aduentures," both "accidents" and "intendments." A heroic person's overriding intention, governed by virtuous habit, ensures an "ensample" of narrative wholeness with many parts. The viewing "mynde" comes to see the wholeness, but only by exercising its coordinated mental faculties in patterned ways. And hero, reader, and poet meet on the same ground, sharing the same ability to see. The exemplary persons fashioned by the poem are the products of the poet's intention expressed in "conceits," however "darke" allegorically, later set forth in heroic characters. Just as their exemplary actions are seen by other characters, so these actions are seen by the reader.

Spenser's visual epistemology is clarified by contrast to Sidney's, which shares the same intellectual seedbed. Both poets assume that poetry bears the humanistic responsibility to move readers to virtuous action on behalf of the community. Poetry teaches the reader to see virtue. Spenser's pictorialism, including earlier incorporation of the emblem tradition and later allegorical tableaux in *The Faerie Queene*, is allied to Sidney's assertion in *A Defence of Poesy* that poetry presents a "speaking picture" (*Defence*, 86). The poem incorporates an "Idea or fore-conceit" (*Defence*, 79), a picture existing first in the poet's mind. Similarly, Spenser asserts to Raleigh that the poet's "conceit" is "sette forth" or pictured in an "ensample" of virtue. For Sidney, poetry combines the "precept" of moral philosophy with the "example" of history in the "speaking picture" (*Defence*, 85–86), a "feigned example" (*Defence*, 89) of virtue that teaches and delights the reader. Epic heroes are feigned examples of specific virtues: Ulysses and Diomedes, of wisdom and temperance; Achilles, valor; Nisus and Euralyus, friendship. More generally, Aeneas is an "example" of a "virtuous man in all fortunes" (*Defence*, 86). In the same vein, Spenser imitating "antique Poets historicall" intends to picture "doctrine" by pleasing fictive "ensamples," not by "rule" or "precept" ("Letter," 737). Both poets conceive examples to be seen by the reader's inner eyes. [29]

The difference between the two poets is equally revealing. Both assume the importance of inner sight, widely acknowledged, as S. K. Heninger notes, as the "mind's eye," [30] but the question is just how, and how much, this eye can be expected to see. Heninger finds in Sidney a successful establishment of poetry on an Aristotelian foundation that derives forms or general "ideas" empirically from the earthly world, not from a preexisting Platonic realm of forms. Although he acknowledges vestigial Platonic vocabulary in Sidney, Heninger argues that for Sidney the "Idea" or "fore-conceit" in the poet's mind and embodied in poetic "speaking pictures" is the universal idea derived from empirical observation of earthly particulars. Sidney's "speaking picture" assumes such a habit of seeing or empirical understanding in the reader. Heninger conjectures that Spenser was influenced directly by the *Defence*, but his grasp of its neo-Aristotelian realism was compromised by a neo-Platonist habit of raising the mind to perceive preexistent harmonies. The stiffness of Spenser's pictorialism reflects a habit of mind that, rather than deriving universals inductively from particulars, imposes preconceived forms and complex, artificial structures on earthly realities. [31] Both poets want the reader to see the "examples" embodying ideal forms of virtue. The difference lies in the source of these ideals.

The reach of allegory and thus the breadth of inner vision are affected by this difference: an example of virtue viewed allegorically complicates the notion of inner sight. A chorus of Sidney critics, including Heninger,[32] claim that Sidney debunked allegory. They ignore Sidney's muted endorsement of allegory in the *Defence*. Blair Worden in demonstrating the political allegory in the *Arcadia* is deaf to this chorus.[33] And its voices are flatly rejected in Kenneth Borris's broad argument that aligns Sidney's *Defence* and the *Arcadia* with a Renaissance allegorical conception of epic.[34] Sidney's "speaking picture" of virtue must, like Spenser's "ensample," be seen allegorically. Thus, the question is not whether Sidney is an allegorist, but what he wants the reader to see. Heninger's Aristoelian claims about empirically constructed universal examples does not, in fact, rule out either political allegory or the civic humanist's anatomy of virtues. In fact, Worden's argument about the virtuous actions of the good ruler, Basilius, allegorically represents a criticism of Elizabethan rule. The reader is invited to see both the moral and political applications, just as Spenser wants us to see morally just behavior as well as issues in contemporary foreign policy. But, unlike Sidney, who rules out a prophetic role for the epic poet, Spenser writes as a prophetic visionary whose epic "darke conceit" leads to an understanding of personal responsibility within an apocalyptic frame. If Spenser had read and misunderstood the *Defence*, as Heninger plausibly argues, it should not surprise us, given the poet's understanding of epic as an appropriate form to express his apocalyptic vision of history invoking John's Revelation.

The apocalyptic dimension is entered first in book 1, then developed most fully in book 5. In the first book, Arthur and Redcrosse both reflect elements in the vision of John of Patmos by killing evil reptilian monsters. They aid the distressed Una, clothed with the sun and identified with the British church, in opposition to Duessa, a Whore of Babylon identified with the Roman church. In book 5 the brush strokes evoking Revelation are less broad, though the political statement is more complex. Arthur vanquishes the evil oppressor, Grantorto, to free the beleaguered, motherly Belge. Artegall succeeds only by half: Irena is freed, but her oppressor escapes. Both actions have rightly been interpreted as political allegory. Arthur's victory recalls the Duke of Leicester's victory over the Catholic Duke of Alva in the Lowlands; Artegall's victory represents Lord Grey's uneasy colonial defeat of the Irish. But as Kenneth Borris has demonstrated, the political allegory is subordinate to an overarching apocalyptic vision. John's prophetic events in Revelation frame the Christlike Arthur's conclusive victory over evil, a foil to Artegall's partial earthly victory. The prophetic foil promises a comic and not tragic end to earthly history, while endorsing Artegall's virtuous effort, however short of its goal to ensure civil order.[35]

Joseph Wittreich likens Spenser to other prophets who teach readers not "with," but "through" the eye.[36] This apt encapsulation of the prophet's visual epistemology is tied to Spenser's "energized" pictorialism.[37] It is not just the poem's more obvious apocalyptic allusions to Revelation, the "continued hieroglyphic"[38] that illuminates Spenser's prophetic mode. Instead, it is the full panoramic mixture of his techniques: the ruptured romance plotting, detailed allegorical tableaux, exfoliating visual counterpoints, and other devices that multiply visual thematic perspectives. Like Redcrosse viewing the New Jerusalem or Britomart before Merlin's magic glass or Arthur visited in dream by the fairy queen or Calidore intrusively viewing the Graces, the reader is disciplined through stunning visual perspectives set forth in Spenser's "vertuous lore."

The panorama of Spenser's combined techniques makes it easy to forget that, basically, we see examples of virtue intended to fashion a virtuous person fulfilling a civic responsibility. Learning to see serves the reader's own right action. The allegorical mode, pointing outward from the narrative event, serves the accumulating prophetic vision that, through the inner eye, leads the reader to see a composite hero inhabiting a complex reality. But the main sequence of events in each book except the fourth keeps the reader's eye trained on a central exemplar, whose virtue is included in the magnificence of the composite hero, Arthur. In any case, the allegorical development through the accumulating vision remains grounded by the "sight" of exemplary persons, whose

bodily presence emphasizes virtue's application within historical time. The prophetic vision allegorically provides additional
perspectives on those grounded events. For example, Duessa's
seduction of Redcrosse addresses the dangers of personal sexuality not guided by faithful conviction. But the seduction that
begins at the most rudimentary personal level also targets papis-
tic culture for having perverted the church's responsibility to
spiritualize the believer's earthly love. The virtue of holiness
must address both levels, but the personal narrative keeps the
reader grounded while revealing more to be seen in the cultural
climate. Grounded experience with a beginning, middle, and provisional end exists in a condition of becoming.

The reader fashioned in virtuous lore, like the fictional exemplars of virtue, exists in a state of becoming. Virtue progressively
governs a person appropriately open to the necessary help of
grace. Like Arthur, the developing person serves others in the
community, while engaging more aspects of the full person.
The composite virtue, magnificence, leads to wholeness and self-
governance, however yet unfulfilled. As Kenneth Borris notes,
the prophetic vision of Arthur's idealized victory in book 5 is a
foil that defines Artegall's earthly limitation while recognizing
his achievement: "Yet Spenser idealistically tends to prophesy a
fulfillment that endorses and validates striving here and now on
a pragmatic basis, despite any frustration."[39] Such obligatory striving works for the ultimate reward prefigured in Arthur's victory
and in the achievement concluding the poem's several books. We
need to remind ourselves that this striving is a progression in virtue
that fashions the reader as a person. The virtuous heroes of the
several books participate in the unifying composite, Arthur, sharing the same *telos* that fulfills the reader/person through serving
the community.

Spenser's triangulation of hero, reader, and poet serves that communal whole. The intermingled assumptions of humanist civic
responsibility and Protestant vocation distinguish the contemporaries Spenser and Sidney. For both, civic humanism binding each
person in virtuous service to the community also binds the poet
vocationally. Responsibility to the community is the tie that

binds. The poet shoulders that responsibility by constructing a lore of moral examples that fashions and instructs virtuous readers. Unlike Sidney, for whom poetry was an "unelected vocation" (*Defence*, 73),[40] Spenser announced himself in his first published poem, *The Shepheardes Calender*, as a Virgilian New Poet for the British nation. Sidney's high-level political ambitions had been blocked by Elizabeth's reaction against his importunate actions. Poetry was "unelected," a choice second to a governor's vocation. No doubt Thomas Elyot would have approved the first. But both governors and poets, especially epic poets, bore responsibility to serve the community. Representation of virtuous and spiritually elevated behavior fulfilled a duty to the community and to God. It can be argued plausibly that by justifying poetry's crucial importance Sidney is putting to rest a lingering fear that poetry is a dubious vocation. Spenser suffers no such qualms in *The Shepheardes Calender*, although he does question whether poets receive their just rewards. Along with Virgilian intentions, the poem introduces the poet's *persona*, Colin Clout, who reappears later in *Colin Clouts Come Home Againe* and in book 6 of *The Faerie Queene*. The proem to the romance epic also pointedly recalls that Virgilian introduction earlier (1.Proem 1.1–9). An earlier time had justified a temporary pastoral "maske" (1); now, the "enforst" (3) vocational responsibility includes the conventional epic subjects of war and love. His readers are the "learned throng" (8) who receive his virtuous lore. To "sing" of "gentle deeds" (5) of knights and ladies underlines civic responsibility; to "moralize" his song with "Fierce warres" and "faithfull loues" (9) prepares for the moral strenuousness of heroic example. His vocational thrust publicly announced in *The Shepheardes Calender* is here represented in strong moral terms notably consistent with the principles of epic poetry conceived in Sidney's *Defence*.

The poet shares with exemplary heroes the moral obligation to serve others while serving the crown. His virtuous lore serves the queen by fashioning virtuous persons. The proem to book 1 of *The Faerie Queene* invokes Elizabeth, along with the muses and Cupid, and identifies Spenser as a servant of the crown. A. C. Hamilton, while suggesting that the proem's first four stanzas are a "prologue to the whole poem rather than to Book I," speaks to the relationship between the poet and queen: "The poet is like his Knight whom he describes in the *L.R.* [letter to Raleigh] as a 'clownish person' who assumes a quest on behalf of the Faerie Queene. Like him, he needs grace to succeed" (Hamilton, 27). Elizabeth is praised as a "Goddesse heauenly bright,/Mirrour of grace and Maiestie diuine"; her presence inspires him, at the poem's outset, to see in her an ideal, Gloriana, the "true glorious type of thine" (1.Proem 4.1–2,7). Like Redcrosse and other heroes, the poet serves the queen; like them, he serves her by serving others. He can fulfill his poetic vocational "quest" and civic responsibility to the crown at once by fashioning a composite heroic person, Arthur, as an "ensample" for his readers.

The claim that Spenser, disillusioned with the Elizabethan polity, broke off his epic "quest," remains debated. Allegedly, he withdrew his Virgilian support from a compromised public weal. Artegall's justice hardened into Talus's automatic violence and Calidore's progressive retreat into a private realm have been claimed as signs of disenchantment. The problematic status of the mutability cantos, published only posthumously, contributes further to unresolved debate about Spenser's vocational role. The abandonment of his public Virgilian role, it has been argued, throws an entirely different light on the chivalric romance epic, especially when seen in tandem with the private sonnets and marriage hymn written to Elizabeth Boyle. That reading of Spenser's changed intention shows *The Faerie Queene* turning back against itself, canceling his Virgilian intention and faith in the goals of civic humanism. However, the broad logic of this reading, pushed *ad absurdum,* also rejects the value of virtuous action that ties individuals together in communal groups. Redcrosse, Guyon, Artegall and Caledore would not remain active in the world as they do in the poem. An alternative, if apocalyptic, reading sees dark shadows in the final two books, while recommending pursuit of a communal ideal represented in composite hero, Arthur, and idealized queen, Gloriana. His experience validates the "adventures" of other exemplary heroes; she represents the possibility of a centralized polity served by virtuous citizens. Whatever the failures of Elizabethan rule, the ideal including Gloriana and Arthur guides human action. This ideal is a source of coherence that assumes continuing responsible civic action, however flawed the public weal may be. Accordingly, the poet continues to fashion persons who serve the community by embodying the ideal through their actions.

The attempt to understand Spenser's sense of his poetic vocation understandably draws discussion beyond *The Faerie Queene* while fixing it centrally in mind. The question of Spenser's disillusionment and abandonment of the Virgilian quest is best considered in the full context of his works. Patrick Cheney argues that the ultimate vocational plan adumbrated in *The Shepheardes Calender* stakes out Orphic, not Virgilian, boundaries. The stated Virgilian intention is subsumed in a Christianized Orphic vision that maintains epic's civic commitment within a broader vision that includes poems of divine praise like the Psalms or, in Spenser's case, the *Fowre Hymnes* and other love poems like the *Amoretti* and *Epithalamium*. The poet is a Christianized Orpheus trained by an Augustinian divine vision. Recurrent avian imagery expressing his inspired flight unifies the Spenserian canon within that vision. Spenser interrupted writing of *The Faerie Queene* with every intention of returning to it. His sense of civic responsibility alluded to in the private *Amoretti* and confirmed in the conclusive "Prothalamium" remains a constant in a poetic vocation that includes his vatic, Virgilian role. For Cheney, the "Prothalamium," like the *Amoretti,* confirms Spenser's intention to return to *The Faerie Queene*. Death, not disillusionment, prevented its completion. In short, the overstated perception of Spenser's disillusionment in books 5 and 6 is nearsightedness that misses the forest for the trees. The critics' Procrustean imposition of a Virgilian model on Spenser's intentions leads to misunderstanding that *The Faerie Queene* is a work still in progress, a major part in a larger whole, interrupted, not abandoned, within his original Orphic flight plan.[41]

Consideration of Spenser's vocational intentions cannot stop short at his poetic work. Comparison with Sidney is again helpful. His distinction between elected and "unelected" vocations endorses both categories and also allows movement between them when circumstances change. As we will see in later chapters, this distinction also allows the categories to exist concurrently as stations within an overarching vocation. Richard Rambus's notion of Spenser's "secret career," by refusing to separate his poetic intentions from his employment as a long term colonial civil servant, contributes fruitfully to debate about Spenser's vocational intentions, provided that we bear in mind Sidney's distinction between vocations. Like Cheney, Rambus warns against imposing restrictive Virgilian boundaries when discussing Spenser's vocation, but for different reasons. For Rambus, *The Shepheardes Calender* does not just introduce Spenser as the new British poet, but encodes him as an educated "secretary" seeking employment. A poem that hides much, including E. K.'s identity, demonstrates the poet's ability to keep secrets, a secretary's primary qualification for employment. This role, when played well on the appropriate stage, could satisfy an educated careerist's ambitions. The success of William Cecil, secretary to the Privy Council and Elizabeth's most trusted counselor, perhaps even "friend," is the century's most noteworthy example. Rambus's essential point is that the vocational poetic role and the professional secretary's role in Spenser's case are "*two* public careers"[42] advancing together. Poetry defined by an encoded ability to keep secrets can attract an appropriate patron. Poet and civil servant are the same careerist person.

Sidney's distinction between two vocations gets covered over by Rambus's modern vocabulary. Sidney's statement is understandable in the contemporary early modern, Protestant context, in which a believer is called to a certain vocational station. Sidney assumed divine approval of both stations. God and Elizabeth willing, he would have proceeded in the first, not the second. Neither was regarded as a secular profession that required specialized training with standardized performance criteria prescribed by a self-regulating body of other professionals. That secular notion was only in its initial stages in the early modern period. While both vocation and career are envisioned as lifelong, one assumes

divine values, the other secular. The vision of Redcrosse beginning *The Faerie Queene* assumes the former, not the latter.
Nonetheless, Rambus's essential point, that poet and secretary
are entwined in Spenser, is well taken, though not only for reasons he gives.[43]

Spenser was a willing colonial secretary in Ireland. Readers arguing that disillusionment with Elizabethan rule eroded Spenser's
humanistic faith in the public weal tend to downplay his long public service in that country. But his two years there as Lord Grey's
secretary and service in several other public offices were both dutiful and successful.[44] Some readers would argue that he might
have regretted necessary military violence, represented in Talus
when unleashed by Artegall used to quell Irish intransigence during Lord Grey's tenure. His suggestions for subduing Ireland
in the prose *A View of the Present State of Ireland* weaken this
argument. In any event, such regrets do not, in principle, reject
Elizabeth's foreign policy, which included colonization of Ireland,
even though he may have been very critical of her conduct of that
policy, as Andrew Hadfield has argued.[45] Spenser performed like
Elyot's governor in what Sidney would have regarded as a vocation. He no doubt experienced periods of great discouragement
as a public servant, but without necessarily loosening his commitment to serve the public body. Even ambitious desire to relo-
cate to England or to upgrade, to use our current careerist argot,
should not be taken as evidence that he questioned the basic
principles of civic humanism. Rambus's essential point about
Spenser's entwined poetic and civic roles encourages the logical
conclusion that they share the same foundation in value. That
logic erodes the claim that, disillusioned, he abandoned *The
Faerie Queene*.

And so does the Edmund Spenser characterized in Lodowick
Bryskett's *A Discovrse of Civill Life*. That Spenser is notably
akin to the author of the letter to Raleigh and also to the "persons," readers and composite hero, to be fashioned by *The Faerie
Queene*. Long-time friends, Bryskette and Spenser were graduates
of Protestant Cambridge, admirers of Sidney with connections to

the Sidney/Leicester circle, civil servants together with Lord Grey in Ireland, and learned students of humanist moral philosophy. Dialogue set at Bryskett's residence near Dublin includes a group of friendly interlocutors representing church, knighthood, military, and civil service. Bryskett's full title spells out his humanistic intentions: *A Discovrse of Civill Life: Containing the Ethike part of* Morall Philosophie. *Fit for the instructing of a Gentleman in the course of a vertuous life.*[46] A thematic kinship to Spenser's letter to Raleigh is unmistakable. The Spenser character, "a gentleman in this company" (*Discovrse*, 25) learned in moral philosophy, excuses himself early on, having "already undertaken a work tending to the same effect." Those present have already read sections of this work in progress, *The Faerie Queene*, quotations from which Bryskett includes in the *Discovrse*. The other gentlemen present are "wel satisfied" (*Discovrse*, 28) by "Spenser's" twofold justification for absenting himself: first, the host, "Bryskett," is himself an authority on humanist moral philosophy and second, the poet has a dutiful need to return to his poetic task.

The drama of "Spenser's" presence then withdrawal endorses Bryskett's thematic purposes in several ways. His presence in a work written earlier in 1582, but not published until 1606, several years after Spenser's death and the canonical enshrinement of *The Faerie Queene*, further credits Bryskett's own work on Italian moral philosophy. The character Spenser testifies, "I haue seene (as he knoweth) a translation made by himself out of the Italian tongue, of a dialogue comprehending all the Ethick part of Moral Philosophy, written by one of those three the formerly mentioned, and that is by *Giraldi*, vnder the title of a dialogue of ciuil life" (*Discovrse*, 27). Further, "Spenser's" withdrawal for a different, but equally important task, alludes to Bryskett's own retirement from public life, telegraphed earlier in dialogue referring to potential medical difficulties. More problematically, Bryskett, when unsuccessfully recommended by the late Lord Grey, for whom *Discovrse* was originally written, to be Secretary of State for Ireland, had withdrawn from public life to his home near Dublin for private study. The apology for this withdrawal is given to "Spenser": "Neither let it trouble him, that I so turne ouer to him againe the taske he wold have put me to: for it falleth out fit for him to verifie the principall part of all this Apologie, euen now made for himselfe; because thereby it will appeare that he hath not withdrawne himself from seruice of the State, to liue idle or wholy priuate to himselfe, but hath spent some time in doing that which may greatly benefit others, and hath serued not a little to the bettering of his owne mind, etc." (*Discovrse*, 28). This gentle ribbing leavens a serious point applicable to both men, that the making of literary or translated philosophical texts no less serves common good than does active service to the state. The dialogue's primary subjects are first education of children, then of young men, and finally, like Spenser's poem, virtues appropriate for adult citizens. Writing either the *Discovrse* or *The Faerie Queene* is an alternative way to serve the public weal. In Bryskett's mind, at least, Spenser's literary and civil service, like the gentleman Spenser, himself "late our Lordships [Arthur Grey] Secretary," embodies vocationally the moral principles of civic humanism.

Like *The Faerie Queene*, Bryskett's *Discovrse*, by instructing a gentleman in "the course of a vertuous life," is virtuous lore. Its goal of "ciuill felicitie" (*Discourse*, 1, 5) is to be achieved through appropriate education of young persons according to principles of moral philosophy that will fashion their personal lives and service to the state. Both Spenser's chivalric narrative and Bryskett's dialogue capture life as humanist action, the "darke conceit" of Spenser's "historicall fiction," as well as Bryskett's fictionalized dialogue with its cast of characters representing real persons, including the two friends. Both men have the same audience in mind, persons like Bryskett's interlocutors, servants of the state learning more about the virtues that should inform their private and public actions. The goal of both writers is to fashion persons for whom the exemplary Arthur, like the Aeneas seen by Sidney, suggests the ideal. Active movement toward that ideal is the reader's task; virtuous lore serving the public weal is the author's.

Few early modern poems in English have taxed our understanding of an author's intentions as much as *The Faerie Queene*. For many modern readers, the poem's reiterative basic frame does not contain the fluctuating, often baffling rhythms of human life allegorized in the poem. The promise of personal coherence built into that frame of individual virtues has tended to disappear in discussion of the poem's allegorical complexities. Readers conditioned by the threatening ambiguities, inconsistencies, and contradictions addressed by our own modern relativism and political skepticism tend to forget that Spenser's basic intention is to offer a vision of virtuous actions reassured by an apocalyptic future. Spenser intends a "vertuous lore" that fashions persons able to face an often-puzzling reality with interrelated, unifying habits of virtuous behavior. He envisions a "person," a self held together by these habits and strengthened by seeing other virtuous "persons" acting together for common good.

Two

Shakespeare's Henriad

Calling the Heir Apparent

Shakespeare's Henriad chronicles the experience of Henry V of England, first as the ambivalent heir apparent to his usurper father, Henry IV, then as the kingly victor over the French monarchy. The problematic Falstaff, his summary rejection by the newly crowned king, the relationships between the plays, the dimensions of legitimate rule, the theatricality of power — debate on all these critical subjects keep the public and private dimensions of Henry's experience in the mind's eye. The notion of self that governs Shakespeare's characterization of Henry, the perspectives shifting from one play to the next, and the protean evasiveness of Hal's behavior have preoccupied students of the work. Quite reasonably, some critics have invoked the help of applicable modern idioms, but the imperatives of Shakespeare's own historical context still offer basic guides to Henry's nature. One imperative is the Reformation doctrine of vocation or calling.

Royal Vocations

The matter of vocation is introduced early in *1 Henry IV*. The king's complaint that "riot and dishonour stain the brow / Of my young Harry" (1.1.84–85)[1] confesses his nagging uneasiness about his successor. Immediately following in scene 2, Prince Hal volleys Falstaff's opening query about the time of day by half seriously calling to account his inversion of redeemed time. Falstaff's return volley shifts to the nighttime working hours of thieves and to Hal's future reign as king. Soon follows a comic exchange on Falstaff's vocational role in that reign, either as a judge or, as Hal would have it, a hangman. When the repartee circles back on thieving, Falstaff's self-defensive debunking of established values makes explicit what remains at the play's thematic heart: "Why, Hal, 'tis my vocation, Hal. 'Tis no sin for a man to labour in his vocation" (1.2.92–93). The timely entrance of Ned Poins wrenches attention to that evening's robbery. First Falstaff departs, then Poins, after he and Hal plan the anti-robbery at Gadshill. Hal is left alone to tell the audience, in a much debated soliloquy, that his rebellious tavern life is only an interlude until he will "throw off" his "loose behaviour" and "pay the debt I never promisèd" (1.2.186–87). Falstaff's "vocation" of thieving, more generally his misrule, by performing a necessary service in Hal's growth, is thus a comically ironic, contrapuntal variation on the primary theme of Hal's vocation.

Another explicit signal in *1 Henry IV* that vocation or calling is a primary concern occurs at the Eastcheap tavern when Hal interrogates the thin-witted young drawer Francis. Hal's stage directions to Poins include the pretext for the interrogation: "But, Ned, to drive away the time till Falstaff come, I prithee do thou stand in some by-room, while I question my puny drawer to what end he gave me the sugar, and do thou never leave calling 'Francis!', that his tale to me may be nothing but 'Anon!' Step aside, and I'll show thee a precedent" (2.5.24–29). The pretext is only half true since Poins like Francis, in obeying Hal's command without fully comprehending his intention, participates in a play-within-the-play that examines implications of calling. While

Hal questions Francis about his "indenture" (43) — how long he has to "serve" (37), whether he wishes to "run from it" (44) — Poins obeys Hal by competitively "calling" Francis to serve him. The young drawer is soon frozen by this competition until his impatient master, the innkeeper, brusquely sends him to serve others in the inn. Hal's carefully staged miniature reflects back on his own vocational experience. Invited to flee, like Francis, he also hears competing calls to duty. The subtler contours in this miniature are available to Hal, but not, ironically, to the ignorant Francis, who serves more than one master at the same time. Most obviously, he serves his legal master, the innkeeper; but as a subject of the crown, he also serves the heir apparent. But he is also being called to serve the prince's agent, Poins, who like Hal claims his service as a drinking patron of the inn. Thin wits can comprehend only the bare thrust of a calling, but the implications of Francis's vocation inform Hal's subtle understanding of the many voices that call one to duty within a vocation.

While students of the play have not ignored the issue of vocations, it deserves to be examined in greater detail for what it can tell us about specific problems which trouble critics. We must ask not only what "vocation" was taken to mean in Shakespeare's time but also what Shakespeare took to be the vocations of heir apparent and king. The vexed question about Hal's evasive use of masques may lead us to a different kind of answer if we find Hal intentionally responding within the limitations of his vocation. Framed by the duties of vocation, the narrative of his experience has a natural coherence less amenable to the modern notion of "role playing" than some readers have been tempted to believe. Questions about the relationships between the plays also need to take that coherence into account.

The secular remains of the Reformation notion of vocation cannot account fully for the irony of Falstaff's labor in his "vocation" of robbery. Falstaff accurately aims his stone to hit more than one bird. His subversive parody would exempt Paul no more than the Reformers and their disciples who built on his injunction: "Let everie man abide in the same vocation wherein he was called"

(1 Corinthians 7: 20).[2] On Paul's authority it was claimed that God called each believer to specific secular work in the world. The believer served God and other persons in the Christian common-wealth by performing the duties of a secular calling. Only a "lawful" calling would serve, with no exemptions and, to press a point, idleness was thieving from the commonwealth. The late-rising Falstaff was not too groggy to see his targets with a clear eye.

Martin Luther laid the foundations of the reformed notion of worldly calling, which, as we will soon see, received its most detailed exposition in Shakespeare's England by William Perkins. Luther heard a double calling from God: a general and a special.[3] The former calls all believers to the Christian faith; and the lat-ter, our primary subject, calls the believer to a particular way of life in the world comprising several "stations" or "offices," includ-ing what we would call an occupation. Luther scholar, Paul Watson, gives this useful characterization of the special calling:

> Now our vocation is given us in and with our stations and offices, as Luther calls them, or in the various relationships in which we stand to our fellowmen, our neighbours. He speaks commonly of three main stations or offices, two of them belong-ing to the worldly, and the third to the spiritual government, which together cover the whole range of life. The former are, first, *Haustand (Hausregiment, oeconomia)*, which includes all that is involved in the relations of husbands and wives, parents and children, masters and servants; and secondly, *Regieramt (Obrigkeit, politia)*, which include all that is involved in the relations of rulers and subjects, magistrates and citizens and so on. In the spiritual government, or *ecclesia*, there is only the *Priesterstand* (or *das Priester Amt*), that is, the Ministry in its various forms, with all it involves for those appointed to it and those they minister to. Now it is clear that any one person will find himself in more than one of these stations, bearing the responsibility of many offices; but no matter how manifold his resultant duties may be, they are all included in his *vocation*.[4]

More than just occupational work, the special vocation or call-ing prescribes all duties regulating the various spheres of service in the world in pursuit of the common good. Watson offers this capsule: "Service is our vocation" (370).[5]

Luther found the essence of this doctrine contained in Paul's injunction to the Corinthians. Whether the Pauline verse is more than a general summons to Christian faith is debatable; nevertheless, it was made to carry the freight of Luther's own assumptions about vocation and its multifarious stations. The Reformation took up this freighted version. For Luther the service commanded by God follows from the command to love one's fellows. The thrust is obedience to God through mutual service in all the stations of worldly existence: political, ecclesiastical, domestic, occupational. In commanding full participation in a common good, Luther's notion was not, as Watson puts it, just the "mutilated and secularized version"[6] of vocation now current.

The power of this notion can be measured by its universality, its multiplicity, and its pervasiveness. All persons called were to be engaged in all stations of their lives: from princes and magistrates to subjects, from masters to apprentices and servants, from parents to offspring, from priests to their parishioners. To answer the call was to obey the command in the vocabulary of both words and actions, attentive to both the external and the internal. The call comes from outside the believer, from God, but is mediated through his many earthly "masques,"[7] his earthly agents who recognize and encourage the believer's special gifts. To obey the call is to take up the cross in prayerful, intimate conformity with Christ, for which the personal costs are effort and suffering. The goal is mutual service according to Christ's model, fully integrated in Christian society while pursuing the common good.

Many essentials of Luther's "vocation" passed undiluted through Calvin into the Reformation mainstream, which included the Elizabethan Puritans. Not surprisingly, the notion was subjected to Calvin's greater emphasis on obedience, order, constraint, and divine power. One casualty was motivating love; nonetheless, the calling remains inclusive and socially productive: "the Lord bids each one of us in all life's actions to look to his calling." Talents are given to be used in disciplined obedience to God's call, in reciprocal service with others. Obedience within the way chosen by

God, in performance of specific duties in different spheres of life, throttles human "restlessness . . . fickleness . . . ambition," the contagions of disorder. A military vocabulary occasionally governs the discourse: "Therefore each individual has his own kind of living assigned to him by the Lord as a sort of sentry post, so that he may not heedlessly wander about through life."[8] Luther's injunctions to serve in conformity with the loving Christ have been subjected to the stiffness of military command; but the notion still requires a full, active participation in the world through dutiful, obedient service of others.

The secularization of this notion in the seventeenth century had only begun when William Perkins, the most widely known Reformation theologian of late Elizabethan England, wrote *A Treatise of the Vocations*. First published posthumously in 1602, this weathervane is the most fully developed English treatment of a staple in Puritan thought. The ideas were not new, and the fullness of detail suggests that it codified widely shared truths. Many identifying earmarks were by then familiar. The keynote text is Paul's injunction to the Corinthians: "Let everie man abide in the calling, wherein he was called" (1 Cor. 7: 20). The methodical Perkins follows at the outset with a definition: "A vocation or calling, is a certaine kinde of life, ordained or imposed on man by God, for the common god [*sic*]." Features in his amplification unmistakably recall Luther and Calvin: "For looke as in the campe, the Generall appointeth to every man his place and standing; one place for the horse-man, & another for the poor-man, and to every particular souldier likewise, his office and standing, in which hee is to abide against the enemie, and therein to live and die: even so it is in humane societies: God is the Generall, appointing to every man his particular calling, and as it were his standing: and to that calling he assignes unto him his particular office in performance whereof he is to live & die."[9] Duties of an office or station are performed within a military structure of command and obedience: Luther and Calvin stand in the background. And the ends are the same: "to do service to God, in serving of man."[10] The discipline of the vocation firmly bound the believer to specific duties and underlined their importance to the society, as Ian

Breward tells us, "The whole point of the treatise was to demonstrate to his readers that the evident disorders of the temporal regiment were due to man's failure to observe the divine laws which would have ensured communal health."[11] Luther and Calvin could only have applauded this requirement of dutiful service.

Perkins was the first English Reformation writer to address in detail some problems created by this requirement. A doctrine advancing the priesthood of all believers necessarily viewed all occupations through God's leveling eye, while the society itself remained essentially hierarchical. Whether the uncertainties were caused by movement within the hierarchy of a rising middle class or by an aristocracy in crisis,[12] social and political stability depended upon orderly fulfillment of duties. Perkins faces these problems within the frame essentially established by Luther and Calvin, ascertaining what justifies a believer in choosing one vocation rather than another. He examines in specific detail what it means to be in specific vocations. He confronts uncomfortably the all-too-obvious question of when it is appropriate to resign from or change vocations. And he asks what problems arise when the duties of one "station" or "office" collide with the duties of another, a dangerous problem inherent in the multiplicity within the Reformation notion. As we will see later, his answers to such questions provide an informative background when assessing Shakespeare's purposes in the Henriad.

Finding a vocation can be a vexing rite of passage in any age. For the Reformation believer the potentially troubled search to hear God's call could be smoothed greatly by ready placement in a hierarchical society. A habit of mutual service trained older members of the society to encourage gifts identified in the young. One could expect a good deal of help in determining one's natural "fitness" for an "office" or "station." The vocation then clearly came from outside the believer in two senses, both from God and from those who mediated His call. It is a long historical path from Luther and Calvin, who saw the vocation as commanded, to our own democratic times when a vocation, at least theoretically, is left entirely to the individual. Perkins, however much he was a primary conduit for English Calvinism, took the initial steps on the path toward examining the role of individual choice in vocation. Unlike his Reformation predecessors, Luther and Calvin, Perkins would seem to have it both ways, taking into account both congenital talents as evidence of God's intention and also the believer's inclination.[13] In loosening the Reformation's rigid obedience to command, Perkins momentarily walked with the humanists, who allowed the individual to choose while observing the injunction to serve God and society. Inadvertently, he stepped along the path toward the economic individualism that in a later time transformed the Reformation.

Strictly interpreted, Paul's injunction to abide where called, if carrying the freight of Luther's interpretation, does not allow the believer to change from one vocation to another. Perkins addressed this problem head on and boldly played the Pauline keynote at the beginning of his treatise while arguing against change. At the same time Perkins wanted to avoid Procrustean constraints, clearly recognizing the rigidity lurking within the received doctrine. Again he wants it both ways, following Luther's Paul while nervously admitting that change is possible, even sometimes necessary. Christ's change from carpenter to Messiah and the disciples' change from fishermen to apostles were unassailable examples in his support. Such allowances for change, despite an ardent defense against inconstancy, are further qualified by the proviso that the change be "lawful," justified by "private necessitie" and the "common good."[14] Need made Paul, an apostle, once again a tentmaker; but he acted later as an apostle to serve the common good. Energies within the late Elizabethan world — the seismic tremors loosening the social hierarchy and the vagaries inherent in the rise of commercial competition —clearly required an elastic notion of vocational constancy. A calling can either be "changeable"; only "imposed" for a "yeare or two or longer"; or "perpetual," lasting a lifetime and terminated only by disability, criminal activity, death, or ultimate Judgment.[15] The balancing act between constancy and change teeters precariously here. Perkins's late Elizabethan conservatism fears the destabilizing "chopping & changing of places"[16] may be fit to serve in more than one calling.

Crucial tensions in the treatise converge in the requirement of "fitness," which distinguishes the whole body of vocational literature. In principle, fitness is a simple spatial notion serving hierarchy: a given place requires a fit resident to fill it. A calling to fill a place within the hierarchical frame naturally exploits the vocabulary of fitness. The gifts bestowed by God make the believer fit to perform the duties of that place. This truth, shared throughout Reformation vocational literature, is summed up by Perkins: "Every man must choose a fit calling to walk in; that is, every calling must be fitted to the man, and every man be fitted to his calling . . . for when men are out of their proper callings in an society, it is as much, as if the joynt were out of place in the body."[17] Not for Perkins but for other vocational writers, the clothing metaphor captured subtleties of vocational fitness, none with more compelling brevity than Herbert with "Aaron's dressed"[18] and none with more ironic attention to the competing stations in a vocation than Shakespeare in designing Hal's pretenses. The search for fitness guides the poetics.

Fitness is crucial not only for entering a vocation, but also when changing from one vocation to another. The play of flexibility within Perkins's doctrine of vocation, especially the latitude allowed to individual choice, necessarily increases the need for carefully scrutinizing fitness. The principle of multiplicity inherent in the Reformation notion naturally complicates this need. Possible stations within the commonwealth, the church, and the family, taken together with the possibility of concurrent occupational stations, such as both lawyer and judge, multiply the requirements for fitness. At times, the notion of calling tends to fly apart in the face of these varying requirements, especially for those persons whose multiple offices require a varied array of suitable gifts. For them, the central requirement of fitness becomes increasingly complex when faced with a vexed historical reality.

Not surprisingly, Perkins's treatise concludes with terms for the resignation of effort and the rendering of an account, the ultimate closure in the matter of vocation. Resignation can occur through disability, criminal activity, death, or the Last Judgment. Appropriately for a discussion of vocation, the issue of justice, which is barely submerged earlier in the discourse, surfaces overtly ; injustice along with covetousness is regarded by Perkins as the major vice compromising obedience in a calling. The crux is that the Christian calling serves the larger Christian frame of justice: actions in a calling, for which fitting gifts have been given by God, are necessary to meet the terms of justice violated by the Fall. An account is rendered and a reckoning made before Christ at the final Judgment. There are no surprises in Perkins's rendition, including the predictable application of Christ's parable of the talents (Matt. 25), a common denominator in vocational literature that later dominates Milton's sonnet on his frustrated poetic vocation ("When I consider how my light is spent"). Perkins notes that the faithful servant invests gifts and other blessings productively: "they are the talents of our Lord, and he lookes for a reckoning."[19] That Christ's final judgment awaits is the ultimate warning for not abiding in the calling where one is called. But the believer is always on trial within a calling. The final appearance at Christ's tribunal is only the final reckoning of the duties to which one is called.

The suggestion by Muriel Bradbrook, that the rejection of Falstaff in *2 Henry IV* recalls the Last Judgment,[20] reverberates all the more if we see him called to account for actions in his vocation. Setting aside until later the complicated ironies, we can say that the threads of biblical allusion woven into this scene become more meaningful in light of the play's concern with vocation. The judgment against the "old man" Falstaff is that it *is* a sin to "labor" unlawfully in a legitimate vocation or in an unlawful one. The newly crowned Henry's "I know thee not, old man" (5.5.45) replays Christ's judgment against the foolish virgins preceding the parable of the talents, as Shakespeare's Christian contemporaries well knew.[21] Even those unfriendly to Hal's iron justice here could not claim that Falstaff, blessed with the undeserved credit for Hotspur's death and bankrolled to conscript soldiers to serve the crown, did not receive "talents" to invest. Nor should it be ignored that, when called to serve Hal at Shrewsbury, he answered not with a ready weapon but a holstered bottle of sack.

This judgment against Falstaff also brings to a climax the new king's first public performance in his new vocation. The incident features his juridical office, introduced earlier in his accepting the Lord Chief Justice as "a father to my youth" (5.2.117). This alliance is the crux of the kingly vocation envisioned by Shakespeare from *Richard II* through the Henriad. Thus, it is with the significance of the Lord Chief Justice that we can begin to construct Shakespeare's conception of vocation as it relates to Henry both as heir apparent and as king. We do well to remember the Lutheran conception adopted by Perkins that a vocation has multiple stations or offices held concurrently. Rule by a virgin queen notwithstanding, the Tudor patriarchal conception of kingship emphasized the monarch as father and, concurrently, the heir apparent as a son. Hal's climactic heroism at Shrewsbury in defeating his "factor," Hotspur, and in protecting his father from Douglas's sword, serves a mixture of patriarchal and military purposes. The prince's vocation is an apprenticeship with both familial and military stations. The son serving the father can later become the surrogate father to his own siblings when, as the new king in part 2, he reaffirms family loyalties. Unlike his father Henry IV, whose defensive use of masques at Shrewsbury elides the military station of the kingly vocation, Hal serves in that station of his princely vocation at Shrewsbury and his kingly vocation at Agincourt. Experience is the testing ground in the stations of both his vocations, first as a prince, then as a king. The climactic structures of all three plays in the Henriad illustrate his performance in the multiple stations of his vocation: fighting on the battlefield in part 1, rendering a public judgment in part 2, and wooing the French princess, Katharine, in the third play, in order to establish the familial foundation of his international kingship.

The alliance with the lord chief justice is the most important. Their testy history creates the justice's expectation that the newly crowned king will not favor him. Hal's earlier physical assault on the judge (1.2.47–48; 5.2.79), who had refused to overturn his conviction of Bardolph, then the judge's imprisonment of the prince, followed by Hal's well-publicized riotous behavior later were reason enough for the judge's low expectations. And the young king clearly plays on the chief justice's fears, briefly rehearsing their earlier history and forcing the older man to justify his earlier actions. This self-conscious staging for Hal's unexpected approval allegorically represents their alliance. Shakespeare's broad point is unmistakable: Henry is committing himself as a king to law and justice. This commitment gains more force in light of the inclusive observation that the Tudor age was "essentially monarchical: that is to say, the king was held to be the source and the centre of all political and social life."[22] Further, Shakespeare is assuming a specific Tudor system of justice with a judicature in which the lord chief justice performs a specific role. A closer scrutiny of what this means tells us a good deal about the judicial aspect of the king's vocation.

The lord chief justice represents more than the principles of law and justice. Elton puts it succinctly, "The chief justice of the King's Bench was lord chief justice of England and the effective head of the judiciary."[23] Parliament is the highest court, and the King's Bench is the most important common law court in the system. And the common law itself is much to our point. Shakespeare's chief justice is not old because, like Henry IV, he is exhausted by the cares of a usurped and tarnished office or, like Falstaff, corrupted by fleshly self-indulgence that the young Henry must reject. Rather, his age represents the centuries-old accumulation of English common law, and his name suggests less a private person than a public fulfillment of his office. In embracing him, and thereby endorsing his earlier judgments against the young heir apparent's violation of vocation, the new king is committing himself to "fundamental law" supporting the whole judicial system and embedded in a body of common law. That body of law held in "profound respect"[24] intimately expresses "the common custom of the realm."[25]

The role of the common law courts in relation to the prerogative courts further explains young Henry's crucial embrace of the Lord Chief Justice. The "ancient" common law courts, firmly established by the end of the fifteenth century, included the Court of the King's Bench, the Court of Common Pleas, and the Exchequer of Pleas. These courts had different, but overlapping jurisdictions. The King's Bench, which dealt with matters relating specifically to the crown, was paramount. In spite of the distinctions between these courts, justices might serve at different times in more than one court; and "the whole body of judges and barons composed the King's legal advisers whose counsel was frequently sought by the crown."[26] Of the prerogative courts, the oldest was the Court of the Chancery, serving the office of the Lord Chancellor; established later were the conciliar courts that served the King's council and included the Court of Star Chamber and the Court of Requests. The so-called prerogative or equity courts were developed to provide a greater flexibility than allowed by the common law courts alone. They served the broader needs of the king's "prerogative," those rights that enabled government of the realm. Not strictly bound by the dictates of common law, but broadened by supplemental recourse to equity — the principles of natural justice, conscience, and common sense — the prerogative courts specifically served the judicial needs of the crown. Potential abuses of royal prerogative were curtailed by the basic Tudor assumption that "prerogative" was granted by the "laws of the realm."[27] That is, the common law remained as the main trunk supporting the branches of this complex, but centralized legal and judicial system. It was the Stuart and not the Tudor monarchs, who began the assault on the common law, and thus upon the "national character, in effect" and on "the common custom of the land."[28]

The domain of the chief justice of the King's Bench suggests the reach of the common law in the Tudor system. The justices of the "ancient" common law courts, King's Bench and Common Pleas, were chosen by the Crown from the sergeants-at-law, the most highly qualified legal experts. These experts were trained at the Inns of Court, the bastion of the Common Law. Despite differing jurisdictions of the "ancient" common law courts, individuals could serve as justices at different times on more than one court. Practiced at "working together,"[29] the body of justices were ever available to advise the crown on a variety of legislative and executive matters. Their duties spiraled outward as "on assize [they] acted as political as well as judicial representatives of the central authority. Besides fulfilling their duties in the superior courts the judges of King's Bench and Common Pleas proceeded at intervals on circuit through the country. For this purpose they were armed with a variety of commissions, which in their collective effect invested their holders with powers almost co-extensive with those which they exercised in the courts at Westminster."[30] The lord chief justice was the primary jurist in this fraternity of Common Law experts. As chief justice of King's Bench, he joined the chief justice of Common Appeals as members of the Court of the Star Chamber. Before the creation of this prerogative court, when the Privy Council was performing its judicial, not governmental functions, the two chief justices had been full council members. Afterwards, when the Privy Council sat as a court, the Common Law[31] sat embodied in the two chief justices, the kingdom's most influential jurists.

The independence of Shakespeare's lord chief justice mirrors the Common Law tradition that "preserved by its insistence on the principle that government must be conducted according to law, an independence of temper that prevented undue subordination to the executive."[32] A shared belief in "fundamental law"[33] serving both king and subject encouraged that independence. In defining the interplay of law and justice in the kingly vocation, Shakespeare underscores that independence in regard to both Henrys, father and son. The young king's staged embrace of the lord chief justice is an attempt to construct the response of the onlookers. Stage-directing the judge's justification of his earlier actions gives Henry the opportunity to answer pointedly according to his father's pattern:

> You are right Justice, and you weigh this well.
> Therefore still bear the balance and the sword;
> And I do wish your honours may increase
> Till you do live to see a son of mine
> Offend you and obey you as I did.
> So shall I live to speak my father's words:
> "Happy am I that have a man so bold

That dares do justice on my proper son,
And not less happy having such a son
That would deliver up his greatness so
Into the hands of justice."

(5.2.101–11)

On both occasions the judge is vulnerable to a king's anger, first the father's on behalf of the son, then the son's in delayed revenge. Both times he is vulnerable to physical assault on the "seat of judgement" (5.2.79) that would forcefully subordinate the common law to the king, not vice versa. The new king's point for his audience, and Shakespeare's for his is that the crown must be the obedient servant of law and justice. The king's supporting point is that, by obediently entering prison, even then he followed the father's commitment to law. This Lancastrian theatrical performance cannot escape the irony that like his son, the usurper king first violated law before he championed it. Nonetheless, young Henry's point, along with Shakespeare's, still stands: like father, like son in endorsing the independence of justice.

A working relationship between the lord chief justice and the king dramatizes the place of law and justice in the Tudor conception of the typical vocation. The lord chief justice's defense of the king's person is specific:

I then did use the person of your father.
The image of his power lay then in me;
And in th' administration of his law,
Whiles I was busy for the commonwealth,
Your highness pleasèd to forget my place,
The majesty and power of law and justice,
The image of the King whom I presented,
And struck me in my very seat of judgement.

(5.2.72–79)

The Tudor monarch's "double capacity" derived from "two bodies," one natural, one politic; hence, two persons as well. "Instead of assigning the royal prerogatives to a natural man, they personified the kingly office."[34] In turn, the chief justice as "image" of the

kingly "person" represents the majesty and power of law and justice inherent in the crown. The chief justice's "very seat of justice" plays adroitly on his double capacity, natural and judicial,
exercised in office; Hal's blow on the judge's head, the seat of natural reason, violated the judicial office, whose power imaged the
crown, the king's "person." Predictably, the judge stands on solid
theoretical ground. The lord chief justice held the highest office
in the Tudor judicial system, a royal court system in which the
crown appointed the judges.[35] In short, it was the "King's justice."
And that justice system applied the common law, which defined
both the system and royal prerogatives.[36]

   The royal vocation as it pertains to the working of law and justice is incomplete without reference to parliament. Shakespeare
again is specific. Henry concludes his accord with the lord chief
justice by announcing his intention to call parliament:

> Now call we our high court of Parliament,
> And let us choose such limbs of noble counsel
> That the great body of our state may go
> In equal rank with the best-governed nation;
> That war, or peace, or both at once, may be
> As things acquainted and familiar to us;
> In which you, father, shall have foremost hand.
>
>   (5.2.133–39)

A dramatic economy compacts much here: the new king's willingness to seek parliamentary counsel; the presence of the lord
chief justice at those deliberations; the juridical nature of parliament. These compacted elements extend Henry's recent accord
with the judge as a fulfillment of the royal "person." Kingly prerogatives, defined by the common law, could be extended only if
parliament, whose prior history as a court "whose judgments . . .
were not considered essentially different from those of other
courts,"[37]ensured that any parliamentary reformulation of royal
prerogative was consistent with the common law and the royal
judicial system. Although increasingly legislative and political in
the Tudor period,[38] its traditional and general designation as the

"High Court of Parliament" expresses the traditional assumption that it was the highest tribunal in the judicial system.[39] Shakespeare pointedly underlines the advisory role of the lord chief justice in that body even though the high judiciary lacked a voice in the Tudor parliament. Generally speaking, Shakespeare is alluding to the Tudor conviction of the mixed sovereignty of king and parliament,[40] a constitutional monarchy based on the common law and the judicial system derived from it. Put differently, it means "though the king in person (*rex solus*) might be equipped with power, he was yet subject to himself in Parliament."[41] Shakespeare's young king is eager to demonstrate his understanding of these terms in his vocation.

His sharp understanding fits him for a crown which he knows from his father's experience will deplete his natural person. We have seen briefly its military and familial offices; in much greater detail we have examined the royal judicial office. It should also be noted in passing that the religious office and its duties are introduced in *Henry V* in his negotiations with high officials of the church. But it is Henry's grasp of his double capacity as a royal "person," taken together with successful performance of the several stations of the royal calling, that is the true measure of his fitness for the royal vocation. The drama at his father's deathbed, in which Shakespeare effectively anatomizes the two persons of the dying king, demonstrates that grasp.

This deathbed scene addresses symbolically many issues concerning the royal self examined in the Henriad. The prince finds the unconscious, bareheaded king in bed, his crown placed at his request beside him on the pillow. For him, the prince notes, there is no nightcap, no "homely biggen" of the commoner for his royal "brow" (4.3.157). The prostrate body and the crown stand respectively for the natural and political persons, for his mortal and his political bodies. After detecting no breath in his father's depleted natural body, the grieving prince takes the crown to an adjacent room and contemplates his inheritance, his new calling. Symbolically, the scene converts possibilities into half-truths, commenting on the ambiguities inherent in the play. If the king is dead, removing and putting on the crown represent lawful succession and coronation; if he still lives, they represent deposition and usurpation, thereby repeating Henry IV's own crime against Richard. The king's earlier command to remove the crown and place it on his pillow is ambivalent: in expressing his expectation of death, it is a resignation from his vocation, thereby justifying Hal's premature possession; its placement nearby reveals his own tenacious desire for possession. Both the presumed death and the removed crown capture one individual's change of vocations and the subsequent passing of a given vocation from one natural person to another, from heir apparent to king. The king's revival and the prince's return of the crown symbolically reverse these changes before our eyes. Shakespeare thus subjects the crown to the ambiguous flux of experience itself, symbolically posing problems necessarily at stake in the play.

Shakespeare continues to probe the uneasy notion of the king's two persons throughout the Henriad. In *Henry V* the disguised Henry debates with a common foot soldier about a king's responsibilities for his subjects' souls. Speaking as one natural person to another, he denies that the royal person bears responsibility for the spiritual condition of subjects killed in battle. Each subject's soul is his own; so, too, is the king's. But the reality is more complex than the disguise itself would first suggest, since the voice is the royal person's. Henry's two persons are only distinct, never separable. And even resignation from a royal vocation is not an exemption from ultimate reckoning for one's actions as a king; in that sense, the individual remains a king, like Richard or Lear, even after resignation. The vexing problem of just how the natural person impersonates the royal prerogatives is illuminated but not solved by the demand for full physical participation in his own social body, the kingdom, as the duty of the office.[42] Young Henry clearly understands that wearing the crown involves an increasing burden of sleepless care, an experience of bodily attrition:

> I spake unto this crown as having sense,
> And thus upbraided it: "The care on thee depending

Hath fed upon the body of my father;
Therefore, thou best of gold art worst of gold."

(4.3.285–88)

Henry IV must scotch rebellion generated by usurpation; his burden of guilt adds more weight to duties of the crown. In turn, the sin of this father, that "fault . . . made in compassing the crown" (4.1.275–76), is visited on the body of his son, Henry V, who diverts further rebellion by fighting a foreign war. Lancastrian guilt increases but it does not create the weight of the royal vocation that necessarily depletes the natural person. The deeper truth is born ironically by Richard II's self-regarding discovery of Christly suffering in his travail. But his self-idolatry obscures true conformity with Christ through the burden of serving others that Luther[43] and other Reformers found in all vocations. Simply put, the royal vocation weighs more; the commoner's "homely biggen" does not fit the sleepless head that bears the crown. Intimate knowledge that the crown in his hands will deplete him as it has his dying father pervades Henry's genuine grief for his father. The son's natural identification with the father, the heir apparent's with the reigning king, implicates him in the king's two persons.

Young Henry's identification with Henry IV has been regarded by many critics as a questionable blessing that mixes too much Machiavelli and too little Falstaff. Some criticism of the *Henry IV* plays has tried and convicted both father and son for coldness, calculation, and suppression of private feelings behind shifting political masques. I have suggested that the grounds for judging Henry's actions, both as heir apparent and as king, be shifted. In particular, Shakespeare's attention to the multiple offices in the royal vocation bears significantly on any account of the king's actions. Moreover, the implications of the judicial office in the king's vocation, understood in terms of the lord chief justice, should guide our understanding of royal responsibility. Questions identified early in this essay concerning the sense of self informing the treatment of Henry, the judgment of Falstaff, and some relationships between the three plays occupy the remainder of the essay.

Royal Selves

Much discussion of Henry pivots on his soliloquy concluding the second scene of part 1. He will "throw off" his "loose behaviour" with Falstaff and his companions, surprising the world by his "reformation" (1.2.186, 191). Many readers find here the formula for his behavior throughout the Henriad. He is a political actor, a role-player without a humane center, committed only to the power of the monarchy. His roles can vary contradictorily: seeming friend to Falstaff; pretended thief in buckram against other thieves; dutiful son to his father's face; prodigal prince behind his back, with Poins a drawer to trick Falstaff again; and a pretended commoner before Agincourt. After continuously permitting "the base contagious clouds / To smother up his beauty" (1.2.176–77), he steps forward as the king and turns Falstaff away. His harshest critics convict him of insensitive political temporizing and cold opportunism.

The "play extempore" (2.5.257), when he and Falstaff take turns playing the prince and his father, asks that we view Hal, Falstaff, and others as actors. Modern Shakespearean criticism has dutifully and often fruitfully done so. The pathways of debate lead inevitably to questions about self laced with intersecting vocabularies from social psychology, psychoanalysis, new historicism, and postmodernism. Hal's repeated "roleplaying"[44] has been taken as evidence of a multiple personality,[45] the "strategies of disguise and inversion" in Tudor power,[46] and the search for "identity."[47] These tempting vocabularies remain useful if they reveal Shakespeare circling around many vexing factors of human behavior. A central question is whether a role-player is many faces fixed to a stable center, or merely a changing set of responses to an ever-refracting historical flux. The concept of the multiple personality is only a rough analogy to the business of being an actor, since it must be borne in mind that this multiplicity is a psychiatric disorder. A more plausible argument can be made that each actor, like every human being, is several selves, each called forth by individual circumstances, but all expressions of a continuing center. Similarly, role-playing, whether taken in its more limited vocational or in its broader social senses, may be required merely by circumstances with no reference to a stable center.

The new historicist project of defining Elizabeth's practice of political power both illuminates and obscures Shakespeare's purposes in the Henriad. A penetrating and justly influential analysis of Tudor political theatricality has shown Shakespeare attentive to the Machiavellian realities of reigning monarchs, including the techniques of what we know as "image politics." The royal actor wears many public faces calculated to serve the interests of power; behind every face there is yet another pretense that meets the emerging occasions encountered in the seat of position and power. Of Henry V it is claimed "that the figure of the monarch breaks apart and disappears into many roles and dialects." This illuminating overstatement, however, is obscured by the overstated corollary that Henry lacks "an internally coherent self."[48] In other words, the many roles have no center in which to inhere; the private self has disappeared. Such an argument about the private self is convincing only if we forget Henry's development in the Henry IV plays. A demonstrable private ambivalence about royal duties characterizes Hal/Henry through all three plays, arguing against an "opaque self"[49] inaccessible to our investigation. His actions as king in the third play are more clearly a consequence of earlier attempts to sort out the implications of both his private and political "persons." Here we find characteristic private energies effectively interrogating the implications of public duties and the consequences of past actions.

There is in Henry, from the first time that we meet him as Prince Hal through his victorious performance at Agincourt, an acceptance of his calling as heir apparent, but that acceptance is contradicted by deep ambivalence about that role. Both acceptance and ambivalence are constant, contradictory though not mutually exclusive, and they caution against claiming too quickly that he is merely a set of masks serving selfish royal power and position. As Shakespeare emphasizes elsewhere, the weight of royal vocational duty, whether anticipated or known, creates its own resistance. Hamlet delays tragically after his dead father calls him as the heir apparent; Lear resigns disastrously from the burdens of his calling; Henry's contradictory wrestling with his calling defines his experience and qualifies any judgment of his role playing.

Henry's roleplaying and his ambivalent acceptance of his calling come into even sharper focus if we recall both the multiple stations in a Reformation calling and its mediation through the expectations of others. His soliloquy leaves no doubt about his intentions as heir apparent, which are confirmed by the unvarying assumptions of his tavern cohorts that he is the crown prince. Certainly, Falstaff has unembarrassed plans to exploit royal patronage when the time comes. Although his vexed royal father may lament his riot, as do many others, Hal gives an early signal to his audience where he stands. Recalcitrance about his responsibilities and energetic avoidance of his father do not cancel his intentions, but suspend them. His performance in the filial and military stations of vocation, in defending his father and confronting Hotspur, carries out those intentions. His clarion-like announcement to Hotspur in part 1 claims his unequivocal identity: "I am the Prince of Wales" (5.2.62). His deference in his father's presence lends support to his promise to mend his ways and, except to his most hardened detractors, suggests a complicated affection for his father. Progressively, he demonstrates a less guarded acceptance of his filial station: a brave defense of his father at Shrewsbury, admission of grief during his father's illness in part 2 that makes him seem a "hypocrite" (2.2.46) to Poins, and his private tears shed at Henry's presumed death.

His ambivalence centers on his relationship to his father, although it continues after Henry's death and is to be understood in relation to both the private and politic persons of the king. The audience first meets the young prince in the presence of Falstaff after hearing Henry's complaint that "riot and dishonour stain the brow / Of my young Harry" (1.1.84–85). This avoidance of king and court, in spite of promising his father to reform and of saving him at Shrewsbury, continues until Henry's death. A continuing ambivalence about the crown, which is instructed by but not identical with the guilt of usurpation inherited by the son, parallels the civil rebellion within the body politic. This persistent ambivalence, understood in terms of a vocational field that includes the several roles he plays, makes him complex, not incoherent. After performing commendably at Shrewsbury, he returns to the tavern disguised as a drawer. As king he again dresses like a commoner at Agincourt while contemplating the royal burden. The same distinguishing ambivalence is at work. His is a nature in which the two "persons," private and politic, do not always reach an easy accord on royal duties. However ambivalent, he does not reject this royal calling, as we are told from the beginning, but he continuously interrogates the implications of its duties. If this is a portrait of Shakespeare's "virtuous king"[50] and "in certain respects — can be called a political hagiography,"[51] then surely his interrogation of his role, without rejecting it, deserves our scrutiny as a paradoxical source of coherence.

The observation that the identities of the two Henrys, father and son, are mutually dependent bears more fruit when both private and public persons are considered. The reconstituted succession is necessary for the identities of both.[52] The father's private guilt can be justified if the son answers his calling as the heir apparent and validates the public person. To put it unsympathetically, the father has entered his own vocation through an illegal threshold and he must drag the son through with him; a sideways glance at the Perkins discussion invites a more sympathetically flexible understanding of the father's need to implicate the son. Perkins acknowledges that an unlawful entrance into a vocation does not rule out a subsequent performance of the duties of that calling if conditioned by repentance. His primary example is the conquering usurper: "A Prince, as W. Conquerour enters into a land or kingdome, & by warre & bloodshed seekes to subdue the people, and to make them subiect unto him: now by this bad entrance, he is no lawfull king: for euery lawfull king is placed by God, and by men that are appointed under God to set up Princes ouer them, according to the lawes and customes of seuerall kingdomes. Yet if the people do willingly submit themselues to this usurper, and been content to yeeld subiections, and the king likewise to rule them by good and wholesome lawes, hee is

now become a lawfull Prince, though his entrance was but tyran-
nicall."[53] By such a standard, Henry IV's kingship is reparable, and
his vocation can modulate from the unlawful to the lawful; establishing a lawful succession with a fit successor would be amongst
his necessary duties. The tarnish on the crown can be rubbed off
with lawful effort.

Henry IV's usurpation of Richard's throne overshadows the
whole Henriad, from Henry's guilt for regicide, to the Percys'
attempted subversion and rebellion against Henry's authority, to
Henry V's penitential commemoration of Richard. The joyously
subversive Falstaff insidiously plays with the shadow on Hal's legitimacy when taunting him to join the thieves at Gadshill: "nor
thou camest not of the blood royal, if thou darest not stand for
ten shillings" (1.2.125–26). Caught out and challenged to "hide"
from his "open and apparent shame" (2.5.243–44), the punning
and shameless Falstaff again ironically plays with royalty as a
measure of truth: "Was it for me to kill the heir-apparent? Should
I turn upon the true prince?" (2.5.247–48). Legitimate succession
to an illegitimate king who stifles any opposition by legitimate
claimants to the usurped throne creates special ambiguities. But
Falstaff no more than Hal questions the reality of possession, however compromised. The prince's succinct but reserved promise to
his father to "Be more myself" (3.2.93) relates not to his calling,
only his ambivalence. For the moment, he promises "more," not
all; the shadows must be lightened further.

If patriarchal succession amplifies the difficulty inherent in all
vocations, a tainted succession takes it one notch further. Perkins's
discussion does not probe the vocational seams connecting the
individual to the group, but inherent in the concept of vocation
is yielding separateness through service to others. This surrender requires patterns of identification that merge the individual
into the group; the sense of distinct being is eroded as duties are
loaded on the back of the self. These patterns of likeness are particularly compelling when the vocation is a patrimony, a vocation given by birth when family likeness is taken as evidence of
fitness for a calling. To be asked to take on a crown tarnished with

the sin of the father threatens to become an entangling corruption. The tarnish can accompany the increasing burden on the self.

Although the young prince has answered the calling mediated through the expectation of others, his ambivalence finds its contradictory way through all three plays. He maintains a space for this individual core while measuring the necessary dimensions for his engagement. His arm's-length accommodation to his father is straitened further by the father's tarnished authority. We find a mirror image in his tavern friendships. There, distancing aggression maintains the fit dimensions of a private self in his engagement.

Hal's distancing of himself from Falstaff has been mistaken by detractors as further evidence of coldness; but in its likeness to the father, it is a vein of continuity, a preparation for succession, or, put differently, a fitness for the royal vocation. The young prince's fitness for the monarchical vocation is also in the clothing metaphor that likens him, but with a distinctive difference, to his father. Hal's succinct pledge to "Be more myself" (3.2.93), preceded and followed by his father's tirade about his degenerate behavior, is amplified by his intentions to divest his shames by claiming Hotspur's honors as rightfully his:

> I will redeem all this on Percy's head,
> And in the closing of some glorious day
> Be bold to tell you that I am your son;
> When I will wear a garment of all blood,
> And stain my favours in a bloody mask,
> Which, washed away, shall scour my shame with it.
>
> (3.2.132–37)

The "garment" of blood and "bloody mask" will prove his fitness for the military station of his calling. The mask, when cleansed away with the purifying sacrificial blood, will remove the undeserved bad reputation, the shame inflated by "any tales devised" (3.2.23). Hal's imagery subtly appropriates Henry's image, but tailors it to remodel their uneasy relationship. Henry's lesson to his heir, drawn from his own experience when Richard was still king, had underlined the royal actor's needs to heed the viewing audience:

> And then I stole all courtesy from heaven,
> And dressed myself in such humility
> That I did pluck allegiance from men's hearts,
> Loud shouts and salutations from their mouths,
> Even in the presence of the crownèd king.
> Thus did I keep my person fresh and new,
> My presence like a robe pontifical —
> Ne'er seen but wondered at.
>
> (3.2.50–57)

The royal player's lesson is that kingship is performance before an audience. Subtle appropriation of the father's clothing imagery demonstrates, in its fineness of linguistic distinction and patient attention in the difficult dramatic station, the son's fitness to succeed his father. The son's success in convincing the father that he will heed this lesson and "more" play his part is measured by the father's dramatic abbreviation of his tirade: "A hundred thousand rebels died in this / Thou shall have charge and sovereign trust herein" (160–61). But the refinement of his father's theatrical sense suggests a greater fitness, since the father's performance was stained by duplicity. Only the anointed King Richard was then entitled to the aura of the Christ likeness; Henry's "humility," is a "courtesy" stolen "from heaven." In contrast, Hal's proposed bloody "garment" (135) and "mask" (136) would be earned against Hotspur, the rebel against the crown, and then removed for other pursuits, after having discharged an unfairly distorted reputation and revealed the true self of the heir apparent.

Hal's response to his father draws fine lines in the play's consideration of fitness. The contemporary notion of fitness recommends that those with intellectual gifts are fit for intellectual vocations, those with natural gifts for handling animals should do so; and persons with craft in their hands should be potters and carpenters. For Shakespeare, not all fitness is so tailored. In part 2, King Henry, faced with Hal's return to the tavern world, expresses his besetting doubts about Hal's fitness for the crown. Warwick counters the king precisely on those grounds, defending Hal's presence there as a necessary acceptance of his apprenticeship:

> The Prince but studies his companions,
> Like a strange tongue, wherein, to gain the language,
> 'Tis needful that the most immodest word
> Be looked upon and learnt, which once attained,
> Your highness knows, comes to no further use
> But to be known and hated; so, like gross terms,
> The Prince will in the perfectness of time
> Cast off his followers, and their memory
> Shall as a pattern or a measure live
> By which his grace must mete the lives of other,
> Turning past evils to advantages.
>
> (4.3.68–78)

Hal's willingness to "study" his low-life companions is his apprenticeship as a future king who eventually will have to "mete the lives" first "known," then "hated." But eventually he will "Cast off" (75) his followers like a garment no longer needed or desired, no longer fit when the apprenticeship as heir apparent is complete. Warwick's attempt to reassure the king cites Hal's willingness to learn from his experience as evidence of his fitness to be king. He knows when to discard the clothing of pretense. But Warwick's claim that Hal hates his low-life companions misses the mark by not understanding his ambivalence. Hal's aggression against his tavern friends could be seen as a kind of hatred, if not for his restrained affection. The garment fits differently than Warwick realizes.

Some critics have found in Warwick's remarks the pattern justifying Hal's flight from the king and court as the apprenticeship that prepares a king to rule a polyglot social body. But Warwick is both more and less correct than he knows. His diplomacy and his logic ignore the energy of Hal's rebellion against Henry, both the private and the political persons. Hal's physical assault on the lord chief justice cannot be written off as a closer participation in the people he will rule. The lord chief justice has it right. The blow on the head is an attack upon the political "person" of the king, upon the royal authority wielded by his father. It is no less a flagrant act of rebellion than the Percys' defection from Henry IV, whom they had joined against Richard. This attack upon the "seat of reason" for the sake of the criminal Bardolph cannot be condoned as a demonstration of fitness, although in an exaggerated form it does express the young prince's distancing himself from his father. The event had occurred before the events beginning part one, and it expresses the same irresponsibility that led to the loss of his place on the royal council to his brother John. But Warwick's claim is true because it comes in the aftermath of Hal's disguise as a tavern drawer in an apron: "From a god to a bull — a heavy declension — it was Jove's case. From a prince to a prentice — low transformation — that shall be mine; for in everything the purpose must weigh with the folly" (2.2.151–54). The self-mockery prevents this incarnation image — the king of gods debasing himself in animal form — from falling into his father's error of likening himself to the incarnate God. But, again, it shows a subtle understanding of the appropriate limits of the figure. An anointed king is a god among men; an heir apparent is one step removed and, if partially rebellious against his calling, dehumanized by comparison. The self-mocking wit that likens the leather apron of the server to the bull preserves Hal's island of individuality in a complex figure. Jove entered the bull, then sodomized the helpless Europa for selfish purposes; so, too, Hal puts on the server's apron to expose Falstaff for further entertainment. The self-mockery keeps Hal in his fit place, subtly aware of the implication of his situation.

But there is more to the figure and more of the prince's fitness here revealed. The self-mockery suppresses but does not erase the syncretic analogy to Christian incarnation. Underplayed allusions to Christ lie behind many events in the play. Hal offers to fight Hotspur one-on-one, like Christ against Satan, to save lives on both sides; he harrows Hell by returning to the tavern; he performs a last Judgment of Falstaff, the Old Man; he is the disguised God who "serves"; he takes on the guilt for his father's sin by succeeding him. The essentially secular vision of the play keeps these parallels in the background and, significantly, the prince keeps them there as well. Unlike Richard and his father, he reveals a fit sense of the divine analogy that instructs our assessment of Shakespeare's use. The royal vocation, like all vocations, is conformity to Christ through suffering effort in service of others. But there is another dimension to that conformity of the king, who heads the corporate body in which all members participate. Unlike the Stuarts, the Tudor monarchs did not exploit the notion of divine right, but it remains as an impinging truth. Nonetheless, Warwick's justification of the Prince's presence in the tavern as a study of his companions falls just short of the mark. To participate in their lives, he has "sounded the very base-strong of humility," becoming "sworn brother to a leash of drawers," and to them the "king of courtesy" (*1 H IV* 2.5.5–9) although he has not stolen this courtesy from heaven. A king of serving men later takes on the disguise of a serving man; he is a "brother" conforming to a pattern of service inherent in the very nature of vocation. Hal does "study" them as members of the same "body" of the kingdom, but more precisely he comes to know the pattern of service through their more limited embodiment of it. He must participate in that pattern with them. His subtle conformity to Christ measures his fitness to be an anointed king; his remaining aggression against all those with whom he must identify preserves his individual separateness from them.

His ironic characterization of himself as a "sworn brother" of the three drawers, Tom, Dick, and Francis, plays ambivalently on the filial station of his vocation. The irony mixes distancing aggression and affection; so, too, he avoids his father and his brothers until his coronation, even though he is grieved by Henry's mortal illness and has had a close relationship with his brother, the Duke of Clarence. The aggression presses his need for his own separation; and the affection fuels his identification and incorporation through likeness. The likeness to Henry is emphasized when Hal passes from one filial station to another, from son to surrogate father to his brothers. As we will see in some detail, he self-consciously steps into his father's shoes, clearly recognizing the fit.

Shakespeare sharpens the ambivalence by playing the real family against the surrogate tavern family. Shortly before his collapse, the rebellion now quelled, the mortally ill patriarch tries also to reorder the royal family in support of his successor. First Gloucester, then Clarence sidesteps his questions about their royal brother's absence while Henry seeks to warm up filial affection, appealing to Clarence, in particular:

> How chance thou art not with the Prince thy brother?
> He loves thee, and thou dost neglect him, Thomas.
> Thou hast a better place in his affection
> Than all thy brothers. Cherish it, my boy,
> And noble offices thou mayst effect
> Of mediation, after I am dead,
> Between his greatness and thy other brethren.
> Therefore omit him not, blunt not his love,
> Nor lose the good advance of his grace
> By seeming cold or careless of his will.
>
> (4.3.20–29)

Both the private and politic persons of the king desire this accord and, however wishfully, Henry desires to excite brotherly affection that would aid the prince in performing the kingly vocation. Clarence first covers for his absent brother, then discloses that he is "With Poins and other his continual followers" (53). This disclosure jars off key in Clarence's annoyed recognition that Poins competes as a surrogate sibling. Falstaff's dubious claim that Poins presumptuously fancies Hal as a brother-in-law to be married to his sister, Nell (2.2.107–19), reinforces this idea. Hal's rebellious presence in the tavern world with a variety of "brothers," including Falstaff, who is also a father surrogate, works out his ambivalence toward the royal family, defining one world in terms of the other. The continuing reference point is the royal father. The return to the dying father and the surrounding brothers acknowledges a return to the public, patriarchal frame. Hereafter, except at his father's deathbed scene, he is framed by brothers prepared by the dead king. He has proved fit for this role, a surrogate father to his brothers.

His first entrance as Henry V plays on his fitness as his father's successor. While confessing the stiffness of his new role, he works to ease his brothers' fears by identifying with the dead father. Though wearing his "new and gorgeous garment, majesty" (5.2.44), he shares their black mourning garb as an image of his own grief. "I will deeply put the fashion on, / And wear it in my heart" (5.2.52–53). The garment of majesty clothes the political person; and sorrow clothes the private person, who is their brother and now also becomes their father:

> Let me but bear your love, I'll bear your cares.
> Yet weep that Harry's dead, and so will I;
> But Harry lives that shall convert those tears
> By number into hours of happiness.
>
> (5.2.58–61)

Just as Henry IV urged Clarence to "effect . . . mediation" (4.3.24–25) between the new king and all the brothers following the father's death, the new king urges a unity through himself. The identification with the old king is completed through replacing him. And, more, as he says to the lord chief justice, he will speak in his father's very words to his own son if necessary: "So shall I live to speak my father's words" (5.2.106). The successor's new and gorgeous garment received from his father, we are told, has become a tailored fit. Identification with the father and vocational fitness merge together.

His accommodation with the lord chief justice hinges on that identification. Once assaulted as the "image" of the King's person, the judge is now welcomed as the "father" (5.2.117) to Henry's youth. Shakespeare is not toying loosely with categories here. By endorsing the lord chief justice's imprisonment of Hal, Henry IV was acknowledging that the king's justice had been rendered through his "image." Effectively, his own justice had been performed on his son. In turn, the new king's endorsement of the judge's action repeats his father's approval in that single action, merging father and son together in the king's "person." The underlying theoretical principle is that only the mortal private person, not the politic person, is subject to time. But the inexperienced young king must be tutored further by experience, and by the judge's own office; this office will be a father to the mortal human who must perform within the continuity of his own political office. By Hal speaking his father's words and promising to repeat them in the future if necessary he becomes the same politic person as his father. This affirmation of likeness in his new calling assures a proper succession, his residual aggression against the judge and against the father notwithstanding.

Henry's death leads inevitably to the new king's rejection and banishment of Falstaff. Assuring his brothers and reaching accord with the lord chief justice both test his fitness; Falstaff's expansively inappropriate public request for acknowledgment forces the most difficult test of Hal's fitness for the kingship. Simultaneously, this meeting is a final trial of Falstaff, who has been repeatedly tried throughout part 2 while evading the constraints of the law, feeding on opportunities presented by the civil unrest, and awaiting Hal's elevation as king. His boasts — that "the laws of England are at my commandment" (5.3.125–26) and that the lord chief justice is at risk — justify Clarence's fear, expressed to John of Lancaster, that Hal's coronation ensures "you must now speak Sir John Falstaff fair" (5.2.33). The king, whom Falstaff possessively, intimately addresses ("King Hal, my royal Hal! . . . my sweet boy! . . . My King! my Jove . . . my heart!" — 5.5.39–44), is accompanied in his inaugural public appearance by the royal brothers and the lord chief justice. In an opposing tableau Falstaff confronts them in the presence of Shallow, Pistol, and Bardolph, known threats to the emergent order. Falstaff's unfettered impropriety tests the new authority of the royal "person," thereby ensuring his banishment "by ten mile" (5.5.63) from the king's carefully tailored political person.

It cannot be forgotten, when assessing the fitness of Henry's judgment, that Falstaff compulsively narrows the possible range of the king's responses. If Henry overreacts, he has good cause. Falstaff's flagrant display of intimacy and possession not only defies necessary proprieties but also misinterprets the mixed signals he had always received from the ambivalent Henry. Mockery and deflation qualified the support given Falstaff as a knight. Falstaff's unsettling impropriety in this sensitive theater of public appearance serves only to underline the tenacity of his disruptive nature at work throughout the play.

> I know thee not, old man. Fall to thy prayers.
> How ill white hairs becomes a fool and jester!
> I have long dreamt of such a kind of man,
> So surfeit-swelled, so old, and so profane;
> But, being awake, I do despise my dream.
>
> (5.5.45–49)

The king's rebuke alludes to the recalcitrance of Paul's Old Man,[54] the disruptive twist in human nature turning away from proper ends. Overreacting or not, the king is compelled to make clear to both Falstaff and to the audience intently viewing his initial public actions that the intrusive Falstaff has no claim on his authority:

> Presume not that I am the thing I was,
> For God doth know, so shall the world perceive,
> That I have turned away my former self.
>
> (5.5.54–56)

Inconsistent with the "person" of the king, the "former self" that inhabited Falstaff's world must be "turned away."

Henry and the lord chief justice stand against Falstaff and Justice Shallow while the rule of law lies in the balance. Falstaff would command the laws of England and stifle a forceful judiciary. The disease in Justice Shallow has already been turned to commodity with the promise of "what office thou wilt in the land" (5.3.114). The token abuse of the outlying system of justices of the peace suggests the general threat to the realm. Falstaff's presence threatens both essential judicial systems, the common law courts and the provincial courts.

Henry acts in the judicial station of the royal vocation. Earlier, dressed in his new robes, he acted in his familial station, taking on his deceased father's place as head of the royal family. Earlier, he acted in the military and familial stations of his vocation as heir apparent. Dissection of the vocational substructure reveals a principle of coherence that can be obscured by our own paradigms for characterizing the self. To point to this coherence is not to ignore the problematical stress lines joining the natural person to the stations of "a certaine kinde of life ordained or imposed" on the individual. The potential for segmentation or splitting inherent in the vocational self applies to both kings and commoners. These problems are even more vexing in the ambivalent *Henry V*, but even there the substratum provided by the principles of vocation should affect discussion in significant ways.

Some Reflections on Henry V

Much recent criticism of *Henry V* hinges on a perception of ambivalence in Shakespeare's characterization of the king. The absorption of the private person into the complex public, corporate role has been a lightning rod for late twentieth century resistance to the practices of *realpolitik*. Accordingly, perceived ambivalence toward Henry in *Henry V* has sparked suspicion, mistrust, and resentment of a hero of English history. The final pages of this chapter examine some implications of the vocational self as a necessary factor in that discussion.

Norman Rabkin's elegant claims about the play's ambivalence toward Henry still inform the critical debate. Rabkin found deliberately mixed signals in Shakespeare's characterization of Henry V, both an "ideal monarch" and a "Machiavellian militarist,"[55] both a rabbit and a duck. Many recent critics perceive more of the Machiavel seeking power, going so far in some cases as to claim that Shakespeare did likewise. But there are dangers in overplaying our late twentieth century mistrust of political power in assessing Shakespeare's characterization, especially if we recall Laurence Olivier's jingoistic version. After all, Rabkin's polarity, in defining a choice between the rabbit and the duck, allows for the legitimacy of the ideal monarch. Even a skeptical voice like Leonard Tennenhouse allows that "In certain respects, *Henry V* can be called a piece of political hagiography."[56] This admission unintentionally strengthens a previous argument by Sherman Hawkins that in *Henry IV* Hal develops the traditional cardinal virtues of temperance and fortitude in part 1; then attains justice and wisdom in part 2; and finally, religion is added to his traditional secular virtues in *Henry V* through divinely approved victory.[57] The Hawkins anatomy of virtues is consistent with Hal's transformation from a wastrel who exasperates his royal father into the guarantor of Lancastrian succession, who unifies British forces in reclaiming lost territory. This movement toward effective governance and focused responsibility — whatever the compromising elements in his behavior — is the central narrative line consistent with the heroic Henry of British history. Maynard Mack spoke for many earlier critics who saw the heroic monarch in this narrative line without even suspecting the outline of a Machiavel when he claimed, "This, the greatest of monarchical success stories in English popular history, traces the evolution of an engaging scapegrace into one of the most admired of English kings. Chicanery and appetite in the first play, apathy and corruption in the second, form an effective theatrical background against which the oncoming sunbright majesty of the future Henry V may shine more bright — as we are assured precisely that it will do on our first meeting with him" (1.2).[58] But a generation of critics exposed to Vietnam era viruses of power politics, militarism, and official duplicity tend to see the Machiavel whose personal qualities have been effaced by a theatrical quest for power. Mack's Hal has disappeared behind a set of masks and a critique of "power" has overridden the vocabulary of "ruling" and "governing" that characterized traditional humanistic discussion.[59] Mack's optimistic narrative has become a problem play, his hero a dubious politician decentered by power lust.

Many objections to Hal in *Henry IV* are also mounted against the more experienced king in *Henry V* and invite similar responses. Earlier objections to the player king's many masks emerge later as the techniques of the impersonal theater of power politics. The private person is nowhere to be found in the decentered monarch. Earlier, I suggested that Protestant vocation with its several stations suggests a different notion of coherence, and that we do well to contemplate in more detail the kingly vocation which Shakespeare signals early in *1 Henry IV* as the norm for assessing Hal/Henry. As a hero of British history, Henry V provides the

frame for the ideal king, however humanized by personal idiosyn-
crasies and human blemishes. The narrative employed by Shakespeare shows Hal developing those qualities associated with ideal
kingship, as Hawkins has shown. Just as that narrative shows
Henry's development in the military, judicial, and familial stations of the royal vocation, Shakespeare extends further his
anatomy of the necessary stations in Henry's kingly vocation, first,
"a true lover of the holy Church" (1.1.24) noted for his theological study and personal spirituality, then as the unifying governor
of disparate ethnic, linguistic, and national constituencies, later
as the military general in combat, finally as the husband-to-be of
the French princess. These components are necessary in the vocation of king.

William Perkins's definition of "vocation or calling" as "a certaine kinde of life ordained and imposed on man by God for
the common good" is instructive here.[60] Three essential ideas are
linked: first, a complete "life" has a fullness; second, a vocation
implicates the self in service to the community; third, an external agent imposes a vocation. The private self is completed
through an outside agent in both Perkins's religious version and
in the derivative secular notion. In the first instance, God creates
the conditions that lead the private self to its public commitment;
in the second instance, society is the source. Perkins says the vocation is "imposed" like a tax or burden identifying the believer.[61]
In both cases, the identified person must bear the burden, pay the
tax, take up the duties of "a certaine kinde of life." This cultural
habit of thought informs the secular legacy as well. Sometime tent-
makers like Paul, hardhanded weavers like Bottom, magistrates
like the lord chief justice, and kings like Henry and Lear all have
certain kinds of lives "imposed" upon them. The stations within
these lives vary accordingly.

A life "imposed" may be neither welcome nor congenial to the
created private self. The choice to obey the call and to take up
the proffered role may be difficult; the cost of obedience may be
ambivalence, even for one naturally fit for the calling. An heir apparent to a tainted crown might justifiably resist the call to labor in
a possibly unlawful vocation. In fact, it might be a sin to labor in

that vocation. Contrarily, such labor could legitimize succession and rightful rule. But even a legitimate crown lies heavy, unlike the simple "biggen" of a commoner; and any heir apparent, even if attracted to the power and privilege of the crown, might instinctively resist the counterweight of responsibility.

The notion of self here is complex. The congenital self has gifts and dispositions that can develop through training and experience. A given calling might selectively exercise specific gifts or dispositions; a later change may exercise others. The carpenter Jesus had craft in his hands; but in a later vocation his parables required the gifts of religious imagination and poetic tongue to express spiritual truths. But the relationship between "private" gifts and dispositions and "public" calling is not seamless. In some cases the congenital disposition may be exercised naturally by the externally imposed requirements of the vocation. In other cases, the response is more complex, ambivalent, resistant. The nature of that resistance may reveal central, private character traits. So it is with Henry.

Henry's disguise as a commoner before Agincourt configures his ambivalence. We meet him initially in *1 Henry IV* with low-life companions; we find him back in the tavern in *2 Henry IV*; then he appears disguised as a commoner in *Henry V*. In all cases, his presence is marked by aggression and resentment against "the base clouds," just as ties to his father are defined by avoidance and rebellion, figuratively a parricidal impulse. A reserve about the demands of responsibility colors his actions throughout *Henry V*; even his defensible claim that each soldier's conscience is his own shifts responsibility for his public actions to someone else. But temporary, patterned avoidance is not refusal; instead, distance and delay are the marks of his nature. In *2 Henry IV* Hal mirrors his own experience in the constructed dilemma of the drawer Francis; likewise, in *Henry V* Shakespeare mirrors Henry's dilemma in the experience of the common soldier conscripted to fight a foreign war where killing offends the private conscience. His father's legacy recommends foreign invasion to unify the nation; by entering the disguise of the common soldier Henry retreats momentarily from the responsibility of leadership and finds a mirror of his own dilemma. For one who offered to fight Hotspur one-on-one to save life in both camps, foreign invasion is inherently problematical. The archbishop's self-serving sanction does not expunge Henry's lingering moral doubts, however much it may justify actions by the Crown. Like his retreat to the tavern world, Henry's trip *incognito* to the camp enacts a retreat from the royal vocation. But the chosen name of Harry Le Roi preserves the connection, ironically translated into the language of the claimed, invaded turf, permitting the distinctness of the king's two bodies, but not their separation.

Shakespeare here traces the seam connecting the private and the public realms of self found in both kings and commoners, created by the idea of vocation. Shakespeare follows this seam later in *Hamlet* where the Prince, faced with a time "out of joint" at first resists his father's call "to set it right" (1.1.189–90). In *King Lear* the old king divests himself of royal duties, then cries in anguish, "Who is it that can tell me who I am?" (1.4.195). Later he refuses to probe the residual meaning inherent in Cordelia's "my Royal Lord" (4.6.37). When the seam is closed, the self leads "a certaine kinde of life" serving within the community. First Hal's then Henry's ambivalence strains but does not open the seam; the stress on the seam lessens but it does not disappear the longer Henry puts on the crown. The vocation with multiple stations interacts with the natural, private person, at times swerving, but not diverted in its general direction by resistance from the private person. His "certaine kinde of life" follows its own proper direction within the public community. Henry's distinguishing ambivalence is no less constant than his overriding commitment to royal responsibilities. Such paradoxical constancy lies at the center of his nature; to say that his nature is "opaque" disallows a recognizable, pivotal, and continuing complexity that develops, but is never effaced. Those elements in the self which are congenital must adapt to vocational requirements which take root, however uneasily, as part of the developing self. Throughout the three plays Shakespeare follows Henry's development in light of his vocational requirements and his ambivalence.

Critical discussion of Henry and self necessarily gravitates to the connections between the Protean "player king" and the King's two bodies. Both notions involve crucial elements in the plays. The first addresses Hal/Henry's theatrical role-playing; the second notion and its variant, the two persons, stress the corporate nature of the crown and a prince's inherent split between private and public. Louis Montrose's analysis of Elizabethan theatricality suggests a natural link between these ideas. Montrose cites a professional self-consciousness in Shakespeare that defends against conservative Christian notions of vocational hierarchy. Shakespearean metadrama includes professional self-justification in "a dialectic between his profession and his society."[62] To Montrose, "from the perspective of long-term historical change, the professional stage-play was still an emergent cultural form; the commercial playhouse, an emergent sociocultural space; and the profession of player, an emergent social calling."[63] Montrose is not invoking the historically specific Protestant notion of calling or vocation addressed in this chapter, but his notion of a self-conscious, "emergent social calling" catches the spirit of Shakespeare's time. This new calling, which was widely regarded as subversive to public morality and order, stimulated vocational self-assertion and the self-defense of drama. The "purpose of playing," as Hamlet puts it (3.2.18–19), is the mirror held up to nature. Plays mirror the *theatrum mundi,* and the actor in many disguises mirrors the human being whose multiple experiences require more than one face. Similarly, the actor's "emergent social calling" mirrors the royal calling. The king viewed as an actor reflects back on the importance of the actor performing his calling. The connection here is a cultural assumption about the role of vocation. The king's "certaine kinde of life" has parallels to the actor's. In both cases the vocational way of life encourages a general coherence of being that comprehends several parts within the whole. The concept of "power" coloring much recent discussion of these plays blurs the subtleties in this idea.

In the mutually reflecting vocations of player and king and in a "certaine kinde of life" that serves the common good, we can connect the king's two bodies. The common good informs the corporate entity in which all participate through their vocations. All vocations inhere in the king's corporate Body ruled by the Crown, its head. Systems of likeness and unlikeness define modes of participation. Hal reflects on the likeness between himself and Francis; so, too, the king at Agincourt strains to define conscience relating respectively to the king and to the common soldier, whose vocational participation differs profoundly. Henry's disguise emphasizes his shared humanity, as a private person who also must deal with his own private conscience. But his translated name (Harry Le Roi) preserves his royal vocation, its claim on French territory, and the vocational responsibility of the royal person. The crown is not the homely biggin, but human likeness binds them together.

Elizabethan obsession with royal succession was driven by an urgent belief in perpetuating the communal body politic represented by the Crown.[64] The crown beside the dying Henry IV's bedside captures the distinction between private and corporate; Hal's self-coronation represents the transfer of royal responsibilities from one private person to another. At the same time Hal is choosing the royal vocation with its several stations. One mythology links to another: the two "persons" with that of vocation. The private person who chooses the royal vocation willingly joins the two persons together. That mysterious jointure can be identified by its characteristics, even if not comprehended rationally, even if not free of paradox.

The jointure includes the strange characterization of corporate activity in terms of private affect. As Claire McEachern puts it, the Elizabethan habit of mind that "employs the tropes of personhood" to conceive "social union" differs sharply from the modern tendency to "segregate . . . power and fellowship"[65] through depersonalized institutions. That difference lies behind our difficulties in accommodating the ambivalence characterizing Henry. Private affects characterize the actions of the public person in whom the body politic inheres. A compelling case in point concludes the action in *Henry V*. The French Catherine is both a private body and a member of the body politic, France, attacked by the conqueror Henry. Brusque, comic wooing anatomizes her body parts within the hard reality of royal marriage. Her body viewed as public booty is justified by the same Salic law that authorizes the invasion of France by a conquering hero. Royal marriage is one further station in the vocation of king that transforms private motive to serve public responsibility. She will be the mate of the private person, whose spousal duties are also part of his vocation as the royal person. However problematic Shakespeare finds this complex and paradoxical relationship, he is sorting through the implications of the cultural frames.

Shakespeare characteristically probes the stress lines in the jointure between the private and corporate persons at the same time that he probes the centrifugal energies inherent in the several stations of royal vocation. But it is no more valid to say that the various elements threaten to break apart the center of Henry's character than to stress the countervailing forces of coherence at work in these notions. Some readers may conclude reasonably that Shakespeare engages more troublesome difficulties in the characterization of Henry than can be contained by the play. And that may be. At the least, it can be safely said that the notion of vocation occupies his examination of the royal self throughout the Henriad.

THREE

"Ego videbo"

Donne and the Vocational Self

In a 1620 Lincoln's Inn sermon Donne boldly impersonated Job's voice in affirming the identity of the self at the resurrection. He, too, would stand face to face, person to person, before the resurrected Christ at the resurrection: "*Ego,* I, I the same body, and the same soul, shall be recompact again, and be identically, numerically, individually the same man. The same integrity of body, and soul, and the same integrity in the Organs of my body, and in the faculties of my soul too; I shall be all there, my body, and my soul, and all my body, and all my soul . . . *Ego,* I, the same person; *Ego videbo,* I shall see."[1] This confident voice spoke before familiar Lincoln's Inn faces, including many members well acquainted with Donne's personal history. First admitted to Lincoln's Inn in 1592, he was appointed Master of the Revels in 1593. After ordination in 1615 and appointment as Divinity Reader at Lincoln's Inn in 1616, he frequently preached there: 21 sermons written for that familiar audience still remain.[2] That "same person" confidently

standing before them physically in time expected to see the resurrected Christ in eternity. The inference to be drawn by the members of this familiar Lincoln's Inn audience is that they — as the
"same persons" — could together physically join Donne and Job.

Donne speaks to them here as a confident pulpit orator ven-
triloquizing the words of a biblical exemplar while filling his
own vocational place. His text assumes that his body is seen in
the pulpit and that his voice is heard by others, body and voice
sealing Job's promise of continuing physical identity after death.
The pulpit performance dutifully incorporates Donne's notion of
the centered, inclusive, vocational "person" in whom others participate: "The person must actuate it self, dilate, extend and prop-
agate it self according to the dimensions of the place, by filling
it in the execution of the duties of it" (*Sermons* 8:178). It is a duty
to incorporate an exemplar: "Be sombody, be like sombody, propose some good example in thy calling and profession to imitate"
(8:180). Paul was his favorite exemplar, but there were others, like
Job, incorporated in this vocational person confidently inviting
the participation of others.

Donne standing confidently before his Lincoln's Inn audience
does not surprise us when we recall his reputation as an orator
in the "theater of preaching."[3] But the parallels between the pulpit and the stage as public spaces, and the preacher and the actor
in relation to participating audiences[4] provide us with more than
just accidental interest if we pursue the informative parallels
between Donne and Shakespeare's fictive Hal/Henry, examined
in my previous chapter. Donne takes on the exemplary model of
Job; the player embodies the fictionalized, but historical royal person; and, in both cases, members of the audience participate com-
munally in these vocational persons. Following his coronation,
the fictive Hal/Henry, dressed in royal robes and wearing his
father's crown, appears in public to pass judgment against Falstaff.
In the new king we find a striking, if unexpected, parallel to John
Donne, ordained four years before (1616) and wearing his priestly
robe while preaching to his parishioners at Lincoln's Inn (1620).
The vocational parallel between Hal/Henry and John Donne is even

more striking and informative since the two men answer the call to their vocations after tainted beginnings, one as the ironic "heir apparent" to a usurper king, the other as an unsettled heir to maligned and illegal religious practices. At first, neither can answer the Protestant call to vocation, to the ready-made cultural role that stabilizes the self. But the same vocational principle that forms both the fictive and the real vocational "persons" contributes to the confident performance at Lincoln's Inn.

Readers of Donne's works written before his ordination have not found this confident, unified sense of self integrated within a community of persons. Quite the contrary. Donne criticism has wrestled long and hard with unsettling elements in Donne's biography and temperament that foster contradiction and indeterminacy in a variety of literary forms. This chapter will rest on Donne's notion of the centered, vocational person, but only after suggesting how the unsettling elements come to be resolved within a unifying vocation serving the common good.

The Struggle to Interpret Donne

Attempts to establish a unifying conception of Donne have been problematical. Vexing contradictions involving witty cynicism, misogyny and spiritualized love in the love lyrics have long bedeviled Donne readers. These contradictions have supported Thomas Docherty's postmodernist claims that several unstable, contingent voices inhabit these poems.[5] Docherty summarily dismisses an article of faith in earlier criticism that an identifiable Donnean voice can be heard throughout the lyric poetry. Instead, the poems are said to configure a postmodernist sense of fragmented, contingent consciousness lacking self-identity.[6] John Carey's portrait of Donne, for which R. C. Bald's authoritative biography provided the basic frame, portrayed a careerist turning his back on his Catholic legacy, doggedly pursuing a satisfying place in the patronage systems, and ultimately settling for protection from the Crown. This largely coherent, albeit unflattering, portrait of apostasy and ambition[7] left a deep mark on Donne criticism. But that mark has been eroded by close scrutiny of texts written, particularly, in Donne's middle years; nor can Carey's portrait withstand criticism for ruling out the validity of Donne's religious experience.

Donne's careerist ambition dominates Carey's portrait, but the texts written between his marriage to Ann Donne and his ordination, although soiled by his search for patronage, are riven by countertensions. For David Aers and Gunter Kress, Donne's verse letters to prospective patrons, particularly Lucy Bedford, are inhabited by two selves: a contingent self requiring recognition and support by the patron and an idealized self true to an independent, stable standard of value by which the contingent world is to be judged.[8] Annabel Patterson's summary claim is that "self-division and equivocation" mark this period.[9] Donne characteristically engages in a "social construction of a self, in which group identity and personal identity are interdependent constructs."[10] Donne "found a way to speak ambivalence."[11] He worked on his potential patrons while simultaneously practicing an oppositional freedom. With David Norbrook, Patterson finds in Donne's parliamentary experience an independent political stance critical of established power. For Norbrook, Donne's connections with the Essex circle and his participation in two parliaments suggest a traditional republican energy that creates oppositional impulses wrestling variously, often contradictorily, against submissive strategies necessary to make his way in the patronage systems. Both critics discover practices in Donne's sermons that contradict what Norbrook aptly calls "the careerist, absolutist Donne of the current critical orthodoxy."[12] Donne's frequently ambivalent and nuanced responses maintain his place within the church while opening critical, oppositional perspectives expressing the "boldness and independence of mind" praised by Thomas Carew in his elegy on Donne.[13]

Although such discussions substantially advance our understanding of Donne's complex self-representations in the works of his middle years and of his nuanced political strategies later as a pulpit orator, they separate Donne as a social and political being from the intense realities of his spiritual life. They step into the same secular trap as Carey, who viewed Donne's religious and theological thought merely as a repository of figures serving his psychological and imaginative needs.[14] Patterson and Norbrook confine Donne within the boundaries of clientage and politics, avoiding his concurrent spiritual turmoil and his searching pilgrimage through theological literature. Helen Gardner's claim that the *Holy Sonnets,* "present an image of a soul working out its salvation in fear and trembling" (xxxi)[15] is one vivid reminder of that intense spirituality. Most of the *Holy Sonnets* were probably written in 1609–11, a few even later, the latest in 1617 after Ann Donne died. Composition of the *Essays in Divinity* spanned roughly the same period from 1610 until Donne's ordination in 1615. The devotional modulations in these "Several Disquisitions, Interwoven with Meditations and Prayers"[16] spiritualize Donne's scholarly, "hydroptique"[17] quest through theological literature.

Patterson illustrates Donne's divided self by his presence at the Mitre Tavern gathering in 1611 amongst a cross-section of ambitious intellectuals of various stripes later "powerfully represented in the 1614 parliament,"[18] many strongly "oppositional" to the monarchy. An even more dramatic self-division is evident in the closely contemporary "Good Friday, 1613. Riding Westward." The tension between the embodied self on horseback "carryed towards the West" (9) by "Pleasure or businesse" (7) and "my Soules forme" bent eastward by memory toward the crucified Christ is unsettling. The concluding request for punitive affliction, in recalling the equally dramatic request earlier to "Batter my heart," suggests a more inclusive context from which the social, political, and economic "selves" of Donne — however divided — should not be removed. This recognizable Pauline/Augustinian self-division plagues Donne's devotional poetry written concurrently with texts situated in more obviously social and political contexts.

However, by its very confidence, the voice speaking to Donne's Lincoln's Inn audience in 1620 opposes the self-division that frays earlier works and invites other ways to construe those divisions. The ordained priest here speaks to an audience familiar with his personal history, thought by some persons, including the Countess of Bedford, to discolor his vocational suitability. Identification with Job is generalized, open to the audience through the priest's confident assertion of an integrated body and soul approved within a human and divine community. The flawed private person known by the audience, the ordained priest fulfilling his vocational role, and the physically beleaguered biblical saint speak together confidently.

Yet this confidence is hard won. The sermon rehearses Donne's phobic obsession with putrefaction, vermiculation, dissolution, and dispersal. "Corruption seises the skinne, all outward beauty quickly, and so it does the body, the whole frame and constitution" (*Sermons* 3:104). Worms soon enter: "*After my skinne, wormes shall destroy this body*" (3:106). Dissolved to basic matter or consumed by other creatures, the body loses its identity and gets lost in the identity of others: "one man is devoured by a fish, and then another man that eats the flesh of that fish, eats, and becomes the other man" (3:96). The terminal *Death's Duell* makes all too clear that Donne did not wear out his obsession, however much he may have tamed it: "Is that dissolution of body and soule, the last death that the body shall suffer? . . . It is not. Though this be *exitus à morte,* it is *introitus in mortem:* though it bee an *issue from* the manifold *deaths* of this *world,* yet it is an *entrance* into the *death of corruption* and *putrefaction* and *vermiculation* and *incineration,* and dispersion in and from the *grave,* in which every dead man dyes over againe" (10:235–36). Conformity to Christ promises resurrection for the individual; only confidence in that promise can defuse the threat to personal identity posed by bodily death.

Donne's obsession with bodily dissolution expresses the fear of annihilation, both of mind and body, which galvanizes his works. Donne's embrace of the doctrine of bodily resurrection is intimately connected to his early rejection of the Mortalist notion that the soul dies with the body. Donne feared the loss of consciousness no less than he feared the loss of bodily integrity. That the soul could enjoy heavenly bliss while the body moldered before the Last Day denied the annihilation of consciousness and assuaged the deepest human fears of a hyperconscious temperament. Still, we may ask skeptically whether Donne is not simply whistling in the dark when he expresses a Jobian confidence that defies fear and self-delusion. Certainly such skeptical questions emerge reasonably given his new confidence.

This confidence in the future integration of an identifiable self that "sees" God in both body and soul deserves further scrutiny. The confidence is circular. It projects the present conviction that the known self standing before his Lincoln's Inn audience will be the same self standing in the heavenly community before God in eternity. The projected future, in turn, reflects back to tame fears that the dualistic human self, a body and soul however compatibly integrated, will become fragmented and dispersed. But it can do so only if there is a present conviction of a continuing self still recognizable as a member of the continuing Body at Lincoln's Inn where Donne had been a member for over 25 years. The component in personal identity that I would underline as the end point of this discussion of Donne is John Donne the priest. We hear a confident vocational voice speaking to his Lincoln's Inn audience.

The dark background for this hard won confidence in the priestly vocational role was unrelenting. The shadows of melancholy and grief in Donne's works come as no surprise in a life so darkened by death, loss, separation, and suffering. His Catholic father died when Donne was four in 1576. His sister Elizabeth died in 1577; then sisters Mary and Katherine in 1582. John and his younger brother Henry were separated from their mother and stepfather, Dr. John Syminges, in 1584 when they were sent to Oxford. Contrary to Isaac Walton's assertion that Donne remained there until 1588, afterwards going to Cambridge, Dennis Flynn argues persuasively that the 12-year-old Donne, facing subscription to the Thirty-Nine Articles, the Oath of Supremacy, and persecution as a Catholic, joined a group accompanying Henry Stanley, the Earl of Derby, to the French court in early 1585. In Flynn's account, this even more radical separation from his family was engineered by his Jesuit uncle, Jasper Heywood, a court friend of Stanley, to protect the young boy's Catholic faith and to place him in a protective Catholic community. Donne then served briefly with a contingent of exiled English Catholic nobles and gentry at the Duke of Parma's recently fortified encampment at Antwerp in 1585 before traveling with the earl's second son,

William Stanley, in Spain and Italy until 1587, and returning to England with William in 1587 to serve in the Catholic Stanley household. On his return Donne was still only 15.[19]

The Catholic undertow carrying the young Donne to and from the Continent kept his family in its grip. In 1593, two years after Donne himself entered the Inns of Court, his brother Henry was arrested for harboring a Catholic priest in his Thavies Inn chambers. Henry's death by plague in Newgate Prison left Donne with only one live sibling, and his mother's stubborn recusancy ensured further separation. Dr. Syminges died in 1588. By 1595 Elizabeth and her third Catholic husband, Richard Rainsford, had sought religious freedom in Antwerp, where they remained for several years. Later, a deep irony ended the separation of son from mother when the widowed and still stubbornly Catholic Elizabeth Rainsford moved into the Protestant Deanery at St. Paul's, remaining there until her death in 1631, just two months before the death of her son.

Death stripped away his last sibling when Anne Lyly died in 1616,[20] but other losses had been even more cruel. Only seven of Ann Donne's eleven children outlived her. After six live births beginning in 1603, she delivered the first of two stillborn children in Donne's absence with the Drurys in 1612. Both Mary and Francis died in 1614. And Ann herself died in 1617, five days after the birth of her second stillborn child. Against this devastation, Donne's injunction "Death be not proud" rings hollow.

Ann Donne resists our understanding, and we sense that Donne's sonnet on her death does not capture the fullness of his bond to her.[21] No doubt "admyring her" did "whett" his mind to seek God. But such praise does not capture their mutual experience of physical love, grief, social ostracism, separation, death, and loss; nor does it capture the ironies of the interrelated watershed events in Donne's life that defined their bond, his secret marriage that predetermined his ordination. Two needs ruled Donne's person: first, a need for intimate mutuality to repair the ruptures from death and earlier separations; second, a need for membership in a stable community for basically the same reasons. These needs became incompatible when he fell in love with Ann Donne.

His gain of intimate mutuality caused his loss of preferment in the dominant culture; the occasion of his greatest gain became the occasion of his greatest loss. In the aftermath he experienced suicidal depression, an aggravated sense of separation, a denigrating search for a solution to his devastated professional prospects, a desperate dependence on male friends, and a practice of marital love that depleted Ann Donne's body in childbirth. In time, Donne satisfied both needs, though more sequentially than concurrently, in spite of the groundswell of death and suffering that continued as a central truth of his life.

The following discussion of Donne's sense of the self assumes a psychology of loss, separation, and depression underlying Donne's autobiographical narrative. That narrative intrudes everywhere in Donne's works, most explicitly in his extensive body of verse and prose letters, in the divine poems, in *Devotions upon Emergent Occasions*, and in numerous asides throughout the sermons. Its implicit presence in the love poetry remains problematical amongst students of Donne's works since strict attempts to avoid the biographical fallacy can be no less restrictive than attempts to extract biographical content from the poems. But the Jobian conviction of sustained identity and the Pauline conception of vocation expressed throughout the sermons, as we will see, are later expressions of a psychology that transmuted loss into gain. In examining the development of this psychology in Donne's representations of the self, the following discussion will center first on the role of the feminine in Donne's thought, then on the prose letters as intimacy yearning for community, and finally on the Pauline conception of vocation that centered his later years. Lastly, the concept of the Jobian self "redintegrates" — to use one of Donne's own terms — the broken fragments of his earlier experience.

Some Interrelationships: Amorousness, Gender and
Its Blurring, Misogyny, Male Readers

His love poetry remains the central focus of Donne criticism, although the filters through which we view the poems change.

Current interest in contextualizing Donne in early modern culture invites us to look at individual love poems less as a record of Donne's own experience than as constructs of his cultural context. For Arthur Marotti, Donne was writing for coterie readers "with whom he chose to associate at the Inns of Court and in the urbane and courtly circles to which he belonged in both the Elizabethan and Jacobean periods."[22] In particular, he wrote for male intellectuals ambitious to make their way within the patronage systems. Various elements in the love poetry reflect codes understandable within the coteries where Donne's manuscripts were circulated concerning misogyny, strategies of wit, varying love relationships, libertinism, and the characterization of women. The codes set up protective screens, allowing political and social commentary on the practices governing general relationships.

The tendency to view Donne as a conduit for the cultural forces of his time tends to exclude the immediacy of his own particular experience. A warning against this exclusion can be found in his anatomy of motivations for accompanying Essex, Raleigh, and Northhampton on the 1597 Azores Island Expedition:

> Whether a rotten state, and hope of gaine,
> Or to disuse mee from the queasie paine
> Of being belov'd, and loving, or the thirst
> Of honour, or faire death, out pusht mee first,
> I lose my end.
>
> ("The Calme," 39–43)[23]

He knows his several motivations, though not precisely which in this case. In any event, the experience of love is central in 1597, during the decade in which the bulk of his love poems were probably written. Unlike Christopher Brooke, to whom he wrote "The Calme," we cannot know whether Donne is referring to one exclusive love relationship or to several. But he does want to "disuse" himself of love's "queasie paine," a besetting, unsettling, and injurious nausea[24] of emotional entanglement. The claim that Donne was a great frequenter of ladies is consistent with this sense of painful and entangling amorousness. But it also suggests that Donne's love poetry is deeply rooted in personal experience, and should be part of any consideration of how the love poetry engages the culture of Donne's time.

Admittedly, recent studies that contextualize Donne have guided our responses to the love poetry in fruitful ways. There is a longstanding criticism that Donne's self-enclosed male subjects desire to dominate their female subjects with "masculine persuasive force."[25] Likewise, the misogyny expressed by some speakers, especially in the elegies, has raised questions about both Donne and his male audience that invite a feminist critique. For Marotti, the answers to such questions must be sought within Donne's Inns of Court coterie, expanded to include other gentlemen readers. Achsah Guibbory suggests a broader envelope enclosing this male coterie in the pervasive power of a female monarch who unsettles male expectations, hence male identity.[26] Disgust with the female body expressed in the blazon, "The Anagram," easily translates into a disgust with Elizabeth's aged body as the focus of power, just as the elegy, "To his Mistris Going to Bed," embodies a colonialism that dominates the woman's body while playfully suggesting with tongue-in-cheek a new spirituality of sexual titillation. Likewise, the forceful strategies of his argument, when read as an attempt to subordinate women, are seen as expressions of standard male-female power relationships displayed for Donne's male readership. Contrarily, Donne may be amusing his coterie by putting these speakers on trial for the very patterns that characterize some members of the coterie.

Accusations that Donne shares the misogynistic aggression, colonialism, and male domination at work in various poems are destabilized by recognition that many speakers are not clearly men. Readers find gender reversals in the love poetry or detect ambiguities that level out gender differences by situating women in rhetorical positions normally falling to the male. Women speak both "Confined Love" and "Breake of Day." The speaker in "Confined Love" argues the case for libertine naturalism on women's behalf, not men's as in poems like "Communitie" and "The Indifferent." The aubade "Breake of Day" pits the world of "businesse" against the necessary leisure of love, berating the male's departure as love's "worst disease." No less than poems that describe woman as a captive hostage of an abortive, patriarchal honor system, such as "The Flea," this poem's male is a captive of the work-a-day world complaining about the "busied man." David Blair cites "Confined Love" and "Breake of Day" for their obvious reversals of gender positions, but he points to the greater subtlety in other poems "deliberately suspending a presumption of maleness." Donne's poems of "marked emotional intensity" demonstrate "an almost complete collapse of differentiated behaviours into a mutuality which generates androgyny."[27]

Such blurring of gender positions takes us back to Donne's readership. Marotti claims that Donne's target audience remains the educated, ambitious male gentry or would-be gentry expanding outward from the Inns of Court and seeking preferment within the patronage networks, including the Court. Donne's relationship with Lucy Bedford notwithstanding, his preferred audience is this male coterie. He speaks to other males about male participation in love relationships. Not sufficiently underlined by Marotti is that the love poetry is merely one of several modes of speaking centered in the same male audience; the satires are another and, more importantly, so are letters written in both poetry and prose. If the audience determines the issues, a speaker's misogyny speaks to attitudes in the audience, either in sympathy or in criticism. Similarly, his satire targets a shared enemy or criticizes a weakness, shared or not. The claim that Donne, like other members of his male coterie, aggressively seeks to dominate or subjugate runs into increasing difficulty the more that we detect gender blurring or androgyny in the love lyrics. To validate female speakers or to blur the maleness of the dominant speaker is to erode the position of male dominance that forms an essential part of that characterization.

Gender blurring goes hand-in-hand with elements of androgyny that run throughout Donne's works. The broad range includes some traditional notions: the female muse, the feminine human soul, "conception" that denotes both thought and impregnation, vocation as a marriage to society, virtue as the feminine "Soules soule." All these notions express Donne's identification with the feminine. It is not just a client's retrospective wit in a letter to Buckingham that contrasts "the mistress of my youth, Poetry" with "the wife of mine age, Divinity."[28]

Donne's recycling of conventional feminine tropes could easily be discounted if not for their frequent appearance in his works. In what Bald calls Donne's "early verse letters,"[29] the idea of the feminine muse is a staple; and given the burgeoning interest in verse letters within the Inns of Court culture, we can assume substantial circulation of this idea. "To Mr B. B.," a verse letter written to Beaupré Bell in the 1590s, turns on this idea:

> If thou unto thy Muse be marryed,
>> Embrace her ever, ever multiply,
>> Be far from me that strange Adulterie
> To tempt thee and procure her widowhed.
> My Muse, (for I had one,) because I'am cold,
>> Divorc'd her selfe:
>
> (1–6)

Donne wittily denigrates the quality of the verse letter; his muse — the putative "Mother" of his "Children of Poetry" — has deserted him for lacking warmth (10, 13). His "Rymes" (9) lack value unless approved by B. B.

The female muse[30] is one idea threading together several verse letters to Roland Woodward. In assuming a shared narrative within a personal friendship, the letters to Woodward illustrate the same principle discovered in an exchange of letters between Donne and Henry Wotton.[31] The most substantial letter ("Like one who'in her third widdowhood") responds to Woodward's request (perhaps 1597)[32] to collect Donne's poetry. The poem joins ideas shared earlier, that virtue is the "soules soule" ("If, as mine is, thy life a slumber be" — 32); and that the muse is female. Donne's purpose in joining these two ideas, in answer to Woodward's request for copies of his poetry, is to deprecate his love poems and satires as a misuse of talent:

> Like one who'in her third widdowhood doth professe
> Her selfe a Nunne, ty'd to retirednesse,
> So'affects my muse now, a chast fallownesse;

Since shee to few, yet to too many'hath showne
How love-song weeds, and Satyrique thornes are growne
Where seeds of better Arts, were early sown.

(1–6)

Rather than poetry, he wishes to cultivate virtue as the soul's soul inhabiting the self:

Seeke wee then our selves in our selves; for as
Men force the Sunne with much more force to passe,
By gathering his beames with a christall glasse;

So wee, if wee into our selves will turne,
Blowing our sparkes of vertue, may outburne
The straw, which doth about our hearts sojourne.

(19–24)

Donne affects "better Arts" (6) dependent on virtue and, as we learn early in satire 1 ("Why should'st thou . . . Hate vertue, though shee be naked, and bare?" — 37, 41) and repeatedly in the letters to Lucy Bedford, virtue is also feminine. Here Donne fudges the matter. That is, he does not eschew poetry, but affects a "chast fallownesse" (3) while, like Stoic "farmers of our selves" (31), he will cultivate virtue. For Donne, the self and the soul animating it are imaginable only in feminine terms.

Woodward's proposed collection, proleptically the Westmoreland manuscript, contributes to the mutual narrative that includes discussion of poetry and virtue in these letters to his friend. If written in 1597, the above letter would have postdated the satires, the elegies, and probably some other love poems, while strengthening the mortar of ideas that bonds friends together. The notion that virtue is the soul's soul also informs the narrative in the clientage letters to Lucy Bedford written more than a decade later. There, Donne appropriately exploits the characterization of virtue as feminine, as we found as early as the first satire, above. Donne's complex strategy in the letters to Lucy Bedford pivots on the idea of virtue, which, as Milgate tells us,[33] is central throughout the verse letters. A client's needs unsettle the moral adviser, who encourages the aristocratic giver of favors to embody

virtue in her practices, particularly at Court. Praise of her virtue
assumes her good behavior; hence such praise is implicit moral
advice. Therefore, she is an embodiment of virtue if she practices
what he implicitly encourages:

> Therefore at Court, which is not vertue's clime,
> (Where a transcendent height, (as, lownesse
> Makes her not be, or not show) all my rime mee
> Your vertues challenge, which there rarest bee
> For, as darke texts need notes: there some must bee
> To usher vertue, and say, *This is shee.*
> ("To the Countesse of Bedford" ["Madame, / You have refin'd
> mee"], 7–12)

Praise identifies Lady Bedford as Virtue *if* she embodies his poetic
"notes" (11) in her actions. Then Donne subtly backs away from
his exaggeration: "Yet to that Deity which dwels in you / Your
vertuous Soule, I now not sacrifice" (31–32). Donne conflates
much here: the exaggeration of clientage stretches orthodox ideas.
The "Deity" he serves — now petitioning ("These are *Petitions,*
and not Hymnes," line 33), implicitly praising while claiming not
to praise, and doing so lavishly — is God's image in the human
soul. The soul within the soul is virtue; the exercise of virtue repairs
the divine image damaged by Edenic failure. The client's inflated
praise thus has a coherent idea as a basis, even though many
modern readers see only the sleazy flattery of a court operator.
The clientage strategy conveniently provided an opportunity to
construct a representation of virtue, which like the human soul
and poetic representation, Donne conceives as feminine.

Elizabeth Drury provided a similar opportunity, this time
Donne's representation of the human soul as feminine, a recurrent idea in his works. A chorus of complaint abused Donne's poetic
strategy of deifying the unknown dead girl. Donne's defense —
that "he described the Idea of a Woman and not as she was"[34] —
would have convinced few members of that chorus, especially Ben
Jonson, who reported Donne's defense to William Drummond. Too
often Donne gets scant credit for the logic of his argument, nor
are his working assumptions recognized fully. An exception is

Barbara Lewalski's influential claim that Elizabeth Drury represents the idealized human image damaged by sin, but reparable through virtue.[35] In Elizabeth Drury we find the quasi-divine godlikeness of the soul before the Fall; her death then participates in the Fall, and her return is a preservation. Donne's praise of her celebrates the regenerate soul deserving the reward of heavenly bliss. The invitation to divine rape in "Batter my heart, three person'd God" is the most flamboyant example of the human soul as female; less flamboyant, but no less obvious and taken for granted, are several instances in the *Devotions upon Emergent Occasions,* such as his prayer that "my soule may looke, and make her use of thy mercifull proceedings toward my *bodily restitution, & goe* the same way to a *spirituall.*"[36] But it was the death of the anonymous Elizabeth Drury that provided the most significant opportunity to represent the human soul in terms of the idea of woman.

And the Virgin Mary remains the norm for assessing Elizabeth Drury. Jonson's complaint that "Donne's *Anniversary* was profane and full of blasphemies" and "if it had been written of the Virgin Mary it had been something"[37] used the appropriate norm, but may have miscalculated the nature of Donne's application. Two feminist readings of the poem use the same norm, but with different results. Maureen Sabine suggests that in *The Anniversaries* Donne extricates himself from an inherited Catholic devotion to the Virgin that was anathematized in the Protestant world he would enter: "By compelling the readers of his *Anniversaries* to accept a wisp of a girl like Elizabeth Drury in place of the Virgin, even if he thus hoped to save some trace of her mystique, Donne was contributing to the deconstruction of the Marian ideal and ultimately to its indeterminacy. Not only far- but partial-sighted as a poet, he now began the work that has recently absorbed literary theory, that of depersonalizing the text, by extracting the essence or pure 'Idea' of femininity from its specificity in Mary's maternal body."[38] Not only Jonson has found Elizabeth Drury's shoulders too thin to bear the symbolism laid on her. With particular trenchancy the sometimes Catholic Jonson judged that Donne should have known better than to write a poem so "profane and full of blasphemies." Sabine's account assumes that Jonson misread Donne's deliberate intentions to set Mary aside as the symbolic vehicle of femininity, although some readers might argue that Drummond of Hawthornden's secondhand account may mask that Jonson knew precisely what Donne was doing. What is clear is that the idea of the feminine so central to Donne's thought cannot be understood without reference to Mary.

Elizabeth Harvey's gynocritical reading of *The Anniversaries*, in linking the pervasive iconography of the Virgin to Elizabeth Drury as the inspiration of Donne's poems, also invokes ideas related to Donne's feminine muse. The chain of ideas cites the woman's body, specifically, the womb, as the locus of creation: "Renaissance physiology privileged the connection between women and the imagination because of the uterus, which was putatively susceptible to the influence of both the moon and the imagination. While this impressionability meant that pregnant women were vulnerable to the image-making capacity of the imagination, it also gendered the imagination as feminine."[39] The womb is linked to the imagination through the negative stereotype of feminine changeability and the conviction that imagination controlled products of the womb; and the womb is associated with words through the negative stereotype of feminine garrulity. These elements are conflated and sublimated in the idea of the feminine muse, who gives the male poet his poetic voice. Elizabeth Drury, whose dead body provides the occasion for a poem "full of metaphors of her sexuality and fecundity,"[40] is to be understood in terms of Mary, whose body also was the occasion for productivity.

The Anniversaries do not celebrate Elizabeth Drury's maternity, however, but her virginity. Paradoxically, her ability to propagate texts is dependent upon that sexual purity. Like the Virgin, her fecundity is asexual. Again, the point is that the Virgin is the standard for measuring Elizabeth Drury, and, when Donne steps back from explicitly identifying her as his muse, his reasons relate partially to basic use of Marian iconology, identifying Mary with the female human soul.

In the second poem Donne makes clear at the outset that, although "poetry is only produced by a chaste muse" and the "dead girl is his poetic source," she becomes the "animating spirit" of the world.[41] For that reason in "a transsexual exchange," she impregnates Donne's muse:

> Immortal Mayd, who though thou wouldst refuse
> The name of Mother, be vnto my Muse,
> A Father since her chast Ambition is,
> Yearely to bring forth such a child as this.
> These Hymes may worke on future wits, and so
> May great Grand-children of thy praises grow.
>
>   ("The Second Anniuersary," 33–38)[42]

Several iconologies serve Donne in developing the symbolism of Elizabeth Drury. As the animating spirit who impregnates Donne's muse, as we will see shortly in Donne's sermons, Elizabeth Drury functions like the Holy Spirit. The key to Donne's application lies in the idea of conception introduced a few years earlier in his address to Mary in "La Corona":

> Ere by the spheares time was created, thou
> Wast in his minde, who is thy Sonne, and Brother,
> Whom thou conceiv'st, conceiv'd; yea thou art now
> Thy Makers maker, and thy Fathers mother,
> Thou'hast light in darke; and shutst in little roome,
> *Immensity cloysterd in thy deare wombe.*
>
>   ("2. Annunciation," 9–14)

Mary's maternal womb conceives the Son, just as God's eternal mind conceived Mary before her birth. Donne's concluding address to the Lamb leads us further toward the necessary equivalencies: "And if thy holy Spirit, my Muse did raise, / *Deigne at my hands this crowne of prayer and praise*" ("7. Ascension," 13–14). Just as Elizabeth Drury must father poetic offspring on the "chast Ambition" of his muse, the Holy Spirit must raise the poetic prayer and praise of "La Corona." Mary's conception of Jesus through the entry of the overshadowing Holy Spirit is the icon for poetic inspiration from the Spirit. This icon frames our understanding of the female Elizabeth Drury as the transsexual "Father" of Donne's "Hymes" in "The Second Anniversary." Several ideas here can be unknotted and displayed by reference to Donne's treatment of Mary in the sermons.

Mary's "conception" is the crucial member in a set of parallels. The Son is generated and conceived eternally in the Father's mind; the Spirit proceeds eternally from both Father and Son.[43] The Son is generated temporally by the Holy Ghost, first in Mary's womb, later in each believer's soul, where conception occurs. The crux is biblical: *"The holy Ghost overshadowed the blessed virgin* (Luke 1.35), and so he was conceiv'd: there was enough done to magnifie the goodness of the holy Ghost in bringing him" (*Sermons* 7:155). Likewise, the female human soul is a womb in which Christ is generated, conceived, and born; both the Holy Spirit and Christ the Son play their roles. The same spirit who "shadowed the whole world under his wings" at Creation will enter the human soul: "Be thou a Mother where the Holy Ghost would be a Father; Conceive by him; and be content that he produce joy in thy heart here" (*Sermons* 7:70). The rational human soul, when consciously responsive to inward motions of Christ's Spirit,[44] can conceive the Son through conformity with Christ. Thus, Christ is conceived and born within the human soul.[45] Christmas manifests this truth rehearsed in Donne's 1625 Christmas Day sermon: "He had a humane birth, by which he was the Son of Mary, and without that he had not been sensible in himself of thine infirmities, and necessities; but, this day (if thou wilt) he hath a spirituall birth in thy soul, without which, both his divine, and his humane birth are utterly unprofitable to thee, and thou art no better then if there had never been Son of God in heaven, nor Son of *Mary* upon earth" (6:335). Mary's womb instructs the receptive human soul.

Other human souls are not chaste, but sinful, and this Christmas Day sermon supplements chaste Mary with repentant Magdalen. Though pure and full of grace, the anomalous Virgin was wrongly suspected of sexual incontinence. Her model comforts other chaste women stained by unjust suspicion; it also comforts women guilty of sexual misconduct, their reputations stained. Repentant behavior can exempt them from God's wrath and remove their stains. All sinners can be reassured by Christ's willingness to be born even in souls stained in the community's eyes or so sinful as to be initially offensive to God: "In that soul, that hath been as it were possessed with *Mary Magdalens* seven Devils, yea with him, whose name was Legion, with all Devils; In that sinful soul would Christ Jesus fain be born, this day, and make that soul, his Mother, that he might be a regeneration to that soul. We cannot afford Christ, such a birth in us, as he had, to be born of a Virgin; for every one of us wel-nigh hath married himself to some particular sin, some beloved sin, that he can hardly divorce himselfe from." Every repentant soul, even the dramatically sinful Magdalene, can be Christ's mother. The Spirit fathers; the human womb conceives; the Son is born, *"Made of a Woman"* (*Sermons* 6:338–39). Every human soul is such a woman.

The spirit that fathers a child in the human soul takes us back to Elizabeth Drury, the "Immortal Mayd," invoked as a "Father" to Donne's muse to "bring forth" an annual poetic "child" (*Sermons* 6:338–39). Put simply, she participates in the iconology of both Mary and the Holy Spirit, both female and male. As noted above, her virtuous but mortal body is the occasion for Donne's poem. And the memory of her virtue fathers his muse to conceive his poetic children. The iconologies of both Mary and the Holy Spirit lie just behind the poem; and the "Idea of Woman" can be said to include both. If Lewalski is right that Elizabeth Drury represents the regenerate human soul freed from its mortal body, then it follows that the residual force of that soul, whose soul is virtue, can imprint others. The very idea of woman paradoxically has an androgynous dimension through its participation in the iconology of the animating Holy Spirit.

Repeated emphasis on the soul, the muse, and virtue as feminine illuminates the gender reversals increasingly discovered in Donne's love poetry and complicates claims of misogyny, male aggression, dominance, antifeminism, and colonialism in these poems. Donne's misogynistic aggression is especially trouble-some when it flatly contradicts sincere praise of women. "Loves Alchymie" is an extreme example. The speaker's bitter denial of "minde" (23) and imagined embrace of dead flesh blame women for dashing love's high hopes of finding love's "hidden mysterie" (5). Disclaimers that Donne is not the speaker cannot mask this current of aggressive misogyny, which circulates throughout the love poems. Blame contradicts praise; misogyny intolerably strains the seams in Donne's androgynous search for the feminine; and a deep ambivalence remains unexplained.

Anna Nardo sees Donne as an amphibian moved by "contra-dictory fears of separation and union." Donne both avoids and desires union with women. Some of his cynical, escapist, or antifeminist speakers staunchly resist commitment; contrarily, others "seek union with the beloved, body and soul." A quite extra-ordinary "one-fifth of the *Songs and Sonnets* . . . are valedictions" that convey Donne's ambivalence, exit lines that reassure union while practicing avoidance.[46] Nardo's insight serves us well, although she shortchanges critics who would take us back to the troubled recusancy of his mother, Elizabeth Donne, and his own apostasy to understand the separation anxieties that shake the love poetry. Nardo abandons "biographical scenarios" as too "speculative"[47] while settling for a more generic solution from object relations thought. But Nardo's fruitful observation begs the question why this ambivalence was so tenacious in Donne; that is, her argument leads naturally to a "biographical scenario" that, in general terms, includes the presence and absence of Elizabeth. All humans need face-to-face union with the mother, while desir-ing independence; this ambivalence lingers with special strength in some adults like Donne.

The presence of dominant imprints in Donne's nature evident in his early works cannot be understood apart from his biograph-ical narrative. These imprints have been greatly undervalued by critics addressing the complex ambivalence and contending voices in the love poems. Donne's experience was deeply scarred by sep-aration, loss, death, suffering, and grief. In his family's ingrained recusancy and protection of Jesuit uncles, his father's early death and Elizabeth's prompt remarriage, an early departure to Oxford at age 12, then a Catholic's exile in Europe before return to England at 1611, we find a history of rupture and separation punctuated with death, disease, and grief that progressively destroyed his family's protective envelope. His mother virtually disappeared after he and his brother Henry left for Oxford; she reestablished her presence, ironically, only at the Deanery of St. Paul's. Significantly, the early Donne was preoccupied with the "queasie paine" of love, the gestures of a congenital, but dissatisfied amorous nature to repair the losses endemic to his life. Donne's identification with the feminine translates into various expressions of androgyny and a hydroptique yearning and search for lost union, for the face-to-face feminine presence lost early in his life, a teeming, paradoxical emptiness not easily satisfied. This yearning ties Donne's amorousness to his other dominant imprints of ambition and covetousness (alternately envy). Just as love seeks approval from the beloved, ambition seeks approval through honor, and covetousness/envy wants the acknowledgment enjoyed by others, the security of possessions that ensures honor. All three dominant imprints create a thirst for fulfillment, discussed in detail below.

The object relations model invoked by Nardo sheds considerable light on Donne's ambivalence between union and separation. But separation taken only as an independent need to identify the self does not explain Donne's misogynistic aggression against women. An alternative object relations model emphasizes the child's aggressive reaction against the mother's intentional separations. Absence fires the child's natural resentment, anger, and aggression against the defecting mother. Satisfaction of the child's needs tames aggression, which is channeled into productive activities as the child develops though readily ignited when satisfaction is blocked. Resentful aggression exacerbated becomes misogyny; even in normal circumstances it resides side-by-side with an amorous desire for reunion, a natural ambivalence.[48] Amorousness and resentment mutually inform each other. Extreme circumstances that exaggerate resentment and aggression can fuel scorn, the stuff of satire; woman, who denies satisfaction, is both a natural target and an object of desire. In Donne's personal narrative the domestic envelope of safety sealed by the mother's presence was increasingly breached, and the idea of woman expressed the desire to repair the breach and restore lost intimacy. In sum, his misogyny expresses an aggressive, resentful sense of injury while his congenital amorousness impelled a desire for union.

Much recent criticism seems ready to abandon the search for the basic Donne. The tendency has been to treat contingencies as a cluttered opaque screen, not as a dark glass through which outlines are still visible. But to detect dominant imprints keyed to a basic amorousness is to see through a glass darkly. Abiding ambivalence between misogyny and the search for feminine intimacy suggest a basic psychic substratum; so, too, the notions of the soul, the muse, and virtue can be seen as part of a basic androgyny that includes an "idea of woman" and expresses hydroptique desire for a lost feminine presence as part of the self. These blurred outlines often may seem to disappear behind contingencies, but they are never completely obscured. To more fully understand them, one must take into account Donne's prose letters, especially those written to his male friends. Even if we resist the full force of Marotti's argument that Donne's poems are written primarily for male readers, it must be granted that the expectations of that audience constitute one circle in which to examine much in the love poems. That circle can be measured with considerable exactness by his communications with friends in the prose letters. Additional contours of the self are drawn quite clearly there.

The Religion of Friendship, the "Exstasie" of Letters, Ambition Reconsidered

Donne has frequently been hauled before the bar and judged guilty of careerist ambition by modern critics. There have been influential prosecutors, especially R. C. Bald, followed by John Carey and Arthur Marotti; and, admittedly, Donne's scrambling to find an appropriate patronage ladder to climb may strain any advocate on his behalf. Influenced by Bald's biographical portrait, Carey argued categorically that ambition and apostasy ruled Donne's life. Marotti fixed him within coteries of aspirants and players in the patronage systems. But Carey left ambition undefined. He also ignored the prose letters, which provide a basic window into Donne's "mind" through his intimate friendships with coterie members. These letters span a period from the 1590s to his last months in 1631, running parallel to his writing in other genres. In their intimate disclosures, letters to close friends expose the psychological foundations of the vocational self that unifies Donne's religious prose. The search for intimacy in the love poetry follows the same emotional current as a similar search in the familiar letters. Donne's ambition is thus more complex than accusations of careerism allow.

Donne's secret marriage to Ann Donne greatly weakens the charges of careerism against him. As a secretary to Thomas Egerton, lord keeper of the seal, later lord chancellor, Donne had a foot on the patronage ladder. Ambition and covetousness, if served wisely by talent and discretion, could achieve honor and wealth as the professional narratives of many Donne contemporaries give ample evidence.[49] A strategic marriage could be a wise chess move. Carey's attempt to protect his careerist portrait of Donne leads him to suggest that in secretly marrying Ann, Donne made such a move, but unwisely. Bald's assessment is simply that Donne grew overconfident and thought he could get away with it. We are asked to ignore the compelling human reality that Donne fell in love. Even if, like most of us, Donne had mixed motives, it seems more likely that his heart overruled his head. A true careerist would know better than to sneak off with the teenaged daughter of a stormy aristocrat. Here is the heartfelt need of an amorous nature for intimate long-term union with a woman.

A singular fact about Donne's life and works is the way his amorous nature, which is embodied in both his secular and divine love poetry, is contextualized by his varyingly intimate friendships with men. Appropriately, Christopher Brooke, to whom he confessed his "queasie paine / Of being belov'd, and loving," also "gave away the bride at Donne's clandestine marriage in 1602."[50]

And, if we accept Marotti's argument, most of the love poetry was written for a male audience. Donne wrote a virtual steady stream of letters to close male friends, first in verse through the 1590s, a few even later, then a sizable number of prose letters dating from his marriage, into his vocational life as a priest, and lasting for roughly 30 years. His letters to women are limited, except patronage letters to Lucy Bedford, none suggesting intimacy. Inexplicably, few are written to Ann Donne, their deep bond notwithstanding.[51] Intimate male friendships sustained in epistolary exchanges coexisted with his writing love poetry and with the full duration of his relationship to Ann Donne. The friendships that sustained him during the spiritually dark years after the marriage that divorced him from his professional hopes are embodied in these letters. The letters, by anatomizing friendship as a necessary mode of participation in the social body, help us understand Donne's notion of the self. Just as heterosexual love provides androgynous completion of the self and relates the lovers to a spiritual Body, the "second religion," friendship, takes the soul beyond itself to union. And Donne's friends are characterized, through their designated roles, by their active participation in the larger world from which his marriage separated him.

For Donne the letter is thus a mode of intersubjectivity that opens into that larger world. His "A Valediction: of the Booke" provides a useful key that indicates close thematic ties between some of his love poetry and his letters. This poem quite likely arises from his relationship to Ann Donne. In the face of separation, the departing lover will "anger destiny" (2) and "posterity shall know it too" (4). His fictional plan is to compose a book from their letters:

> Study our manuscripts, those Myriades
>> Of letters, which have past twixt thee and mee,
>> Thence write our Annals, and in them will bee
> To all whom love's subliming fire invades,
>>> Rule and example found.
>
> (10–14)

As a shared narrative, these texts not only have value for the lovers, but for other readers. Donne may have in mind his own coterie readers privy to his experience with Ann Donne. In turn, the projected "annals" could be a group of poems, perhaps including "The Canonization" with its "sonnets" built of "pretty roomes," arising from his love of Ann Donne. In any event, a working analogy here tells us much. Connected love poems like skeins of connected letters are shared narratives embodying intersubjectivity; and as texts available to additional readers, they serve an expanded audience. Poets and letter writers both enter a larger community.

Donne's frequent correspondence with a group of male friends absorbed in the outside world provides the context for evaluating his theoretical statements about both friendship and the letter form. Donne's numerous extant letters in poetry and prose express a remarkable sociability as well as a capacity for abiding friendship. Letters were the medium for maintaining the presence of friends even in absence, as separation plagues the letters no less than the love poetry. This textual medium connected him to the greater world where he sought an active place. As I will argue below in relation to the sermons, the same sociable needs were satisfied later by a vocational spirituality also involving a textual medium.

Donne's sociability, friendship, and amorousness express a deep need for mutuality as the shield against separation, loss, and resulting grief. Friendship, like mutual love, is a selective sociability when two souls meet. No less than spiritualized heterosexual love, same-sex friendship exhibits godlikeness through mutuality. Much more than a poetic figure, Donne's "second religion, friendship" (30.74)[52] captures his conviction that spiritual union is possible between close friends. His understanding of that "second religion" and the central role of letters is most explicit when writing to long-term, close friends like Henry Goodyere, George Garrard, and Henry Wotton. Both words and actions, both spoken and written words, are necessary; and the relationships between language and self, between texts and souls, are spelled out.

Donne's opening strategy in his 1598 verse letter to Henry Wotton gives a useful keynote for examining the "religion of friendship" and the role of epistolarity: "Sir, more than kisses, letters mingle Soules; / For, thus friends absent speake" (1–2). Donne builds in three parallels: one between heterosexual and homosocial love, a second between spoken and written words, a third between absence and presence. A prose letter from Donne to Wotton written much later in 1612 while at Amiens with the Drurys explicitly names affection as the engine that drives their longstanding practice of exchanging letters:

> You (I think) and I am much of one sect in the Philosophy of love; which though it be directed upon the minde, doth inhere in the body, and find piety entertainment there: so have Letters for their principall office, to be seals and testimonies of mutuall affection, but the materialls and fuell of them should be a confident and mutuall communicating of those things which we know. (41.104–05)

The claim that both of Donne's 1598 verse letters to Wotton, including "Sir, more than kisses, letters mingle Soules," are part of a sequence [53] is made even more persuasive by Donne's statement here that his various letters "make but one long Letter," just like the "affection continuall and uninterrupted" that "suggests and dictates them" (104). Further, a 1607 letter to Magdalen Herbert claims that his letters "interpret one another."[54] In short, love motivates union in friendship; the mutual narrative embodied in letters sustains it.

Souls mingled by letters between friends recall the mixed souls gone out of their bodies in the "The Exstasie." In a letter to Thomas Lucey in 1607, Donne explains, "I make account that this writing of letters, when it is with any seriousness, is a kind of extasie, and a departure and secession and suspension of the soul, which doth then communicate itself to two bodies: And, as I would every day provide for my souls last convoy, though I know not when I shall die, and perchance I shall never die, so for these extasies in letters, I oftentimes deliver my self over in writing when I know not when those letters shall be sent to you" (6.10).

A characteristic pun on "deliver" opens up further dimensions in the idea. As Donne says to George Garrard (1630–31), "our Letters are our selves and in them absent friends meet" (86.207). To Henry Goodyere he calls letters "conveyances and deliverers of me to you" (36.94). The text of the letter embodies the self then delivered to the friend; the spiritual selves are mixed in an exchange of letters. The epistolary texts present souls to each other.

The pun on "deliver" implies conception and pregnancy while carrying the notion of friendship as religion. In 1612 he writes on reception of two connected letters from George Garrard, "the mother and the daughter," assuming that the last letter delivered to him has been conceived by Garrard in light of the preceding letter (94.222). The letters are conceived by the self and thus embody it. In 1609 Donne treats Goodyere to a variation of the same idea: "Because things be conserved by the same means, which established them, I nurse that friendship by Letters, which you begot so: though you have since strengthened it by more solid aliment and real offices" (24.59). Here friendship is the child fathered by Goodyere; Donne is the mother nursing the child through letters.

The implicit idea of spiritual conception leads Goodyere a step further toward the sustaining religious sphere always perceptible in this notion. Creating friendship is a godly act: "There is some of the honour and some of the degrees of a Creation, to make a friendship of nothing" (22.56–57). The divinity of friendship requires the sacrifice of letters, which requires not only the disposition but, as he writes to Goodyere, the regular practice, "some certain times for the outward service thereof, though it be but formall and testimoniall" (39.100). Donne stresses that the spiritual divinity lies not in friends, but in friendship, in the shared experience. Perhaps Donne has in mind an analogy with the mutuality of persons of the godhead.

Friendship as a creation from nothing exposes the emotional quick in Donne. The competition between creation and annihilation in Donne's thought[55] formalizes the opposition in his nature between being and nonbeing, between life and death, between fullness and emptiness, between union and separation.

His self-representation as "nothing" throughout his works is prominent during the difficult years after marrying Ann when he felt exiled from the world of London. The "nothing" that resonates within Donne's deepest anxieties is never completely silent in his inner self, but his cries are most anguished in those troubled middle years between his marriage and his ordination. The most unsettling moments occur in letters to his closest friends, especially Henry Goodyere. Such letters have been too readily exploited as evidence of his careerist ambition.

Knocked off the patronage ladder, then kept off by wary patrons, Donne describes himself with telling poignancy in an often-quoted lament to Goodyere from Mitcham in 1608. He complains about separation from the dominant social Body, distinguishing his isolation from "primitive Monkes" whose "retirings and enclosures of themselves" were "excusable" because of their self-sufficient lives of "meditation, and manufactures," which respectively fulfill "soul and body" (18.42). The monkish parallel serves two purposes: one, to characterize the religious practices of his Mitcham isolation that serve a powerful "thirst and inhiation after the next life" (43) that is potentially destructive through suicidal excess in Donne; two, to underline the need for bodily action to supplement spiritual life with active involvement in the world: "Therefore I would fain do something; but that I cannot tell what, is no wonder. For to chuse, is to do: but to be no part of any body, is to be nothing. At most, the greatest persons, are but great wens, and excrescences; men of wit and delightful conversation, but as moalls for ornament, except they be so incorporated into the body of the world, that they contribute something to the sustentation of the whole." By marrying Ann Donne, he "stumbled" in his "service" to Egerton; he became a "nothing" without preferment, separated from active participation in the dominant culture (44–45).

That concept of "nothing" is vocational, but it addresses disorders of an excessive nature, rather than careerist "ambition." His retrospective analysis of that disorder is penetrating: "I have often suspected my self to be overtaken . . . with a desire of the next life." That desire asserted itself even earlier when his worldly "hopes" were "fairer," and, he implies, a religious suicide could now tempt him from necessary worldly involvement. Earlier, he had been "diverted" from legal studies by the "worst voluptuousnes, which is an Hydroptique immoderate desire of human learning and languages: beautifull ornaments to great fortunes."[56] But he lacked such fortune; he needed an "occupation"; and therefore he submitted himself in "service" to Egerton. Life in Mitcham now presents a parallel situation; he is "nothing, or so little that I am scarce subject and argument good enough for one of mine own letters" (45). In losing his vocational foothold, he had simultaneously annihilated the London social context that had sustained him, even when earlier "overtaken" by religious desire or "diverted" by studious retreat.

His intense depression further darkens the melancholy and suffering inherent in the separation and isolation clouding his personal narrative. The need for intimacy that caused his exile is met on two fronts, by Ann Donne on one, and by his male friends on the other. The sometimes whining, self-indulgent complaint to Wotton and Goodyere — he is "nothing" and it is unimaginable that persons busy in the world can be interested in someone separated from real events — is expressed only more strategically and less pathetically in a 1610 New Year's verse letter to Lucy Bedford. There, he is merely "One corne of one low anthills dust, and lesse" ("This twilight of two yeares," 28). He is virtually nothing without a vocational role in a world defined by secular patronage. His male friendships can "create him," but not in fullness. His grief, melancholy, and depression are not new; they are longtime companions exaggerated by his separation, which he regarded as isolation, as nothingness. The basic alienation recalls those love poems, perhaps contemporary with these letters, where there is a spiritually bonded inner community. The lovers are available for an inner community of other lovers who are also alienated, separated from the dominant community. In prose letters written during this period, Donne is bonded to his friends, but separated from the social Body. In contrast, his friends participate in that Body, while also sharing a religion of friendship with him. He cannot manage the threat of nothing until he also participates fully in that larger world.

The language of the letters constantly places the "nothing" Donne outside the boundary of the established world, while playing on the means of engagement there. Friendship is characterized in terms of business, the duties of office, and legal contracts, thereby drawing attention to the active world that engages his friends, but excludes him. A 1607 letter to Wotton signed "Your unprofitablest friend" wittily mingles the language of religion and commerce to characterize their friendship. Uncertain where to send his letter, Donne playfully writes anyway, thereby satisfying both duty and conscience, "and so in all Pilgrimages enterprised in devotion, he which dies in the way, enjoys all the benefit and indulgences which the end did afford. Howsoever, all that can encrease my merit; for, as where they immolate men, it is a scanter devotion, to sacrifice one of many slaves or of many children, or an onely child, then to beget and bring up one purposely to sacrifice it, so if I ordain this Letter purposely for destruction, it is the largest expressing of that kinde of piety, and I am easie to beleeve (because I wish it) your hast hither" (45.121–22). The mingled "Pilgrimages enterprised in devotion" play on two kinds of "businesse" that keep Wotton in London and from visiting Mitcham. One is "true businesse" spurred by his "fortune and honour." The other is competing "*Quasi negotia*," minor "visitations, and such, as though they be not full businesses, yet are so near them that serve as for excuses." The letter implicitly chides Wotton for allowing such minor "businesses" at "Courts and the houses of great Princes and officers" to "serve as for excuses" for delaying more important matters, by implication, the visit to Mitcham. Donne's rather self-pitying "Your unprofitablest friend," as the Mitcham resident in exile, admits his envy of Wotton's busy involvement and his own "extream idelenesse" (122–23); but his chiding assumes that friendship itself is a competing "businesse" as he readily states in a letter to Goodyere, also written from Mitcham: "As you are a great part of my businesse, when I come to *London*, so are you when I send" (180.195). Like Donne in London, Wotton was expected to tend the business of friendship in Mitcham.

A crucial point is that the friends with whom he mingles selves determine Donne's conception of friendship. Donne was a gentleman, if we take Louis Montrose's flexible designation to include not just hereditary gentility, but all persons enabled by education and talent to advance their positions.[57] Donne's ties through his mother to the Heywood and More families, together with his Oxford education and ties at the Inns of Court, ensured almost exclusive association with other gentlemen, both hereditary and not. His intense sociability and unprecedented economic mobility in Jacobean England widened his circle of friends to those circulating, doing "businesse," within the patronage systems, both inside and outside the Court.[58] Donne's exile from preferment was anomalous for members of his immediate circle; his desire to reestablish himself through secular preferment is to be expected for a "nothing" excluded from his natural ambience.

Such friends determine his conception of friendship. The vocabularies of business, service, and obligation that distinguish Donne's conception of friendship express his desire to enter the world where his friends participate. He can contact this world, and did so through regular trips to London, even sitting as a member of parliament and developing a network of patronage ties. But he no longer had an established vocational place within it, hence remained separated and indebted to friends through whom he participates in it vicariously. Letter writing is the currency of this "businesse" of friendship. In a 1607 letter Donne wittily calculates the debt of letters owed to Goodyere: "I owed you a Letter in verse before by mine own promise, and now that you think that you have hedged in that debt by a greater by your Letter in verse, I think it now most seasonable and fashionable for me to break" (30.76). A letter to George Garrard while traveling with the Drurys in 1612 calculates this relationship more exact: "It is one ill affection of a desperate debtor, that he dares not come to an account, nor take knowledge how much he owes; this makes me that I dare not tell you how manie letters I have received from you since I came to this Towne; I had three the first by the Cooke, who brought none but yours, nor ever came to me, to let me know what became of the rest" (92.218). In a letter written just two days earlier, while commenting on "the offices of so spirituall a thing as friendship," he underlines the importance of rereading letters, lavishly praises Garrard's letter, and promises to pay his "great debt" with "small summes weekly" by writing regularly (89.212–13).

The vocabulary of friendship as "businesse" blends into the even more pervasive vocabulary of service. Predictably, Donne's letters to patrons like Lucy Bedford script a servant's role for himself, an appropriate protocol for subordinates within hierarchical power relations. Less predictable, but more revealing is his conception of friendship as service with duties, obligations, and offices to perform; it is a habit of obedience to commands. To Goodyere he is varyingly "Your very affectionate servant and lover" (27.71); "Your very true poor friend and servant and lover" (26.66); "Your very affectionate friend and servant" (65.171), and others. These concluding epithets are not mere formulaic courtesies. The spirituality of friendship assumes the mutual delivery of selves, a mutual "service" mingling souls. The exchange of letters and mutual service in practical matters follows. This mutuality does not rule out a greater dependence by the "exiled" Donne in the wake of his marriage. Donne requested favors from his established friends throughout those difficult years, leaning at times too strenuously on his "servant's" dependency. Such service can seem more like self-pitying servility. However, a 1621 letter to Goodyere at Polesworth, playing usefully on the ways mutual friends serve each other, suggests the underlying principle at work even in his earlier dependency.

> Though I be not Dean of *Pauls* yet, my L[ord] of *Warwick* hath gone so low, as to command of me the office of being Master of my game, in our wood about him in *Essex*. I pray be you content to be my officer too, the Steward of my services to all to whom you know them to be due in your walk, and continue your own assurance that I am
> *Your affectionate servant in Chr. Jes.*
> J. Donne
> (81.196–97)

As "Steward," Goodyere serves as the emissary of Donne's will; in turn, Donne as a clerical friend serves Goodyere "In Christ" and through conformity to Christ's humble service upends the hierarchy. To serve is to submit the self to another's will; mutual submission prevents an unequal power relation while satisfying the need for intimacy.

The mutual "service" in friendship can be brought into sharper perspective through contrast to the cultural practices that deny mutuality in the love poetry. The hate-filled speaker of "Oh, let mee not serve so" transforms an embittered sense of injury against a "faithlesse" (13), libidinous lover into rebellion against servile one-way love service. Self-hatred likens his experience to "Idolatrous flatterers" of the great who get nothing substantial in return:

> Such services as I offer as shall pay
> Themselves, I hate dead names: Oh then let mee
> Favorite in Ordinary, or no favorite bee.
>
> (8–10)

Thwarted expectations of mutuality transform the recusant speaker into a rebel against the cultural habit of abusing proper service. So, too, the speaker of "The Will" frames his playfully murderous rebellion against love service by reference to a cultural fabric of imbalances:

> Thou, Love, hast taught mee heretofore
> By making mee serve her who' had twenty more
> That I should give to none, but such, as had too much before.
>
> (7–9)

The speaker plays with suicide as revenge against serving an older woman who recompenses his love only with, at best, "friendship" shared with other "yonger lovers" (44–45). His "will" playfully addresses pandemic imbalances by wittily attacking practices of love service; but his failure to encourage mutual love as a radical shield against imbalance merely leaves him a dissatisfied participant. In poems like "Loves Deitie," "Loves Diet," and "Loves

Exchange," Donne energetically extends his satirical critique of love rituals that mirror violations within a hierarchical society. His conception in the prose letters — that true friendship is mutual service — expresses the same assumptions that widespread cultural habits stifle the bonds of mutuality necessary to satisfy essential emotional needs. Letters to friends busying themselves within that hierarchical world with its complex service relationships assume that mutuality offers a proper fulfillment of service. This assumption honors their business there while admitting his own need to incorporate himself within that world.

A final point to be underlined about Donne's prose letters is that the medium is inextricable from the message. The number of extant prose letters, plus evidence of regular correspondence only minutely represented in the extant collections,[59] suggest that Donne wrote hundreds of letters. Rapid growth of the letter form in his time, in both verse and prose, cannot account for Donne's outpouring of letters for 30 years. Written with crude pens, the numerous letters to a variety of persons, especially intimate friends, would have been a laborious and constant effort. If, in fact, he wrote every Tuesday to Goodyere for 25 years, those letters would have exceeded a thousand. All told, the number written during his lifetime would have been extravagant. The motivation seems obvious in one so ingrained by separation and absence. In a 1618 sermon, not too long after his ordination, he characterizes his sense of the form: "An Epistle is *collocutio scripta*, saies Saint *Ambrose*, Though it be written far off, and sent, yet it is a Conference, and *seperatos copulat*, sayes hee; by this meanes wee overcome distances, we deceive absences, and wee are together even then when wee are asunder" (1.285).

Letters simulate the presence of persons together. Donne catches this complex reality simply: "we are together." The self is delivered to the receiver, translating absence into presence, a surrogate union that salves the pain of separation.[60] The exile's self-pity that, unlike his friends in the thick of London's activity, he was nothing, mounted its own logic: his letters contained nothing since he was nothing; neither could have substantial news. But paradoxically he did send them the presence of the mediated self, as he tells Garrard: "our Letters are our selves and in them absent friends meet" (86.207). In contrast, the devastated speaker in "A Nocturnall upon S. Lucies Day" is "rebegot / Of absence, darknesse, death; things which are not" (17–18). Spiritual annihilation frequently occurred when "absences / Withdrew our soules and made us carcasses" (26–27); without mediated spiritual presence there is "death in absence" (86.211). But the text of the letters to friends presented the self.

"Redintegration" and Service

The ironies emerging from the last stage in Donne's life play against each other. The long-avoided priestly vocation satisfied the basic needs of his complicated nature, but an appropriate secular career might have served just as well. Some readers still find his unrelenting pursuit of secular preferment compromising. Even though his religious vocation opened the path to what may be his finest literary achievements and to a creative satisfaction of his hydroptique nature, accusations of compromising insincerity and last ditch opportunism remain. Unforgiving critics find grist enough for their mill, and Donne will never escape the indictments for insincerity that have dogged accounts of his life. However much this play of ironies may continue to vex Donne readers, the retrospective elements in his later works indicate that much in his troubled nature was resolved in the various dimensions of his religious vocation. His habit of retrospection keeps exposing the basic grounds in his own nature and contributes to the reformulation of basic powers.

His identification with Paul is the key. Paul was his favorite biblical saint: understanding Donne's ventriloquism of Colossians 1:24, a favorite verse, returns us to his hydroptique nature, immured to suffering, annihilated by absence, and struggling for fullness in concert with others. Paul's model invited affliction as the means of incorporation in the community: "Who now rejoyce in my sufferings for you, and fill up that which is behind of the afflictions of Christ in my flesh, for his bodies sake which is the church" (*Sermons* 3:332). The crux is Donne's simultaneous conformity with Paul, in Christ, through suffering on others' behalf. The transformation of Donne's suffering, the source of his life-long pain, becomes the avenue of his joy.[61] To understand the complicated psychology and theology of this Pauline truth is to probe the center of the later Donne, the essence of his mature work, and the gist of his conception of vocation. At the center is conformity with Christ that subsumes the androgyny, dominant psychological imprints, and desire for participation in community that color his thought throughout his previous works.

Donne's habit of retrospection continues to highlight the dominant imprints in his nature, most obviously in the *Holy Sonnets*, but no less significantly elsewhere. Profane love must surrender to spiritual love in the sonnets; later in the sermons we are told that Solomon was imprinted with an amorous nature:

> *Salomon* whose disposition was amorous, and excessive in the love of women, when he turn'd to God, he departed not utterly from his old phrase and language, but having put a new, and a spiritual tincture, and form and habit into all his thoughts, and words, he conveyes all his loving approaches and applications to God, and all Gods gracious answers to his amorous soul, into songs, and Epithalamions, and meditations upon contracts, and marriages between God and his Church, and between God and his soul.
>
> (*Sermons* 1:237)

But Donne is still thinking about himself as well. Self-retrospection explains the cluster of sins — wantonness, ambition, covetousness, and their variants[62] that appear in the sermons. The frequent reappearance of these standard Christian targets as a cluster — often arranged in the same chronological order — owes not just to their personal importance to Donne since they were common targets. But Donne can revisit a personal truth while pointing to their generic significance. In a 1618 churching sermon, he admonishes that a pardoned sin requires continuing good behavior: "When I returne to my repented sinnes againe, I am under the burden of all my former sinnes, and my very repentance, contracts the nature of a sinne." The history of one's sins continues to threaten, especially "all the wantonnesses of your youth, all the Ambitions of your middle years, all the covetous desires of your age" (*Sermons* 5:182). The voice returning to "my repented sinnes" while laboring under "the burden of all my former sinnes" includes himself with others; this is the representative "I" identified by Joan Webber.[63] There is an unmistakable fit between Donne's own life and the generic pattern.

Donne's reiterated consideration of his own dominant imprints, even in his years as a priest, is broadened to an examination of other affections while expressing the same understanding of human nature. Like Solomon, Donne had an amorous nature; his task was to turn lovingly toward the right love object, to change "*amorousnesse* into *devotion*" (*Sermons* 6:203). Donne speaks through Augustine: "But *purga amorem*, saith hee, I doe not forbid thee loving, (it is a noble affection) but purge and purifie thy love" (9:384). Similarly, a person given to choler must change it "into *Zeale*," another must change "*wastfulnesse* into *Almes* to the poore" (6:203). Building the new spiritual habit required retrospection on the old sinful habit: a dominant imprint must be converted.

The threat of relapse, of returning to old habits, required the discipline of retrospection, and then renewed resolve. A "covetous mind" lives in an "insatiable whirlpoole" (*Sermons* 3:236), given to idolatry (4:140) of material riches. An "ambitious" surrender to the "wayes of preferment" (4:51) expresses a perverted desire for "honour" (6:159) that seeks the regard of other persons. Such desires must be converted to "holy amorousnesse . . . covetousnesse . . . ambition . . . voluptuousnesse" (7:390). To love, possess, and enjoy God's attention through proper devotion is to fulfil the needs that dominate one's nature. The groundwork for understanding human nature lies in Donne's own experience and in his recognition that one must contemplate one's own sinful history in order to consider the direction of new habits.

To explain just how the hydroptique Donne satisfied his amorousness, ambition, and covetousness in the priestly vocation is an ultimate goal in this chapter. But, first, the ways that the androgyny in his thought is implicated in this satisfaction must be understood. The central idea is the feminine soul, so dramatically signified in "Batter my heart." There, the soul is betrothed to Satan and needs to be overcome by a divine forcefulness to prepare for the spiritual marriage to God. The sermons provide a striking cognate in the sinful slave woman whose affections must be "circumcised" in preparation for marriage to Christ:

> As by the Law a man might mary a captive woman in the Warres, if he shaved her head, and pared her nails, and changed her clothes: so my Saviour having fought for my soul, fought to blood, to death, to the death of the Crosse for her, having studied my soul so much, as to write all those Epistles which are in the New Testament to my soul, having presented my soule with his own picture, that I can see his face in all his temporall blessings, having shaved her head in abating her pride, and pared her nails in contracting her greedy desires, and changed her clothes not to fashion her self after this world, my soul beeing thus fitted by himself, Christ Jesus hath maried my soul.
>
> (*Sermons* 3:251)[64]

The soul is doubly "captive," both to sinful affections like the entrapped self bethrothed to Satan in "Batter my heart" and also to Christ, the husband. The female soul burnt by the "fires of ambition, or envy, or lust" (3:251) must be disciplined in marriage to the male Christ: "so captivate, subdue, change thy affections" (6:203). The reach of androgyny is no less arresting in the "heart" to be battered, which William Kerrigan tells us stood for both the male and female genitalia in Donne's time.[65] Here, the audience is told to "Circumcise thy heart to him, and all thy *senses* and all thy *affections* . . . change thy *choler* into *Zeale*, change thy *amorousnesse* into *devotion*, change thy *wastfulnesse* into *Almes* to the poore, and then thou hast circumcised[66] thy *affections*, and mayest retaine them" (6:203–04). The captive woman modulates into the male penis, the offending male member in Donne's youthful wantonness, a personal figure for misguided affections, the lasting emblem of the impure self that pursued "prophane mistresses" and now must submit like a loving wife to Christ.

Our understanding of the female in the human soul is incomplete without the idea of conception. Mary's conception of Jesus stands for the presence of Christ generated and conceived in the believer's soul. Each person is Mary; each must conceive Christ in the soul; and each can give birth to Christ by conforming to his truth. Christ is thus both the child and the husband of the soul. Conception leads to fruitfulness, to children, to good thoughts, desires and actions in the world; on the other hand, "woe unto inconsiderate Christians, that think not upon their calling, that conceive not by Christ . . . wo unto them that are with child, and are never delivered; that have sometimes good conceptions, religious dispositions, holy desires to the advancement of Gods truth, but for some collaterall respects dare not utter them, nor bring them to their birth, to any effect. The purpose of his mariage to us, is to have children by us: and this is his abundant and his present fecundity, that working now, by me in you, in one instant he hath children in me, and grand children by me" (*Sermons* 3:252). Each Christian soul, disciplined, circumcised, and pregnant with good conceptions, serves others through conformity to Christ the Bridegroom. Androgyny is an essential aspect of that conformity.

Service to others through conformity to Christ is the essence of Calling. Just as the Head serves the members of the communal Body, so does the believer, through conformity to the head, serve other members of that Body. Conformity to Christ welds the personal to the social through a set of androgynous equivalencies incorporating individuals in mutual service and participation with others. The Bridegroom simultaneously marries the Bride, the individual soul, and the female church. In turn, the individual believer commands the female soul to conceive children, the good actions that serve others in the communal body. Such conformity with the Head leads to a designated mode of service, a specific vocation. For Donne as a priest, vocation was the social side of conformity; the personal side of conformity included the moral, spiritual, and devotional whereby the priest disciplined his own female soul. His prayerful devotions to Christ satisfied his personal needs for intersubjectivity that drove the secular love poetry and his compulsive letter writing. In the traditional notion of conformity, Donne thus experienced a complex and subtle fulfillment of his own emotional nature.

Conformity with Christ likewise solved the problem of separation, annihilation, absence, and exclusion that were Donne's birthright. Although conformity did not dispel suffering and the anxiety of separation, it harnessed them through participation in the community. For this reason Colossians 1:24 is pivotal in Donne's mature thought.[67] The Cross represents suffering as a mode of serving others; in Paul's footsteps, Donne sought joy by turning suffering into service, thereby addressing the problem of absence, alienation, isolation, and nothing, "things which are not." Like Christ and like Paul, Donne became a preacher. An intellectual like Paul, he wrote letters and sermons, following a path of conformity that through the right use of words promised joy in service.

To conform is to take up the cross, to be crucified with Christ, to fulfil Christ's suffering in one's own place. "And when I am come to that conformity with my Saviour, as to *fulfill his suffering in my flesh* (as I am, when I glorifie him in a Christian constancy and cheerfulnesse in my afflictions) then I am crucified with him, carried up to his Crosse" (*Sermons* 2:300). But the Cross is personalized; it is not just any affliction, but those specifically selected by God; nor is the Cross those afflictions that are necessary correction or punishment for past sins, "So that that onely is my crosse, which the hand of God hath laid upon me. Alas, that crosse of present bodily weaknesse, which the former wantonnesses of my youth have brought upon me, is not my crosse; That crosse of poverty which the wastfulesse of youth hath brought upon me, is not my crosse; for these, weaknesse upon wantonnesse, want upon wastfulnesse, are Natures crosses, not Gods, and they would fall naturally though there were . . . no God." Instead, the crosses specifically laid on by God are "tentations or tribulations in my calling" (2:301). The designated cross taken up by the believer is a means of identification: "my calling" to suffer for others. The self achieves identity in the community through suffering. The "nothing" separated from the social Body in Donne's earlier prose letters has become an identified "I" with a God-given place.

It is no accident that Paul's verse encapsulates for Donne the essence of *calling*. Nor is it merely enough to note that Paul was Donne's favorite saint. Donne is categorical: each believer must seek models within a given calling. That principle is clearly set out in a 1627 sermon on Stephen, who as a preacher was also one of Donne's models. Three dicta shape the sermon: 1) every person is "bound to be something, to take some calling upon him"; 2) each "is bound to do seriously and sceduously, and sincerely the duties of that calling"; and 3) "the better to performe those duties, every man shall do well to propose to himself some person, some pattern, some example whom he will follow and imitate in that calling" (*Sermons* 8:175). Stephen is a generic good man laboring in his calling through conformity to Christ, suffering pain while performing his duties as a deacon. Not just a generic pattern to imitate, he was also a more personal model for Donne as a preacher of Christ's truth. But Paul was the most important personal model.

Donne's affinity to Paul was natural. The intellectual Saul was first a persecutor, then Paul the preacher fulfilling the suffering of Christ in his own flesh for the Body's sake. So, too, Jack Donne, who crucified Christ daily through his own sins,[68] became John Donne, a preacher like Paul. The compulsive writer of letters knew the greatness of Paul's letters. Just as those persons "erre not much, that call the whole new-Testament Epistle" so did Paul's epistles contain the "vehemence, the force of the holy-Ghost" (1:285–86) in his letters. Like Stephen, Paul made sermons, but he also readily adapted his literary gifts as situations required, a facility that Donne repeatedly demonstrated. A sermon on Colossians 1:24 expresses his admiration for Paul's literary adaptability and passion: "But when Saint *Paul* being now a prisoner for the preaching of the Gospell, speaks still for the advancement of the Gospell, that he suffers for, and finds out another way of preaching it by letters and epistles, when he opens himselfe to more danger, to open to them more doctrine, then that was very credible which he spake, though in prison; There is in all his epistles *impetus Spiritus sancti,* as *Irenaeus* says, a vehemence of the holy Ghost, but yet *amplius habent quae è vinculis,* says St. *Chrysostome,* Those epistles which Saint *Paul* writ in prison, have more of this vehemency in them" (III, 336). Paul addressed his own profound sense of guilt through service to the community, by submitting to Christ's superior pattern. Conformity with Christ as the linchpin in Donne's mature thought depends on Paul.[69] Suffering in Christ's pattern on behalf of others reforms the dominant imprints in Donne's nature deformed by sin and guilt. Paul's pattern was Christ; Donne's pattern for the preacher, the maker of words, was Paul in Christ. Donne stands in Paul's lengthened shadow when he claims that "It is an unexpressible comfort to have beene Gods instrument, for the conversion of others by the power of Preaching, or by a holy and exemplar life in any calling" (9:318–19).

Donne's discussion of vocation everywhere reflects his own experience as a priest, but the more general principles applying to all believers are set forth in two sermons on Matthew 4:18–19 delivered at the Hague in 1617, just two years after ordination, then revised in 1630 shortly before his death in 1631. In these verses, Christ calls Peter and Andrew to follow him and become "*fishers of men,*" in that name capturing the basic principles "of labour, of service, and of humiliation" in an honest and lawful vocation. Although chosen to be apostles, they remained fishers, their basic talent enhanced spiritually within the vocation: "He does not call them from their calling, but he mends them in it" (*Sermons* 2:304–05). To follow requires humility, not thrusting pride of self, plus hard work in serving Christ and the members of the communal Body. Donne's emphasis on Peter and Andrew as humble fishermen applies broadly to all professions while targeting prideful expectations of a hierarchical honor code. All human functions are insignificant in contrast to divine functions, but they can be elevated spiritually through divine summons: "Christ makes heaven all things to all men, that he might gaine all: To the mirthfull man he presents heaven, as all joy, and to the ambitious man, as all glory; To the Merchant it is a Pearle, and to the husbandman it is a rich field. Christ hath made heaven all things to all men, that he might gaine all, and he puts no man out of his way to come thither. These men he calls Fishers."

Specific qualities are necessary for all: "names that tast of humiliation, and labour, and service, are most properly ours; (fishers we may be) names of dignity, and authority, and command are not so properly ours." His attack on "empty, aery, frothy love of Names and Titles," conscious or not, reflects ironically on his earlier assiduous search for secular preferment (2:305). But the idea of the apostle is ambiguous since a chosen few were called to preach. Some callings do have more honor and dignity than others, and standing behind this discussion is Donne's claim that preaching has a special value. Donne's emphasis on humility to some readers may seem to protest too much. But the point is clear: Christ calls each believer within the limits of that particular ability and temperament to rise to answer the divine call.

Not surprisingly, Donne's conception of vocation is integral in his mature theology of Creation. The threat of nothing, of annihilation, that sends shock waves through his earlier writings expressed his birthright of separation, suffering, loss, and marginalization. Annihilation, in general, and lack of vocational certainty, in particular, expressed that inherited burden. But in his mature thought, the balance leans toward Creation and its optimism, and away from annihilation and pessimism. His burgeoning theology of the Holy Spirit,[70] both as the agent of Creation and of spiritual re-creation, expressed this new optimism. The overshadowing Spirit, who generated the Christ child in Mary's womb and illuminated a believer's heart (*Sermons* 6:174), shall edify the believer: "God shall raise thee peece by peece, into a spirituall building; And after one Story of Creation, and another of Vocation, and another of Sanctification, he shall bring up, to meet thy selfe, in the bosome of thy God, where thou wast at first in an eternall election" (6:175). For Donne, vocation was necessarily connected to his theology of Creation through the Holy Spirit. The vocation of John the Baptist provided a ready example. John, who called others to Christ, was himself called by the Spirit to serve God. John was another figure for the true preacher and a model for Donne himself: "those onely who have a true in*ward Calling* from the Spirit, *shall turn the people from their evill wayes, and from the wickednesse of their inventions.*" This "*vocation* of his *internall Spirit*" (4:156) is necessary to perform his mission. The same Spirit who presided at Creation and now enters the sanctified believer is the divine agent of calling, of vocation. We remember that the believer "conceives" when the Holy Spirit generates within the willing soul. A fullness of conception yields the vocational mission that joins the believer in service to the communal Body. John's example armed Donne against his fears of separation and annhilation: "He that undertake no course, no *vocation*, he is no part, no member, no limbe of the body of this world; no eye, to give light to others; no eare to receive profit by others." Those without vocations may only be "excrementall *nayles*" scratching favors from others, or "excrementall *hayre*" entertaining others with wit or mirth (4:160). This 1622 sermon on John the Baptist touches the same tender nerve as his 1608 letter to Goodyere anguishing that he is a "nothing" without vocational identity, but earlier depression and alienation have given way to the preacher's authority and vocational confidence.

We heard that confidence in the Jobian voice of the 1620 Lincoln's Inn sermon. Here, the "redintegrated" self pours scorn on "excrementall *nayles* . . . and *hayre*," defensively lengthening the distance from its own earlier scratching and entertaining (4:160). Vocational purpose can hold at bay the swelling fear of "things which are not." The preacher's authority and confidence characterize his sense of membership in a social Body. Fear of isolation has been tamed by conformity with Christ, who "loves not singularity" and who offered a model of vocational service to the Body. That vocational model "redintegates" the self and, by defying annihilation and marrying the self to the Body, restores its created nature. Vocation is a marriage that recreates the androgynous self in relation to others.

Common vocational language in Donne's sermons resonates with a special life when we consider the twisting path leading to his priestly vocation. Paul's familiar injunction to "walk in the calling to which you are called" (1 Cor. 7:20) undergirds the sermons, along with the standard Protestant command to "labor" or "work" in a "lawful calling."[71] His listeners are told that "we also must labour in our severall vocations, and not content our selves with our own spirituall sleep" (*Sermons* 2:227). Elsewhere, God's command that Adam and Eve "increase and multiply" (Gen. 1:28) takes an identifiable Reformation coloration in Donne's pastoral claim that vocation requires a presence in the material world: "there is a law, or obligation laid upon us, to endeavour by industry in a lawfull calling, to mend and improve, to enlarge our selves, and spread even in worldly things" (2:291). Likeness to God determines this labor or work in a calling; like the Creator, the human creature must continue to work. "God hath not accomplished his worke upon us, in one Act, though an Election; but he works in our Vocation, and he works in our Justification, and in our Sanctification he works still" (8:368). A minister's labors of words and deeds embody conformity with Christ, advancing Christ's suffering in human words and exemplary actions for the sake of the social Body; the cooperating Holy Spirit aids these labors in vocational responsibilities that recreate the individual. The *Devotions upon Emergent Occasions,* which interprets Donne's own bodily experience on behalf of the social Body and the King, is such a labor. The *Devotions* is a "work" in more than one sense.

Donne's labor as a political counselor should be viewed in this vocational light. The *Devotions,* in speaking to a public audience, enacts Donne's incorporation in the social Body. Dave Gray and Jeanne Shami have shown that the work also offers political counsel to King James and to Prince Charles, the heir apparent.[72] Donne walks this same political tightrope in the sermons, risking criticism of royal actions while supporting the monarchy. Shami shows how Donne's nuanced support and criticism of James's 1621 *Directions for Preachers* assumes his pulpit's watchful political role in relation to the Crown.[73] Specific Donne sermon texts, in addition to their other purposes, offer independent commentary on important political issues of the day. Donne's labor in "the publicly authorized vocation of minister as 'conscience' of the Church"[74] frees him to speak throughout the sermons. Paul

Harland discovers in Donne's 1629 Whitehall sermon a pointed intervention in the parliamentary crisis that basically supports the Crown while independently criticizing Charles's excesses.[75] Donne's claim that a minister is not a prophet with the right to upbraid kings (*Sermons* 3:298) resists a more intrusive admonitory role, at the same time that he saw his responsibility as a working member of the Body to influence contemporary affairs. The emerging picture of Donne as a moderate, forceful, but subtle critic of royal and parliamentary issues suggests a mature vocational sense of duty. Such counsel is labor in his lawful profession; the risks taken by conscience are crosses shouldered in that role.

Donne's more obvious labors as a vocational person in the pulpit were ecclesiastical and theological. We have examined Donne's notion of the natural person, enhanced and completed through vocational actions, in his case as a preacher. Donne in the pulpit, that central cultural space, the "theatre of preaching,"[76] while impersonating models like Paul and Stephen, is such a vocational person through whom other community members participate. Shami portrays Donne as a moderate voice in a contested public sphere, where more strident voices compete for interpretive authority in both ecclesiastical and theological matters. With a clear sense of the "distinction between fundamental and indifferent matters,"[77] Donne maintains a "middle voice" in controversy,[78] speaking rather to defuse polemics and seek unity within the church and elsewhere in the communal body. He envisions a church that "achieves unity through orderly process of doctrinal debate."[79] I think it fair to say that his voice for unity, based upon shared, fundamental Christian values, expresses a centered person or self unified and dilated by his vocational role as an important participant in the community.

Donne's labors included both texts and their pulpit performances, both words and exemplary actions. No less than his performance of the 1629 Whitehall sermon during the parliamentary crisis or *Deaths Duell* delivered in his dying body, the words of his Jobian voice spoken to his Lincoln's Inn audience in 1620 express a sense of vocational responsibility that informs the whole person, body and soul. His confidence that he and his audience will see God with their own eyes assumes the integrity of the full person at the resurrection. That assurance is the strength of self earlier threatened by "things which are not," then later dilated and "redintegrated" through a defined vocational role in the community. The person or self that speaks occupies a vocational place in the same community that includes Job.

FOUR

Jonson

The Truth of Envy

Ben Jonson's famous poem on William Shakespeare begins with
a disclaimer. Jonson will draw no envy on Shakespeare's name
through inflated praise, even though neither man nor muse can
praise Shakespeare's writings too much. And "'Tis true" that "all
men's suffrage" (*UV* 26.5) confirms Shakespeare's high worth. This
truth claim, by further authorizing the disclaimer, pointedly links
truth with envy, two abiding subjects in Jonson's own works.
The "Beloved . . . Author" of Jonson's title, elsewhere called a friend
much "loved . . . on this side of idolatry" (*Disc* 664–65), was
Jonson's most gifted rival in a cultural environment too often
discolored by envious detraction and malice. Within this competitive environment, the self-assertive Johnson defined his own
humanistic role as an arbiter of truth.

Addressed to readers in this environment, the poem stands at
the poetic threshold of the 1623 posthumous First Folio of
Shakespeare's plays. The virtual poet laureate, Jonson may have

written the dedicatory address, and he likely had a hand in arranging the volume. Publication of his own 1616 Folio, in dramatically breaking new ground for professional poets, had established an immediate precedent for Shakespeare's first folio. Appropriately, Jonson was invited to write a commendatory poem; predictably, the self-assertive Jonson addressed his own complex relationship to Shakespeare as a friend, a rival, a dramatist, a poet, and a critic; and, not surprisingly, the poem has fueled continuing debate about this relationship. Though he admired Jonson, John Dryden groused that the poem was "an insolent, sparing, and invidious panegyric."[1] Alexander Pope bluntly disagreed, "I cannot for my own part find any thing *Invidious* or *Sparing* in those verses, but wonder Mr. *Dryden* was of that opinion. He exalts him not only above all his Contemporaries, but above *Chaucer* and *Spenser*, whom he will not allow to be great enough to be rank'd with him; and challenges the names of *Sophocles, Euripides, and AEscylus*, nay all *Greece* and *Rome* at once, to equal him."[2] Later discussion of Jonson's panegyric falls somewhere between these two poles. Much significant commentary addresses the nuanced personal content — however allusive or implicit — as Jonson's medium for defining Shakespeare's poetic achievement. Jonson claims possession of Shakespeare: "My Beloved, the Author Mr William Shakespeare" and "My Shakespeare." For Jonson, poets personally inform their writings; these writings inform readers' lives; readers thus possess the truth of these writings. Jonson's possession celebrates both Shakespeare's achievement and, assertively, Jonson's critical measure of that achievement. As Shakespeare's primary rival, he knows, perhaps enjoys knowing, that his self-assertion invites charges of envy.

Both poets sought recognition in a centralized, hierarchical culture of competitive patronage networks and emergent market forces. Competition for place stimulated envious detraction and threatened truthful judgment. Jonson assumed the poet's traditional humanistic stance as a moral counselor critical of that competitive world and its moral failures. He addressed those failures as an individual participating within the community, subject to its strengths and weaknesses. Unlike his rival, Shakespeare, who removes his own personal experience from texts written for a public audience, Jonson inhabits his works. But, like Milton after him, his commentary on his world is too often charged with the affect of immediate engagement. As we see later in chapter 6, the intemperance of pamphlet warfare stimulated Milton's aggression and self-defensiveness. Similarly, Jonson personally wrestled with habits of envy and detraction that he attacked as cultural dangers. Jonson's humanistic praise of Shakespeare's achievement deliberately confronts those dangers that threaten the common good. The following discussion first addresses Jonson's conception of a centered self contributing to common good, then the vocabulary of truth identifying his humanistic role as a poet, and finally, the cultural habit of envy that detracts from community, destabilizes the self and corrupts poetic responsibility. This chapter assumes that, for Jonson, it is in commitment to truth that the self establishes its stable center and its defense against envy.

The Compass of the Self

Like Donne and Milton, Jonson can be found everywhere in his works. He often speaks personally in the poetry and in the prefaces to the plays with aggressive candor and unmuffled feeling. A natural aggression straitens his humanistic sense of duty as a poetic adviser and critic of culture. For Jonson, individual duties of place are supported by a notion of true self that included the poet, as well as others. The intrusive Jonson we hear in his works is no less a representative "example" of that notion than are various subjects of his praise. Jonson was not given easily to self-criticism, but even his own shortcomings, such as his wrong steps on the patronage tightrope by compromising legitimate praise with flattery, can represent struggles of self in relation to community. As we will see, that notion of true self, inflected with his own experience, reappears frequently in his works.

Thomas M. Greene's seminal essay on the "centered self" in Jonson identifies the circle and its center as unifying images: "In

Jonson, the associations of the circle — as metaphysical, political, and moral ideal, as proportion and equilibrium, as cosmos, realm, society, estate, marriage, harmonious soul — are doubled by the associations of a center — governor, participant, house, inner self, identity, or, when the outer circle is broken, as lonely critic and self-reliant solitary."[3] The centered self is the "Stoic individual soul, self-contained, balanced, at peace with itself even in isolation."[4] The compass is a fellow image: a stable central foot with an outer leg moving to complete the circle, stability serving motion, not stasis. Additional to Greene's discussion, Richard Peterson links this "paradoxical combination of motion with fixity"[5] to Jonson's habits of imitation. Active assimilation of traditional learning and exemplary human behavior assures the self's natural roundness.

Paradoxically, a true self is not only "round," but "straight," and "gathered" as well. The first of two companion epigrams praising Thomas Roe, a Jonson friend, plays with these paradoxical complexities: "He that is round within himself, and straight,/ Need seek no other strength, no other height" (*Epig* 98.3–4). Round and straight, the soul can withstand buffets of Fortune. Both metaphorical notions assume a circular self, its natural roundness ensured by virtuous actions, its center straightened by rectitude.[6] Jonson counsels Roe to "Be always to thy gathered self the same" (9). Such constancy recalls Neo-Stoic self-defense, an inner fortress standing against Fortune's outer threat. Admittedly, self-containment in "isolation" suggested by Greene is more notional than affective in the irascible Jonson himself. But, as Peterson rightly notes, the "gathered" self paradoxically achieves constancy by assimilating previous learning and exemplary actions of others.[7] Stretching outward like a mobile compass leg, the live self continuously gathers and assimilates new truths.

A companion poem, by identifying Roe as an "example," illuminates the assumptions of the first poem and indirectly confirms themes related to the centered self that unify the *Epigrams*. Jonson's deceptively simple title ("To the Same" — *Epig* 99) serves these ends by addressing the stability dependent on exemplary, praiseworthy deeds that sustain praise. Thomas Roe is the same subject; further praise is built into the same 12-line structure. The title directly invokes the moral counsel of the first poem ("Be always to thy gathered self the same / And study conscience more than thou wouldst fame" — 9–10); this counsel serves as a prelude to ultimate counsel in the second ("let truth encourage thee" — 12); and the title also prepares for the ironic "self-same deeds" (8). Regrettably, deference to station and wealth "diversely" skews praise of the "self-same" (8). Otherwise, the virtuous Roe would be a "great example" (5), even though "thy name less than our great ones be" (11). A truthful Jonson assures Roe: unlike other poets, his "praiser's judgement" (10) of "thy fact" does not suffer. The "truth" (12) binds Jonson and Roe. The first poem affirms that Roe "hast begun well" (1). The second affirms that, encouraged by truth, his exemplary deeds, by earning Jonson's subsequent praise, will serve both himself and others.

Poetic praise offers examples of virtue to readers, that, when imitated, help develop moral roundedness in the centered selves of others. A circle's center and rounded circumference are mutually defining, distinct but not separate. So, too, a self gathered and centered through assimilating other examples cannot be isolated from the social circumference on which it depends. When centered, an individual self is straightened by a constant, strengthened disposition to gather, accumulate, judge, and assimilate. The individual self prepared for further assimilation, in turn, serves as an exemplary influence on other persons.

All true selves enact this principle. Jonson's readers included Roe, who will imitate the example of others, for whom Roe is an example. Likewise, Jonson himself will copy the exemplary actions of others and assimilate works of other poets whose role, like his, is to provide appropriate examples for imitation by others. Another turn of the screw is that Jonson's further poetic praise depends on Roe imitating his own example in the future. The literary cast of Roe's exemplary actions expresses a further component in Jonson's humanistic conception of the centered self. The second poem itemizes those actions emerging as words:

> That thou hast kept thy love, increased thy will,
>   Bettered thy trust to letters; that, thy skill;
> Hast taught thyself worthy thy pen to tread,
>   And that to write things worthy to be read
>
> (1–4)

Roe has progressed through constant desire, disciplined will, practice, and now increased literacy to substantial writing. Jonson's praise assumes the primacy of language in building, increasing, and expressing the self through assimilation of truth in "letters." A constant disposition to gather from appropriate literary sources is a condition of the soul's straightness, a conception following from the central role of imitation in Jonson's thought. Claiming that Roe's imitative "trust to letters" makes him an "example" splices two sides of the same truth. Jonson's theory of panegyric assumes that the centered self must imitate the best in literary sources as well as exemplary human actions. This assumption applies no less to poets than to all humans. However, a poet's special gift, though accidental to his essential humanity, incurs the responsibility to identify and praise worthy literary sources and human behavior as the mode of instructing others.

In two companion epigrams written to Henry Goodyere, we find Jonson expanding his conception of a literate, centered self. Knowledge, learning, and books were inextricably linked in Jonson's mind with friendship. The two poems gracefully addressed contradictions in Goodyere's nature through these links. Knighted in 1599, later appointed a Gentleman of the King's Bedchamber, Goodyere was a courtier of easy nature, whose pursuit of courtly pleasures, including hunting, cost dearly. Yet his heartfelt, lasting intimacy with John Donne drew on an intellectual, literary, and spiritual bent evident in Donne's numerous letters to him.[8] Donne's Prince Henry elegy addressed not only the learned Edward Herbert's but also Goodyere's poem on Henry's death.[9] Also, Donne's Good Friday poem was written at Polesworth, Goodyere's Welsh estate (1613). A "few days' sport" of hawking with Goodyere (*Epig* 85. 2) provided an occasion for Jonson's elegant, but critical assessment of Goodyere: "I both learned why wise men hawking follow, / And why that bird was sacred to Apollo" (3–4). Experience had instructed Jonson; his poem would instruct Goodyere that, not just a means of pleasure, a hawk represents the knowledge and learning essential to wisdom. Whereas true knowledge elevates, hawk-like, stooping only "to strike ignorance" (7) of the "fool" (10), Goodyere's pleasures raise questions about his wisdom: "Now, in whose pleasures I have this discerned, / What would his serious actions me have learned?" (11–12). Exemplary actions teach. Jonson's concluding question challenges Goodyere to study his own actions and their effects on others.

These companion poems praise without retracting this challenge. Unlike substantial friends such as Camden, Selden, and Donne, whose studiously serious actions Jonson greatly admired, Goodyere was less substantial, more loved than admired. The epigram's praise turns on a familiar human reality that our choice of friends and books reveals much truth about ourselves:

> When I would know thee, Goodyere, my thought looks
>   Upon thy well-made choice of friends and books;
> Then do I know thee, and behold thy ends
>   In making thy friends books, and thy books friends.
>   (*Epig* 86.1–4)

Like books, exemplary human actions are studied, interpreted and imitated. Goodyere's "well-made choice" (2) after necessary "study" (6) reveals him through his literate choices. In turn, Jonson after "Attending" (6) and studying Goodyere can "voice" (5) his praise of Goodyere.

Such coterie poems as these assume habitual studiousness shared by centered selves with others in a "commonwealth of learning" (*Disc* 936): the study of books was a humanistic bond connecting Jonson to his friends. Jonson's praise includes at least Donne and his intellectual ties to his closest friend, Goodyere. Not a passively received notion, but a learned habit of mind shared with his closest friends and most admired patrons, this "commonwealth of learning" served the political commonwealth. In turn, it should be ruled by a good king, the primary "public servant" (1246–47), whose "best counsellors" are books (1252). After all,

"A prince without letters is a pilot without eyes" (1248). In sum, true friendship included study of true knowledge in the commonwealth of learning, and true friendship required true, centered selves.

Jonson's closest friends and most admired patrons included notable antiquarians, scholars, and writers of his day. Many were distinguished servants of the state. Early on, the great antiquarian William Camden, Jonson's former teacher at Westminster School, had introduced him to Robert Cotton. In Cotton's famous library, generously open to other scholars, researchers and intellectuals, Jonson met the most studious, lettered men of his time. Included were distinguished close friends like Camden, Cotton, John Selden, and others. Jonson's own personal library, though devastated by a 1623 fire, was available to others, while scholarly friendship inspirited other spaces as well. Cotton hosted Jonson at his country estate during the plague in 1602; the scholarly patron, Esmé Stuart, Lord D'Aubigny, hosted Jonson at his Blackfriars mansion for substantial periods beginning in 1604 and again in 1613. Life in the commonwealth of learning assumed habits of friendly, laborious, scholarly study.

For Jonson such a disciplined habit of study enjoyed with true friends expressed a centered self most intimately. His dedicatory epistle, first prefixed to John Selden's influential *Titles of Honor* (1614), shows us in an arresting, literary way how intimate friendship concentrated that habit. A distinguished legal expert, jurist, linguist, and scholar, Selden was a fast friend to Camden, Cotton, and Jonson. He frequented Cotton's library and dedicated two scholarly works to him, the *Analecton Anglobritannicon* (1607) and the much-debated *Historie of Tithes* (1618). Selden shared an Inner Temple chamber with his closest scholarly friend, Edward Hayward, also a friend of Jonson. Jonson's lavish praise of Selden's achievement in *Titles of Honor* widens to embrace Hayward, who "having wrought" with Selden in the "same mines of knowledge" (*Und* 14.75–76), was a reliable witness to his scholarly effort and integrity. Notably, Selden's dedication bypasses influential patrons to honor "my most beloued friend and *Chamberfellow, M. Edward Heyward.*"[10]

Jonson's verse epistle reflects components of Selden's published volume. The poem first asserts the truthfulness of Jonson's
praise (1–28), then addresses Selden ("Stand forth my object," 29)
and lavishly praises the book's embodiment of his admirable
qualities (29–60) and, finally, discusses the laudable dedication to
Hayward (61–80). This structure captures the friendship of all three
men, as does the published volume that includes Jonson's epistle, Selden's dedication to Hayward, and the text of *Titles*.[11] In sharp
contrast to other contemporary volumes, Selden's valuable text
emerged within an exemplary, studious friendship that defined
all three men.

Jonson's opening self-justification, in linking character to poetic
method, prepares for his praise of Selden's methodology:

> I know to whom I write. Here, I am sure,
> Though I am short, I cannot be obscure;
> Less shall I for the art of dressing care,
> Truth and the graces best when naked are.
>
> (1–4)

Simple, undisguised, direct, clear praise befits honest Selden. Just
as Jonson trusted Donne's honest judgment on his poems,[12] Selden
trusted Jonson's by sending him a gift copy to assess:

> Your book, my Selden, I have read, and much
> Was trusted, that you thought my judgment such
> To ask it.
>
> (5–7)

Such trust is the mark of true friendship, whereas the wrong
kind of "friend's affection" (10) is a "Pernicious enemy" to "study"
and honest evaluation, to be guarded against. Jonson's own fail-
ings instruct that "even good judgements" (13–15) are vulnerable. He himself had "praised some names too much; / But 'twas
with purpose to have made them such" (21–22). Jonson's strategic confession has it both ways, admitting honest error while
defending his intention. Now, still honest, he wisely guards
against "being deceived" (23) to ensure a friend's true evaluation

appropriately expressed in language "short" and not "obscure," thus befitting honest Selden.

Jonson's detailed praise considers style and method as expressive of Selden's virtuous character. The familiar compass figure, "one foot still / Upon your centre," introduces Selden's research method of filling his "circle" of general knowledge without traveling elsewhere (31–33). The ambiguous "Ever at home" (30) locates Selden in England, but also points to his moral center essential in "gathering" (38) knowledge to "instruct and teach" (37). A repeated structure of questions ("Which grace shall I make love to first?" — 35) modulates into a series of exclamations which capture Selden's breadth of attention, patient respect for fact, will to verify, refusal to accept distortion, and wise evaluation of legitimate authority. Selden's honest, methodical, and patient search for truth, which progressively fills his circle of general knowledge," is richly illustrated and expressed with "manly elocution" (56). The style is the man.

A final measure of both man and book is Selden's dedication to Hayward, not to a "great name" (69), but to a true friend. Unlike other dedications, which seek favor and profit from ungenerous, ignorant patrons, Selden chose the kindred Hayward, "learnèd chamber-fellow," who can pay "true respects" (72–73) to the book, knowing the effort involved in its making. Such an objective study of social structure will generate "envy" (79); scholarly Hayward's honest voice can defend the book's integrity and methodology against detractors.

Jonson's praise comes to rest on friendship that sustains true learning. His poem makes clear that Hayward, the learned friend, informs Selden's "centre" (32) through mutual, exemplary scholarship. True learning in centered selves earns and deserves true praise. Jonson presses hard against distorted practices in literary panegyric: pursuit of personal gain bends judgment and compromises literary and scholarly duties of objectivity. Jonson speaks for a higher value:

> O how I do count
> Among my comings-in, and see it mount,

The gain of your two friendships! Hayward and
Selden: two names that so much understand;
On whom I could take up, and ne'er abuse
The credit, what would furnish a tenth muse!

(79–84)

The ironic ambiguity of "count," the profitable "comings-in," the borrower's "take up" and unlimited "credit" speak to an accumulating moral "wealth" (85) that cannot be tallied. Jonson personally gains from Selden and Hayward's shared example, while his praise seals his participation in their disinterested search for true knowledge.

For Jonson, selves grow more rounded through a shared search for true knowledge that joins studious readers bound by friendship. Jonson was a man of prodigious memory holding alive a full array of humanist texts while laboriously searching for new knowledge. His compass, like Selden's, ever stretched outward to fill his own circle of general knowledge. For Jonson, then, the commonwealth of learning includes works of dead writers alive in memory and living friends searching in concert for new knowledge. The book, a visible object, is currency in this commonwealth among its participating, studious friendships.

Circulation of this currency, as we see in a verse epistle written in response to a gift book from an anonymous friend (*Und* 37), may require honest diplomacy. The poem breaks sharply in two parts: first, gratefully acknowledging receipt of a gift book (1–15); second, apologizing for perceived harshness (16–33). Reappearance *verbatim* of the last five stanzas in a different verse epistle (*UV* 49) suggests that we have two versions written to the same person. In its thanks for the book (*Und* 37), this version acknowledges his friend's own generous attempt to strengthen friendship. The earlier verse letter locates the perceived harshness in Jonson's criticism of his friend's poetry. Jonson begins by quoting from that friend's own epistle to Jonson: "'Censure not sharply then, but me advise / Before I write more verse, to be more wise'" (*UV* 49.1–2). Friendship requires particular diplomacy in exchanges between poets of differing levels of talent. Arrival of the book would have inspired Jonson to recast his apology and salve his friend's perceived wound, while preserving his earlier thought that friendship traces an uneasy boundary between honest criticism and unnecessary injury. Jonson's later version first addresses the value of their friendship, then the gift book, setting aside the friend's sense of injury until later in the poem:

> Sir, I am thankful, first to heaven for you;
> > Next to yourself, for making your love true;
> > Then to your love and gift. And all's but due.
>
> You have unto my store added a book,
> > On which with profit I shall never look
> > But must confess from whom what gift I took.
>
> > > (*Und* 37.1–6)

The book's "profit" in learning enriches a friendship through literary means despite differing stations:

> But as a friend, which name yourself receive,
> > And which you, being the worthier, gave me leave
> > In letters, that mix spirits, thus to weave.
>
> > > (10–12)

Gift book and letter exchange cement a friendship sustained by the friend's true love (2), a literate union of mixed spirit[13] and the shared name of friend.

Conscientious diplomacy resists the careless injury that inhibits the rounding of self through such friendship. On a different occasion, Jonson's confident invitation that Donne critically assess his poetry may risk injury, but less so in friendship balanced between intellectual, social, and literary equals. Diplomacy requires added sensitivity when different levels of talent or social station are involved. Ambiguity in Jonson's apology in the letter allows for either the injured friend's overreaction or excesses of Jonson's critical nature, or both. That ambiguity does not erode the general truth enunciated almost verbatim[14] in both versions:

> It is an act of tyranny, not love,
> > In practised friendship, wholly to reprove,
> > As flattery with friends' humours still to move.
>
> > > (*Und* 37.25–27)

True friendship must preserve the liberality of honest exchange that risks either tyranny or flattery, although Jonson labors "to be free" (28) from both. His ambiguous diplomacy requests forgiveness "if" (29) he has failed. After all, "no man" is immune to "passion's sway" (31), and Jonson's diplomacy, ever protecting his own credibility, subtly speaks to the poem's other readers as well.

A letter mixing the spirits of literate friends carries a heavier burden if also intended for secondary readers, such as a personal letter assuming a coterie readership. Jonson's verse letter prefixed to Selden's *Titles of Honor* is an even more complex example. It addressed Selden and, *in tandem*, Hayward, but readers of Selden's published book were also intended. Here, again, Jonson celebrates the exemplary mixed spirits of Selden and Hayward, while the title implicitly includes himself in the mix ("Ben Jonson: To His Honord Friend Mr Iohn Selden"). Personal, not intimate, the verse letter aims at a public readership to celebrate exemplary, studious friendship as a true sinew in the commonwealth of learning. Thereby, the poem in capturing mixed spirits, like the text it celebrates, serves the larger political commonwealth.

Selden's dedication to Hayward in 1614 and again in the 1631 second edition do likewise. Here, by considering Jonson's poem in light of Selden's new dedication, we can advance our understanding of selves rounded through others. Selden's 1631 replacement is remarkable for its stubborn refusal to honor a different, more powerful person or an important patron. The 1614 edition of *Titles of Honor* was Selden's first significant achievement before he became increasingly important. By 1621 when he entered Parliament, he was distinguished for "vast knowledge of constitutional law and of the records of the law courts and of parliament."[15] Expanding public involvement included his influential *Historie of Tythes* (1617) and its unsettling effects on habits of ecclesiastical financing. Even more important was his role in the 1626 impeachment proceedings against the Duke of Buckingham. But Hayward was little known outside the Inner Temple, where he no longer shared chambers with Selden by 1631.[16]

Nonetheless, both dedications honor Hayward exclusively. The 1614 version leaves little doubt that few persons are worthy

receivers of true scholarship: "Bookes should most fitly be consecrated to true lovers of Goodnes and all good Learning." Hayward
is a rare human, his "Qualitie" having "speciall worth," as if different in kind from those in "that world of Natures infinitely
varied by basenesse of Spirit." One of a select, virtuous few, he
is "Generous . . . Ingenuous . . . proportion'd to good." Selden's
definition of "book" is no less selective. And Jonson, who viewed
books as a true currency among friends, would no doubt have
endorsed Selden's delimited notion of books: "I would call *Books*
onely those which haue in them either of the two objects of
Mans best part, *Verum or Bonum,* and to an instructing purpose
handled, not whateuer onley speaks in Print and hath its litle worthy ending in its many words. In this of Mine dealing with *Verum*
chiefly, in matter of *Storie* and *Philologie,* I giue you the greatest
interest, that in a thing of so Publique right may be enioyed."[17]
Such a book should be consecrated only to such a man. The 1631
dedication also specifies Hayward's other essential qualities in their
shared learning earlier, stating "That affection, which thus gaue
you, some sixteen yeers past, the first edition of *Titles of Honor*
was justly bred out of the most sweet Community of life and
Freedom of Studies which I then happily enioyd with you. And
your excellent constancie to Virtue and good Arts, besides the
mutual habitude of no intermitting friendship between vs, hath
so strongly since confirmed it, that, although you had not such
a former right to this Second also, yet you only or a Name of such
Worth (in what ranke soeuer) I should have sought for, if any, to
haue placed here."[18] Committed to free inquiry, Hayward and
Selden stand together against the "disualuing" of learning by the
"common enemy Ignorance."[19] A true scholar like Hayward can
understand Selden's content drawn from "rich and most select
Stores and Cabinets of Ciuill Learning."[20]

The 1631 edition honored Jonson's friendship more subtly.
Left intact to speak for itself, Jonson's verse letter continued to
affirm scholarly friendship between Hayward and Selden. In turn,
Selden's subtle allusion to Jonson's poem included him in that
mutual bond while affirming implicitly the natural intercourse
between poetry and other true knowledge. The poem praises

Selden, "Ever at home" (*Und* 14.30)[21] while filling his "circle" of "general knowledge" (32–33) through "unwearied pain / Of gathering" (37–38) in "all countries" (30). Just as a new dedication amply extended praise of Hayward, an elegant development of Jonson's figure honored him in his own poetic medium. The weight is upon mutual love and respect of true friends in the commonwealth of learning: But the truly Generous soule well knowes and freely vses its owne strength, not only in prudently gaining and iudging of what it selfe selects and loues best within the vast Circle of knowledge, but iniustly [i.e., in justly] valuing also what another chuses there. It is said that all Iles and Continents (which are indeed but greater Iles) are so seated, that there is none, but that, from some shore of it, another may be discouered. Some take this as an inuitation of Nature to the peopling of one soile from another. Others note it, as if the publique right of Mutuall Commerce were designed by it. Certainly the seuerd parts of good Arts and Learning, haue that kind of site.[22] Jonson had seized the 1614 occasion to honor the mutual friendship of all three men; Selden followed his lead in the 1631 edition.

Assimilation of Jonson's poetic figure in Selden's new dedication to Hayward subtly ties Jonson to the "mutuall habitude of no intermitting friendship" between the two scholars. Mutual respect for true knowledge includes Greek-like respect for "mutuall use that one Art or discipline had of another."[23] Though distinct and "severd," Selden's studies in "civil" subjects and Hayward's in nature and mathematics enjoy a "habitude" consistent with their friendship; civil states are derived from nature, just as "Geometicall proportion" informs understanding of distributive justice affecting "Dignities and Titles."[24] The presence of Jonson's verse letter admits poetry as a site in the circle of general knowledge. Notably, Hayward's commendatory poem, which along with poems by Selden and others prefaced Jonson's 1616 Folio, praised his "love of truth" and intellectual substance: "Words speak thy matter; matter fills thy words."[25]

The mutual habitude binding Jonson, Selden, and Hayward in friendship assumes individual selves strengthened through reciprocal values and practices serving the commonwealth of learning. Here is shared example, essential imitation personally serving public good. Katharine Maus locates the foundation supporting Jonson's notion of true intellectual friendship, which simultaneously informs private and public virtue, in a Roman moral tradition indebted to Stoic values.[26] Centered in virtue and knowledge, any true self bears a civic responsibility, participating through exemplary actions. A humanist poet participates in this model of self through specific tasks: assimilating learning, identifying praiseworthy human examples, guiding virtuous action, and providing counsel. Poetry serves public good. This humanist model invests a poet with special responsibilities based upon personal virtue and justified only by demonstrable achievement and merit.

Jonson's humanist emphasis upon virtue, intellectual achievement, and social responsibility did not rest easily with arbitrary patronage, the power of wealth, and the incrustations of inherited title. Emergent market forces were no friendlier to a stable, ethical commonwealth of humanistic principle than were hierarchical privilege and the favoritism in patronage. Unsettling strains caused by market forces and a loosened hierarchy[27] did favor the humanistically trained new man, but Jonson's beginnings were dramatically unfortunate. Birth as a bricklayer's stepson placed him far outside the boundaries of social possibility and favor. Even with the happy accident of humanistic education at Westminster School under William Camden, he failed to win a university scholarship. He fell back into hated bricklaying, followed by military service in the Netherlands, then life as an actor and dramatist in the problematic world of commercial theater. His humanistic study under Camden at Westminster School, curtailed by early necessity, resurfaced when, returning from military service, he independently "betook himself to his wonted studies" (*Conv* 198–99). A heartfelt tribute to his teacher and longtime friend, which was included in the 1616 Folio edition, clearly locates the nursery of Jonson's deep humanist root: "Camden, most reverend head, to whom I owe / All that I am in arts, all that I know" (*Epig* 14.1–2). Jonson's stunning rise to literary importance at James I's court while espousing humanist principles speaks to his remarkable talent, will, and ambition. This rise is all the more notable given what David Riggs calls the "powerfully subversive streak" of a "chronic transgressor."[28] But Jonson's generous praise of Camden indicates just how crucial was early planting of his humanistic root in preparation for eventual achievement in the face of contending forces.

Among the forces confronting an ambitious new man was a far-reaching patronage culture. And Jonson's conception of the centered self, which included literate, studious friends, also assumed exemplary patronage relationships. Patronage networks ruled governance and administrative placement, as well as artistic sponsorship. Those at higher levels of the social hierarchy, however opposed by factional rivals, exerted most control over the patronage networks. Ambition in a new man could be served only through judicious personal ties to patrons with appropriate network connections. Jonson viewed personal ties with exemplary patrons, however less intimate than with true friends, as essential constructs in the rounded self.

But, as Robert C. Evans tells us, the immediate world of patronage from which Jonson's poetry emerged was anxious and competitive.[29] Rivals for favor and recognition were perpetually scrutinized and judged by patrons and one another. Only the king at the hierarchy's apex escaped competition. In a highly socialized world, anxious competition for favor while under constant scrutiny was heightened by the personal nature of watchfulness. Every person watched every other person in hopes of benefit. Knowledge that current judgments might affect future benefits heightened suspicion and anxiety. So, too, epideictic rhetorical skills could be a two-edged sword either benefiting or endangering the poet.[30] Poems of blame or praise can create lasting ripples, and the friction of anxiety wears in both cases. Ambition demanded self-promotion, while anxious fear of disapproval required subtlety and care. Threats to the self were endemic. A dramatic instance was Jonson's friend, John Donne, who by his own admission felt annihilated by life without appropriate patronage.[31]

For Jonson, the true self was stabilized by imitating human examples, not just intimate friends, but appropriate persons with power and status essential to a healthy commonwealth. The self's outer compass leg works to incorporate appropriate patrons, strengthening the center by identifying with those patrons worthy of praise. In turn, the poet's humanistic praise complements the importance and influence of exemplary patrons. The trick, of course, lies in establishing beneficial ties with deserving patrons. No less varied than were the benefits received, Jonson's collection of patrons included the king; nobles like William Herbert, Edward Sackville and Thomas Howard; plus high government officials like Thomas Egerton, Robert Percy, and Thomas Weston.[32] Patronage benefits included a 100 pounds annual royal pension, the extended hospitality of Esmé Stuart, an annual twenty pounds from William Herbert for books, timely financial gratuities, commissioned panegyrics, and favorable recommendations to other patrons.

Like Donne, Jonson has been accused of a demeaning surrender to patronage from undeserving patrons, but living outside the patronage system was no real alternative for a talented new man. His incriminating, though doubled-edged admission that his muse had "betrayed me to a worthless lord" (*Epig* 65.2), perhaps Robert Percy, a substantial concession for the aggressively proud Jonson, is only partially cleansed by an underlying honesty ploy. Commentators on the 1616 Folio have noted that persons of power and high station are primary subjects in the *Epigrams,* and exclusively so in *The Forest.* Publication of the Folio was an eye-catching promotion of a professional writer aimed at a general audience while clearly tying Jonson to exemplary persons high in the social pyramid. Admittedly, Jonson's strategy is a figure for his ambition. But, as Richard Helgerson notes, Jonson faced the unsettling competition between "a system of ascribed status and personal patronage belonging to the traditional feudal order" versus "a system of earned status belonging to the newer market economy and to the meritocratic state imagined by Renaissance humanism."[33] For a striving, savvy new man like Jonson, success in that world hinged on patronage.

The key to Jonson's uneasy peace with patronage can found in his dedication to William Herbert introducing the *Epigrams:*

"TO THE GREAT EXAMPLE OF HONOUR AND VIRTUE, THE MOST NOBLE WILLIAM, EARL OF PEMBROKE, L[ORD] CHAMBERLAIN, ETC." (Donaldson, 221). Unlike Thomas Roe, "great" only in virtue, not in "name" (*Epig* 99.11), Pembroke is both noble by birth and honorable by his virtuous actions. Poetic praise identifies great persons who are exemplary members in the body of the commonwealth. Pembroke's "protection of truth, and liberty," while true to his "own goodness" (11–12), presents an example worthy of imitation. In turn, Jonson serves the commonwealth further by enunciating that worth: "My Lord: while you cannot change your merit, I dare not change your title; it was that made it, and not I" (1–2). Herbert's family title had been based on merit, hence was deserved; his own personal merit was truly noble. Jonson's possessive "My Lord," in claiming a personal tie, implies mutual virtue that serves both their necessary roles. By singling out Herbert as an example of *vera nobilitas*, Jonson obeyed a humanist mandate necessary for common good to identify and encourage persons ennobled through virtue. Any true, centered self would endorse Jonson's dedication to such a worthy, noble example.

Michael McCanles sees in *vera nobilitas* the foundation of Jonson's panegyric.[34] In merit, not lineage or wealth, lies true nobility, although inherited place may provide conditions more favorable to virtue. Jonson did not step backward like some humanists to concede that inherited place is a necessary condition for nobility. Instead, he agreed with Juvenal that "'tis virtue alone, is true nobility."[35] Many modern readers find only distasteful ambition in Jonson's alleged readiness to stroke persons of high station; *The Forest* is cited as ready support. Blair Worden finds a harder line taken in Jonson's choice of subjects: "The men most earnestly praised by Jonson are carefully chosen. He favors political failures or half-failures, whose antique virtue the court cannot accommodate: the Earl of Pembroke, Sir Robert Wroth, Sir Robert Sidney, Sir Henry Neville, and the Earl of Arundel (who is Camden's and Cotton's model too)."[36] This harder line may well have softened too much in later troubled years when, felled by a stroke, strung out financially, and shouldered aside in the Caroline court, he was not so restrictive.[37] Nevertheless, a moderated application of *vera nobilitas* sets a basis for working honorably within the patronage networks. McCanles rightly argues that Jonson's letter to Edward Sackville, Earl of Dorset, in its sincere gratitude for a timely, unsolicited financial gift approves that basis. The poem assimilates Seneca's *De Beneficiis*, an interpretation of Roman *amicitia*, a patronage institution of benefits exchanged reciprocally between persons of both equal and unequal status. A practice of personal exchange between friends (*amici*) served the same ends as some impersonal agencies in modern societies. Jonson adapts Seneca's sublimation of exchanged benefits, likewise using commercial language as a paradoxical foil to emphasize a higher, moral intent. Seneca recommends a habit of generosity and good will that confers benefits without expectation of repayment. Such unselfish gifts stimulate gratitude in the recipient, who, in the same spirit, owes a return not expected or calculated by the giver.

Like *De Beneficiis*, Jonson's poem, a grateful return for a generous gift of money, sublimates patronage through reciprocal goodwill and respect. It is a detailed attempt to capture the mutual benefit possible in a patronage relationship beneficial to both persons. Not just Sackville is offered as an example:

> Keep you such,
> That I may love your person (as I do)
> Without your gift, though I can rate that too,
> By thanking thus the courtesy to life,
> Which you will bury; but therein the strife
> May grow so great to be example, when
> (As their true rule or lesson) either men,
> Donors or donees, to their practice shall
> Find you to reckon nothing, me owe all.
>
> (*Und* 13.156–64)

Jonson concludes by counseling Sackville to remain the same: the person not the gift earns the poet's praise. Yet, the tangible gift expressing the person cannot be ignored; the poet must "rate" it

(58), assess its value, take a reckoning (*OED*). The ironic commercial foil established earlier in the poem denotes assessment of worth and prepares for the sublimated "reckon" in the last line. To rate the financial gift that meets Jonson's needs, however necessary that actual gift, is gratefully to praise the humane "courtesy to life" that moves the donor. Earlier, the poet examines his habit of giving appropriate thanks for a "courtesy." Attitude, not size of gift, determines thanks; even "smallest courtesies" (16), "noblest benefits" (19), are gratefully acknowledged unless the donor's good "will" (26) is wanting. True to the Senecan spirit, Sackville expects no return, unlike strategic patrons, "hunters of false fame" (65). He will "bury" out of mind his own generous actions. In grateful return, Jonson's poem read by Sackville and others pays the debt of thanks owed though not expected, for a benefit freely, generously given. Sackville's true fame will stimulate ("strife," 160) imitative actions in others. The giver, Sackville, and the grateful giver of praise, Jonson, become thereby "example" (161) to other "Donors or donees" (163).

A visual pun caps Jonson's discussion of reciprocal, exemplary deeds in patronage that contribute to rounded selves. The satisfying habit of true reciprocity between virtuous persons elevates clientage beyond self-interest through "fortitude" (105) to serve "honesty and public good" (111). Variations of do (did, done, does, doth, deed) unify the poem, beginning in the first line ("If, Sackville, all that have the power to do / Great and good turns," 1–2) and ending in the visual pun on "Do[nors] or do[nees]" (163) who will imitate the exemplary Sackville and Jonson. Benefits must be given and gratitude returned in the same spirit of doing good deeds:

> No! Gifts and thanks should have one cheerful face,
> So each that's *done* and ta'en becomes a brace.
> He neither gives, or *does*, that *doth* delay
> A benefit, or that *doth* throw it away;
> No more than he *doth* thank that will receive
> Naught but in corners, and is loath to leave
> Least air or print, but flies it: such men would
> Run from the conscience of it, if they could.
>
> (39–46; my italics)

Pieces of the latinate "benefit" (*bene* + *factum*) serve Jonson's wordplay on doing mutual good deeds. Patrons must "time" their gifts, knowing "how and where" (2). Clients should accept courtesies only from worthy patrons and true nobles like Sackville. Reciprocal action assumes growth in virtuous deeds: "'Tis by degrees that men arrive at glad/ Profit in aught; each day some little add" (131–32). Incremental growth requires self-knowledge of personal faults ("I have the list of mine own faults to know, / Look to and cure" (114–15) and the intention to address them one-by-one, elevating laboriously by degrees, not overnight. Only the last "keystone" (136) can complete the "triumphal" (139) arch appropriate for the true noble Sackville if he continues ("Keep . . . such," 156) to perform deeds that deserve the poet's "love" (157).

The visual pun on donor and donee, like the stressed variants of "do" feeding into it, stresses active reciprocity but may not ensure equality, an ambiguity that tests all readers, not just Sackville. One example informs another "with the same mind" (5) while fulfilling their interdependent roles. It is debatable whether their personal reciprocity erases class differences in a friendship of equals, as McCanles claims: "In the Epistle to Sackville and other poems concerned with Jonson's financial dependence on aristocratic and royal patronage, the poet transforms the patron-client relation implicit in financial dependence into one between equal friends."[38] If so, it follows that the friendly patronage of true nobles would erase differences existing in explicit friendships with persons like Selden and Camden. A similar erasure might apply to clientage relationships with William Herbert, Lucy Bedford, Robert Sidney, and other high-born nobles. Here, some readers may hesitate. Is that really Jonson's intention? The logic of *vera nobilitas* does allow this deduction, and Jonson's invocation of Roman *amicitia* implicitly brings patrons and clients together as *amici*. The Senecan sublimation of Roman patronage so liberally imbedded in the poem would seem to encourage this erasure of differences between persons "with the same mind." Seneca stands immediately behind Jonson: "Eodem animo beneficium debetur quo datur" ["A benefit is acknowledged in the same spirit in which it is bestowed"].[39] However, the vocabulary of *amicitia* may allow no more latitude than the modern over-statement of professional associates as "friends" or the British parliamentary practice of so addressing allies.[40] Elsewhere, in contrast, Jonson's usage is categorically explicit as in "The grain of your two friendships! Hayward and / Selden!" (*Und* 14.81–82). Still, Jonson's injunction to Sackville seems to gesture in that direction: "Keep you such, / That I may love your person (as I do)" (156–57), though Dorset's noble status puts Jonson on thin ice. On a different occasion discussed earlier, Jonson noted that a social superior had first signaled that he was Jonson's "friend, which name yourself receive, / And which you, being the worthier, gave me leave / In letters, that mix spirits, thus to weave" (*Und* 37.11–12). Perhaps, the ambiguity present in Roman *amici* is skillful diplomacy that leaves the choice to the recently named Earl of Dorset.

Appropriate patronage ties, whether they are friendships or not, are essential fibers in the poetic self, contributing to common good through the alliance of true selves. Jonson was an assiduously social being: lifelong intimate friend to a selected few, father to a tribe of protegees, house guest of patrons, dramatist in commercial theater, maker of Court masques, fellow scholar and poet, dinner party host, tavern conversationalist. He viewed the quality of human ties as a lifetime's labor, although the "list" of "mine own faults" too frequently marred his labor. A true self can arrive at "glad profit" in support of the common good only laboriously "by degrees" in concert with other virtuous human beings. I have suggested that, for Jonson, studious friendship and exemplary patronage strengthened the center as the compass leg moved outward in its various discoveries. But more needs to be said about the stationary leg at the individual center, and for that we need to consider further Jonson's commitment to "truth."

The Vocabulary of Truth

The vocabulary of truth so conspicuous everywhere in Jonson's works is inextricably related to his concept of the rounded and centered self. Two dedications, one already discussed, and an epigram to William Herbert provide us with a useful point of departure. Products of the same short time period, all three texts were included in the 1616 Folio. Jonson deliberately linked the Folio to selected patrons while paradoxically advancing his professional independence to a public readership. The first dedication had appeared in the quarto edition of *Catiline His Conspiracy* just after the play's maligned 1611 performance; it was reprinted in the Folio. The *Epigrams* had been readied for publication as early as 1612; Drummond of Hawthornden claimed to have read it that year. Few if any works had been written after 1612,[41] by which time Jonson was in full sail. His greatest plays had been performed; he was established at Court; his virtual laureate status was building. Thus, the 1616 Folio edition not only promoted Jonson further; it also advanced Herbert as *vera nobilitas* and as a touchstone of truth and virtue essential for the common good. Less explicitly, but no less pointedly, the work advanced Jonson himself as an arbiter of truth, investing the poems with special importance.

The two dedications praising Herbert as a "great example of honor and virtue," along with the epigram's claim that to name him is an "epigram on all mankind" (*Epig* 102.1–2), belabor several standard oppositions. A virtual Manichean reduction stands Herbert beside Jonson on the side of good versus evil, virtue versus vice, knowledge versus ignorance, nobility versus baseness, truth versus opinion and error. Herbert's "noblesse keeps one stature still, / And one true posture" even though "besieged with ill" (*Epig* 102.13–14). His constant goodness will support Jonson's call for "protection of truth and liberty" (Donaldson, 221.12) against expected detraction. A "study" in virtue principled by truth, Herbert has the "iudgement," understanding, knowledge, and goodness to confront the "so thick, and darke an ignorance"[42] and "ill deeds" (Donaldson, 221.7) of the age. A grateful "posterity" (15) can study his exemplary benefit to the commonwealth along with other names included in the "theatre" (29) of the epigrams, where Cato, the touchstone of tough-minded Roman virtue might enter without scandal.

These concise texts honoring William Herbert encapsulate interrelated, broad notions in Jonson's conception of truth. The common currency of these notions in Jonson's time makes them no less significant. Judgment, understanding, and knowledge are actions of the rational soul informing virtuous deeds and necessary for goodness. The social, political, and cultural emphasis here is characteristic but not exclusive in Jonson. God-given principles of truth that inform right reason are available to a rational being through study that incorporates sensory experience, imitation of good example, received knowledge, and Christian belief.

Timber or Discoveries, a borrowing from Justus Lipsius that is indebted to Seneca and Tacitus, suggests broader dimensions of truth while maintaining a social and political emphasis: "Truth is man's proper good, and the only immortal thing was given to our mortality to use. No good Christian or ethnic, if he be honest, can miss it; no statesman, or patriot should. For without truth all the actions of mankind are craft, malice or what you will, rather than wisdom (*Disc* 540–45). Jonson's pervasive vocabulary of truth expresses that "proper good." Other borrowings in the *Discoveries* address the nature of truth, its role in knowing, reason's central control, and truth's corruption through deceit and falsity. But the status of this incomplete work remains uncertain: posthumous publication; unknown editor; debatable intentions guiding choice of parts. Such uncertainty requires that we first assess the appearance of truth in the poetry; and, again, the verse letters to Selden and Sackville serve our understanding.

The poem to Selden is immediately categorical. Like Selden's book, truthful directness rules Jonson's literary mode: "Truth and the graces best when naked are" (*Und* 14.4). Selden's *Titles of Honor* emerged from honest discernment that much deserves the poet's exclamatory praise:

> What fables have you vexed, what truth redeemed,
> Antiquities searched, opinions disesteemed,
> Impostures branded, and authorities urged!
>
> (39–41)

Such scholarly practice requires a clear, methodological eye and a moral way of being that assumes truth as the bond with others. Selden has chosen Jonson and Hayward as first readers able to do the book "true respects" (73). In turn, the letter to Sackville, though more about virtue than intellectual truth, assumes their mutual dependence. Both Sackville's benefits to Jonson and the poet's thanks follow from virtue. The intention of such benefits is not "false fame" (65) or fame at all, although in fact, the poet's verse praise grants true fame, an unexpected but proper return for generosity, however unexpected. Such virtue is an accumulative, daily labor: "this is not true / Alone in money" (133–34). Its achievement in Sackville is based on "fortitude" (105) serving "honesty and public good" (111), which becomes for others a "true rule or lesson" (162). For both Selden and Sackville, right action requires the honesty to discern what is true and what false.

This traditional link between truth and virtue comes as no surprise. But the reiteration of "truth" distinctly marking Jonson's works, notably the 1616 Folio, in whole and in part, is worthy of special attention. Variations on this theme of truth erect structural lines in both the *Epigrams* and *The Forest*, two major components in the Folio. As we have seen, Jonson's dedication in the *Epigrams* to William Herbert invokes his "truth, and liberty" as well as "goodness." His protective benefit wins "the honour" in the *Epigrams* "of leading forth so many good and great names as my verses mention on the better part, to their remembrance with posterity" (Donaldson, 221.13–15). These persons stand together against blameworthy, anonymous subjects unwilling to "remit anything of their riot, their pride, their self-love, and other inherent graces, to consider truth and virtue" (23–25). Willingness to learn from the "study" and the "studiers of humanity" starkly separates these two groups (27). An epigram to William Camden follows hard after an early series scornful of transgressors. Jonson's surpassing personal debt to the learned, but modest Camden includes "All that I am in arts, all that I know" (*Epig* 14.2); the "country" (3) itself has gained by Camden's scholarly achievement. A witty poetic strategy serves Jonson's praise. Only an appeal to

Camden's inherent truthfulness can gain a hearing for that praise: "Pardon free truth, and let thy modesty, / Which conquers all, be once overcome by thee" (11–12). Camden's virtuous respect for truth ties to his scholarly integrity, including factual objectivity ("faith . . . in things," 7), searching scrutiny of cultural remains, and judicious language. Another "name" led forth by the Herbert dedication is studied more literally in the commemorative acrostic on Margaret Ratcliffe, a favorite maid of honor to Queen Elizabeth. Whereas the learned Camden was honored for intellectual truth, the deceased Ratcliffe was defined by "true passion" (*Epig* 40.16) expressed in her overwhelming grief at the deaths of four brothers that hastened her untimely death. The brightness of her intelligent spirit ("wit," 9–16) and deep familial love suggest a divine likeness:

> A ll the gazers on the skies
> R ead not in fair heaven's story
> E xpresser truth or truer glory
> T han they might in her bright eyes.

(5–8)

In her true passion, distinct categories of virtue and truth stressed in the dedicatory letter to Herbert naturally merge. Interactive like heart and mind, these categories are distinct, but not ultimately separate. Principles of virtue are defined by truth; applications of truth are an act of virtue.

The *Epigrams* initially requires that readers as "studiers of humanity" (Donaldson, 221.27) must "understand" (*Epig* 1.2) the natural interplay between truth and virtue. Later poems exercise this requirement. The concluding injunction to Thomas Roe that "truth encourage thee" (*Epig* 99.12) includes a virtuous life guided by "letters" (2) and "conscience" (*Epig* 98.10). Taken together, poems to Roe point to a studious holism attentive to principles of truth. Jonson's praise of the intellectual noble William Herbert steps even further in that direction:

> If men get name for some one virtue, then
> What man art thou, that art so many men,

> All-virtuous Herbert! on whose every part
> Truth might spend all her voice, fame all her art.
>
> > (*Epig* 106.1–4)

The epigram praises an exemplary field of virtues guided by truth and deserving study by others. That field includes Herbert's learning, wit, valor, uprightness, judgment, and piety. The intellective habit of studious, learned attention informs right reason's habitual governance of virtuous, active life. Truth guides both habits in meeting the realities of existence, and both depend upon received learning that feeds true discernment. Jonson's epigram to Sir Henry Savile is not just one scholar's praise of another's important achievement. In Savile's translation of the *Annals*, it seemed that the rational soul of Tacitus, through Savile, "lived to us" (*Epig* 95.4). So enlivened, a man could truthfully face unsettling realities of Britain's own political history:

> We need a man can speak of the intents,
> > The counsels, actions, orders and events
> Of state, and censure them; we need his pen
> > Can write the things, the causes, and the men.
> But most we need his faith (and all have you)
> > That dares nor write things false, nor hide things true.
>
> > (31–36)

Just as the epigrams distinguish good examples from bad, the learned Savile could emulate the true, rational discernment of Tacitus.

Jonson's poem invites Savile to become a Tacitus to English readers by undertaking a truthful history of Britain. Serious readers of the 1616 folio, with its heavily annotated version of *Sejanus*, might also conclude that the souls of Tacitus and other writers inhabited Jonson's vision of public affairs. Notably, the formula for political history that concludes the letter to Savile is borrowed from Cicero's thinking on the necessary linkage between textuality and truth.[43] Jonson clearly assumes that the selective accumulation of texts is a source of truth, just as he assumes that study and "studiers of humanity" inform truth. At the outset, the dedication to William Herbert leaves no doubt that relationships between virtue and truth are central in the *Epigrams*, and a reiterated vocabulary of truth draws readers to that center.

The vocabulary of *The Forest*, which follows immediately after the *Epigrams* in the 1616 folio, fixes an even more precise structural principle, despite the work's far greater formal variety. A major break occurs in the linkage of "And must I sing?" (*For* 10) and "Epode" (*For* 11). The first poem, after questioning which traditional poetic genre is best for the poet, ends by celebrating his independence:

> Nor all the ladies of the Thespian lake
> (Though they were crushed into one form) could make
> A beauty of that merit that should take
>
> My muse up by commission: no, I bring
> My own true fire. Now my thought takes wing,
> And now an epode to deep ears I sing.
>
> (*For* 10.25–30)

This showy promotion of poetic "true fire," self-ironic in its inspired overstatement, yields in the epode to a sober reflection on reason's necessary rule over the passions. Such sharply contesting tones paradoxically underline the thematic linkage between the poet's gift and poetry's rational power of definition, which is immediately addressed in the second poem:

> Not to know vice at all, and keep true state,
>   Is virtue, and not fate;
> Next to that virtue, is to know vice well
>   And her black spite expel.
>
> (*For* 11.1–4)

Regrettably, virtue's "true state," a benign ignorance of vice, is not possible. The alternative is knowledge of vice guided by a "wakeful reason" (13) on guard over the affections. That alternative is itself all too fallible: "But this true course is not embraced by many — / By many? scarce by any" (19–20). But, when all is said and done, the little embraced "true course" does remain plausible, notwithstanding reason's lapses from truth when blinded by rebellious passions. On those occasions reason's deluded "intelligence" (25) falsely swears, and the "cloud of error" (35) grows in the face of "usurping" (31) passions that "invade the mind" (29). In contrast, a major business of the poem is to exonerate "true love" (43) by distinguishing it from the culprit "blind desire" (37). The poet's own right reason makes this distinction, clearing away falsehood and error. By definition, "true love" itself submits to right reason:

> This bears no brands nor darts
>   To murther different hearts,
> But in a calm and god-like unity
>   Preserves community.
>
> (51–54)

The poet places "true love" on an idealized, higher plane consistent with dictates of truth and freed from destructive passion. The poem's final task is to characterize a person moved by such love guided by reason.

Appropriately dignified for a rational discussion of virtue and its constituents, the epode contributes to the ideal of virtue undergirding *The Forest* and its noble subjects. Early portraits of Penshurst (*For* 2), of the coherent family estate, and of Robert Wroth (*For* 3), an appropriate resident for such an idealized rural society, share this ideal. These portraits precede "To the World: A Farewell for a Gentlewoman, Virtuous and Noble" (*For* 4), the death lament of a virtuous woman scornful of a "False world" (1) inimical to such ideal virtue. In stressing virtue's connection to truth, *the* epode prepares for side-by-side verse epistles to two other virtuous women (*For* 12–13), and for the birthday ode to William Sidney, the Penshurst heir (*For* 14). These two epistles, in praising women, who are true nobles like Robert Sidney and Robert Wroth, and persons appropriate for the aristocratic ideal of *The Forest*, further address a woman's place in relation to that ideal. The birthday ode provides advice on continuity in that ideal. However, his praise has a double edge by harshly judging a society unworthy of that ideal.

The two noble women praised in the companion epistles play important, but differing roles. A New Year's verse epistle to Elizabeth, Countess of Rutland (1600), praises a subject whose poetic heritage, natural talent, and friendship with a significant cultural patron, Lucy, Countess of Bedford, assure respect for poetry as a monitor of truth. In an age in which "all virtue now is sold" (*For* 12.1), Jonson's verse is coin with different value. He can see the "truth of times" (21) and, like poets "rapt with rage divine" (63), is worthy to praise such women as Lady Rutland and Lady Bedford. Jonson promises future praise akin to poetry of the "god-like Sidney" (91), Lady Rutland's late father. Such grandiloquent claims may elicit amused gasps from modern readers but, more to the point, they are strategically positioned in *The Forest* to amplify the "true fire" predicted in "And must I sing?" A true noble gifted poetically, she is a proper subject for a poet placing himself genealogically as her father's poetic heir.[44]

Jonson speaks to a much harsher "truth of the times" in the companion epistle praising Katherine, Lady Aubigny. Written in 1612 just before the birth of her first child, the poem targets more than gold's debasement of virtue. Harsh strictures warn of serious dangers:

> 'Tis grown almost a danger to speak true
>   Of any good mind now, there are so few.
> The bad, by number, are so fortified,
>   As, what they've lost to expect, they dare deride.
> So both the praised and praisers suffer: yet,
>   For others' ill, ought none their good forget.
>
> (*For* 13.1–6)

However reviled and threatened, the poet "in love / With every virtue" will remain "at feud / With sin and vice" (7–10). Poetic true fire will cauterize vice while illuminating the virtuous Lady Katherine, a true wife carrying the first child of "great Aubigny" (105), Jonson's long-time patron. Unafraid, the poet wi12ll "draw true lines" (20) in her portrait, a "character" (24) in which she can see herself. Her physical beauty, like her "great title, birth" (49), is taken for granted. Instead, the poetic "mirror" reflects back the "beauties of the mind" (43–44), her true greatness that rejects surfaces for inner worth. This mirror stands in harsh poetic judgment against those who reject "truth's complexion" for superficial "masks," for ephemeral "fashions and attires" (70–71). Distant from "the maze of custom, error, strife" (60), she remains sequestered in virtuous retreat like other exemplary true nobles in *The Forest*. She is "truly that rare wife" (110) bonded in love to her husband, a presence that could induce a conscientious "blush" (111) in her less truly noble counterparts. She is not "fashioned" (115), Jonson puns, for either the Court or strangers' eyes, only for her husband.

Concluding couplets in looking both forward and backward add structural support to *The Forest*:

> Live that one still; and as long years do pass,
>   Madam, be bold to use this truest glass,
> Wherein your form you still the same shall find,
>   Because nor it can change, nor such a mind.
>
>   (121–24)

The "truest glass" recalls the poem's initial promise to "speak true" of a "good mind." That backward glance further reminds us that appropriate bonds between poets and proper subjects are essential in a healthy commonwealth. The poet's "true fire" and *vera nobilitas* join. The poem looks forward in its encouragement that the pregnant Lady Aubigny will revisit her "truest glass" in the future. Her inner beauties reflected there bear continuing responsibility to her husband and his true cultural line. The poem's forward glance looks beyond to future children born by her "blessed womb, made fruitful from above" (95). The conclusion also leads beyond to the penultimate text in *The Forest*, the birthday ode to William Sidney, the son of Robert Sidney, master of Penshurst. There, Jonson flips the coin, looking at its other side. The letter to Lady Aubigny addresses her duty to bear offspring; the birthday ode, likewise assessing actions in time, addresses an offspring's duty to "outstrip your peers" (*For* 14.26) by advancing in virtue: "'Twill be exacted of your name, whose son, / Whose nephew, whose grandchild you are" (41–42). Urgency of time requires that William Sidney now advance in "honour as in name, / If with this truth you be inspired" (51–52). If he does so, then this day, in time, will deserve a memorial backward glance.

The poem places Jonson, wisely standing back, advising William and the Sidney family. That placement recalls the "truest glass" held before Lady Augbigny, another family great in status and in virtue. The "truest glass" claims much, both for its subject and for the poet. Beauties of mind mark true nobility. And only a poet with true fire can discern those beauties and the other distinguishing factors that can sustain the ideal enunciated in *The Forest*. Similarly, the poet stands to help an aristocratic family see itself and to judge its responsibilities. The poet is a necessary interpreter of truth.

Jonson's broadly reaching vocabulary of truth attests to its central role in his thought and, in particular, his conception of self. Jonson's succinct, borrowed claim in *Discoveries* that "Truth is man's proper good"[45] is strongly endorsed by the pervasive truth claims in his writing on poetic inspiration, exemplary members of the commonwealth, virtue, scholarship, letters, and learning in general. That "only immortal thing . . . given to our mortality to use" (*Disc* 540–41) was detected in the "bright eyes" and "true passion" of Margaret Ratcliffe (*Epig* 40.8,16). Jonson put himself "to use" it in judging the "truth of the times"; he saw himself inspired by "true fire" that consecrated his praise of *vera nobilitas*. This succinct borrowing from the *Discoveries* conforms to Jonson's poetic practices and brings us back to a more detailed use of the problematical *Discoveries* in understanding that, for Jonson, the self is centered and straightened by truth. Truth's immortal fixity is the measure of earthly straightness, which is subject to the relative circumstances of life. Conviction of truth helps one resist abrasions of fortune and detractions of vice while strengthening bonds with other virtuous persons.

Several terse statements suggest much. The claim that truth is man's proper good links to the claim that "Knowledge is the action of the soul" (*Disc* 823) and recalls the letter to Selden:

"Truth and the graces best when naked are" (*Und* 14.4). A similar statement in *Discoveries* holds that "Truth lies open to all" (*Disc* 141). But there is a catch: truth is clear only when known and understood, and it is not clear to the ignorant or deceived. Even more important, no person monopolizes truth. Though open to all, truth is known only in part from many sources, never whole: "it is no man's several" (141–42). Terse, apparent simple statements belie the necessary, laborious study in common with the living and the dead. We do well to recall what Jonson's congenial study with true friends suggests about the centered self: only accumulated, shared knowledge through laborious study can reveal truth's clarity.

Learning yields knowing. Jonson could speak in unison with Bacon that "all learning is knowledge acquired"[46] for, Jonson tells us, they are the "true tillage of the mind" and occur together (*Disc* 483). Like Bacon, whose support is respectfully cited in *Discoveries*, Jonson makes the scrutiny of language in its relationship to sensory experience and judgment of right reason essential to knowledge of truth. The human soul is served by sense organs, "the same conduits" by which "she takes in errors" as "she doth truths" (830–31). However potentially deluded or misguided its judgment, reason exercised by study can learn to cut through entangling "cobwebs" (2013) of error that distort knowledge of truth. The crux is language, a sensible medium subject to error, but essential for learning truth. Quoting Bacon that the "study of words is the first distemper of learning" (2110), Jonson fixes on language as both a sensory barrier, if flawed, and a necessary avenue to truth.

A famous dictum about language substantially addresses much in his thought. "Language most shows a man: speak, that I may see thee" (*Disc* 2049). The ambiguous "show" and "see" collapse the heard into the seen. Deliberate blurring plays on spoken language as sensory communication that expresses the quality of a mind. Jonson continues: "It springs out of the most retired and inmost parts of us, and is the image of the parent of it, the mind. No glass renders a man's form or likeness so true as his speech. Nay, it is likened to a man" (2050–53). Language as a "glass," an image developed at length in the verse letter to Lady Aubigny, further complicates the necessity of sensory experience. The verse letter, a sensory medium, is a "glass" reflecting "beauties of the mind," not the body. Metaphorically speaking, the poem, a physical medium, is the mirror that gives back an image of her spiritual, not physical person. The compelling irony is that proof of her "beauties of the mind," which unite her faithfully in one spirit with her noble husband, is her pregnant womb. Sealing the poem's truth is the unborn fetus. Metaphorical truth advanced by the poem requires true perception and an understanding of physical realities. Words that generate learning and knowledge are conveyed by the senses.

The "example" of virtuous behavior imitated by the centered self is conveyed through the senses in a variety of media. Sackville's gratuitous benefit, William Herbert's annual gift of twenty pounds to purchase books, Selden's and Heyward's friendship — all include physical objects submitted to the senses and subject to the judgment and understanding of Jonson's reason. Most virtuous actions include speech and written language. Jonson could "see" Camden in his spoken teachings at Westminster School and in his books; Selden, in his giving Jonson an advance copy of *Titles of Honor;* Donne, in his judgments of Jonson's poems; Cotton and Aubigny, in their expressions of hospitality. All these linguistic actions are like books to be studied. Similarly, performances of Jonson's dramas and masques through speech and gesture present sensory likenesses of individual human form to be interpreted.

Paradoxically, Jonson warns against the senses while defining their nuanced role in knowledge. Surrender to the senses can corrupt virtuous action, but "if we will look with our understanding and not our senses, we may behold virtue and beauty . . . in their brightness" (1443–45). The same reserve about sensory experience emerges in his Platonic-sounding statement that the soul "is perfect without the senses, as having the seeds of all science, and virtue in itself" (823–25). But the nagging ambiguities of Lady Aubigny's "glass" that cling to a sensory grasp are not satisfied alone by a reminder of right reason's watchfulness. We get closest to Jonson's notion of sensory knowledge and its ambiguities through the importance of "picture." When assessing kinship between poetry and oratory, with an ear to Cicero, Jonson claims that "conceits of the mind are pictures of things, and the tongue is the interpreter of those pictures." Sensory images provide the stuff of rational thought. Jonson goes on to say that rudimentary sensory perception embraces the truth of the created world: "The order of God's creatures in themselves is not only admirable, and glorious, but eloquent; then he who could apprehend the consequence of things in their truth, and utter his apprehensions as truly, were the best writer, or speaker" (2149–54). Accordingly, an artist's true "picture" can capture an uncluttered, elemental knowing whereby the senses serve an affective grasp. Jonson's stringent, often shrill, attacks upon Inigo Jones for alleged willingness to divorce masque from language do not deny that sensory grasp. Profundity of a true picture lives in its likeness to created nature, the order of God's creatures immediately grasped through affections. Superiority of poetry to picture is that, as a "speaking picture" (1525), it can through language "speak to the understanding; the other but to the sense" (1529–30). Nonetheless, Jonson admits a natural profundity in sensory experience that informs "conceits" of rational thought. Imitation of nature is the crux in poetry and picture, just as it is in learning and knowing: "Whosoever loves not picture is injurious to truth, and all the wisdom of poetry. Picture is the invention of heaven: the most ancient, and most akin to nature. It is itself a silent work, and always of one and the same habit; yet it doth so enter and penetrate the inmost affection — being done by an excellent artificer — as sometimes it o'ercomes the power of speech and oratory" (*Disc* 1536–42). Both art forms, the so-called "sister arts,"[47] imitate nature; one embodies a likeness that acts primarily on the senses; the other, on the understanding. Both forms "serve nature" in order to better minds through learning and knowledge. Imitative by nature, the human being learns and knows through perceiving and understanding likeness; as the senses perceive, the reason judges and understands according to principles of truth. Picture and poetry, imitative art forms also based on likeness, must also be judged according to the principles of truth. It follows that learning embraces likeness and that knowledge incorporates it. More complex imitative learning is stimulated by "examples" of human behavior and by "letters" shared in the commonwealth of learning. In all these instances, principles of truth stabilize apprehension and knowledge of likeness while concentrating on the self.

The poet's role in the commonwealth of learning occupies Jonson's primary attention in *Discoveries*. Readers learn imitatively from poets, just as poets learn imitatively from other writers. Making a poet requires "nature, exercise, imitation, and study" plus "art" (*Disc* 2515–16). A poet's gift of "natural wit" ["Ingenium"] (*Disc* 2434)[48] becomes practiced art through exercise, study, and imitation. Jonson advises a poet to learn by copying "one excellent man above the rest" (2492–93); this exercise in likeness along with wide reading in "the best and choicest" authors (2531–32) yields knowledge. Learning through "exactness of study and multiplicity of reading . . . maketh a full man" (2507–08); learned fullness through assimilation develops poetic art. The same basic patterns are followed by all human souls who assimilate human examples and the best in letters.

Learning through imitation trains knowledge, the action of the soul. In short, likeness is the way of knowing and of being. The abiding problem is that "likeness is always this side of truth" (*Disc* 896). Essential "letters" inadvertently chafe at the problem, since literary texts necessary to study are feigned imaginatively by poets.[49] The "true artificer" (784–85) will "feign" (1526) a "likeness of truth" (786) by copying nature and life. A copy can be only a likeness, however true, but right reason through study, labor, and accumulating knowledge can learn to distinguish true likeness from false. Reason's arbitration in making these distinctions centers the self.

The abiding threat to imitation, and thus to truth, is calculated false likeness. Unlike poets and painters who truthfully "invent, feign and devise many things" (*Disc* 1526–27), others feign to serve dubious ends. Pretenders to learning "feign" knowing whole books (744) while "great and popular men feign themselves to be servants to others to make those slaves to them" (1123–25). Also, opinion in the guise of truth can manipulate persuasively the tools of rhetoric and logic to false ends.[50] Other false likeness is even more destructive. Jonson emphasizes with Bacon that one "distemper of learning" is deceit, or the misleading "likeness of truth; imposture held up by credulity" (2110–12). Lying is a cousin to deceit, a false likeness threatening to others. Jonson's satire targets flattery, the lurking dark side of praise, along with lying and deceit as false likeness destructive to both the individual and the society.

The greatest threat to an individual self resides in its own imitative nature. The mandate to seek worthy examples outside the self drives the self, but Jonson admits the dangers lying in wait for a naturally imitative creature: "I have considered our whole life is like a play: wherein every man forgetful of himself, is in travail with expression of another. Nay, we so insist in imitating others, as we cannot, when it is necessary, return to ourselves; like children that imitate the vices of stammerers so long, till at last they become such, and make the habit to another nature, as it is never forgotten" (*Disc* 1105–11). The implicit injunction to remember the self lays claim to a created identity at the center. The imitation necessary to develop the rounded self can be a troublesome and dangerous gift.

So far in examining the importance of truth in Jonson's thought we have concentrated on the lyric at the expense of drama. But his sense of human life as imitation in a play necessarily leads to drama as well. A former actor, he was an inventor of dramatic characters and narratives of mask and disguise, even as he was a lyric poet filled with the words of others. His theatrical experience fueled a fear of centrifugal disintegration. Jonson played out his fear of losing stable identity in characters like Face, Mosca, and Volpone, who effortlessly changed from one mask or disguise to another, igniting their natural wit through pleasure in variety. In defense, right reason judges the truth and virtue of examples, welcoming new dimensions to the self only while preserving and asserting the stable center.

The ability to judge the "truth of the times" (*For* 12.21) and to decry false likeness hinges on knowledge essential to the virtuous self through interaction with others. The well-being of both the individual and the group is at stake; "they are ever good men that must make good the times; if the men be naught, the times will be such" (*Disc* 249–51). Without virtuous citizens centered in truth and as examples serving public good, the commonwealth becomes unsafe; and in a society gone wrong, false likeness corrupts truth and serves criminally unjust power. The tragic world of *Sejanus* represents Jonson's worst fears of political tyranny. Poisonous deceit, lying, dissimulation, flattery, and disguise pervade both private and public behavior. Powerless, good men are ignored, destroyed or inadvertently conscripted to serve corruption. Other dramas play on such fears less forcefully, but no less significantly. In the witty comic world of *Epicoene*, all participants are selfishly complicit in false likeness. These two plays express Jonson's fears about dangers threatening public truth in his own times.

For Jonson, each person faces a world of contending likenesses, and each must be a judge of what is true and what is false. Individual and community well being depends upon judgments based in virtue and truth. The poet, an arbiter of truth serving the public good, aids the individual person's labor of judgment. Jonson's vocabulary of truth persistently urges his reader to imitate his judgments on the "times." With special force his dramas portray a contest of likeness that fills political and social worlds facing his audience. *Sejanus* and *Epicoene* provide, respectively, tragic and comic examples.

Fear of tyranny drives *Sejanus*. Elizabeth's demise and James's accession created an uncertain political watershed vulnerable to political disruption, corruption, and abusive power. Roman history serves Jonson's warning about the consequences of losing order and public virtue. He writes as a historian heavily indebted to Tacitus, as well as Dio Cassius and Suetonius; and his richly annotated folio edition of *Sejanus* clearly documents its Roman sources. Jonson embraced the Ciceronian commonplace that history is the "light of truth,"[51] and in the 1605 preface, "To the Readers,"[52] his justification of the play as a tragedy claimed its "truth of argument," or presentation of content was historically true. His warning about political tyranny incorporates citations from Roman history copiously documented in the marginalia. He writes as a poet informed by history, the "light of truth."[53]

The actions of the Roman emperor, Tiberius, violate the simple foundation of Jonson's discourse on the duties of princes in *Discoveries*. "A good king is a public servant" (1247–48). Tiberius does not only subvert an essential principle that power guided by virtue advances the common good. He joins those evil princes who "neglect their proper office" (1238) when he empowers an ambitious subordinate like Sejanus, first acting in the prince's stead, then competing subversively. They share like motivations, tactics, and a claim on absolute power based on deceit, duplicity, flattery, secrecy, espionage, and ruthless killing.

A foil opposing their corrupt power includes the surviving family of the late Germanicus, its sympathizers, and other virtuous citizens. This stark opposition is expressed structurally in groupings of virtuous observers, silenced and powerless, standing aside watchfully in fearful judgment on corrupt power. Their observations ironically counterpoint the pernicious espionage feared everywhere, just as their necessarily private commentary contrasts ironically to the deliberations of the emasculated Senate. The play's initial scene establishes the counterpoint. Two former associates of Germanicus, later destroyed, meet by chance and commiserate that the Court has become a dangerous place. One is Sabinus, a knight and friend of the deceased Germanicus. The other is Silius, a former general, now consul, who tersely seals their categorical agreement: "'Tis true: indeed, this place is not our sphere" (1.3). Their exchange, observed at a distance by two dangerous "clients" (23) of Sejanus, catalogues widespread corruption of truth and virtue. Sabinus agrees ironically that they lack the "fine arts" (5) to serve corrupt ambition:

> We have no shift of faces, no cleft tongues,
> No soft and glutinous bodies, that can stick,
> Like snails, on painted walls; or, on our breasts,
> Creep up, to fall from that proud height to which
> We did by slavery, not by service, climb.
>
> (7–11)

Sabinus summarizes the counterpointed arts practiced by nearby "clients" of Sejanus: "These can lie, / Flatter, and swear, forswear, deprave, inform, / Smile, and betray; make guilty men" (27–29). Their criminal deceit serves corruption and abuse of power destructive to others.

Silius and Sabinus are joined by two other truthful citizens, two stand-ins for Jonson's own experience. The historian, Cordus, represents *lux veritatis* posing a threat to corrupt power, while the expostulating Senator, Arruntius, laments in frustration the corrupting loss of public virtue and liberty once embodied by the exemplary Cato. He endorses an earlier claim by Cordus: "'Tis true, that Cordus says, / 'Brave Cassius was the last of all that race'" (103–04). Both agree that the late Germanicus had represented potential for common good. Now, fear that Cordus's "light of truth" would illuminate current actions, though he had specifically addressed a more distant time, leads eventually to a trumped-up indictment against him. His praise of Cassius and Brutus is interpreted as a coded attack on Tiberius (3.379–406). His books burned, injustice drives him to suicide. The stifling of Cordus is tied strategically to Sejanus's ploy to let Arruntius speak freely, ironically becoming an unwitting screen for further corrupt action:

> By any means, preserve him. His frank tongue
> Being lent the reins, will take away all thought
> Of malice in your course against the rest.
> We must keep him to stalk with.
>
> (3.498–501)

Censorship and captive free speech are deceitfully conjoined to suppress truth.

Dissimulation between the plotters themselves accents the poisonous reach of their deceit. Sejanus plots to overtake Tiberius's power by encouraging his removal to Capreae and by marrying Livia, the widow of Tiberius's murdered son. Overstated flattery prepares his request for Livia's hand: "I not sooner would commit my hopes / Or wishes to the gods than to your ears" (3.506–07). This request having alerted the emperor's fear of Sejanus's dangerous ambition, Tiberius answers with a series of disingenuous reasons why the marriage would create political risks. The exchange leads each man to plot duplicitously against the other, while pretending mutual support and benefit. Privately, Sejanus vows to consolidate his power and advance his boundless ambition. For his part, Tiberius commissions Macro to spy on Sejanus during his own retreat to Capreae, encouraging these "two poisons" (3.654) to believe that he trusts them both. Like Sejanus, Macro is unconstrained by either the "trodden paths that truth and right respect" or that "narrow thing" virtue (3.737–39). The absentee Tiberius, endangered by Sejanus's competing power, plots through Macro an elaborate entrapment in the Senate. One poison works to drive out the other.

Prior to the climactic senate arrest, Tiberius deceitfully unsettles attempts to interpret his intentions. An observer's uncertainty is generic in a world of false likeness, while fear of dangerous, corrupt power acutely sharpens that uncertainty. Whereas fear of Sejanus openly consolidating his power in Rome is immediate, fear of the unseen Tiberius, his relationship to Sejanus increasingly uncertain, is less tangible though no less dangerous. From a distance he sends messengers with contradictory signals, verbal and written. Many senators at the staged arrest of Sejanus had expected that Tiberius's public reading of the letter would honor Sejanus with further power. Others had confused expectations, and only deceitful Macro and his henchmen have certain knowledge that a trap will be sprung. Mixed uncertainties before the Senate event are expressed most compellingly in opposing interpretations by two virtuous citizens, the perpetually observant Arruntius and the stoical consul, Lepidus, who counters Arruntius's alarmism and overstatement. Together, they eavesdrop to overhear how others are interpreting the mixed signals and false likenesses, emitted broadly from the emperor. Arruntius judges that Tiberius is either unaware of Sejanus's intentions or obtuse about his capacities. Lepidus rightly judges that the artful Tiberius follows a "doubling line" (4.465) while biding his time:

> I'll ne'er believe but Caeser hath some scent
> Of bold Sejanus' footing. These cross-points

Of varying letters and opposing consuls,
Mingling his honours and his punishments,
Feigning now ill, now well, raising Sejanus
And then depressing him, as now of late
In all reports we have it, cannot be
Empty of practice. 'Tis Tiberius' art.

(446–53)

Arruntius counters that a "politic tyrant" capable of disguising his intentions would be direct, not roundabout; instead, "feigned honest," he would return straightaway to "cut his throat, by law" (474–77). Lepidus proves to be right, but he might not have been. Contradictory interpretations underline the vexing indeterminacy that burdens the judgments of right reason in a morally and politically compromised Roman society of false likenesses.

Jonson's Rome differs from less urgent dramatic settings only by exaggerated degree. Stark differences between a dangerous, criminal world in *Sejanus* and a witty, sophisticated English gentleman's world in *Epicoene* do not obscure their common ground. In both cases, the arbiter, right reason, is strained by false likeness. Causes include self-serving plots, secrecy, deceit, lies, plotting, disguise, entrapment, targeting, espionage, dissimulation, and duplicity. Like Tiberius plotting with Macro against Sejanus, Dauphine plots with Epicoene to target Morose. Both plays climax in a secret trap sprung to catch victim, and onlookers, by surprise. Both work variations on the theme of cosmetics, an art that can obscure nature and mask truth. The Roman physician, Eudemus, advises Lydia about appropriate cosmetic mixtures; Clerimont and Truewit debate wittily on the propriety of cosmetics. Both plays thus represent reason's labor in interpreting the mixed signals created through false likenesses.

Like tragedy, comedy establishes standards of truth for interpretation. In *Sejanus* the historian's "light of truth" is manifested in historical accuracy, the "truth of argument." Similarly, *Epicoene* incorporates the Ciceronian definition expressed earlier in *Every Man Out of his Humour*, that comedy is "*imitatio vitae, speculum consuetudinis, imago veritatis.*"[54] Two poems ("Prologue" and "Another")[55] prefacing the folio edition of *Epicoene* define boundaries within that comic truth. The first invokes the authority of traditional "Truth" (1) to justify the play's appeal to a broad "popular" (6) audience. Jonson exploits a commonplace that the play is an edible feast, concluding that its substantial variety will feed later discussion even after its performance, if the poet's "muse be true" (28). The poem thus circles back on its traditional claim to "content the people" (2). The second poem ("Occasioned by some person's important exception") denies that the play targets actual persons. Again, comic tradition is invoked. A play should "profit and delight" (2); real "persons" are "not touched"; instead, their generic "crimes" are taxed (4). *Epicoene* presents not literal "truths," but "things like truths well feigned" (10). Just as *Epigrams* do not name actual persons, but characterize generic foolishness, the play gives "well-feigned" imitations of foolish behavior. Otherwise, Jonson would have made "a libel," not a "play" (14). Both poems invoke Jonson's vocabulary of truth to make claims about his intentions in the play.

Epicoene addresses infringed and blurred categories. At the center is a boy disguised as a nubile young woman, a hired pawn in a secret counterplot. Epicoene's feigned identity is known only to Dauphine, a gentleman plotting to claim a first installment in his inheritance from a misanthropic uncle. The reclusive uncle, Morose, a one time courtier, pointedly plots to produce an heir and thereby disinherit his nephew. In short: Epicoene is no woman; Morose is an unnatural uncle. Other categories suffer infringement. Knights only in name, the well-named Jack Daw and Amorous La Foole lack both honor and courage. And more, the would-be intellect and poet, Daw, egregiously abuses language and glibly dismisses great humanist writers as models. As for the indiscriminate La Foole, his compulsive sociability, lack of embarrassment and clownish wastefulness ensure universal scorn, not respect for a knight. Women fare no better. The epicene Collegiates, a klatch of aggressive bluestockings, more masculine than feminine in their behavior, are would-be courtiers. Their group name signals competition with communities of male scholars. Their epicene aggression, including sexual predation, parallels Mrs. Otter's purchase and subordination of Captain Otter. He submits to domestic tyranny of his "Princess" according to a marriage contract that ensures his financial support. This gender reversal, however, does not impede the irrepressible, amphibious Otter from reemerging as a disguised legal expert along with the barber, Cutbeard, in Truewit's unsolicited, parallel plot against Morose.

Such blurred categories exercise reason's judgment, both intellectually and judicially. Edward Partridge observes that the three gentlemen not only plot, but also judge: "The fine gentlemen are not just playing with the fools, though they are certainly playing. They are also judging. Truewit thinks that his plot against Daw and La Foole is a legal process in which a charge is drawn up against these presumptuous fools and delivered by a sheriff (himself), and which involves a trial with judges (Dauphine, Clerimont, and himself) who shall render a verdict and mete out the proper punishment. . . . But while they are judging the fools, we are judging the judges's"[56] Just as Daw and La Foole are "caricatures of true knights," the "authentic gentlemen are not always gentle, however genuinely manly they are."[57] There are no innocent victims here; all sufferers get what they have coming. But entrapment, imprisonment, and engineered violence against Daw and La Foole raise ethical questions. Even more so, the unwelcome trespass and occupation of Morose's house, followed by stage-managed ridicule, cannot be whitewashed despite his reprehensible behavior. Ironically, our judgment becomes more, not less complex, through our enjoyment of the ingenious plotting and refusal to be too sober-sided.

The more subtle the ironies, the more indeterminate are the judgments. The judicial theme is pursued assiduously in the mock divorce hearing by fake legal experts, one in civil,one in canon law, schooled by the learned Truewit to bewilder Morose with Latin terminology ("only remember your terms" — 5.3.14–15). Subcategories and conditions prolong presentation of canon law "cases" allowing divorce. Jonson plays implicitly on the difficulty of rendering judgment in "true" legal situations while pointing to the bewildering permutations in marital situations that require reason's arbitration. Necessary judgment includes reasoning itself, legal categories and, most importantly, the standards of truth. An audience's task is to judge the relevance of these issues in Truewit's showily brilliant strategy of ridicule and punishment that is preempted by Dauphine's secret plot. We expect the sprung trap in *Sejanus*; in *Epicoene* the audience is caught along with the ignorant Truewit. Dauphine secretly plots not to dumfound, only to prevent interference. In contrast, the poet springs a deliberate trap to catch both Truewit and the audience. We are challenged to judge why.

Ambiguity in Truewit's name is at the center of the challenge. We must judge in what sense his "wit" is "true." One ready answer is that a "true" wit has no debility. Partridge helpfully reminds us that contemporay "wit" was "more of ingenious inventiveness than of sophisticated repartee."[58] In *Discoveries* Jonson's notes on the poet's "goodness of natural wit" are further suggestive, as is the marginal *Ingenium* broadly glossed by Donaldson as "talent." Jonson tells us that "the poet must be able by nature and instinct to pour out the treasure of his mind." This observation stretches further to the "divine instinct" of "poetical rapture" (*Disc* 2435–43). Dimensions of Truewit's expansive "wit" include linguistic readiness, cleverness, quick reason, inventive stage-managing, ingenious plotting, penetating understanding of others, and associative leaps. Like Face, Mosca, and Volpone, he resembles the poet. His first meeting with Morose is a stunning linguistic performance that, like Volpone's ironically rapturous address to the sun or *carpe diem* lyric to Celia, demonstrates a poetic gift. Like Mosca and Face, his inventive plotting and stage-managing suggest a dramatic gift, but like them his plots fall short. This failure invites an ironic judgment on the "truth" of his wit.

Introductory poems to *Epicoene*, alerting the audience that what is "true" is at stake in the play, are consistent with his poetry elsewhere. As we have seen, Jonson's vocabulary of truth cites actions that promote the common good. There is true nobility in William Herbert, "free truth" that guides Camden (*Epig* 14.11), and naked "Truth" perceived by honest, virtuous persons like Selden (*Und* 14.4). In contrast, Truewit's dazzling performance is self-indulgent; his glib cruelties, uninvited intrusions, and ultimate

ineffectiveness are troubling. From the outset the play suggests
that he has put a higher set of values out of gear. He appears at
Clerimont's house in the first scene and ironically censures his
friend: "here's the man can melt away his time, and never feels
it!" (1.1.22–23). Clerimont is enjoined to "esteem" time "at the
true rate" (29), then glibly invited to take part in trivialities
"wherein fashionable men exercise themselves" (37). Clerimont
ironically responds to the undercurrent of seriousness in Truewit,
"Foh! Thou hast read Plurarch's *Morals* now, or some such tedious
fellow, and it shows so vilely with thee, 'fore God, 'twill spoil thy
wit utterly. Talk me of pins, and feathers, and ladies, and rushes,
and such things; and leave this stoicity alone till thou mak'st
sermons" (56–60).

Truewit quickly backtracks in the face of this polarity. Plutarch
and "stoicity" might not suit a young gentleman's choice, but
Jonson himself would not dismiss them so lightly. Even if we judge
Truewit's censure of melted time as only a young man's playful
irony, more serious values are invoked by the play itself. Plutarch
emerges later with Seneca in a "sackful" of traditonal "names"
(2.3.65) in mocking, judgmental exchanges between the gentlemen, Clerimont and Dauphine, and the foolish Daw, who dismisses
traditional learning except in promiscuous name-dropping. The
play thereby points to the humanist birthright of educated gentlemen, while they, ironically, act as a leisure class committed
only to their own pleasures and class interests, not to the common good. Daw is not the only satirical target of the sackful of
names.

Truewit's ambiguous name identifies him, along with his gracefully ingenious, gentleman friends, as another target. He is and
he is not a "true" wit. One measure of his ingenious invention
is our pleasure in his brilliant performance. But class interest and
self-display, not "truth," guide his actions. Morose denies Dauphine
500 pounds *per annum* that would sustain his life in a leisure class;
Truewit seizes this occasion to parade his wit while advancing
his friend's selfish interests. Jonson pulls the rug out from under
him, and us, at the end of the play, advancing a conclusion that

Truewit has misdirected his admirable talent and suggesting strongly that his efforts may be irrelevant. A true wit, like a true noble, would deliberately contribute to public good.

Judgment against Truewit is incomplete without asking why Jonson subtly entraps his audience. We can find an answer in the analogous relationship between the individual self and the poet as arbiters of truth. The play introduces a recognizable world in which characters infringe on set categories by pretending to be what they are not. The audience is invited to share the true judgments of Clerimont, Dauphine, and Truewit on their fellow citizens. One difficulty lies in judging these judges, and Jonson's surprise ending shakes the audience's confidence in its own judgment. Jonson's introductory poems remind us that comic truth instructs and delights us. Truewit clearly delights us, but the sprung trap questions our confidence in just how we have been instructed. For this, we need the poet's help as an arbiter. A primary segment in Jonson's audience would have been educated gentlemen, proud of their learning and their intelligence, but careless of their responsibilities to the common good. Jonson's ironies do not end abruptly there since Truewit, Dauphine, and Clerimont do the right things, but for the wrong reasons and in the wrong spirit. They judge and punish fools to please themselves, not to serve common good. Having enjoyed the best of humanist education, they know better, especially Truewit, who we learn in the first scene is acting against his higher impulses. The ultimate irony — and Jonson's play leads us to this judgment ourselves — is that they may serve the common good, in spite of themselves. The poet as the arbiter of truth, while delighting us has instructed us how to make that ambiguous judgment, not by creating likenesses of real people, but "truths" about generic qualities well-feigned.

Both *Epicoene* and *Sejanus* provide examples of how Jonson's ironies and indeterminacies, by disturbing judgment, slow the accessibility of naked truth and pose questions about the centered self. Truewit's pleasure in his own gift, his *ingenium*, diverts him from a straighter path. The prologue to *Epicoene* reminds us that comic truth delights and instructs while the play itself allows that both the audience and the poet, like Truewit, can be waylaid by delight. Unlike Volpone, Truewit is not punished; unlike Face, he is not grounded. Not at all chagrinned, he concludes genially by praising his friends' achievements, then recapitulates the foolishness of his victims, but not his own. If Truewit is a stand-in for the poet, as Jonas Barish argues,[59] he may represent the ambiguity of Jonson's own comic delight set loose in the play. In *Sejanus*, judgment can be no more categorical about the appropriate response to dangers portrayed there. There is enough in Jonson's works to invite claims that the "centered self" was shaped by the neo-Stoicism of Justus Lipsius,[60] and Lepidus recommends Stoic self-containment while waiting for ill times to improve:

> None, but the plain and passive fortitude
> To suffer, and be silent; never stretch
> These arms, against the torrent; live at home,
> With my own thoughts, and innocence about me,
> Not tempting the wolves' jaws; these are my arts.
>
> (4.294–98)

In sharp contrast, the exasperated Arruntius is too outspoken in his truthful criticism to go unheeded by dangerous spies. Jonson himself had personally experienced the dangers of addressing political realities freely.[61] A sharp difference in responses between Lepidus and Arruntius exercises our judgment while, ironically, the only certainty lies in the continuing tyranny of Tiberius.

Jonson's "truth of argument" in *Sejanus* warns against similar dangers near the surface in his own world. Roman competition for corrupt power renders tragically the competitive and often dangerous English world in which Jonson labored to establish himself. Rivalry for favor, recognition, and advancement in a hierarchical culture generates envy, detraction, and malice. The aristocratic, pastoral ideal in *The Forest* and images of harmony in the Court masques can be viewed as alternatives to competitive antagonism eroding the common good. Jonson's visible success made him a vulnerable target of envy; his natural aggression, rebellion, and rivalry encouraged both abuse and counter accusations of envy. He saw in envy an infection of truth threatening the individual self and the common good. A reluctant self-knowledge admitted his lack of immunity to its infection. A rounded self in its labor for coherent judgment must truthfully confront threats from within and without. It follows that envy, as a natural enemy to truth, is inherent in Jonson's consideration of self.

The Truth of Envy

Jonson returned repeatedly to the problem of envy. Two poems most read in our time, "To Penshurst" ("not . . . built to envious show" — *For* 2.1) and the memorial to Shakespeare ("To draw no envy . . . on thy name" — *UV* 26.1) pointedly begin with the problem. Both poems confront an envious habit of mind destructive in a tight social world. In "To Penshurst" architecture designed to make rivals feel inadequate invites envy and resentment. A general climate of resentment automatically awakens feelings of inadequacy and envy in rivals over any significant achievement, such as Shakespeare's. Habits of envious detraction corrupt truthful circulation of praise and blame that ensure common good. Written at the zenith of Jonson's career, these poems appeared respectively in the 1616 (Jonson) and 1623 (Shakespeare) folio editions designed for broad public readership.

A much later poem honoring Richard Weston's elevation as the Earl of Portland in 1632 encapsulates the conventional literary features of envy. Emergence of these features in a complex patronage context suggests their importance. The poet's ill health and diminished importance at the Caroline court only emphasized the importance of patrons to his well being. He honored Weston and his son Jerome with commendatory poems on several occasions in the 1630s, including Jerome's 1632 wedding to Arabella Stuart. (Weston died in 1634, Jonson himself in 1637.) An experienced administrator, most recently as the lord high treasurer, the tight-fisted Weston had served his own financial interests as he served the crown. Jonson shies from overly praising Weston while anticipating inevitable detraction. The poem toys with an allegorical taunt. The speaker goads the sleeping "seed of envy" (*Und* 73.1), that "sluggish spawn" (8), to observe the king's elevation of Weston, the wakeful "eye of state" (5). In contrast, the willfully blind envy with its "faint, and narrow eyes" (2) is unable to see "virtue, and true worth" (10). Envy's dilemma is punishing. Viewing Weston's elevation would only "Feed" its ineffective "spite" (9) and hatred, hence increase its frustration. By taunting Weston's detractors with his success, Jonson tempers praise of a compromised subject, an alert public servant, though no true noble.

Jonson's cameo depiction of envy incorporates conventional iconographic details[62] developed more fully in the prologue character, Envy, of *Poetaster*, a central text in the so-called War of the Theatres against John Marston and Thomas Dekker.[63] This "comic satire" was performed in 1601, two years before the first version of *Sejanus*. Both plays were set in Rome; both were included in the 1616 Folio. In *Poetaster* two plot lines feature Augustan poets. One plot opposes the talented satirist Horace, a stand-in for Jonson, to Crispinus and Demetrius, two poetic pretenders standing in for Marston and Dekker. Another plot line follows Ovid's wrong steps in an alternative poetic pathway of love poetry. Aloof from trivial involvement, the serious, but witty Horace is supported by the patron Maecenus and protected by Emperor Augustus. Unwise Ovid spends his talent on love poetry to Augustus's daughter and socializes with shallow social climbers familiar with Horace's envious detractors, Crispinus and Demetrius. A monstrous, "infected bulk" ("The Induction," 21),[64] Envy emerges from midstage, seemingly from her darkened and deep-set Ovidian home. Her "sunk eyes" (4) recall the "faint, and narrow eyes" in the Weston poem. She seeks an appropriate target for the "forced stings" of her poisonous snakes to "hide themselves within his maliced sides" (10). Vexed by the unexpected Roman setting, not "the present state" (34) of England, she seeks "players" and "poet-apes" (35) armed with her snakes to attack the author:

> Spit it forth
> Upon his lines, and show your rusty teeth
> At every word or accent; or else choose
> Out of my longest vipers, to stick down

> In your deep throats, and let the heads come forth
> At your rank mouths, that he may see you armed
> With triple malice, to hiss, sting and tear
> His work and him; to forge, and then declaim,
> Traduce, corrupt, apply, inform, suggest.
>
> (46–54)

Venomous malice is augmented by rusty teeth able to penetrate even metal.

The prologue character, "armèd" against a "dangerous age" (67), comments on "the allegory and hid sense" (73) of his presence. His foot on Envy's head conclusively suppresses her malice and spite, while he warns that any author faces "base detractors and illiterate apes" (70) driven by "pride" and "folly" (75). The envious "spawn of ignorance / Our fry of writers" who would "beslime" the author's fame with an "adulterate name" (79–81), are akin to the envious, "sluggish spawn" (*Und* 73.8) expected to attack Weston. Envy's dark underworld suggests illiteracy and ignorance of the "fry," whose untruthful detraction can damage an author when an audience is not warned.

Two kinds of eyesight distinguish Envy's detraction. One kind is "sunk eyes" suggesting illiteracy and ignorance. Accustomed to darkness, these "eyes" cannot tolerate the light of truth that obliges truthful perception of surrounding circumstances: "Light, I salute thee, but with wounded nerves, / Wishing thy golden splendour pitchy darkness" (1–2). The second kind is assaulting "basilisks' eyes" (35). Here we find the malicious evil eye (*in* + *videre*) that, like the "forkèd tongues . . . steeped in venom" (36–37), intends malicious injury to the good. These "basilisks' eyes" immobilize in order to kill: detraction puts fame, name, reputation, and honor at risk.

Jonson's prologue locates malicious envy and detraction within the play's broader work signaled by the alternative title: *Poetaster, or The Arraignment: A Comical Satire*. Both plots address the vocational role of poetic talent within the commonwealth and its constitutional frame. Ovid rightly rejects a legal career to exercise his poetic gift, but love poetry and trivial socialization divert him from public responsibility. He is less punished than his self-indulgence is thwarted. In contrast, Horace embraces responsibility, but learns how just power must protect a true satirist serving the common good. The arraignment of envious detractors censures their calumny against a true poet; the just power of Augustus, encouraged by wise poets and the patron Maecenus, turns the tables judicially on envious detractors. Augustus's justice acknowledges true poetry as an essential in the common good; Horace is vindicated and assured of judicial support. Seen in the best light, *Poetaster* steps above the arena of spite-filled, *ad hominem* attack to suggest that poets should revalue their talents in broader terms. A less generous interpretation would indict Jonson for whitewashing his detractions against his rivals.

Nevertheless, Jonson's play categorically establishes envy as a source of calumny and detraction against true poets. Horace's detractors, smarting from "sharp yet modest rhymes, / That spare men's persons and but tax their crimes" (3.5.133–34), falsely accuse him of libel. Their sole evidence is an emblem text pilfered from Horace, then misinterpreted: "A libel, Caesar. A dangerous, seditious libel. A libel in picture" (5.3.43–44). An agent of justice, Augustus hears both sides, then judges promptly against informer Lupus, and false witness Aeneas, as enemies of public order. Then, Augustus deputizes poets to judge poets; Virgil presides as judge over Crispinus and Demetrius. They are indicted, "to be arraigned, upon the statute of calumny" (208–09) as acting "contrary to the peace of our liege lord, Augustus Caesar, his crown and dignity" (214–15) in an attempt "to deprave and calumniate the person and writings of Quintus Horatius Flaccus" (218–19). Found guilty, Demetrius admits to being goaded by a competitive, personal envy: "In troth, no great cause, not I, I must confess, but that he kept better company for the most part than I, and that better men loved him than loved me, and that his writings thrived better than mine and were better liked and graced. Nothing else" (5.3.441–45). Appropriately punished with an emetic pill, a comic device imported from Lucian. Crispinus must vomit his stock of vocabulary that offends linguistic decorum. Jonson's summary truth is that personal envy leading to calumny against true poets threatens public order.

Revealing elements in *Poetaster* are derived from the essay on slander by Lucian, whose influence on Jonson ever broadened. Lucian's works were revived in Renaissance new learning, and the Greek's essay on slander, centering on an allegorical painting by the Greek artist, Apelles, was first translated into Latin in 1408, then progressively circulated in Greek, other Latin translations, and vernacular versions well into the seventeenth century throughout western Europe.[66] Literary effects were widespread. An example is Thomas Elyot's chapter, "Of Detraction and the ymage thereof made by the paynter Apelles" in *The Boke Named the Governour* (*Disc* 911).[67] In *De Pictura* (1436) earlier, Alberti recommended the allegory of calumny in Lucian's essay as a subject for painting.[68] Later visual works on the subject in various media include paintings, drawings, woodcuts, engravings, and wall paintings in public buildings by major artists including Botticelli, Montegna, Raphael, and Durer. One of many minor artists, Antonio Toto, presented a painting, "Calumny of Apelles," to Henry VIII in 1538.[69] Taken together, the literary and visual works generated by Lucian's "Scandal" (*De Calumnia*) form a minor, but significant stream in humanist culture.

In Lucian's account, Apelles's unfortunate personal experience generated his allegorical painting. An envious rival wrongly accused Apelles of conspiring against a general in the army of Ptolemy IV. Gullible Ptolemy believed the rival artist's false accusation; Apelles escaped execution only when the truth emerged belatedly; then, repentant, Ptolemy set things right. Lucian's account of the allegorical painting featured a seated, Midas-eared authority figure reaching toward Calumny, a beautiful woman led by emaciated, hollow-eyed Envy in the presence of Artifice and Deceit. Close to the seated figure stand Ignorance and Suspicion. At a distance shamefaced Repentance turns away from the bystander, Truth. The gist: competitive envy inspires calumny, formed by deceit; ignorance and suspicion mislead the foolish seat of judgment and authority, necessarily shamefaced and repentant when confronted by the truth. Renaissance humanist readers of Lucian's text would take special note that a literary work about a visual artifact contains this allegory.

Versatile application of Lucian's essay in the Renaissance extended its influence. David Cast elucidates, "The virtue of the allegory of the *Calumny of Apelles* lay in its generalities, in the range of virtues and vices it encompassed."[70] Calumny and envy as threats to both personal and civil well-being were primary Renaissance concerns. Deceit, calumny, and detraction that corrupted truth were seen to undermine systems of justice and authority. Also, circumstances featured in Lucian's essay reflected on the disruptive envy found in rivalry between artists competing for patronage favors. Lucian's essay was also endorsed implicitly by Apelles's importance to Renaissance humanism as the ancient Greek model of the painter. In sum, Lucian on the calumny of Appelles knotted together interrelated themes of high importance to the Renaissance. Literary and visual imitators could pick and choose which related themes to represent, but the full complement had enduring cultural importance.

Jonson's *Poetaster* is an example. Our early introduction to the allegorical prologue Envy clearly prepares us for Demetrius's confession that envy prompted his deceitful participation in libel against Horace. The indictment's broad legal and judicial foundation is crucial. Calumny violates law and, more important, political authority that ensures public good. The offenders transgressed Caesar's "peace . . . crown and dignity" while breaching "the form of a statute" (5.3.214–16). His judicial inquiry of the facts completed, Augustus as legal guarantor of the arts deputizes Virgil. Other poets serving Virgil must understand the broad foundation of their judicial agency:

> You shall swear
> By thunder-darting Jove, the king of gods,
> And by the genius of Augustus Caesar,
> By your own white and uncorrupted souls,
> And the deep reverence of our Roman justice,
> To judge this case with truth and equity,
> As bound by your religion and your laws.
>
> (5.3.249–55)

Under Caesar's auspices, Virgil invokes truth and equity broadly sanctioned by highest civil and divine authority. Jonson's comic fantasy, in marrying arts with high authority, addresses themes first introduced in the divide between the talented Ovid and his rigid father. Son and father together entrench poetry and law in irrevocable opposition. The patron Augustus's judicial protection of Horace closes the divide between poetry and law, squelching disruptive rivalry. Unlike Ptolemy, Augustus gets matters straight at the outset. The seat of justice and authority, unmoved by deceit and artifice, protects a true artist from his rival's envy and calumny.

Jonson's standard opposition between truth and ignorance informs *Poetaster* as it does Apelles's *Calumnia*. The armed Prologue prepares against "base detractors and illiterate apes" ("Induction," 70) and warns against "that common spawn of ignorance / Our fry of writers" (79–80). This preparation leads to Crispinus and Demetrius's stark opposition to learned poets informing the imperial seat. The lettered Augustus affirms that poesy "True born and nursed with all the sciences" can "mould Rome and her monuments" (5.1.20–21). Augustus surrounds himself with true poets, like them enlightening his judgment with truth. His final speech censures "the discords of those jangling rhymers" that "Bring all true arts and learning in contempt" (5.3.602–04). Virgil, who finds his natural place highest amongst Caesar's chosen poets, speaks like him with Jonson's vocabulary of truth. He judges "with truth and equity" (5.3.254), while assuming a normative "true and perfect merit" (342). With Augustus he unites justice, truth, and learning against envy, ignorance, detraction, and calumny.

Like Lucian's essay on calumny, the *Poetaster* addresses malicious envy in artistic rivalry. Literary and visual lines derived from this essay encouraged applications in both media, and *Poetaster* gestures toward other media as well. Competition between singers at the home of the social climbers Chloe and Albius parallels rivalry between poets. The text pilfered from Horace and used in evidence against him combines both visual and literary media. Given

Jonson's habits at work elsewhere, this choice of the emblem genre seems odd, unless taken as a pointer to similar issues affecting artists in visual media as well. Jonson's interest in painting would support this suggestion.[71] Also, by combining visual and literary in the emblem text, Jonson may be alluding more specifically to the combination in Lucian's essay. In any event, both Lucian's essay and Jonson's play address envy in artistic rivalry.

That essay knotted together issues that informed Jonson's vocational concerns during the War of the Theatres period. His "comical satires" beginning with *Every Man Out of His Humour* (1599), followed by *Poetaster* (1601), then *Cynthia's Revels* (1602), address poetry's cultural value and the poet's role in the commonwealth. In examining modes of satire in relation to envy, the first two plays share a vocabulary with enemy dramatists. Events precipitating satirical hostilities remain unclear, and Roma Gill suggests that there may have been more swagger than emotional heat in the conventions of envy that distinguish satire of the 1590s.[72] These conventions may have been primarily attention-getting devices, shadowboxing between young poets testing their artistic skills. Jonson's accord with Marston and Dekker before and after the "war" might seem to support the claim, if Jonson's continuing preoccupation with envy in his career had not gone beyond mere shadow boxing.

A key lies in his close attention to the psychology of envy and its various applications to himself. In *Poetaster* Demetrius's confession of the selfish envy driving his calumny condenses an analysis in *Every Man Out* developed at length in the humorous character, Macilente, a scholar driven by aggression, envy, and self-pity to scourge foolishness. The Juvenalian author figure of the Induction, Asper, becomes the envy-devoured Macilente in the play itself, then re-emerges at the play's end while pointedly keeping Macilente's identity. Together with the rational Cordatus, the author's choric "friend,"[73] these two characters represent aspects of Jonson's own experience. Viewed in hindsight, Macilente's envy is an early stage in Jonson's recurrent self-scrutiny that includes his subtly ambiguous celebration of his rival, Shakespeare.

A lank scholar, Macilente embodies the traditional assumptions that envy naturally targets virtue or good fortune in others. His spare frame conveys his poverty and the gnawing frustration of envy visually represented in the Apelles allegory. We first meet him rejecting the Stoic inner "Kingdom" of the "Mind" (1.1.14) as a defense against Fortune's capricious unfairness:

> I look into the world, and there I meet
> With objects that do strike my bloodshot eyes
> Into my brain; where, when I view myself —
> Having before observed, this man is great,
> Mighty and feared; that, loved and highly favoured;
> A third, though wise and learned; a fourth, rich
> And therefore honoured; a fifth, rarely featured;
> A sixth, admired for his nuptial fortunes —
> When I see these (I say) and view myself,
> I wish my optic instruments were cracked;
> And that the engine of my grief could cast
> Mine eyeballs like two globes of wildfire forth,
> To melt this unproportioned frame of nature.
>
> (16–28)

Like the prologue Envy of *Poetaster*, Macilente's eyes cannot tolerate truthful perception. Grief torments him with the advantages of others; hateful aggression and frustration seek to retaliate. Cordatus identifies him as traditional envy: "'*Invidus suspirat, gemit, incutitque dentes, / Sudat frigidus, intuens quod odit*'" (34–35). An outsider looking in, he overreacts to the good fortune of fools, then plots to expose foolishness and drive his victims out of their respective humors. Cordatus rightly predicts that his stored "malicious thoughts" in a "torrent of his envy" will "break forth" (4.5.155–56). His primary victims are the womanizing and foppish courtier, Fastidious Brisk; the doting husband, Deliro, and his unfaithful wife, Fallace; and the vainglorious Puntavolo given to romanticized, self-indulgent performances. Some of Macilente's actions are restorative. He first warns his host, Deliro, against dotage, then exposes his wife's duplicity; and he saves

Deliro's brother-in-law from an unjust debt burden. Cordatus's correct assessment in act 5, that Macilente's teeming envy will soon erupt, fails to note that all his victims are foolish. Macilente claims that his plotting has purged him of envy:

> Why, here's a change! Now is my soul at peace.
> I am as empty of all envy now
> As they of merit to be envied at.
> My humour, like a flame, no longer lasts
> Than it hath stuff to feed it, and their folly,
> Being now raked up in their repentant ashes,
> Affords no ampler subject to my spleen.
> I am so far from malicing their states,
> That I begin to pity 'em. It grieves me
> To think they have a being. I could wish
> They might turn wise upon it, and be saved now
> So heaven were pleased: but let them vanish, vapours.
>
> (Variant passage after 5.3.573. See Ostovich, 375)

This claim contradicts his introductory complaint about virtuous, not just foolish beneficiaries of Fortune. By that logic, scourging only fools would not purge his envy. Nor is it certain that Deliro is cured of dotage or Puntavolo of extravagant delusions. Nor does Macilente's concluding assertion explain his redundant soliloquy before Queen Elizabeth in the coda: "in her graces, / All my malicious powers have lost their stings" (2–3). Nor can we overlook that the coda follows Asper's reentry while maintaining Macilente's guise: "returned to you as I was Asper at the first" (5.9.69).

Cordatus's early analysis of Macilente's envy contrasts it with hate. The second choric figure, Mitis, is puzzled by Macilente's statement, "'I envy not this Buffon, but I hate him'" (1.3.171). Cordatus explains that Macilente envies only those blessed by fortune. Carlo Buffone, "an impudent common jester, a violent railer, and an imcomprehensible epicure" ("Prologue," 337–38), a man with no principles and no loyalties, as Cordatus explains, lacks good fortune or virtue. He cannot be envied, only hated, "For the true condition of envy is *Dolor alienae foelicitatis*, to have our eyes continually fixed upon another man's prosperity — his

that is, his chief happiness — and to grieve at that" (1.3.164–67).
In contrast, the contemptible, would-be courtier, Sordido, though
willing to play the fool, possesses land and wealth envied by the
impoverished scholar, Macilente. Cordatus's early analysis clearly
isolates Macilente's envious "dolor" when facing others' fortunate wealth and well being. This analysis likewise explains his
overstated hatred of foolishness. What it does not account for is
the "land flood" of malice, indignation, and frustration that colors his judgment against them. Nor does it explain why Elizabeth's
favor is so satisfying.

The traditional background to Renaissance conceptions of
envy helps to clarify this issue. Plutarch's basic distinction
between envy and hatred is not too far from Jonson's mind.
Prosperity and virtue are magnets for others' envy; desirable
good attracts envy, not hatred, which is reserved for persons
"bad either in general or toward oneself."[74] Envy is desire for the
good possessed by others; hatred is ill will toward the bad: "The
intention of the hater is to injure, and the meaning of hate is thus
defined: it is a certain disposition and intention awaiting the
opportunity to injury."[75] For Plutarch, the hateful intention to injure
includes malice. The reasons why Jonson on some occasions
includes malice and spite in envy, as in the prologue Envy of
Poetaster, deserve further attention.

Aristotle defines envy in light of other emotions including
indignation and emulation. Whereas indignation is the pain felt
at others' "undeserved good fortune,"[76] envy is pain felt at any
good fortune of others, deserved or not: "The deeds or possessions
which arouse the love of reputation and honour and the desire
for fame, and the various gifts of fortune, are almost all subject
to envy."[77] Possession by others of desired objects causes pain; their
possession is an implicit reproof for our failure. In contrast to envy,
emulation is pain caused by the "presence" of "good things that
are highly valued and possible for ourselves to acquire."[78] The
difference from envy is that emulation is "a good feeling felt by
good persons, whereas envy is a bad feeling felt by bad persons."[79]
Emulation stimulates action to acquire the good for its own sake,
not just enviously because others possess it.

Competition with others is a common denominator in Plutarch's and Aristotle's notions of envy, as well as Jonson's prologue Envy in *Poetaster* and Macilente in *Every Man Out*. Aristotle could approve Cordatus's more limited definition, which suits Jonson's thematic purposes. *Every Man Out* pivots on the relationship between the Juvenalian author, Asper, who enters into, but never completely exits out from impersonating the malcontented scholar, Macilente. Cordatus's attempt to moderate the rough, outspoken Asper in his reproofs of the "world's abuses"[80] correlates with his choric commentary on Macilente. Connections between Asper and Macilente work both ways. Asper's intemperate goal to "strip the ragged follies of the time" ("Induction," 1.15) prepares the audience to see that Macilente targets only fools, his envy and malice not withstanding. The pained and wounded soul with a generalized envy of all fortunate persons does not translate into an indiscriminate, unprincipled railer like Carlo Buffone. Moral truth distinguishes them. Folly scourged, Macilente claims a spirit now peaceful and emptied of envy and malice. Not good fortune, but actions serving the common good have purged his envy. At this point Jonson reminds us that Asper inhabits Macilente ("I should have gone in and returned to you as I was Asper" — 5.4.51–52), inviting the turnabout question whether Macilente's experience inhabits Asper. In Asper, tempered by Cordatus, then later in Horace, Jonson personates alternative vocational roles while seeking patronage at court. Asper has already established a role; the talented outsider, Macilente, is progressing toward one. His "lank hungry belly barks for food" (1.1.15). Envy and malice follow, then allegedly disappear as he exercises his merit in the face of deprivation. In Macilente resides the raw motive of Asper and of Jonson, sublimated in a satirical reproof of follies and vices in his society. Thus, the destructive energy of envy, allegorized in *Poetaster*, can be harnessed against social ills.

In Macilente's concluding address to Queen Elizabeth in the play's coda, Jonson looks further at the psychology of envy while angling for royal recognition and patronage. Elizabeth is praised for her effects on the kingdom that diffuse envy's destructiveness: Asper / Macilente asserts that "in her graces / All my malicious powers have lost their stings" (5.4.7–8). Here we return to the ambiguity of Macilente's claim to be emptied of envy and malice since, after all, scourging a mere handful of fools cannot eliminate foolishness. Also, her alleged perfection has not tamed the kingdom enough to make unnecessary the hopeful prayer that a flawed kingdom can prosper. A prayerful final half of the coda confronts contingencies with fanciful hopes, for example, that war's threat be stifled and "turtle-footed Peace dance fairy rings / About her court" (32–33). But the concluding admission that the "strongest wall" against ruin (36) will fall at her death fearfully undercuts wish fulfillment and returns us to the ambiguous claim about purged envy. Identification with Macilente or at least with his experience, suggests envy in Jonson himself. At the same time he suggests that in an ideal world, the grounds for envy would disappear. An elusive, critical self-knowledge reveals itself here.

That revelation indicates that Jonson's continuing attention to envy and distraction is not only a shared cultural concern about their damaging effects. His critics addressed his personal envy much more openly. John Davies's ironic epigram, "To my well'accomplish'd friend Mr. Ben Johnson" (1611), wittily praises his achievement in light of his alleged envy. The edge of the poem's wit is the condition that his detractors, if correct, only confirm the rivalrous Jonson's high standards. The poem's primary irony rests in the speaker's own implicit envy of Jonson's alleged envy:

> I loue thy *Parts;* so, must I love thy *Whole:*
> Then, still be whole in thy beloued *Parts:*
> Th'art sound in *Body:* but, some say thy *Soule*
> *Enuy* doth vlcer: yet corrupted hearts
> Such censurers may haue: But, if thou bee
> An enuious *Soule,* would thou couldst enuy me:
> *But (ah!) I feare my Vertues are too darke*
> *For* Enuies *shadow, from so bright a* Sparke.[81]

Davies neither confirms nor denies Jonson's ulcerous envy explicitly. Ambiguous syntax makes "corrupted hearts" a reference either to Jonson's "*Soule*" (3) or to "such censurers" (or both). The conditional "if" (5) sets up the witty affirmation that Jonson would envy only the most valuable achievements, which the speaker wistfully admits would exclude his own limited poetic *"Vertues"* (7). Allegations of envy cited but not categorically dismissed are implicitly confirmed, not condemned. The poem reflects on a hierarchy of talent in a competitive environment where the aggressive Jonson had stepped on "some" (3) toes, but where his excellence is self-justifying.

Jonson's continuing concern about envy in that environment affirms dangers of an "ulcer" within and the venom without. The "ulcer" gnawing insatiably within is envy's incurable dissatisfaction. Jonson's self-analysis discovers beneath that dissatisfaction a congenital psychic substratum that in its expression may catch us by surprise. Macilente's wishful prayer in praise of Elizabeth longs for an idealized world free from abrasion. That same longing emerges as "envy" in Jonson's epigram on his dead son, a poem that few parents can read, or reread, untouched. A self-imposed logic of Christian farewell works to control grief for a dead son too much loved and enjoyed, in whom too much hope was invested. The exercise of the logic as much as the assurance of its truth diverts grief:

> Oh, could I lose all father now! For why
>   Will man lament the state he should envy?
> To have so soon 'scaped world's and flesh's rage,
>   And, if no other misery, yet age?
>
> (*Epig* 45.5–8)

The word "envy" catches us by surprise. In this epigram Jonson apprehends an envious longing for a world that could satisfy a congenitally unfulfilled self. Making children or a "piece of poetry" (10) expresses a longing for recognition. In Demetrius's envy of the recognition received by Horace such longing goes awry, whereas Macilente feeds his longing, at least for a time, by serving the common good and enjoying the queen's blessing. As a "new man," Jonson knew the thrust of longing skewed by aggressive competition for recognition. His war on the injurious bent of detraction includes an elusive self-knowledge that envy is natural in the congenitally unfulfilled human self.

Jonson's preoccupation with envy is fraught with personal ironies. To Sackville he admitted to a "list of mine own faults to know, / Look to, and cure" (*Und* 13.114–15). This admission concurs with the self-knowledge essential in keeping the centered self straight. The broadly nuanced understanding of envy incorporated in Macilente, along with others' unabashed accusations of Jonson's envy, make it seem likely that his competitive envy and detraction were on the list of his faults without diluting his sense of social dangers in envious detraction. However, such an admission in Jonson is inhibited by his well-fortified self-defenses or masked in dramatic representations like Macilente. His attacks upon envy in others, especially artistic rivals, are charged with a personal animus that disallows the "pity" (5.11.56) that Macilente begins to feel for his foolish victims. Jonson's attacks upon rivals and detractors can be gratuitous or bullying, or both. His "humble petition" that Charles I follow James I's lead in paying the 100 pounds annual pension is appropriate; so is the pointed justification that his accomplishment exceeds that of lesser poets and detractors. But personal animus infects the decorum necessary for addressing a king. Jonson attacks the detractive "envy of the rhymes / And the rattling pit-pat noise" of "the less poetic boys" with their "pot-guns" and "pellets of small wit" (*Und* 76.18–22). His animus devises an inappropriate strategy whereby the king's payment makes him complicit against Jonson's detractors: "This would all their envy burst" (30). A petition that the Crown should fulfil a financial obligation hardly seems the appropriate occasion for spiteful detraction against his detractors' "spite" (28). No more becoming were spiteful hostilities with Inigo Jones that spoke well for neither rival. Jonson wittily preempts just accusations of envy: "I am too fat to envy him; he too lean / To be worth envy" (*UV* 34.69–70). Jones's belittled size is maliciously identified as the root of his envy while made to signify a mindless achievement and paltry talent in contrast to the larger man's more substantial literary gift. Mock refusal to "pity" (71) wittily upends nascent human sympathy like Macilente's. Jonson's strategy is to parade a wit so brilliant that it proves his immunity from envying any rival. Ironically, he has merely armed his envy with his best weapon.

Such ironies express contradictions in a complex nature performing a difficult cultural role. He accepted a humanistic social responsibility to praise and blame according to standards of truth. These standards center the individual self and stabilize participation in the community. But the exercise of praise and blame can drift into cross-purposes as the poet competes for the support and approval that sustain poetic activity. Praising a true noble can ignite envy and malice in a rival patron; likewise, blaming a rival poet's shortcomings may ignite envy and deceitful detraction that compromises reputation. Perhaps no poet, even a "laureate" of Jonson's importance, can be fully immunized against envying the praise received by a rival poet or against the impulse to detract from it. Achievement and virtue, by definition, invite envy and detraction.

At times Jonson seems to enjoy this malady; at other times a truthful self-knowledge recognizes his own inability to find the necessary antidote, supporting David Riggs's portrait of Jonson's disruptively competitive and subversive nature. Attention to Jonson's all too public weaknesses in recent criticism has set aside an earlier emphasis upon Jonson the public moralist. Yet that older vision of Jonson serves to remind us that his competitive personal envy does not always escape the truthfulness of self-knowledge enriching his humanistic criticism of the world around him. Jonson leaves us unprepared for the depth of this self-knowledge, only occasionally revealed and too often suppressed. The devotional lyric, "To Heaven," with which Jonson ends *The Forest*, is such a revelation.

This prayer to God concludes the 15 related poems in *The Forest* incorporating Jonson's humanistic notion of an ideal, civilized society. Jonson's publication of the 1616 Folio, which included *The Forest*, was a competitive act of self-identification displaying various poetic skills. A self-abnegating devotion, "To Heaven," strikes off-key. Jonson was a Christian humanist, but unlike Spenser, Donne, and Milton, little in his works is overtly Christian. And unlike Donne, he wrote little devotional poetry. The following lines would seem at first glance to belong to someone else:

Dwell, dwell here still: Oh, being everywhere,
How can I doubt to find thee ever here?
I know my state, both full of shame and scorn,
Conceived in sin, and unto labour born,
Standing with fear, and must with horror fall,
And destined unto judgement, after all.

(For 15.15–20)

These ideas are conventionally Christian, and his competitive urge
to demonstrate command of one more poetic *genre* cannot be discounted. But a peculiar juxtaposition of "shame and scorn" suggests an honest self-awareness too often suppressed by Jonson's
competitive aggression. The poem admits sinful guilt, offenses
against God, without labeling individual actions; but it claims as
well a fullness of "shame," an admission of having wrongly dis-
honored himself in injuring others, and of "scorn," the satirist's
hurtful, derisive contempt toward human targets. Here, I think,
there is a truthful self-awareness that Jonson too often denies.

Jonson wants his readers to find in "To Heaven," his confessional ending to *The Forest,* the same abiding standard of truth
embodied in the exemplars praised earlier in the aggregate work.
That ending projects a prayerful, inward likeness, a devotional complement to his humanistic commentary on the outward "truth
of times" in *The Forest.* His ending can be seen as a parallel to
Lady Aubigny's poetic "glass" reflecting her likeness of virtuous
subjectivity, an exemplary model that will guide herself and other
readers in the future, a contribution to rounded and centered
selves. The poet's praise endorses and elevates such virtuous
examples, especially patrons supporting poetry's necessary role,
to be gathered and assimilated in Jonson's readers. His verse
letter praising Elizabeth, Countess of Rutland, daughter to Philip
Sidney, describes her inheritance of her father's "love unto the
muses" (*For* 12.33) and her own poetic gift. Throughout *The
Forest* Jonson identifies himself as a necessary celebrant endorsing and elevating examples of common good idealized in *The
Forest.* But his prayerful confession of personal weakness implicitly reminds his readers that centered selves exist in a state of gathering, of becoming, while confessional self-criticism based on

commitment to truth helps to reinforce the center. His truthful self-awareness of "shame" and "scorn," I would suggest, reflects his own personal habits disruptive of the common good, in particular, the corrosive envy that threatened his embrace of truth.[82]

This truthful self-awareness encourages us to side with Pope, not Dryden, when evaluating Jonson's poem introducing the folio edition of Shakespeare's works.[83] For Pope, Jonson "exalts" Shakespeare above all English poets as a worthy rival of the Greeks. A simple question comes to mind in considering that poem with which this chapter began: why does Jonson bother to mention envy at all when beginning that poem? Admittedly, a person greatly praised can be a target of mean-spirited envy and its consequent detraction and malice; so, too, the person giving the praise. But the real issues about truth and envy are implicit. Jonson's readers knew his reputation for rough handling of rivals, which many blamed on his own envy of the recognition they received. Jonson's opening is implicitly preemptive, setting aside all envy to allow for a truthful estimate of Shakespeare's achievement by the other great poet of that time, Jonson himself. Jonson's estimate is not just generous: it is truthful. Literary history of the last four centuries has proven that Shakespeare, unlike Jonson and most other writers we might mention, did write for all time. Jonson's humanistic achievement is that in a public poem he confronted one of his own demons, envy of a rival, to give Shakespeare his highest praise. That truthful estimate of Shakespeare can be seen as the work of Jonson's centered self.

FIVE

Milton

Self-Defense and the Drama of Blame

John Milton's pride in being chosen to defend the new English republic against attack was unabashed. He welcomed "the glorious task of defending the very defenders" of "civil life and religion."[1] His *A Defence of the People of England* (1651)[2] earned widespread European approval, and even after the republican moment faded, his pride in this *First Defence* remained unabashed. In his layered characterization of himself as a defender of defenders can been found an essential truth of his nearly 20 years as a prose polemicist, stretching from his prelatical tracts to his last futile attempts to stave off restoration of the Stuart monarchy. His is an increasingly defensive self defined by participation in an adversarial community: a centered Protestant vocational self engaged in holy war along with other defenders of truth, pursuing a strenuous Protestant ideal of common good. The implications of this conception reach beyond the prose works of his "left hand"[3] to his late poetical works.

Such defensiveness came naturally. The period of Milton's active political involvement was intensely adversarial, both before and after the death of Charles I. Milton's self-representation as an epic hero in *A Second Defence of the English People* (1654) assumes a holy war with both sides exploiting the militant infrastructure of Christian thought. Paul's warfaring Christian warrior[4] and John's polarized battle between Christ and Antichrist[5] clearly informed the adversarial, contentious thinking on both sides in this holy war. Not even the strategic hypocrisies of European realpolitik could erase the sense of a cosmic opposition between good and evil. With other militant defenders of the Reformation, Milton viewed not only the papacy as the Antichrist, but also the English alliance between the monarchy and the prelacy. Battle lines were clearly drawn in pamphlet warfare, where the practices of defense dictated both literary form and working vocabulary. The formal prose defense is only the most obvious example.

The adversarial stance taken by Milton after his return from Italy in 1639 dominated his middle years until the Restoration. At first anonymous in his defense of the Smectymnuans against the church hierarchy, Milton progressively established his fame throughout Western Europe as the bold defender of church reform, divorce, regicide, and the new republican government. He characterized that boldness as the programmatic defense of religious, domestic, and civic liberty;[6] and the full force of his commanding sense of vocational and prophetic duty is at work. But the stated ideals justifying his boldness cannot mask a pugilistic aggression, leading to counterattacks which, in turn, called forth his abusive and combative self-defense.[7] To understand his disposition, at times flagrantly unleashed as in his misguided attack on Alexander More, is to better understand Milton's conception of the vocational self serving the common good.

This chapter examines the ways in which Milton's defensive vocational stance informs his works. The formal defenses written during his life as a polemicist are essential in this discussion, but we find elements in that defensive stance emerging as early as *Lycidas* and revisited as late as the great poems of his maturity. Some broad similarities to Jonson provide a useful backdrop here. Both writers acted from a sense of personal responsibility for the common good; both took an aggressive stance in the public sphere that deliberately elicited strong responses from their audiences; both defended themselves aggressively, sustained by a strong sense of centered self; both reflected critically on their personal behavior in their works. The differences are equally informative. For Jonson, the self is centered in a notion of "truth" that stabilizes his humanistic sense of social responsibility; for Milton the center is Protestant self-esteem as God's chosen, vocational servant recognized by others. His aggression and defensiveness are inextricable from his self-esteem, as are the related issues of blame, justice, and deserved fame that distinguish his sense of vocation. In the great poems of his maturity, we find Milton reflecting critically on the often excessive defensiveness of his earlier vocational experience in contentious pamphlet warfare.

Habits of Blame

Nowhere does Milton defend himself so combatively and lengthily as in two works published in 1654–55, the justly admired *A Second Defence* and the underrated *A Defence of Himself Against Alexander More*.[8] In early 1650 Milton was asked by the Council of State to rebut *A Defence of the King* (1649),[9] the work of the great European scholar, Claudius Salmasius. Aimed at a broad European audience, this influential work had been commissioned by the exiled Prince Charles to discredit the regicidal republican government. Milton was a logical choice to defend the new republican government against this attack. His defense of the regicides in *The Tenure of Kings and Magistrates* had been published two weeks after Charles I was beheaded in 1649. A month later Milton had been appointed secretary of foreign tongues to the Council of State. And still later that year he was commissioned to write *Eikonoklastes* to refute the widely influential *Eikon Basilike*, which claimed to be a work of the executed king. A few months later he was asked to rebut Salmasius.

Enormously honored to be asked, Milton was also applauded throughout Europe for his learned, convincing, and highly successful rebuttal in *First Defence,* published in 1651. Milton waited in vain for Salmasius to respond; but in 1652 *The Cry of the Royal Blood to Heaven Against the English Parricides,*[10] a scathing anonymous attack on the English and on Milton in particular, was published. Milton mistakenly thought the author was Alexander More, a French cleric connected to the Salmasius household. More had edited the work, aided in its publication, and included his own dedication to Charles II. In fact, the author was Peter Du Moulin, an Englishman living in London, who had sent the work to Salmasius for publication. Milton did not discover Du Moulin's identity until much later, in 1670.

While further defending the English actions against Charles and the monarchy, Milton's eloquent counterattack in *Second Defence* also included a protracted defense of Milton's own person against More, the putative author of *A Cry to Heaven.* The badly outmatched More, whose disastrous dalliance with Elizabeth Guerret, a lady-in-waiting in the Salmasius household, was widely publicized in *A Second Defence,*[11] feebly attempted to defend himself in 1654 against Milton's unjust charge of authorship in *The Public Faith of Alexander More, Preacher and Professor of Sacred literature Against the Calumnies of John Milton.*[12] By the time Milton wrote the virulently satirical, punitive, crushing, and misguided *ad hominem* response in *Defence of Himself* the same year, he had convincing evidence that More was not the author, a fact he admitted evasively while punishing More without mercy.[13] Here, uneasily, we encounter the dark and malign side of a great writer, but we also find a crucial text for examining Milton's defensive conception of the self and its abuses in relation to the community.

A good place to begin investigating this defensive self is Milton's 1653 translation of the first eight psalms. These translations contain many of the crucial issues claiming Milton's attention during the period of the prose defenses: *First Defence* (1651), *A Second Defence* (1654), and *Defence of Himself* (1655). Milton's psalms embody a sense of the self as God's military champion standing against God's enemies. The speakers stand against "Mine enemies" (Psalm 6.21), the "workers of iniquity" (5.13), those "many millions / The populous rout . . . encamping round about / They pitch against me their Pavilions" (3.15–18). The beleaguered champion(s) looks to God for his "defense" (7.40) against the unjust hordes. Milton's characterization of himself as a warrior in the prose defenses finds its close parallel here:

> Push them in their rebellions all
> Still on; for against thee they have rebelled;
> Then all who trust in thee shall bring
> Their joy, while thou from blame
> Defend'st them, they shall ever sing
> And shall triumph in thee, who love thy name.
> For thou Jehovah wilt be found
> To bless the just man still,
> As with a shield thou wilt surround
> Him with thy lasting favor and good will.
>
> (5.31–40)

Just as the champion's aggressive shield recalls the prose defenses, so also does Milton's sharpened langue in contrast to the King James Authorized Version (1611). There, believers who love God's name will "shout for joy" (KJV, Ps. 5.11), but they "triumph" in Milton's version (5.36). The petition to "cast them out in the multitude of their transgressions; for they have rebelled against thee" (KJV, Ps. 5.10) is hardened further to "Push them in their rebellions / Still on" (5.31–32).

The self is distinguished by the shield provided by God against the enemy, and the nature of the shield reveals much. Milton gives a more generalized identification in "Psalm III": "But thou, Lord, art my shield, my glory" (7). Later in "Psalm V" Milton is more specific. It is God's "lasting favor and good will" that surrounds the just man "As with a shield" (38–39). This God "Defend'st" those who "trust in thee," significantly protecting against "blame" (33–35). The besieged champion, the attacking horde, and God's shield coalesce in blame, which designates both the mode of attack and the nature of the damage. Here is the controversialist's fear of enemy words that poison the sources of honor. The protecting "favor and good will" point to the friendly audience, inspired by God, dissipating the evil blame of God's enemies. The more general "my shield, my glory" is made more particular, its meaning more defined: man's glory is honor that defies blame and participates in God's glory, establishing the champion in the eyes of God's other servants. But this self is nonetheless galvanized by fear of blame or the disparaging words and attitudes of the enemy.

An angry fear calls upon God's vengeance and anger to satisfy the righteous champion's sense of outraged justice. Only powerful anger and just righteousness can defeat the force of the assembled enemy. The speaker will empower his own hatred and anger by identifying with God's. He asks God who "hat'st . . . All workers of iniquity" (5.12–13) to "Rise . . . in thine ire" (7.20). God will empower just believers and their champion, in particular, against the enemy nation and their leaders (2.1–5), including the "Great ones" who "My glory have in scorn" (4.7–8). Retribution will turn the tables to assuage dishonor and damaged glory:

> Mine enemies shall all be blank and dash't
>   With much confusion; then grow red with shame;
> They shall return in haste the way they came
>   And in a moment shall be quite abash't.
>
> (6.21–24)

Fear of blame and its accompanying shame will be turned back upon the enemy who are the cause.

The embattled self at work in Milton's 1653 Psalms comes as no surprise to the reader of Milton's formal defenses against Salmasius and his lieutenants, Du Moulin and More. Supported by a just God and standing for the community, he carries the weapons of righteous anger and deep conviction into battle against the champions of a tyrannical, unjust, but formidable enemy of his community. He fights fire with fire, turning defense into offense, armed with wrath and blame against champions of a multiple enemy, the monarchical supporters of western Europe. Milton's defensive vituperation and angry aggression in *Defence of Himself*, weapons razor-honed by the personal fierceness at work in Milton's earlier polemics, may besiege the modern reader's notions of justice and fairness. But relationships between anger, blame, and justified self-defense provide us with direct access to Milton's conception of the self in the community. The role of blame in pamphlet warfare, where mutual recriminations define the terms of engagement, is predictable, but my claim is that Milton's notion of self is inexorably linked to the practice of defensiveness and to patterns of blame.[14]

Before proceeding to the patterns of self-defense and habitual blame that inform his defenses of the English people and himself, I would like to take a retrospective look at *Lycidas* (1637), perhaps Milton's most important early work. The purpose here is to establish that the connections in Milton's thought between defensiveness, habits of blame, expectations of fame, and demands of justice in relation to vocation were not mere reactions to pamphlet combat. Rather, in *Lycidas* the rude swain's catalog of blame expresses Milton's own sense of justice disturbed by Edward King's death. The connections between the swain and Lycidas and between Milton and King lie in the vocational gift of poetry. Expectations of using this gift express that sense of justice and inspire a search for the perpetrator when death violates that gift. Initial blaming of the nymphs by the rude swain expresses the limitations of his youthful vision and inexperience:

> Where were ye Nymphs when the remorseless deep
> Clos'd o'er the head of your lov'd *Lycidas?*
> For neither were ye playing on the steep,
> Where your old *Bards*, the famous *Druids*, lie,
> Nor on the shaggy top of *Mona* high,
> Nor yet where *Deva* spreads her wizard stream:
> Ay me, I fondly dream!
> Had ye been there — for what could that have done?
> What could the Muse herself that *Orpheus* bore,
> The Muse herself, for her enchanting son
> Whom Universal nature did lament,
> When by the rout that made the hideous roar,
> His gory visage down the stream was sent,
> Down the swift *Hebrus* to the *Lesbian* shore?

(50–63)

The abrupt contradiction advances the awareness that the muse could not protect Orpheus. A two-edged blade finely scores a muse too weak to protect even her own son Orpheus, let alone Lycidas, while attacking the scheme of justice that motivates a desire for fame. Only Phoebus's admonishing reinterpretation that fame does not grow "on mortal soil" (79) diverts blame away from the ultimate target, Jove, whom Phoebus serves and under whose seat the muses reside ("the sacred well/ That from beneath the seat of *Jove* doth spring" — 15–16). Thus diverted, blame later targets the wolfish clergy, who abuse the Good Shepherd, his surrogates like Lycidas, and the sheep they serve.

   Phoebus's clarification of fame vindicates the system of justice implicitly questioned by the attempts to fix blame. True fame rewards the poet with lasting praise from Jove himself:

> *"Fame"* is no plant that grows on mortal soil
> Nor in the glistering foil
> Set off to th'world, nor in broad rumor lies,
> But lives and spreads aloft by those pure eyes
> And perfect witness of all-judging *Jove*;
> As he pronounces lastly on each deed,
> Of so much fame in Heav'n expect thy meed.
>
> (78–84)

The Christian God syncretized as Jove presides as judge, ensuring the reward system that honors all true activity whatever its earthly misfortunes. The frame of divine justice can protect the poet's vocation from death's claim. While the vindication of divine justice extinguishes the implicit murmuring against God, it identifies the search to blame as a search for justice. The rude swain continues the search as the poem cinches more tightly the connection between blame and justice:

> But now my Oat proceeds
> And listens to the Herald of the Sea
> That came in *Neptune's* plea.
> He ask'd the Waves, and ask'd the Felon winds,
> What hard mishap hath doom'd this gentle swain?
>
> (88–92)

Language suggesting legal accountability for criminal action characterizes the offense to Lycidas and the desire for retribution. Both Phoebus and Neptune are agents of the justice maintained by Jove, but Neptune's need for self-defense keeps alive the question of ultimate accountability. Blame still seeks justice:

> It was that fatal and perfidious Bark
> Built in th'eclipse, and rigg'd with curses dark,
> That sunk so low that sacred head of thine.
>
> (100–02)

This displacement of blame onto an inanimate object is a natural step backwards from putting Jove on trial, but it also leaves unresolved whom to blame.

Phoebus's intervention serves as the gods' defense against blame, and it introduces the long transition including the outburst against the clergy that leads to the resolution of the need to fix blame. Milton puts this attack against the corrupt clergy in the mouth of Peter, the "Pilot of the *Galilean* Lake" (109), who is angered by the selfish "Blind mouths" (119) who violate their shepherd's responsibility to the "hungry Sheep" (125). The hard edge of Milton's satire once again joins blame and justice, deeply scoring clerical abuses and threatening them with the ultimate justice of the "two-handed engine at the door . . . ready to smite once, and smite no more" (130–31). Peter parallels Jove as a powerful judge who maintains a system of justice against abuse. But a crucial shift has occurred. Unlike *"Camus,* reverend Sire" (103), who still seeks those responsible for Lycidas's death, Peter attacks those who have violated the shepherd's trust. Justice is no less offended, but blame now aims at a different target, not those responsible for Lycidas's death, but those violating their vocations.

This shift away from blaming God further exacerbates the irony that Lycidas could not have died without divine approval. The poem's conclusion that Lycidas still lives is a half-truth clouding that irony while deepening the truth of God's justice. An even deeper irony is that the righteous impulse to blame sometimes may serve a justice beyond immediate rational grasp.

Here, the self, in defending against the threat to justice, becomes a judicial agent in reformulating Lycidas's role. Phoebus' declaration opens up the ultimate truth that Lycidas in his new role as the genius of the shore while singing in the heavenly choir is not the victim of injustice, but an agent of true fame. And the swain's song is not just the vehicle of blame and an instrument to establish Lycidas's fame serving others, but also the agency for enacting justice. The truth that this realization would not have occurred without God's permission is not explicitly expressed in the poem, nor is the principle that the swain, as his anger dissipates, achieves poetic fame as the maker of the song made known by the second speaker.

The swain's inarticulateness expresses doubts about divine justice caused by thwarted vocation. We will return below to the theme of frustrated vocational gifts that recurs in Milton's works. Here, it is sufficient to establish that interconnections between self-defense, blame, fame, justice, and vocational responsibility were present in Milton's thought as early as *Lycidas* before he entered the lists of pamphlet warfare in 1641. The characteristic interconnections were exacerbated but not created by the hostilities of textual warfare.

Self-Esteem in Textual Warfare

By the time he defended himself in *A Second Defence* against Du Moulin's *Cry to Heaven*, Milton was a veteran defender in the hostilities of mutual blame and a public champion of the new republican government. Although there is good reason to argue that Milton's self-defense is excessive, he could not leave Du Moulin's *ad hominem* attack unanswered. Blame must counter blame. Just as Milton had belittled Salmasius as a henpecked victim of Madame Salmasius in order to assail his defense of the monarchy and Charles I, so Du Moulin had ridiculed Milton to subvert the validity of his defense of the regicides. He had belittled Milton's ability as a defender of truth while claiming untruthfully that, after being expelled from Cambridge, Milton had fled to Italy in shame, to be recalled later for the purpose of furthering his interests against the king (4.2.1050). Not just a "blockhead" and a "foolish shrewmouse," Milton was a "vile buffoon," "filth soaked in black blood" (1078–79), and "a worm voided lately from the dungpit" (4.2.1050). Du Moulin's argument strained to outdo its own invective while assailing the truthfulness of Milton's argument against Salmasius and attacking the presumptuous mite who dared to joust with that giant. The defender of the republican cause needed to respond. But in that necessary response, the practice of mutual blame in pamphlet warfare overstepped a reasonable boundary. As we will see, Milton's own principle of vocational self-esteem, centered as it was in a conviction of being chosen by God, sits in judgment against his actions at the same time that he himself tries, judges, and convicts Alexander More for a lack of self-esteem leading to violations of justice.

The counterattack as a necessary weapon of self defense is not the issue, but its excess. If unchallenged, such a strong attack by More (Du Moulin) could validate distorted claims and under-cut the truth of Milton's own cause. And even if the construc-tion of his self-defense seems to exceed its cause, the logic of Milton's *ad hominem* sniping[15] at Salmasius is that the defender is the measure of the cause. A silent response to Du Moulin's tar brushing would justify the tar's black truth and injure the repub-lican cause. Du Moulin's own attack followed this logic, imme-diately ridiculing the choice of Milton as defender in order to undermine the republican legitimacy. Milton's self-defensive retaliation against More, whom he mistakenly took to be the author of the *Cry to Heaven,* applied that logic once again.

Milton bases his vindication of his protracted self-defense on clear principles relating to the common good of the self and oth-ers in the community. These principles are clearly established in *A Second Defence.* He gives three reasons for freeing his name from the potential disgrace resulting from the lies told about him: first, to convince "many good and learned men" in other coun-tries that his previous words will never be disgraced by his "dis-honorable conduct" or "slavish deeds"; second, to reassure those "distinguished and praiseworthy" English leaders that they have been praised by a good and honorable man; and, third, to show the English people "whose defence their own virtue has impelled me to undertake" that his "pure and honorable life" prevents his *Defence* from causing them "shame or disgrace" (4.1.611). Pivotal in these three reasons is the way that virtuous communities and their champions are mirrored in their actions and words. Consistency between good actions and good words is essential to the system of honor binding together the members of a virtuous community in a common good. Untruth can weaken the voices of truth heard by a virtuous audience, thereby weakening the praise of virtuous deeds. Conversely, the fulfillment of virtuous deeds in praise ensures the continuity of virtue through recognition by others. For this reason, praisers of virtue, in turn, are recognized for their goodness in the words of praise. When slander and unjust blame damage reputations, the mirrors of mutual recognition become cracked and the bonds of community loosened. In the *Second Defence* Milton works to justify his energetic self-defense in terms of these mutual mirrors and the bonds necessary for community.

Mutual recognition identifies the good, and the exercise of goodness requires vigilant defense against attack, both "by arms" and "by reason" (4.1.553). The republican government must defend itself with the word as well as the sword, with a Milton as well as a Cromwell. The republicans defended liberty against tyranny, the people against the monarch; and Milton was called by "vote and decision" to the "glorious task of defending the very defenders" (4.1.554). From the mutual recognition between defender and defenders, it follows that Milton's self-defense is necessarily implicated in the defense of the people who have chosen him to defend truth "by reason — the only defence truly appropriate to man" (4.1.553). The English "people" includes only those who pursue virtue and truth, although his conviction is that England possesses more of these than other countries. However, his broadest claim is that God has blessed him with the gifts to defend not just "on behalf one people nor yet one defendant, but rather for the entire human race against the foes of human liberty" (4.1.557–58). Milton's barely masked pride in his people's divinely inspired choice of him to defend the cause of liberty imposes his own image on his respect for the people. To "congratulate myself" (4.1.553) is to congratulate their virtue for recognizing his. Mirrors facing each other ensure that their images reflect the common good.

A further dimension in mutual identification between Milton and the people, between the self and the community, is Milton's defense of Cromwell. Several principles converge in this defense. In defending the defenders, Milton necessarily singles out those heroes whose actions most significantly advance the republican cause, the common good; he especially singles out Cromwell for military and political reasons. The mutual recognition between Milton and a virtuous people likewise explains Cromwell's relationship to the people. He is the "very patron and tutelary god of liberty, as it were . . . than whom no one has been considered more just, more holy, more excellent" (4.1.673). That he is the spirit of liberty suggests that the capacity for liberty in the people is most fully expressed in Cromwell. Milton's praise of Cromwell is constructed to reflect glory not only on the English people, but on Milton himself. Whereas Milton is a primary defender of England "by reason," Cromwell is the primary defender "by arms." They mirror each other in subtle and complicated ways that profoundly affect the structure of the whole *A Second Defence*. Well before praising Cromwell, he has informed us, while praising England's glory "by arms," that defense "by reason" is the most appropriate means of human defense. But Milton's self-congratulation wrestles ambivalently with his defensive admission that he was not a participant in military glory. On one hand, Milton works hard to defend himself against the possible accusation of failure to participate in dangerous public actions, while praising the heroism of those who did. On the other hand, he emboldens his identification with these events to suggest that he, too, is a warrior involved in danger: "For I did not avoid the toils and dangers of military service without rendering to my fellow citizens another kind of service that was much more useful and no less perilous" (4.1.552). Modern readers looking for more than thrusting ego in this argument may at least grant that Milton is constructing his intricate self-defense with adroitness.

Readers more sympathetic to Milton will find in his concluding admonition to the English readers — that they prepare themselves morally and spiritually for the "warfare of peace" (4.1.681)
through piety and virtuous behavior — the larger principle at
work, which puts the heroism of military activity in perspective.
The assumption is that all virtuous "people," warriors or not, are
the Christian warriors of Paul's letter to the Ephesians, appropri-
ated earlier in the "warfaring" Christian of *Areopagitica* (2.515).
This identification closes the gap between actual warriors, like
Cromwell, and others who took risks for the republican cause.
These include Milton who risked his eyes, just as earlier he had
displayed his Reformist colors in Catholic Italy. Milton exploits
the potential of the Pauline infrastructure to strengthen his own
self-portrait in Christian military terms. He had been "so bold as
to risk combat with Salmasius," refusing the advice that "I was
a tyro about to join battle with a veteran" and could "be conquered
and leave the field with serious damage" (4.1.602–03).

The brilliance of Milton's argument lies in the risks he continues to take in comparison with Cromwell. The admonition
to fight the "warfare of peace" is first prefaced by his ambivalent
praise of Cromwell as the "very patron and tutelary god of liberty" who must guard against any inclination to "attack that liberty which he himself has defended" (4.1.673). The defender in
arms must become the defender in reason, exercising the power
of persuasion guided by virtue in the warfare of peace. Like Milton
he would then pursue the more "appropriate" defense of liberty.
Cromwell must take a different kind of risk, just as Milton risks
offence against Cromwell himself. This kind of warning, with its
strong kinship to Marvell's warning in the Horation ode, expresses
Milton's genuine fear about Cromwell; it also puts Milton at hazard especially since he is offering himself as an example of reason to the Protector.

A thrust against More (Du Moulin), the enemy whose blame
is transformed into praise of the defender, demonstrates the use
of such reason while adroitly illustrating the hazard he runs:
"Continue to curse me as being 'worse than Cromwell' in your
estimation — the highest praise you could bestow on me" (4.1.595).

Proving his enemy a fool allows Milton to exploit the inversion that subordinates Cromwell to Milton in the eyes of the enemy's representative: "For if you hate me most of all, surely I am the one who has injured you most of all, hurt you most of all, and damaged your cause. If such is the case, I am also the one who has deserved most highly of my fellow-citizens, for the testimony of judgment of an enemy, even if in other circumstances somewhat unreliable, is nevertheless by far the most weighty when it concerns his own suffering" (4.1.595). Having established his enemy as a fool, Milton protects himself behind the pretense that there is no real seriousness in that argument. At the same time Milton can pursue the sense in which he *is* greater than Cromwell, as the enemy rightly perceives. An epic parallel between Milton and Ulysses is fitted for his purposes, maintaining the continuing comparison between himself and Cromwell as Christian warriors while underscoring the higher calling to defend by reason. This skillful transformation of the enemy's censure into praise recalls that Homer let the enemy Trojans judge the contest between Ulysses and Ajax for the weapons of Achilles. So, too, Milton traps the enemy defender into preferring Milton's Ulysses to Cromwell's Ajax. The risk to Milton, whose readership includes More (Du Moulin), Cromwell, and the English people depends upon how well Cromwell understands the real subtleties of the argument. Ulysses is both a warrior and a counselor, using both arms and reason. So can Cromwell if he fights the warfare of peace according to Milton's example of virtuous reason. Milton has it both ways: after first offering himself as a Christian warrior like Ulysses, he then leaves the field to Cromwell: "For although I should like to be Ulysses — should like, that is, to have deserved as well as possible of my country — yet I do not covet the arms of Achilles. I do not seek to bear before me heaven painted on a shield, for others, not myself to see in battle, while I carry on my shoulders a burden, not painted, but real, for myself, and not for others to perceive" (4.1.595–96). Only Cromwell, not Milton, can be Ulysses.

The warrior image serves Milton most intimately when defending his physical person. This defense is deeply revealing in its apparent superfluousness to the main line of his defense, while confirming our suspicions that the whole defense verges on overreaction. But while it serves psychological needs characteristic in Milton, to be examined later, it likewise contributes substantially to the portrait of Milton as a warrior and stresses this attack upon the new enemy, whose sexual behavior expresses his moral monstrosity. An attack on the physical Milton in *Cry to Heaven* attempted to discredit the English by suggesting the monstrosity of their defender. Milton was likened to the Cyclops: "A monster, dreadful, ugly, huge, deprived of sight"; then, contradictorily, he was depicted as "Yet not huge, for there is nothing more feeble, bloodless, and pinched" (4.1.582). Milton countered this unjust attack with a characterization of his physical person and the athleticism of his swordsmanship, allowing the implicit claim that he could have been a real warrior: "Girded with my sword, as I generally was, I thought myself equal to anyone, though he was far more sturdy, and I was fearless of any injury that one man could inflict on another. Today I possess the same spirit, the same strength, but not the same eyes" (4.1.583). This self-defense supports the central claim that he is a warrior of a higher kind anyway, defending with reason and not arms. Buried in his rejection of the Cyclops characterization, since it is More that is really the monster, is the further claim that the blind seer Milton has the true rational sight. And we recall that the rationally insightful Ulysses, to whom Milton likens himself elsewhere in *Second Defence,* blinded the monstrous Cyclops.

Whatever the deepest psychological sources of his virulent attack upon More later in *Defence of Himself,* Milton's continuing role as the champion against Salmasius increasingly required More as a target. To measure the truth of an argument by the virtue of the person advancing it erected constraints for Milton as well. To attack Salmasius as obtuse, limited in learning, and henpecked, then to attack More as even less intelligent, less learned, and possessing even less self-control in regard to women could endanger Milton's proud victory over Salmasius if Milton had the wrong man, especially since the divorce tracts had discolored his own reputation for sexual integrity. Although More's sexual history made him an easy target,[16] Milton's earlier attack was the petard that could hoist Milton himself if he had the wrong man. The truth of the English cause stood to suffer inadvertent damage at Milton's hands, to be exploited by the enemy. When the disturbed More published his *Public Faith,* flatly denying authorship of Du Moulin's anonymous *Cry to Heaven,* he seemed to put the now blameworthy Milton at a disadvantage.

The intensity of Milton's reactive blame and vituperation strikes many modem readers as especially perverse.[17] And it is. But Milton's strategy reveals much about his conception of the role of justice in personal self-defense and of authorship in relationship to public truths. However disingenuous we may find it, the claim that More was the author, even if he had not written the text,[18] assumes the close identification between individuals and public truths that they embody. Milton was identified by the English truths he championed. More's contribution to the publication of *Cry to Heaven* similarly identified him with the substance of the work, whatever its actual authorship.

Milton conceives of the mutual blame and vituperation in judicial terms, more obviously applied to More, but no less significantly to Milton himself. While defending himself against More's unjust charges, he is putting More on trial for present and past wrongs in Amsterdam, Geneva, and elsewhere. He makes no "fabricated charges against More . . . but real ones, already published and attested." Milton and others are "his judges" who with "all reason and justice" will "justly deliver a verdict" against More who "first judged us" (4.2.798). More's previous moral, legal, and ecclesiastical infractions, especially in regard to his abandoned mistress, Elisabeth Guerret, are grist readily milled in Milton's *ad hominem* attack. Milton is not only the accuser, but also the judge; and by bringing More to trial, Milton delivers him to the "judgment of all the ages" (4.2.767). The linchpin in Milton's judicial theme is the "testimony" and witnesses against More's defense. The accuser Milton recycles the previous accusations of that "mass of men who testify against you" (4.2.780), while building his own prosecution of More and allying himself, in his own charges and judgment, with men of "great honor and reputation" (4.2.779) in Geneva and everywhere who reject the actions of such a criminal.

Milton interplays legal judgment and testimony, on one hand, and rational judgment and fame, on the other, taking advantage of the natural kinship between them. The legal judgment against More is an exercise in reason, and the testimony against him includes an analysis of his reputation. Milton's argument must unhinge the central claim of More's *Public Faith* that the witness by others about his character invalidates Milton's censure of him in *A Second Defence.* More offers the testimony of his supporters as evidence of communal faith in him and requires that Milton give contrary evidence. Milton counters with the written and spoken testimony of witnesses giving evidence of More's immoral and criminal actions in several countries: "But as for that adulterous spousal of yours with Pontia [Elisabeth Guerret], which has rendered you everywhere in those provinces a marked man and the common talk, there is much less reason why you should demand from me 'witnesses and proofs.' Call into judgment, if you wish, common and constant Fame, and those hundred, or rather thousand, mouths. There are many witnesses" (4.2.758). One stanchion in Milton's argument is the distinction between good and bad testimony. He does not settle for the simple distinction that some persons are unreliable witnesses, but assumes that corrupted testimony is a serious threat to justice and truth. Milton is especially strenuous in criticizing the verdicts of both the civil and synodical courts that heard Elizabeth Guerret's charges against More for breach of promise. According to Milton, the infected judicial proceedings with their perverted testimony and bad judgment embarrassed even More, the source of the infection: "More himself was ashamed of so lax a sentence; he pretends afresh that he is disturbed and that he takes it ill that those volumes of his crimes were not read forth" (4.2.808). Milton is inviting his readers to put More on trial, judging his self-defense both rationally and legally in light of Milton's cross-examination of More's own testimony and of the record of his actions preserved in his reputation.

Seen against More, a corrupted foil, Milton himself stands forth before his reader as the model of reason needed to judge More's perverted testimony and the details of his life. Constantly assessing the evidence and freely exercising rational judgment according to the principles of morality and justice, Milton's judgment of More will testify to the value of Milton's own person called by God "above all others to the defence of liberty" (4.2.735). Rational judgment is the exercise of liberty and the answer to that call. More importantly, it fulfills the self.

The ultimate charge against More is his damage to the self through the abuse of both reason and liberty. Milton's charge that More is in "flight from yourself" (4.2.779) assumes a witting perversion of his God-given essence while portending Milton's crushing judgment on Satan's self-destruction in *Paradise Lost* (4.20–23). The perverted self becomes its own punishment: "Nothing is more offensive than to live with yourself, to be in your own company; no one do you avoid more willingly than yourself. In vain, poor worthless man, for you fly with yourself, you follow yourself" (4.2.776). Flight *from* the self and, paradoxically, *with* the self seem contradictory since perversion is a departure from the created self. But the perversion accompanies the culprit everywhere. This apparent contradiction casts light on the warring effects of such a nature, the entanglements that twist intentions: "For if you deny that you cry slanders, your very words, in spite of yourself, confess that which you deny; if you confess, those same words of yours deny the very thing which you confess" (4.2.765). Milton's own rational judgment sorts out the perversions of a damaged self on trial for its abuses.

Milton's charges against More, by enacting judgment in both its rational and judicial senses, are simultaneously basic to his own self-defense against More's blame. Whether or not he convinces us that he has "never praised myself" (4.2.735), he does coherently offer himself as the foil to the enemy. The skillful maneuvering of his judgment dramatizes the healthy rational self, freely pursuing the call to defend liberty against its enemies according to god-given standards of justice. Overturning More's arguments in order to discredit the testimony of his witnesses exposes, censures, and charges his crimes; that is, it blames the wrongdoer for his violations. Such blame is primary in Milton's self-defense as a champion who defends liberty by fulfilling the potential of the free rational self. By demonstrating that More deserves his name ("Morus"), Milton displays his own fulfilling capacity of judgment.

Such a defense requires that Milton be correct in his accusations. An admission that he was wrong earlier in singling out More for blame as the author of *Cry to Heaven* is damaging. Milton's vituperative defensiveness cannot be accounted for only on these grounds, even though his position is precarious. The relentless censure of More's sexual indiscretions protests too much in light of Milton's grudging admission that More might not be the actual author of *Cry to Heaven.* The attention to More's nocturnal trysts, to the geography of the garden locale, and to his scratched face — however brilliantly introduced and exploited by Milton — seems off center. The basic charge that More wrote *Cry to Heaven* deserves to be thrown out of court, that is unless we grant Milton's sophistic definition of authorship that allows him to treat the three works, respectively by Salmasius, Du Moulin, and More, as essentially one text.

So, too, are Milton's three formal defenses to be taken as one text, its parts to be viewed in terms of the whole. We can usefully approach the vituperation against More's sexual indiscretions, including his face scratched by the insulted "Pontia" and his undignified nocturnal activities, in light of Milton's defense of his own bodily self in *A Second Defence.* His characterization of his medium sized, but youthfully athletic frame, his clear and bright eyes, in spite of blindness, and his luminous skin are connected to his skill as a swordsman. And the claim that "Ugly I have never been thought by anyone . . . who has laid eyes on me" (4.1.582–83) works to free him from the comparison with the Cyclops. It also serves a larger intention to present an ideal self, in both body and mind, proper for a heroic defender of liberty. That attractive physical self is the foil for More's scratched face, the text against which the world can measure More's immoral use of his physical self. More is an ironically "warlike Alexander" defeated by the "Amazon," Elisabeth Guerret, his scratched face an "engraved tablet . . . a codex, on which the avenging Pontia has set down her arguments with a new stilus" (4.2.748–49). In the text of More's damaged face can be read the consequences of his perverted sexual ethics and also an inversion of the heroic pattern that Milton has constructed for himself: Alexander More as the "warlike Alexander" unequal in battle with an "Amazon" falls foolishly short of the Milton patterned after "Scipio Africanus" (4.2.699–700).

For Michael Lieb, the language of military violence in Milton's attack on More / Du Moulin in the *Second Defence* and *Defence of Himself* expresses Milton's deepest psychological roots. Milton's "sparagmatic mentality"[19] so central to his person and thought is rooted in a deep personal fear of destructive, violent, bodily mutilation, and dismemberment; paradoxically, the trauma of personal injury can be transformed into a retaliatory, generative violence that serves the good by violently destroying evil. Violent language, a weapon against the self, can be turned against the enemy in a violence of regeneration. More/Du Moulin's attack on Milton's person stimulates a violent sparagmatic counterattack that aims to destroy the enemy. This verbal counterattack includes a regenerative self-portrait of the physical Milton, the satirical foil for judging More's scratched face, debased in his battle against a woman. Lieb's important argument expands our understanding of Milton's aggressive self-defensiveness, but the threat to the self must be understood more broadly through Milton's notion of self-esteem in relation to blame. Self-esteem in Milton's thought requires a confident sense of honor in relation to other persons.

Milton's deft satire against More/Du Moulin works the same notion introduced earlier in his self-defense on behalf of the Smectymnuans. We are told that an epic writer must first be a "true Poem," his life a moral text, a "composition, and patterne of the best and honourablest things" (890). Milton's characterization of himself in *Second Defence* as a warrior assumes his person as a true epic poem adversarial to More, a corrupted text. The

Smectymnuan defense clearly affirms the need to experience and to practice all that is praiseworthy, taken together with a "certaine niceness of nature, an honest haughtinesse and self-esteem" (890). The text of the self requires honorable behavior buoyed by self-esteem. This notion helps account for Milton's muscular resistance to blame throughout his works.

But it does not account for the obsessive attack upon More's illicit sexuality expressed in his facial disfiguration. A modern reader may find in this ingenious attack upon More's sexuality an expression of Milton's own complicated uneasiness about sexuality. His personal history included an intense early friendship with Charles Diodati, his dubious renown as the Lady of Christ's College, the celebration of chastity in *Comus*, marital difficulties with his runaway young wife, and a defense of divorce that opened him to charges of libertinism throughout Europe.[20] His defense of his bodily self in *Second Defence* and his inventively scurrilous criticism of More's sexuality, while defending himself against the charge of unchaste language, reveal a text of the self more complicated than he intends. Milton struggles to manage these complications: "He who describes you and your villainies must speak obscenely" (4.2.744). While he admits his uneasiness about his invention of obscenities, he compulsively continues, "Vile, prostituted man, high priest of the stews. There is as much need for a buckle on your private parts as there is one on your lips" (4.2.760). We struggle to find the "true poem" of Milton's ideal self, while suspecting that Milton himself is struggling with a more complicated textuality of the self. Just as Pontia's nails leave the text of More's face "deeply lettered" (4.2.749), Milton's defense against More's censure, his blame, calls forth troubling aspects of himself, and the defense of his physical person resonates with the unresolved history of his sexuality. Not just the unbuckled More invites a consideration of the connections between language and the troublesome physical self. More's blame threatens the integrity of the full self.

That threat evokes a highly problematical self-esteem, which, as we will see, occupies a central place in Milton's conception of the defensive self. Milton's conviction about his own integrity is expressed in his definition of self-esteem in *Defence of Himself.* This self-esteem, which centers the self, should muffle the need for public testimony as well as the need to retaliate against villainous blame, "for a good man, content with himself, does nothing to make himself known. If he needs commendation, he has always with him that virtue which is the best commender; if defence — and, of a truth, he will be attacked not infrequently with envious detractions and slanders — he surrounds himself with his own integrity and the invincible knowledge of rightous deeds, by which, as if by the strongest bulwark and garrison, he both receives the vain attacks of vicious men and frustrates their spears" (4.2.791). Milton invokes this principle to censure More's manipulation of public testimony in his defense against Milton's attack. But Milton's overstated defensiveness, abuse, and revengefulness force the question of why his own self-esteem cannot temper his aggressive retaliation against More's blame. The work's aggression against More ironically undercuts the confidence attendant on self-esteem.

Much earlier in *Reason of Church Government* (1642), Milton stressed self-esteem in rejecting the spirituality of domination and the servile fear that sustained hierarchical church government. Self-esteem is essential in "honourable shame," the reverence for goodness in both oneself and in others. This reverence assumes that the respectful fear of giving offence to good persons encourages the government of virtuous behavior. So does self-esteem: "But there is yet a more ingenuous and noble degree of honest shame, or call it if you will an esteem, whereby men bear an inward reverence toward their own persons" (1.841). Even more than fearing disapproval of good men, the virtuous person "dreads and would blush at" his own self-reproach for offending "the dignity of God's image upon him" and the mark of his redemption that raises him "to a new friendship and filiall relation with God" (1.842). This celebration of self-esteem ensures actions of mutual reverence within a virtuous community honoring God. Such assurance would support the assertion of self as the elected champion of God, but it should also subdue the angry defensiveness turned on Alexander More.

But it did not. Significantly, self-esteem in *Defence of Himself* has taken on a militaristic cast. One's own "integrity" and "invincible knowledge of righteous deeds" build "the strongest bulwark and garrison" (4.2.791) against the onslaught of blame. Earlier, Milton spoke of "pious and just honouring of our selves" as a "radical moisture and fountain head" giving rise to praiseworthy actions. This "moisture" powerfully restrains "the mixture of any ungenerous and unbeseeming motion" (1.841–42) and rises upward from earthy stains of damaging soil. The metaphorical direction here is a spiritual process, in contrast to a military construction walling in the self from the outside. In the one instance, self-esteem encourages an elevating familial relationship with God; in the other, it builds a hard shell against the armies of blame. As Milton's translation of the first eight Psalms would suggest, the onslaught of blame deeply troubled Milton.

This embattled self comes as no surprise to the reader of Milton's controversial prose. Milton, who advised Cromwell to ready himself for the "warfare" of peace after subduing Scotland with the New Model Army, repeatedly invoked the familiar terminology of Christian warfare. Milton and his fellow Puritans regarded themselves as warriors in the archetypal battle fighting for truth, justice, and liberty against tyranny, custom, and oppression. The hated bishops, tyrannical magistrates, and others who constrained liberty were regarded as Satan's followers. Paul provided the spiritual model for these Puritan warriors (Ephesians 6), and the pamphlet wars flaunted the lineaments of this model at every turn. The "warfaring" Christian saints called singly to champion God's cause served God by jointly serving the church and God's chosen people. Both words and deeds were weapons for Puritan warriors; and vehement words advocated and defended vehement actions in the events leading up to and following the civil war. The gift of talent was returned to God through zealous service in His cause; it enlisted the self in championing the people chosen by God and committed to the common good.

At worst, the vehement conviction of Puritan polemics was aggressively self-righteous; at best, it expressed a single-minded clarity and focused pride of purpose. Milton was a complex mixture of both qualities. The Christian warrior coalesced with the chosen prophet opposed to the false prophet[21] and, in Milton's case, with the divine poet and teacher as well. The Lutheran notion of multiple vocations[22] flowered dramatically in Milton's role modulations between poet, prophet, teacher, citizen-pamphleteer, and public servant. Unshaken in his conviction of God's favor, Milton proudly, aggressively, and unrelentingly attacked God's enemies and, out of necessity, defended himself and the chosen people from enemy assaults. Milton's Reformism conscripted his humanism; the warrior and prophet subsumed the classical orator and satirist. Both Old Testament prophecy and classical oratory tutored his polemic.[23] Milton did not abandon his vocation as a poet while writing the works of his "left hand" during the middle years, although, as he tells us more than once, he did leave it standing and waiting. Meanwhile, the Christian warrior carried the battle of words to God's enemies.

Christian warfare framed Milton's notion of self-defense. The cosmic warfare between God and Satan had political and personal consequences after the Fall. The damage to God's image in the individual human caused by Adam's transgression engendered wrong and, as Milton stressed in *Tenure of Kings and Magistrates*, caused damage within the human community. Mutual self-defense became obligatory: "Till from the root of *Adam's* transgression falling among themselves to doe wrong and violence, and foreseeing that such courses must needs tend to the destruction of them all, they agreed by common league to bind each other from mutual injury, and jointly to defend themselves against any that gave disturbance or opposition to such agreement. Hence came Citties, Townes and Common-wealths" (3.199). The "authoritie and power of self-defence and preservation" were a birthright, both "in every one of them, and unitedly in them all"; by covenant they agreed to cede "autority and jurisdiction" to a king or a magistrate as their "Deputies and Commissioners" (3.199) bound by laws devised by the people's chosen representatives. Christian kings and magistrates as protective deputies defended their people

against enemies both from within and without. Just as enemy king-
doms abused liberty and public safety, tyrant kings abused the people's trust. Thus, English "defenders of the faith" became its
enemies, suppressing civil liberties while the church hierarchy
suppressed religious liberty.

By the time Milton joined the Smectymnuans in major battle
against the prelates, he was a confirmed bishop hater and a
defender of shared truth. The bishops were fighting on the papal
side in Christian warfare, enlisted by ambition, pride and greed:
"But if ye take that course which *Erasmus* was wont to say *Luther*
tooke against the Pope and Monks, if yee denounce warre against
their Miters and their bellies, ye shall soon discerne that *Turbant*
of pride which they weare upon their heads to be no *helmet of
salvation*, but the meere mettle of horn-work of Papall jurisdiction; and that they have also this guift, like a certaine kinde of
some that are possest, to have their voice in their bellies, which
being well drain'd and taken downe, their great Oracle, which
is only there, will soone be dumbe, and the *Divine right of
Episcopacy* worthwith expiring, will put us no more to trouble
with tedious antiquities and disputes" (1.953). The worldly thriv-
ing of prelatical entrenchment, power, wealth, and domination
had corrupted the "speciall warfare" (1.951) of the clergyman's
vocation. Leagued with those still fighting that "special warfare," Milton's angry attack on Bishop Hall in *Animadversions,
Upon the "Remonstrants" Defence, against Smectymnuus* had
inspired the anonymous and scurrilous counterattack (probably
by one of Hall's sons) on Milton.

His rejoinder sets the theoretical foundation supporting his literature of self-defense. In defending himself, the champion defends
God's truth shared with the community: "But when I discern'd
his intent was not so much to smite at me, as through me to render odious the truth which I had written, and to staine with
ignominy that Evangelick doctrine which opposes the tradition
of Prelaty, I conceav'd my selfe to be now not as mine own person, but as a member incorporate into that truth whereof I was
perswaded, and whereof I had declar'd openly to be a partaker"
(1.871). A proper self-defense has two sides: one is defending the

participating community; the other is guarding against the enemy within. Later, Milton tells us that Cromwell had first defeated "whatever enemy lay within — vain hopes, fears, desires" before he defeated the enemy on the battlefield: a "Commander first over himself, victor over himself" (4.1.667–68). Reason and conscience defend against the affections, readying the self to defend against external enemies of the community.

Thus, the vocabulary of warfare so pervasive in Milton's works[24] assumes interlocking principles of Christian warfare. Cosmic, political, military, ecclesiatical, and personal spiritual battles are common elements in "Puritan" militancy. Milton never doubted that God was on his side; and, as long as they defended liberty and truth, on the side of his fellow reformers as well. Traditional lineaments in Milton's militancy are no more surprising than his zeal in a time of polarized values. But the roots of his defensiveness seem especially deep even for this historical soil, and his zealous reaction formed against blame seems overstated for one so convinced of the truth. In welcoming a shield specifically against the enemies of blame, Milton's Psalmist seems at odds with an earlier claim in *Apology* that an enemy's blame ironically praises God's champion, that an attack by the bad confirms the good. Milton would "dare not wish to passe this life unpersecuted of slanderous tongues, for God hath told us that to be generally praise'd is wofull" (1.883). Seemingly compulsive strategies of self-defense reverberate throughout Milton's works, sometimes unabashedly, other times more subtly, but too often overstating the stimulus.

Habits of defensiveness tend to overstate threat and set up targets for aggression. These habits have roots running deep in the self. To trace Milton's reaction formed against "blame" is to follow these roots to the base of the rational self in its essential need for appropriate recognition from others. The frenzied attack on Alexander More aggressively displaces a fear expressed repeatedly in Milton's works that recognition will be denied. The belittling, mocking attack on More's incompetent claims of supportive "public testimony" would be less unsettling if Milton were not the ironic victim of his own displaced fear. He contrasts More's unseemly scrambling for "public testimony" to self-esteem, the "strongest bulwark and garrison" against "envious detractions and slanders" (4.2.791). But his own self-esteem, so obtrusive elsewhere, does not protect him from overreaction in his attack on More.

A more searching look at Milton's notion of "blame" — a portmanteau packed with slander, libel, calumny, censure, reproof, accusation, and defamation — is helpful here. Simple blame imputes responsibility for wrongdoing. When motivated by malicious intent to injure and defame, it is slander, libel, or calumny. Publicly expressed, blame assaults reputation for honor bestowed through the approval of others. It *de-fames.* Milton's virulently defensive counterattacks against untrue accusations of sexual promiscuity energetically reject slanderous blame.[25] He defends his good name — his fame for virtue — against evil defamation. Renaissance writers bore the Roman legacy of seeking fame variously; Milton's search was a genuinely sublimated desire for virtuous achievement recognized by the virtuous community, human and divine. His formal defenses beginning with the *Apology* served that end, and his angry vindication of himself against slanderous abuse was predictable.

But the affect too frequently outran the occasion. Admittedly, in the arena of pamphlet warfare, preemptive self-defense and overreaction endorse blame as a postlapsarian compulsion to pursue justice. Blame paid for blame is the crude economy of pamphlet warfare. Milton's defensiveness against suffering blame is the reverse side of his own impulse to cast blame as the necessary instrument of justice. In *Lycidas* we have seen this Reformist tendency in Milton's nature more subtly present as a way of understanding the demands of ultimate judgment. To say that the accidents of arena warfare coarsen this subtle grasp of blame, however, is not enough to account for Milton's public overreaction to blame. An underlying danger shakes the self.

Once again *Lycidas* is instructive. The prospect of death weakens the "spur" of fame that requires disciplined labor, the "uncessant care" (64), necessary for an earthly poetic vocation. Phoebus stifles this objection by defining true fame: it is "no plant that grows on mortal soil" (78). The true "praise" (76) that rewards vocational achievement is the approving "perfect witness of all-judging *Jove*" (82) that outlives death. The implicit corollary to Phoebus's explicit truth is embodied in the poem's praise of Lycidas. Vocational achievement in conformity with divine truth earns lasting praise both from God and his community that spans earth and heaven. Milton's desire for true fame — and his rigorous objection to blame —is reaffirmed frequently and variously later, as in the ironies of a "fit" audience, however "few."

This desire lies deep in the essential social nature of the created self, its individuality paradoxically deformed by loneliness. The keys that open this essential truth are everywhere in Milton's works. One key is the "honourable shame" that he would fix at the center of church discipline in *Reason of Church Government*. In attacking the tyranny of prelatical power and custom, he replaces malign with benign fear: "For where shame is there is fear, but where fear is there is not presently shame" (1.841). Benign fear motivates true "shame," which put differently is "reverence of our elders, our brethren, and friends" (1.840). It is fear of losing their approval. This benign fear ensures pity and virtue, especially by not offending those "put in autority, as a healing superintendence over our lives and behaviours" (1.841). Fully extended, this fear is "religious dred of being outcast from the company of Saints, and from the fatherly protection of God in his Church" (1.841). Here in the individual human's need for mutual acknowledgment — for dialogic recognition — we can find Milton's defensiveness against blame and infamy. Recurring claims that Milton's thought drifted increasingly toward individualism must be tethered by this congenital need for acknowledgment from others.

The self 's other essential root, which is also clearly set out in this discussion of church discipline, is the complementary self-esteem: "But he that holds himself in reverence and due esteem, both for the dignity of Gods image upon him, and for the price of his redemption, which he thinks is visibly markt upon his forehead, accounts himselfe both a fit person to do the noblest and godliest deeds, and much better worth than to deject and defile, with such a debasement and such a pollution as sin is, himselfe so highly ransom'd and enobl'd to a new friendship and filiall relation with God" (1.842). Self-esteem that honors God's image in humans desires congenital friendship and filial relation with God through dialogue. Again, the self that reverentially fears disapproval by other virtuous souls in the church fears even more the stringent self-reproach that acknowledges divine disapproval for sin: the self "dreads and would blush at the reflection of his own severe and modest eye upon himselfe, if it should see him doing or imagining that which is sinfull" (1.842). In sum, self-esteem, honorable shame, and honoring God merge together in the desire for dialogic completion.

That desire for acknowledgment fears loneliness and isolation from other beings, human and divine. A raw nerve in the divorce tracts, this desire seeks cheerful conversation between rational beings; it is a burning, "inbred desire of joyning to it self in conjugall fellowship a fit conversing soul" (2.251). Without mutual acknowledgment and solicitude through "cheerfull and agreeable conversation" (2.248), there is punitive loneliness and isolation that is "dishonourable to the undervalu'd soule of man, and even to the Christian doctrine it self" (2.249). Later in *Paradise Lost* the "native Honor" (4.289) paradoxically clothing the naked Adam and Eve is expressed in courteous conversation, mutual appreciation, shared pleasure, ceremonious respect, lack of embarrassment — in sum, an unbroken communion of mutual acknowledgment. The Fall disfigures this happy conversation, leaving bruised and angry isolation until Eve takes the initiative to heal the lesions between them. To their fallen heirs they leave the same painful task of constructing an agreeable dialogic fit between fallen souls.

The struggle to regain God's acknowledgment is hereditary. Before the Fall the mutual honor between Adam and Eve closely parallels their communion with the living God, both directly and indirectly through angelic go-betweens. An elegant narrative complexity captures the drama of these parallel relationships. The account of the celestial "Colloquy sublime" (8.455), the "trial" (8.447) in which the newly created Adam expresses his natural need for Eve, his "likeness . . . fit help . . . other self" (8.450), is Adam's contribution to his colloquy later with Raphael. Mutual pleasure warms these dialogic exchanges. Raphael's summary speaks for both himself and Adam: "for I attend, / Pleas'd with thy words no less than thou with mine" (8.248–49). God who is "not displeas'd" (398) when Adam, expressing his nature freely, reasons that other creatures cannot satisfy his need for "fellowship . . . fit to participate / All rational delight" (8.389–91). God was "pleas'd" through this colloquy "to try" (8.437) Adam and, in turn, will "please" (8.449) Adam by bringing Eve his natural other self. The natural pleasure between man and woman, between human and angel, and between man and God is for Milton a condition of mutual acknowledgement. Such acknowledgment denies human loneliness while exercising the distinctness of individuality.

The fine balance between individuality and acknowledgment by others rests in self-esteem. God's exercises of Adam's judgment sharpen awareness of himself as the receptacle of God's "Image, not imparted to the Brute" (8.441). Adam's colloquy that pleases God is not the first event that occurs in his conscious history. When "new wakt" (8.253), he surveyed his surroundings and moved with joyful vigor amongst his fellow creatures and, with a gesture ironically, paradoxically predicting the tormented Satan's entry into Eden, asked the sun, then other creatures how he might "know" and "adore" (8.280) his Maker, the "shape Divine" (8.295) that guides him in the vision immediately following. A conscious self-awareness precedes the colloquy that honors his nature in a rational exercise; the newly made human, having "presum'd" (8.356) freely to examine the implications of "solitude" (8.364), honors both himself and the Creator, who explains his Lordship over lower creatures. Such self-esteem earns God's pleased approval. In Eve, self-consciousness appropriate to her nature also precedes completion later through another human being. Discovery of her image in the pool, which she experiences with pleasure, sympathy, and love, is a natural appreciation of her distinct being. Her "vain desire" (8.466) for her image, a potential misdirection of those psychological energies, will be tutored through the approbation of Adam. This connection is ensured first by the warning divine voice, then by the seizing hand of Adam in whose image she is created and in whose acknowledging presence she is to be completed. But the pool first gives back the image of her own value. Just as man's self-esteem lies in recognizing God's Image within, hers lies in honoring the distinct and valuable physical being created in Adam's image as his other self. Memory preserves ("I oft remember" — 8.449) her estimable sense of distinctness and self-esteem.

Self-esteem and true fame are coterminous. Honoring the self necessarily leads to virtuous actions honored by other good beings, human, angelic, and divine. And Milton's own assertive self-esteem and expectation of true fame are constantly on display in his works. Arthur Barker rightly speaks of Milton's "lofty pride"[26] in being elected by God to champion his cause. Clearly, Milton regarded himself as "elected" for special purposes. His poetic, prophetic, pedagogical, and oratorical gifts served these purposes; the expected reward was true fame. As noted above, Milton's defensiveness against blame jars inconsistently with the very resiliency of his self-esteem and conviction of true fame. This inconsistency is directly related to the mentality of trial and judgment explicit in his adversarial vision of existence.

For Milton the defensive self assumes the juridical nature of Christian warfare. Exercised by a "trial" of contraries, the "warfaring" Christian of *Areopagitica* must know the good cleaving to its evil twin (2.515). The juridical ground on which this warfare is fought is God-given, and the purifying exercise or test assumes the principles of justice. Behind this closet oration intended for the English Areopagus lies the traditional notion of the "high court of parliament";[27] and for this tribunal he clarifies the necessary conditions of warfaring. The optimism of *Areopagitica* soft-pedals the punitive meaning of trial, which emerges boldly in the formal defenses in the vocabulary of crime, accusations, charges, judgments, sentences and punishment. In their litigiousness, the prose defenses suffer the irony that Christian pamphlet warfare was fought virulently between rival Christians alleging crimes against the same divine laws and frames of justice.

The notions that Christian life is militant trial and that the threat of judgment and possible punishment await all chosen actions were too frequently enlisted as weapons against the enemy rather than as goads to spiritual improvement as Paul intended. Reformed Christianity straitened the rigors of justice; and historical crises ignited the flames of litigiousness, blamesaying, and defensiveness that fanned the conflagration of Christian warfare. In the instinct to blame the enemies of God, Christian warriors on opposing sides ironically dramatized the universal blameworthiness of the sinful enemy. Seemingly, blame tries all human beings, even God's champions, on both sides of a battle that Milton often fought with virulent aggression.

The recognition expressed in *Lycidas* — that blame is the natural agent of justice, even to the point of impatiently questioning God — leads to a two-edged compulsion to accuse and to defend excessively against defamation. The ironies of overreaction are natural on a polemical battlefield. Milton blisters Alexander More for assembling character witnesses when self-esteem based on personal integrity and a history of righteous deeds should have been the "strongest bulwark and garrison" against attacking "spears" (4.2.71). Self-esteem should have disarmed Milton's need to retaliate by flinging brutal spears at far weaker, errant beings. But Milton's own bulwark was not strong enough in that litigious political warfare, and the irony prevails, only to serve a more profound irony of self-awareness enriching the great poetic works. As we will see in the second half of this discussion, there is much in those works that reflects back on the excesses of the defensive self. For Milton these reflections are intrinsic to a vocational narrative constantly submitted to his interpretation.

Narrativization, Vocational Conviction, and the Centered Self

The defensive self that progressively emerges in the polemical prose between Milton's return from Italy and the restoration of Charles II is most clearly on display in the three prose defenses. For this defensive self, the sense of participatory belonging in a common good is vocational; even in the virulent *Defence of Himself,* where intense personal feeling assumes Milton's public responsibility. Raw aggression and angry retaliation do not blur the devastating satirical focus that, by implication, also defends the defenders of truth and justice. We need to examine these vocational sinews somewhat further before assessing subjectivity represented in the late poetic works, especially against the history of lingering claims about Milton's individualism and retreat from the community as the revolutionary government faltered. Milton's postscript in the revised edition of the *First Defence* (1658) substantially weakens such claims: "Now that my toil has won the richest rewards I had hoped for in this life, I do delight in them with all thankfulness, but at the same time I am earnestly seeking how best I may show not only my own country, to which I devoted all I have, but men of every land and, particularly, all Christian men, that for their sake I am at this time hoping and planning still greater things, if these be possible for me, as with God's help they will." His vocational aspiration stair-steps, first on behalf of England, then "every land," particularly those Christian (4.1.537). Assurance that "English people" are vindicated in "the eyes of all men yet to come" (4.1.536) justifies that aspiration. This revised text expresses satisfaction with Milton's labors for the revolutionary government, which lasted until 1659,[28] whatever his reservations about Cromwell and the Protectorate may have been.

This service to the political community, along with his proud "hoping and planning still greater things" after nearly 20 years in the political arena, 11 in service of the revolutionary government, reveals strong unifying sinews in the vocational commitment that centers his self. That unifying continuity resists Jonathan Goldberg's strained Derridean attempt to find in Milton's self-representations "a range of Miltonic self-productions . . . various Miltons"[29] constantly under "revision and rewriting."[30] He rejects the "narrativization" of Milton acknowledged in Milton scholarship as "always the same, always himself . . . self-unified, self-identical."[31] Goldberg's argument usefully draws attention to the implications of Milton's constant revision, which destabilizes identifications from one self-representation to another. In his Derridean vision of Milton, contingent selves proliferate and presence is endlessly deferred, unsettling the consistency of linear time.

However, the autobiographical texts contested by Goldberg paradoxically resist historical contingencies through a confidence in a divinely inspired and unifying vocational responsibility elided in Goldberg's argument. Milton expects blame on two counts: first, if he fails to attack prelatical abuses with his left hand in "defence" of the church and, second, if he uses virulent language in making that polemical defense. *Reason of Church Government* vindicates the "left hand" (1.808) of prose polemics, which bears Jeremiah's prophetic burden in following "divine inspiration" (1.802). Practice of the right hand is deferred, although "inward prompting" (1.810) has guided its preparation for epic poetry as an "interpreter & relater of the best and sagest things among mine own Citizens throughout this Island in the mother dialect" (1.811–12). He may also be called to divine poetry with "the inspired guift of God" (1.816) to serve the same end. The left hand is thus joined to the right by vocational faith in being chosen to work by God. The temporal moment is contingent, but not the conviction of divine election to serve his community.

To say that the self-representation in the *A Second Defence* may "mark Milton's arrival at the subject position of *Paradise Lost*" admits to sameness in spite of the caveat that this identification is not the "end."[32] Milton's ongoing textual revisions do not erase the consistent pattern of sameness in relation to faithful conviction about vocational inspiration. The ambidexterity established in *Reason of Church Government* underwent revision in the face of historical contingencies most dramatically in *A Second Defence* in his self-representation as a prophet, as an epic writer, and as an epic hero fighting for the English people.[33] The prophetic and poetic vocations merged; the left hand merged with the right; and divine inspiration guided the merger. And the habits of self-defense remained essentially the same. The habit of revision — in which Shawcross finds the compulsion of the "anal retentive"[34] — suggests the defensive constancy of narrative retrospection that defines Milton.

Yet there is a nagging half truth in the claim that Milton's revisions compound historical contingency and destabilize the presumed objectivity in dating individual texts. A revised text can no longer claim to be the same text constructed earlier and that contingency paradoxically confronts the stabilizing vocational conviction. A more flexible "narrativization" is necessary to accommodate the "burden of interpretation."[35] A tenacious impulse in Milton scholarship to find him everywhere written into his texts[36] supports the claim that his works constitute a constant interpretation of the narrative text of the self. And Milton's habit of writing himself into his texts is no less compulsive than his revision of those texts. It is also possible to view each revised text as a preemptive self-defense, one more self-defense by the defender of the defenders.

Goldberg rightly views Milton's self-representations as a "narrativization" of his experience. But Goldberg's narrative of several destabilized selves constantly under revision cannot accommodate Milton's conviction of a divinely inspired vocational narrative running throughout the works. This vocational narrative is identified by interpretive strategies of self-defense simultaneously resisting blame and working to earn fame in the eyes of a virtuous community spanning earth and heaven. As I will suggest in the discussion below, *Paradise Regained* and *Samson Agonistes* are mutually reflecting vocational narratives. They embody Milton's maturest interpretation of the defensive patterns that framed his own vocational experience.

Perspectives indebted to modern hermeneutics are helpful here. Marshall Grossman's examination of *Paradise Lost* in light of Adam and Eve as "Authors to themselves" (3.122) is usefully informed by principles from modern hermeneutics, specifically from Paul Ricoeur. A basic assumption is that actions are to be understood as a narrative text. Adam and Eve are free agents who bear responsibility for their own lives within a teleological, providential order. Though situated in history, they freely exercise "authority . . . to determine the narrative of their lives by judging and choosing."[37] Several principles interact within the hermeneutic model undergirding Grossman's argument: the narrative self is viewed as a text; this text undergoes constant interpretation; it is unified in historical time through habits and disposition; and it constructs itself though language. According to Anthony Kerby's paraphrase of Ricoeur, "the self is generated and is given unity in and through its own narratives, in its own recounting and hence understanding of itself. The self . . . is essentially a being of reflexivity, coming to itself in its own narrational acts."[38] For Kerby there is a "prenarrative," the actual experience in time expressed in the linguistic narration of that experience.[39] By definition, that linguistic narration is a constant interpretive act for, as Ricouer has it quoting Charles Taylor, human beings are "interpretive animals."[40] The self is constituted through that narrative interpretation of its own experiences; and the unifying "connectedness"[41] of that life experience is itself constantly subject to reinterpretation. Also, individual narratives necessarily develop through interconnections with the narratives of others drawn together in many cases by the habits of "participatory belonging,"[42] including the sinews of responsibility by which individuals can count on each other. In this way, a similar sense of the self, its narrative unity, and its interconnectedness to others through vocational responsibility inform the three great works of Milton's maturity.

More richly complex than the focused vocational narratives of *Paradise Regained* and *Samson Agonistes,* the narrative structure of *Paradise Lost* with its vocational subplots embraces the whole cosmic hierarchy of active agents. The discipline of obedient service within a clearly demarcated hierarchy of vocational stations includes all rational beings from the Son of God downward through the orders of angels to Adam and Eve. Their narrative interconnections are vocational: the begotten Son, designated "Vicegerent" (5.609) to enact the Father's will as victor in the heavenly war, as judge of Adam and Eve, then proleptically as deliverer; the archangel Michael, as military general and prophetic dispossessor; the archangel, Gabriel, as military general and commander of the Edenic guard; the angel, Raphael, as divine ambassador and teacher;

the seraph Uriel, stationed as a guard under Gabriel's command; and Adam and Eve, as progenitors of the race and caretakers of Eden with "work . . . assign'd" (9.230–31).

A reflecting mirror in which these interconnecting narratives are to be interpreted is the epic poet's own vocational narrative. Now blind, "fall'n on evil days," defamed by "evil tongues," and "with dangers compast round," the epic poet Milton seeks to define his own dependence upon God's inspiration while writing to a much reduced "fit audience . . . though few" (7.25–31). At the outset he confirms his dependence on God: "What in me is dark / Illumine, what is low raise and support." But his epic purpose is summarily intent to "assert Eternal Providence, / And justify the ways of God to men" (1.22–26). This purpose connects to his claim in *Reason of Church Government* that God moved him to prepare for this epic role; it also connects to *A Second Defence*, where he grasped that epic responsibility with his prose left hand. Now it is to be grasped with his poetic right hand. His self-representation absorbs many of the interconnected events in his vocational narrative: the interpretation of his blindness, the consequences of public service, the threat of death to his person after the Restoration, the experience of defamation, the need for an approving and enlightened readership, and the conviction of divine inspiration necessary to fulfill an epic responsibility. Like the faithful Uriel, fulfilling his vocational responsibility while defending Eden, he serves the divine will with his given talents.

His narrative is also a mirror in which the skewed counter-narrative of Satan is to be interpreted. Few contemporary readers would endorse Blake's claim that Milton belonged to the Devil's party without knowing it. But much in Satan's presence continues to tax us. A subtly ironical self-defense essential to the poem locates in Satan many of the same dangers to which Milton is susceptible. William Riggs points to one, "the explicit comparison of poet and devil in *Paradise Lost* intended by Milton to demonstrate an undeluded recognition of the satanic potential of his poetic act."[43] The parallels follow accordingly. Both poet and devil have high aspirations: one to replace God, the other to praise him with "Things unattempted yet in Prose or Rhyme" (1.16). Milton must defend against the pride to which Satan surrenders; the poet must humbly repeat his need for divine inspiration, constantly alert to his "fear of self-delusion." But "invocation of a heavenly muse" is not "his only defense against presuming too much."[44] Admitting his potential likeness to Satan is the bulwark of his defense.[45]

The ironies work to undermine the defensive bulwark under construction. Milton knows that prideful self-assertion can be found lurking within confessional honesty. And interconnected events in Milton's textual history may resonate even more ambiguously behind the poem. The prideful Satan who rejects the vocational service required of his place in the hierarchy is hardened further by repeated actions. His inner hell is portable: "Which way I fly is Hell; myself am Hell" (4.75). So, too, Alexander More could not avoid himself: "no one do you avoid more willingly than yourself. In vain, poor worthless man, for you fly with yourself, you follow yourself" (4.2.776). More's habitual philandering and violation of vocational responsibilities are self-entrapping; that notion of punishing entrapment within the self informs Milton's later conception of Satan's inner hell. But, if we recall More, we also recall Milton's obsessively defensive reaction to blame accompanied by the dishonesty and injustice of his virulent attack on More. The memory of Milton's defensive overreaction can be found behind Satan's habitually defensive refusal to admit conscientious self-examination, except briefly when first arriving alone in Eden.

The poem, which contains not only Milton's most subtle and paradoxical strategies of self-defense, but also his most searching examination of the psychology of self-defense and blame, can be viewed as an extended interpretation and criticism of elements in his own vocational self-narration. Preemptive strategies that defend against blame paradoxically through their very defensiveness invite further blame. The bold intention to justify God's ways to man anticipates blame, but cannot dissipate it by invoking necessary divine help. He fearfully defends not just against human, but also divine blame, as he later admits: "May I express

thee unblam'd?" (3.3). The poem's representation of Satan's patho-
logical defensiveness addresses the dispositions which Milton
himself cannot flee, but which have defined his own vocational
narrative.

The poem begins *in medias res* with the defeated Satan immobilized in chains and speaking with his cohort Beelzebub. His
immobility ironically undercuts his revengeful vaunt to wage "eternal War" (1.121): he will remain powerless until released by his
omnipotent enemy. The irony is complicated further by his self-
defensive pretence before his followers: "Vaunting aloud, but
rackt with deep despair" (1.126). Genuine shock and fellow feeling for Beelzebub — "But O how fall'n! how chang'd" (1.85) — is
subordinated to overweening political manipulations that self-
defensively serve his pride. The leader of a failed rebellion, he is
the natural target of blame. His preemptive strategy of self-defense
protects not just against political blame and subsequent rebellion,
but also against his own despair and self-censure. Political pretence and self-delusion are mutually sustaining strategies of self-
defense; their apparent success is ironically confirmed when God
releases Satan, now the unwitting agent of the divine plan. Satan's
misreading of this event dramatizes the larger implications of his
own defensiveness and fear of blame. He continues to protect himself against the blame from his followers while blaming God for
his own debacle. The ironies of his self-defensiveness and blame-
setting are only briefly stripped away when, alone in Eden, his
conscience acknowledges his full responsibility for creating his
inner Hell:

> Pride and worse Ambition threw me down
> Warring in Heav'n against Heav'n's matchless King:
> Ah wherefore! he deserv'd no such return
> From me, whom he created what I was
> In that bright eminence, and with his good
> Upbraided none; nor was his service hard.
>
> (4.40–45)

But conscience surrenders to the habits of pridefulness; the
moment quickly passes; and his Hell deepens.

In *Paradise Lost* Milton's own disposition to self-defense and his affective response to blame are contextualized as shared qualities of fallen psychology, first dramatized in Satan, then in Adam and Eve. The breach between Adam and Eve can be bridged only when they stop blaming each other as a defense against admitting their respective guilt for the Fall. The fear of reprisal that follows after slaking their new born lust generates their first marital argument. Each defends the self by blaming the other. Adam berates Eve for her solitary wandering; then Eve, "mov'd with touch of blame" (9.1143), retaliates that he did not command her to remain. The narrative voice pinpoints their self-defensive refusal to take responsibility for their actions:

> Thus they in mutual accusation spent
> The fruitless hours, but neither self-condemning,
> And of thir vain contést appear'd no end.
>
> (9.1187–89)

The quasi-legal vocabulary of accusation and condemnation predicts the Son's judgment later. Then, faced with the vicegerent Judge, the defendant Eve "with shame nigh overwhelm'd" (10.159) readily admits her own responsibility: "The Serpent me beguil'd and I did eat" (10.162). Her "abasht" (10.161) simplicity and the juxtaposed "Serpent me" that identifies her with Satan contrast starkly with the tenaciously self-defensive strategies of Adam. He still shifts the blame to her and, more slantingly, to God:

> This Woman whom thou mad'st to be my help,
> And gav'st me as thy perfet gift, so good,
> So fit, so acceptable, so Divine,
> That from her hand I could suspect no ill,
> And what she did, whatever in itself,
> Her doing seem'd to justify the deed;
> She gave me of the Tree, and I did eat.
>
> (10.137–43)

Adam's distribution of the blame between Eve and God weds betrayal to impiety. Such tenacious defensiveness in its stark contrast to Eve's bare, almost breathless confession works to suppress his greater responsibility for their fall. Eve is the target of his immature name-calling: "that bad Woman" (10.837), "thou Serpent" (10.867), "this fair defect / Of nature" (10.891–92). A sophistical argument holds the creator at least partially responsible for the creature's actions:

> Did I request thee, Maker, from my Clay
> To mould me Man, did I solicit thee
> From darkness to promote me, or here place
> In this delicious Garden?
>
> (10.743–46)

But Adam's evasive drive to blame others stifles his emerging conscience until the humbled Eve, in a selfless attempt to take all responsibility upon herself, delivers him from his compulsion. His recognition that they must "no more contend, nor blame / Each other, blam'd enough elsewhere" (10.958–59) is an essential step in the path towards a just distribution of responsibility. Self-defensiveness must yield to conscience, to reasoned practicality and, most important, to mutual love. Unlike the unrepentant Satan, Adam by following Eve's example accepts responsibility for his actions.

Just as the narrator's experience is defined in terms of Satan's, so are Adam and Eve's. Throughout *Paradise Lost* one narrative reverberates against another through patterns of likeness and difference. The basic cosmic opposition between God and Satan is contested in the experience of Adam and Eve. Satan's defection from God leads to heavenly war, then to his infiltration of Eden and the defense attempted by both angels and humans against the destructive enemy. The poem examines how individual narratives necessarily develop various defenses against both internal and external threats while performing their God-given responsibilities. The poet's own preemptive self-defense against blame for exercising his vocational gifts assumes that defense is the natural posture for a fallen being caught in a metaphysical battle between good and evil. Whether or not individuals deserve blame or fame for how they use their gifts in their vocational roles depends on how well they interpret the implications of their developing narratives. The chastened Adam wisely reasons that he and Eve can still fulfill their vocational responsibility as progenitors of the race by assessing their shared failure properly, but they must control their destructive likenesses to Satan. Likewise, the narrator, through preemptively admitting his likenesses to Satan, must manage the residual patterns of his own pridefulness and aggression in fulfilling his role as an inspired creator.

Retrospective Ironies in the Late Poems

In the two companion poems, *Paradise Regained* and *Samson Agonistes*, the vocational narratives are more narrowly focused than in *Paradise Lost*, while reflecting further on many of the same issues. In each poem, a lone individual is tempted to betray a major vocational responsibility. Standing alone, each must defend the self while striving to interpret the divine will directing his actions in serving a common good. Emptied of previous divine knowledge, the rationally composed Jesus of *Paradise Regained* must patiently stand and wait, first "revolving in his breast" (1.185) his previous experience, inwardly anticipating the nature of his vocational role and assessing the implications of Satan's temptations. Samson's task is darkly discolored by earlier failures leading to humiliation, depression, and imprisonment by an enemy nation. Milton's complex diptych, in playing its differing histories and responses against each other, further reflects his own experience of the defensive self.

In *Paradise Regained* Milton pointedly constructs the adversarial context in which the vocational narrative is to be told. The Spirit has led Jesus "Into the Desert, his Victorious Field / Against the Spiritual Foe" (1.9–10). He will gain the "Victory and the Triumph" (1.173). This is one more major battle in the cosmic war first fought in heaven in *Paradise Lost*. The focused central action is "one man's firm obedience fully tried / Through all temptation, and the Tempter foil'd" (1.4–5). The exercising "triall" of virtue that "purifies" the "true warfaring Christian" (*CPW* 2.515) must exercise the pure as well. In *Paradise Lost* Adam and Eve are tried before and after the fall, and in *Paradise Regained* the Father's plan for the pure Son follows accordingly:

> But first I mean
> To exercise him in the Wilderness;
> There he shall first lay down the rudiments
> Of his great warfare, ere I send him forth
> To conquer Sin and Death the two grand foes,
> By Humiliation and strong Sufferance.
>
> (1.155–60)

Satan is allowed to try the Son by "whate'er may tempt, whate'er seduce, / Allure, or terrify, or undermine" (1.178–79). Obedient and patient like Job before him, Jesus must maintain a virtuous defense against the evil "Adversary" (1.33). The "great warfare" mixes defense with offense; and the new hero will be "far abler to resist" (1.151) the "stratagems of Hell, / And devilish machinations" (1.180–81) than even the heroic Job. The Adversary's goal is clear: he would "subvert whom he suspected rais'd / To end his Reign on Earth so long enjoy'd" (1.124–25). He would prevent Jesus from performing his vocation, the "glorious work . . . to save mankind" (4.634–35) by first raising Eden in the "waste Wilderness" (1.7).

The mode of Jesus' defensive resistance governs the drama in the work. He is the composed center of action deliberately and patiently awaiting the next stage of his progress. Acted upon by Satan, he must engage rationally the issue of each temptation, such as the attractions of classical learning to his studious temperament, while resisting the dangers of inappropriate emotional responses that would place him at risk. To overreact impatiently, intemperately, and angrily — as Milton himself did earlier to Alexander More — is to become a victim by allowing Satan, not God, to set the terms of his existence. The strength of his defense is rooted in his reflective understanding of his own experience.

For this reason Satan's temptations are contextualized as current events in Jesus' full narrative, beginning with the Annunciation and, proleptically, ending with the Passion. Jesus can shoulder his vocational responsibility only by interpreting the God-given implications of each event in his personal narrative. Trial by Satan's temptations unfolds within that larger history and its continuing interpretive experience. We first meet Jesus in the desert, where the Spirit has led him. He is "Musing and much revolving in his breast" (1.185) the events of his experience:

> O what a multitude of thoughts at once
> Awak'n'd in me swarm, while I consider
> What from within I feel myself, and hear
> What from without comes often to my ears,
> Ill sorting with my present state compar'd.
>
> (1.196–200)

He recalls his nature as a child ("Serious to learn and know, and thence to do / What might be public good" — 1.203–04), his reading of the "Law of God" (1.207), and his trip to the temple and discussion with the teachers of the Law. He also recalls his consideration of military means to free his Israelite nation from the "*Roman* yoke" (1.217) before concluding that initially "winning words to conquer willing hearts" is "more human, more heavenly" (1.221–22). And he recalls his conversation with Mary about his "matchless Sire" (1.233); he also recalls her report of the Annunciation and the birth at Bethlehem followed by the Magi's visit. His most recent recollection is baptism by John, the Dove's descent, and his endorsement by the Father's voice. In sum, the Jesus we meet is actively interpreting his own narrative experience in light of his vocation.

Milton's received assumptions about vocation account for much in the poem's narrative structure. The first event is Jesus' baptism, a divinely staged public event at which John's "witness" (1.26) of Jesus' greater role is confirmed by both the Spirit and the Father. Two responses to this event immediately follow, one by Satan in council, the other by God to Gabriel before the full angelic audience. Then, Jesus himself interprets the baptism in light of his vocational considerations to date. Thus, mutually interdependent narratives by Satan, God, and Jesus place Jesus' attempt to understand his God-given vocational duties within the polarized opposition between good and evil. Led by the Spirit and attentive to divine directions, he intends to serve God by furthering the public good. The interconnections between his narrative and those narratives of the members of the nation he intends to serve, such as Mary's and the Galilean fishermen's, also shape the poem's structure as a vocational narrative.

All told, we are given four different reports of Jesus' baptism included within separate, but interconnected narratives. There is the poet's own account (1.18–32), the first event in the poem's containing narrative; next, Satan's report to the hellish council (1.70–85) while recalling the history of his defensive espionage since the prophecy that Mary's seed would bruise his head; then, Andrew and Simon's brief examination (2.50–53) in relation to their own attempt to interpret Jesus' significance; and, finally, Mary's second hand account gathered from persons present at the Baptism and the "pondering oft, and oft to mind / Recalling" (2.105–06), her unique motherhood. By fixing this event as the point where several related narratives intersect, Milton captures the interconnectedness of human and divine events by which individuals participate in communities. And this interconnectedness captures how the lives of heroic members, whose vocational presence serves the whole community, become present in other narratives.

In short, these selves, through participatory belonging, share in that experience as part of their own narratives. The poet will "tell of deeds / Above Heroic, though in secret done" (1.14–15), offering a divinely inspired narrative beginning with the public baptism of Jesus. Subsequent undisclosed events related to Satan's temptation of Jesus, by implication, will become part of the narrative experiences of his readers, just as the narratives of Job and Elijah formed parts of Jesus' experience. As a vocational narrative, the poem embodies the ways that duties within a vocation serve the community and its common good, just as the inspired poet's narration of "unrecorded" deeds (1.16) will serve his English readers. Telling of these "deeds" is the most recent event in the poet's own narrative recalled at the outset: "I who erewhile the happy Garden sung" (1.1). His vocational narrative also belongs to the community.

The "unrecorded" deeds are an exemplary, virtuous defense against temptation in preparation for his "great warfare" (1.158), the "glorious work" (4.634) of his vocation. His "firm obedience . . .

defeated and repuls't" (1.4, 6) the Tempter. The military *"defeated"* alludes to the "great warfare," the adversarial opposition; so does the multifarious *"repulst,"* which also includes strong refusal, rebuttal, rebuke (OED). Voluntary obedience, in conforming the human to the divine will, is the muscle that strengthens deed and word; it assumes Job's exemplary "patience" (1.425) that recalls its root, *patior*, to suffer events in time. Like Job, the patient Jesus suffers Satan's temptation while deliberating on his service to God. Obedience to God's will requires the habit of waiting patiently while interpreting the God-given meaning of temporal events. This habit enables the temperate Jesus to repel temptation and not overreact to the tempter's evil even when his passions are moved. Jesus repels Satan "temperately" (2.378), "patiently" (2.432), "calmly" (3.43), "unmov'd" (3.386; 4.109), "sagely" (4.285). Yet he "fervently" (3.121) repels Satan's accusation that pursuit of glory motivates the Father and thereby would justify the Son's own worldly pursuit. His authoritative command that Satan "reason" (3.122) to true understanding of divine intention subjects his own righteous anger to the discipline of truth. His passionate, scornful reaction to Satan's impiety is disciplined, but not suppressed:

> Who for so many benefits receiv'd
> Turn'd recreant to God, ingrate and false,
> And so of all true good himself despoil'd,
> Yet, sacrilegius, to himself would take
> That which to God alone of right belongs.
>
> (3.137–41)

As Milton learned in his scornful attack on Alexander More, an implicit temptation to overreaction is lurking here. Later, Jesus "answer'd with disdain" (4.170) the impudent temptation that he worship Satan:

> I never lik'd thy talk, thy offers less,
> Now both abhor, since thou hast dar'd to utter
> Th'abominable terms, impious condition
>
> (4.171–73)

The anger, hatred, and disgust within righteous scorn naturally modulate into disdain; but disdain can easily escalate to prideful, obsessive defensiveness. Elsewhere, Jesus repels temptation with more protracted argument; here the brevity of his fervent and disdainful responses constrains the danger of excessive counterattack. He is a king "who reigns within himself, and rules/ Passions, Desires, and Fears" (2.466–67). That reign is defensively disciplined against overreaction by obedience to God and the habit of patient self-reflection.

Jesus' restrained defense consistently derails Satan. A defining irony is that Satan's temptations of political power and military glory fall lifeless because the reflective Christ has already rejected these options. Even before Satan tracks him down in the wilderness, Jesus has resolved that the first task in rescuing Israel from the "*Roman* yoke" (1.217) is not military deeds, but "winning words to conquer willing hearts / And make persuasion do the work of fear" (1.222–23). Similarly, his own experience of thoughtful self-rule leads naturally to the notion of true kingship, the personal rule of virtue and sense of public responsibility that easily repel Satan's temptation of kingly wealth:

> But to guide Nations in the way of truth
> By saving Doctrine, and from error lead
> To know, and knowing worship God aright,
> Is yet more Kingly.
>
> (2.473–76)

Had the fallen Satan been patient, self-reflective, and obedient to God's will and not his own, he would have been able to interpret the principle of spiritual kingship, and would know that his temptations to earthly glory and empire would prove untimely. Instead, his fallen nature ensures his ironic failure when growing frustration hastens intemperate, self-defeating overreaction. By contrast, he faces a hero of patient deliberation, who habitually takes the time to interpret events for evidence of God's will in his own developing vocational narrative.

When Milton "added" *Samson Agonistes* to *Paradise Regained* (1671),[46] he arranged the two vocational narratives to reflect on each other; and they mirror both compelling parallels and bold differences in their two heroes that must be interpreted.[47] God publicly confirms both deliverers as superior members of their communities: Jesus at his baptism and Samson at his birth. These communities stand in adversarial relationships with dominating colonial powers, the Romans and the Philistines; these adversarial relationships, in turn, are contained within larger cosmic confrontations between God and Satan and Dagon. Consequently, both are the targets of resulting espionage and sabotage: Jesus by Satan, Samson by the woman of Timna and Dalila. Both are tempted to disclose private knowledge essential to fulfilling their vocations while they undergo an experience of absorbing inwardness. And both deliverers must defend against temptations from without and within to betray their responsibilities to deliver their communities from old oppressions. Death awaits both heroes after delivering their communities from oppression.

The differences between the two works pivot on Samson's failure and its problematic aftermath. For the flawless Jesus, emptied of his divine knowing, temptation is an exercise in understanding his mission to create a new spirituality, the nonviolent paradise within. For Samson temptation has precipitated a fall, followed by a later battery of temptations repelled, but only with new interpretive difficulties. The fallen Samson is guilt-ridden, desperate, and constrained by God's enemies; reconstructed, he kills himself while violently killing thousands of his Philistine enemies. Whereas Jesus unerringly awaits divine prompting before acting, Samson's responses are less transparent. Some readers see in his punishment of the Philistines the climax of his divinely inspired renovation, even regeneration; other readers doubt that he is divinely inspired at all, only pridefully willful and violently revengeful. Recent Milton scholarship has perceived a widening field of indeterminacies in the text, contributing further to what Barbara Lewalski has called "a cacophony of interpretations."[48]

In particular, the Samson spiritually regenerated through temptation, and climactically heroic, has suffered a major frontal challenge. Joseph Wittreich's seminal argument — that Milton viewed Samson as a violent, tragic failure — invoked an unsettled, traditional debate about Samson based on difficulties in the biblical text and the history of contested interpretation, especially in Milton's own time.[49] For Wittreich, Milton's Samson is a prideful, violent, savage murderer, not a regenerated champion of God. Samson's delusion that God moved him to pull down the Philistine temple is undercut first in the biblical text, then in Milton's play. Neither his "rousing motions" (*SA,* 1382) before going to the temple nor his stance before destroying it "as one who pray'd / Or some great matter in his mind revolv'd" (1637–38) proves God's endorsement. After all, Samson had been wrong before when bodily desire bent his logic, wrongly concluding that it was "lawful" (222) to marry Dalila. In his second major study of the poem, Wittreich approached the Samson story as a historically contested field of meanings for Puritan soul-searching after the restoration. The uncertainties and ambiguities perceived in the received Samson story serve Milton's complex interpretation of his culture's recent failures.[50] Milton's condemnation of Samson's prideful delusion about God's inward motions and his resulting mass murder rules out the renovation and regeneration found by others in the text.

Paradoxically, Wittreich's important argument about the historically conflicted perceptions of the text allows widely differing interpretations of Samson's actions. For example, Milton's text neither confirms nor denies God's presence in Samson's "rousing motions" leading him to the Philistine temple and mass killing. David Loewenstein argues plausibly that the 1671 diptych incorporates two possible, but opposed choices available to Milton's continuing radical Puritan politics. One choice is Jesus' inward rule through humility and persuasive language. The other choice, consistent with Milton's continuing iconoclasm, justifies Samson's violent, revengeful destruction of enemy culture.[51] Michael Lieb does not find this ambivalence in Milton's approval of Samson's climactic killing of the Philistines. That act expresses the "sparagmatic mentality," the streak of violence running throughout the works of Milton, who is temperamentally disposed to celebrate Samson's multiple killing.[52] But by effectively extracting *Samson*

Agonistes from the diptych structure that mirrors one poem in the other, Lieb does not engage the ambiguities established by Milton's chosen structure, which are incumbent upon the reader to interpret. Even if, as Lieb believes, the Samson poem was written much earlier during the period of the prose defenses, its oppositional placement in the 1671 volume raises questions about violence.

The interpretive difficulties generated by the play invite open questions not only about Milton's attitude to Samson and about Milton himself, but also about his God, whose actions can vex any interpreter. Even if God does not endorse Samson's violent revenge, God could prevent it; instead, God seems to use it; at the very least, allows it. God's apparent complicity chafes against the divine intention to establish the spiritual "Eden rais'd" (1.7) by the nonviolent Jesus in *Paradise Regained.* Not unreasonably, some readers may wonder if Samson is, after all, not tempted beyond what he is able to bear. If so, God's justice is at stake. God creates his basic disposition, selects a place for him, and sends an angel to prepare his mother. His likenesses to Jesus are obvious; the differences raise questions. Jesus is inherently studious, thoughtful, cerebral: a natural-born teacher who thinks before he acts, whose pleasures are of the mind, not the body. By contrast, Samson has the kinds of stunning physical gifts that magnetically attract public attention: an athletic warrior with vast sexual appeal, superhuman strength, explosive violence, and dramatic bravery. The directions of their respective vocational paths seem overly determined by their divinely created natures. Samson thinks he is moved by God to marry a Philistine woman; he obeys, but clearly against the competing wishes of his Israelite parents:

> they knew not
> That what I motion'd was of God; I knew
> From intimate impulse, and therefore urg'd
> The Marrriage on; that by occasion hence
> I might begin *Israel's* Deliverance,
> The work to which I was divinely call'd;
> She proving false, the next I took to Wife

(O that I never had! fond wish too late)
Was in the Vale of *Sorec, Dalila.*

(221–29)

Sexual appeal would at first seem to serve divinely ordained vocational responsibility; and no evidence from the poem blames
Samson for the infidelity of his Timnan wife. The line of argument that leads him to another Philistine woman seems much
less bent when we add together his given sexual nature, his
intended obedience to God's motions, and his changed circumstances. A maker of riddles, Samson is not without intelligence,
unlike the gormless Harapha. But he lacks the studious, thoughtful nature, and scriptural resources that yield precedents like
Elijah and Job. His vocational task is constrained by the liabili-
ties and limitations of the old dispensation. In contrast, the pure
Jesus seems far less likely to fall unjustly as the victim to his own
nature.

Milton's own relationship to Samson likewise vexes interpretation. A gifted blind hero in defeat, frustrated earlier in serving
his nation's misguided leaders, his actions now circumscribed
by the enemies of his God — the parallels are there, even if merely
accidental, or misleading. In the much-prized *First Defence,*
Samson was viewed as a hero who, either "prompted" by God
or by his own "valor" (4.1.402),[53] defied his nation's leaders to
destroy a tyrannical enemy. For John Guillory the play's central
issues are vocational, and Milton's identification with Samson
includes "*ressentiment* of blindness or defeat" plus "the self-
sacrifice of the artist."[54] Entangling strings are attached to such
identification and, the closer the identification, the more vexing
are Samson's sense of guilt and revengeful violence. Nevertheless,
Samson's reconstructed self-esteem determines a necessary interpretive pivot for measuring Milton's approval of his flawed hero.

A potent irony governs the vocational narrative so intrusive
in Milton's works. His dramatization of shared human sinfulness
and guilt in *Paradise Lost* and in *Samson Agonistes* contrasts with
his own personal evasiveness earlier. His two vocational sonnets
are primary examples of this evasion, which is encouraged by his

conviction of being chosen by God. In contrast, Donne's sonnet sequence connected devotional exercises of intense self-censure, presenting "an image of a soul working out its salvation in fear and trembling."[55] Such is not the case with Milton, whose individual sonnets mostly address occasions and virtuous exemplars. His sonnet on his twenty-third birthday ("How soon hath Time") defends against the accusation of idleness by shifting the responsibility to God. Milton's "hasting days fly on with full career" and "no bud or blossom show'th" (3–4); but his "great task-Master," he concludes, presides over his slow ripening. Vocational work has been deferred by God, not sinfully neglected by Milton. Characteristically, his self-defense denies guilt and extracts the tooth from potential blame. In the nineteenth sonnet ("When I consider"), vocational frustration knows fear of divine punishment in the face of time's passage. The biblical "murmur" (9) that God, who has not used Milton's "work" or his "gifts" (10), may punish his lack of productivity ("Doth God exact day-labor, light denied" — 7), is calmed by patience, but not before the return of doubts about God's justice that we saw emerging in *Lycidas*. Once again, self-defense evades guilt by shifting responsibility to God. But Samson's admission of personal failure as a cause of frustrated ability prevents such a shift. Just how much Milton is to be identified with Samson is one more indeterminacy in the play; nonetheless, in the late poetry his repeated attention to the psychology of admitted failure contrasts sharply with his own earlier evasive strategies of self-defense. Viewed in retrospect, these strategies can be interrogated as the prideful struggle to maintain self-esteem and avoid accountability in the face of mounting difficulties.

The recurrent issue of self-esteem in Milton's thought is crucial here. In *Defence of Himself* (1655), he berates Alexander More's scramble to offer public testimony as a failure of self-esteem, suppressing the irony that his own overreaction to blame calls his own self-esteem in question. Self-esteem is implicitly at stake in the nineteenth sonnet, written sometime around 1655[56] when Milton was sorely tried by enemy blame and personal tragedy. Inevitably, Milton's wide-ranging examination of trial and

312   *The Self in Early Modern Literature*

defense in the great poetry addresses self-esteem. In *Paradise Lost* the unfallen Eve applies Milton's principle of necessary personal trial in justifying her separation from Adam. Against Adam's argument that a seducer's approach might shame her, she counters that though "single" and not "combin'd" (9.339) with Adam she will possess "like defense" (9.325):

> But harm precedes not sin: only our Foe
> Tempting affronts us with his foul esteem
> Of our integrity: his foul esteem
> Sticks no dishonor on our Front, but turns
> Foul on himself.
>
> (9.327–31)

Milton flailed More with a similar argument that true self-esteem gives immunity to foul esteem from others. The ironies eventually entangle Eve: inexperience is weakness; a "single" defense *should* sometimes be "combin'd"; increased self-esteem can increase vulnerability to pride. These ironies serve the larger irony that her successful argument exercises Adam' s own self-esteem. Earlier, Raphael's "contracted brow" (8.560) telegraphed his fear of Adam's disposition to uxoriousness, and the terms of his warning against "subjection" are clear: "Oft-times nothing profits more / Than self-esteem, grounded on just and right / Well manag'd" (8.571–73). Lacking esteem for his role as Head, Adam fails to defend his place in the hierarchy against her temptation. Eve, stripped of self-esteem, fallen at Adam's feet, and "vile" (10.971) by her own cruel judgment prepares us for the desperately self-loathing Samson, who hates his "vile" folly (377).

And the parallels that hinge *Paradise Regained* to *Samson Agonistes* measure Samson's despair by the exemplary self-esteem of Jesus. His composed self-rule and sense of vocational direction confirm a self-esteem exercised but never shaken by Satan. By contrast, Samson bitterly indicts his lack of wise "command" (57) over his physical person. He might withstand strong drink, but not Dalila's subtly managed attractions:

> But what avail'd this temperance, not complete
> Against another object more enticing?

What boots it at one gate to make defense,
And at another to let in the foe,
Effeminately vanquish't?

(558–62)

The blind, enchained, and self-loathing Samson is thus a diametric opposite to the exemplary Jesus.

But it follows that Samson's renewed self-esteem, by resisting his tempters, likens him to Jesus. We are expected to approve the beginnings of that renewal in his admission of personal fault and to find in the poem, as John Shawcross puts it, "Samson's recovery of self through trial and repentance, his renovation."[57] Claims that the revengeful Samson remains imprisoned by his pride cannot account adequately for our identification with his self-esteem reconstructed through a series of temptations perhaps designed, at least allowed by God. Commendably, Samson admits his guilt, refuses to blame God, and defends himself against the temptation that earlier led to his failure. Most important, his affirmation that his "trust is in the living God" (1140), as Stanley Fish emphasizes, is the essential constant in Milton's thought.[58] Like Manoa and the Chorus, we may struggle laboriously to comprehend fully the meaning of Samson's experience, but must recognize the importance of his reconstruction. Divine intention that allows Satan to tempt Jesus in *Paradise Regained* allows the second round of Samson's temptations. Attraction to Dalila is the pivot, and he must prove that he can defend the "gate" through which he "let in the foe." Samson is given the opportunity to revisit the site of his failure; Manoa's temptation prepares him; Harapha's allows him to connect his regained strength and conviction to his faith in God. Laudable reconstruction of his self-esteem occurs before Samson's "rousing motions" and decision to go to the temple.

The reconstruction takes place within his vocational narrative. Defaulting on his vocational responsibilities defines his shame, guilt, and despair; and, even though his self-esteem has been temporarily stripped away, a bedrock identification with Israel and its God remains. That bedrock is visible in his defense against temptation, first against Manoa, a member of his own Israelite nation, then against Dalila and Harapha of the enemy Philistines. Manoa offers him not pleasure, but cessation of painful imprisonment and enforced labor. Samson stands on the bedrock of his vocational identity, a deliverer called by God, when he repels temptation in terms of service to nation and obligation to work. Intense shame for failing the nation and guilt for failing God invite punishment: "let me here, / As I deserve, pay on my punishment; / And expiate, if possible, my crime" (488–90). He had "brought scandal / To Israel" (453–54) that weakened the faith of others. Returned home, he would be a "Vain monument of strength" (570), a living reminder of failed promise that could weaken the members of his nation further. Remaining responsibility to Israel and to God is still central to his person, along with his need to avoid idleness and to perform responsible work, to "drudge and earn my bread" (573) as part of justified punishment for vocational crimes. Repelling Manoa's temptation confirms the vocational core of his self.

Dalila's temptation penetrates that core in the most intensely personal terms. Created a charged physical being with a vocational mission, the obedient Samson, faithful to what he perceived to be God's command, had married the Timnan woman, then wrongly followed his powerful sexual attraction to Dalila. Placed at risk by his own physicality, the deluded champion of Israel and God, by submitting to an enemy agent, first unwittingly then involuntarily served the Philistines and Dagon. Dalila's temptation matches her sexual desire and "bonds of civil Duty / And of Religion" (853–54) against his: Samson in her Philistine bed while satisfying her sexual desire would be a living monument to her Philistine achievement. Both know that simple touch will ignite powerful mutual attraction suppressed only when Samson threatens violent, methodical dismemberment:

> *Dalila.* Let me approach at least, and touch thy hand.
> *Samson.* Not for thy life, lest fierce remembrance wake
> My sudden rage to tear thee joint by joint.
>
> (951–53)

Memory blames his failure on her betrayal; self-defense fights fire with fire; and a warrior's explosive violence overrules sexual desire.

Blame serves an irony here. Unlike Adam in *Paradise Lost,* a self-loathing Samson has quickly stifled the impulse to blame God:

> But peace, I must not quarrel with the will
> Of highest dispensation, which herein
> Haply had ends above my reach to know:
> Suffices that to mee strength is my bane,
> And proves the source of all my miseries.
>
> (60–64)

Nor will he participate vicariously in Manoa's blame: "Appoint not heavenly disposition, Father" (373). He clearly blames himself for not defending the "gate" (560) against the enemy, Dalila. Yet, like Adam's against Eve, his compulsive name calling against Dalila defensively shifts the blame to "my Traitress" (725), "Hyaena" (748), "sorceress" (817) "viper" (1001). The rage awakened by her offered touch expresses the core of his charged physical person, the bodily medium divinely created for his vocational mission. The ironic dubiety of blame here captures his emergent self-esteem while excessively censuring Dalila's betrayal in order to repel his powerful sexual desire, the source of his failure. Invoked by Dalila's need, his desire would betray him again.

Having closed the bodily gate and "Repuls't" (1006) Dalila, he has reconstructed the self-esteem necessary for a champion of God. His easy victory over Harapha, Dagon's champion, confirms his defense against the Philistine Dalila and further exercises self-command fortified by "trust . . . in the living God" (1140). He challenges Harapha to fortify himself with devotions to Dagon before testing in combat "whose God is strongest" (1155). He counters Harapha's scorn for his earlier failures with "confidence" (1174) in God's pardon. Without hesitation, he assumes that he is God's champion and his own body a medium of God's strength. Harapha withers in the face of such confidence, and God's Israelite champion categorically defeats Dagon's Philistine champion.

The reconstruction of Samson's self-esteem is a step in the vocational narrative that concludes with the destruction of the Philistine temple. The narrative invites interpretation by several audiences. The Israelite chorus is present at all three temptations, at the events preceding Samson's departure for the temple, and at the report of its destruction by the Philistine messenger. Both the Chorus's evolving interpretation through dialogue with Samson and its summary conclusions will enter Israel's oral culture. Manoa comes and goes in the play: first, through report as a participant in Samson's early narrative; later, as an agent for his ransom; finally, as the custodian of Samson's remains and of the prospective Israelite shrine interpreting Samson's heroic deeds:

> Home to his Father's house: there will I build him
> A Monument, and plant it round with shade
> Of Laurel ever green, and branching Palm,
> With all his Trophies hung, and Acts enroll'd
> In copious Legend, or sweet Lyric Song.
>
> (1733–37)

The audience intended for this interpretation, which is embodied in visual artifacts, written text and song, will be "valiant youth" (1738) and "Virgins" (1741), the new generation to revive Israel. The poem's readers form the largest audience. And we must approach Samson's vocational narrative not only in terms of the interpretations it generates within the Israelite nation, however uncomprehending these several audiences, but also in relation to the biblical text interpreted by Milton's text.

Samson's self-esteem is necessarily an issue in the interrelated questions about interpretation raised by the two companion poems. The broad range of questions includes the role of biblical texts, events in the narrative, the interpretations by participants in the action, the interplay between the two poems, and the reader's uncertainties. Mary Ann Radzinowicz has pointed to the "hermeneutic combat"[59] between Jesus and Satan in *Paradise Regained* in their respective applications of biblical texts. Dayton Haskin has claimed that Milton's "burden"[60] of interpreting indeterminacy in biblical texts weighs heavily in both poems, especially in *Samson Agonistes*. More broadly, Stanley Fish finds a "radically indeterminate"[61] and mysterious Samson who resists our need to interpret his actions, but who convinces us of his faith in God. Much debate on the poem continues to center on the vexing task of interpreting Samson's motivation. But even if Samson's various inner motions are not God-given, Samson has faced down those who would deter him from acting out his sense of duty to God. The exercises in temptation have reconstructed the bulwark of self-esteem, which Milton found so lacking in Alexander More.

Joseph Wittreich's argument that a prideful, murderous Samson deserves God's punishment for destroying the Philistine temple wrongly takes us down a darkened interpretive path: that God, after deliberately allowing conditions for Samson's reconstruction as Israel's deliverer, allows him to perform a punitive mass murder as his own punishment. Instead, Samson's reconstructed and defended self-esteem leads in a different interpretive direction. Self-esteem would be a necessary foundation for the much-contested "spiritual regeneration"[62] in Samson, although its presence gives no interpretive guarantees that this more fulfilled state has developed. Instead, its presence allows Ashraf Rushdy's middle ground interpretation that Samson — however incomplete spiritually — willingly obeys God's command to act as a divine agent at the Philistine temple.[63] Self-esteem also leads back to questions about Milton's own possible identification with Samson, a final consideration in the above discussion of self-defense. Samson's hard retrospective eye censures the pride in competitive aggression and in God's favor that blinded his defense of vocational duty:

> after some proof
> Of acts indeed heroic, far beyond
> The Sons of *Anak*, famous now and blaz'd,
> Fearless of danger, like a petty God
> I walk'd about admir'd of all and dreaded
> On hostile ground, none daring my affront.
> Then swoll'n with pride into the snare I fell
> Of fair fallacious looks, venereal trains,
> Soft'n'd with pleasure and voluptuous life.

> (526–34)

By stark contrast, the thoughtful composure of Jesus serves God's glory by stifling the prideful impatience vulnerable to destructive annoyance from others. The "perfect man," Jesus never lacks the bulwark which the failed Samson must reconstruct in defending the self against the temptations of destructive enemies. No less stark is the contrast between Jesus and the proud defender of the English defenders, whose aggressive, ruthless, and revengeful overreaction to the troublesome Alexander More inadvertently shadows his attack on More's failed self-esteem with his own vehement reaction to external blame. Much in the two companion poems reflects on that irony.

Ambivalent threads in Milton's vocational narrative prepare for this reflection. By moving Milton's fear that death would frustrate vocational gifts, Edward King's death provoked questions about divine justice. Earlier, the ambivalent Sonnet 7 suppressed fears of vocational inaction by sidestepping responsibility and leaving the measure of "ripeness" to the great Taskmaster. In Sonnet 19 patience wrestles with the frustrated vocational imperative from a God who needs neither "man's work" nor "his own gifts" (10). Characteristically, Milton confesses vocational frustration and anger, but evades personal guilt as a cause. In the failed Samson's guilt Milton can be seen opening up the possibility of his own guilt in his vocational narrative. Milton's capacity for prideful evasion, impatient anger, aggression, virulence, and revengefulness in a divine cause stand a far cry from the composed spirituality and patient self-command of Jesus. However, a residual evasiveness exercises our interpretation. Unlike *Paradise Lost* and *Paradise Regained*, the dramatic *Samson Agonistes* provides no narrator identified with Milton to tutor our responses. Instead, we meet a defeated blind man whose natural disposition and strong sense of divine mission entrap him in their excesses. But Samson's gifts are largely physical, not mental, and his remodeled Old Testament vocational narrative is mined with interpretive difficulties. Still, the vocational sonnets had muffled an inbuilt ambivalence, self-defensively suppressing fear of vocational guilt, while implicitly allowing its threat in a postlapsarian world. Some readers may find a similar evasion in Samson, a foil constructed to distinguish Milton's own achievement. I find a subtler self-defense worthy of the complexities in Milton's nature. His conviction that he was God's champion was the bedrock of his self-esteem, but in Samson's guilt he examines the disposition to prideful excess inherent in his own given nature. Historical contingencies may have tempted Samson more than he seemed able; so, too, Milton. Yet he settles with the opposed valencies: personal responsibility for his excesses and evasions versus nagging uncertainties about divine justice. His ultimate self-defense is that he stands firm on vocational bedrock with Jesus and Samson.

The Bacon Family

The intention of Edmund Spenser's "vertuous lore" is to fashion persons serving the common good. In Spenser, and many other writers with similar intentions, such transforming lore includes the lives of poets as expressed in their works. As Spenser's admirer, John Milton, puts it, the true poet must be a true poem appropriately present in his texts. The lives of Spenser, Donne, Jonson, and Milton are everywhere intrusive in their works as part of their "vertuous lore" contributing to the common good. In word and deed, like the fictive heroes or representative speakers they create, these writers, however palpable their weaknesses may seem to us, intend to express the values that will fashion readers. The exception, Shakespeare, hides himself from his readers in his plays, but many of his heroes also personate recognizable foundational values serving the common good. There is a conviction at work in these writers that a self indebted to these values can resist the decentering force of historical dislocations.

My introduction to this study points to the reinforcement of that foundation through Protestant vocation and Christian civic humanism. In the linked chapters that follow — to adapt another working term of Spenser — we have "ensamples" that fix on distinguishing aspects of individual poets and poetic works standing on this cultural foundation. An appropriate conclusion for this accumulative structure, differing as it does from arguments rising progressively toward a logical climax, is a final "ensample," but from a complementary dimension in the early modern formation of self. This concluding "ensample," while pivoting on Francis Bacon, views him as a member of an entire family standing on the same cultural foundation. Interwoven issues of formal education, selective textuality, religious bent, commitment to common good, and gender roles, which are all suggestively present in the Bacon family, point us to a fuller understanding of the early modern self, or "person," and its formation. The vocational role of Anne Bacon in relation to her sons is especially suggestive for study beyond the scope of the present project.

By any standard, the achievement of her son, Francis Bacon, was remarkable. Like Philip Sidney he was trained to follow an important father into a life of public service. Unlike Sidney, he outdistanced his father while serving two monarchs continuously for four decades. Part time with his left hand, then full time with his right hand after the abrupt end to his public career at age 60, he produced a varied body of important texts based upon his vast learning. The heroic proportions of an achievement that included a growing burden of official duties and ambitious intellectual projects were motivated, as Brian Vickers notes, "by a typically Renaissance wish to improve life by applying the fruits of his studies *pro bono publico*."[1] No less than any writer examined in the preceding chapters, his works were guided by the common good. The biographies of few early modern writers illustrate so compellingly the formation of self through the coalescence of humanist and Protestant influences that shaped that commitment. And few early writers illustrate so informatively the continuing legacy of these influences left by one generation for another, and by both father and mother.

At first glance, his father's influence seems most significant. Distinguished by eloquence, judgment, political wisdom, and deep learning in the law, Nicholas Bacon was a trusted and astute servant of the Crown. He served as member of Parliament then as secretary of state, later as lord keeper of the seal, still later as a member of Queen Elizabeth's Privy Council. He enjoyed friendship with other high level political and Protestant ecclesiastical figures. At Cambridge he became a close friend with Matthew Parker, an archbishop under Elizabeth, and with William Cecil, later her most trusted counselor and, next to the queen herself, the most powerful politician in the kingdom. For many years under Elizabeth, Bacon and Cecil together oversaw development of a state church responsive to Reformed values. Bacon's own pathway — first Cambridge, then a brief sojourn in Paris, later Gray's Inn for legal training, finally extended public service — was the pattern for Francis and Anthony, his two sons by his second wife, Anne Cooke Bacon.

The pattern assumed training, studious practical experience, and public responsibility. The sons were first tutored privately by a recent Cambridge cleric serving as chaplain to the Bacon household, then at Cambridge by the young John Whitgift, an archbishop in his later years. By his father's arrangement Francis's three years at Cambridge were followed by a stint in France as secretary to Sir Amias Paulet, the Queen's ambassador to France, as Vickers puts it, "presumably studying statecraft and performing routine diplomatic duties."[2] Nicholas Bacon's sudden death precipitated a return to England where, along with his brother Anthony, Francis followed his father's footsteps into legal training at Gray's Inn. From there he proceeded into public life along a pathway ascending naturally in responsibility: member of Parliament (1581–1604), king's counsel (1604), solicitor general (1607), clerk of the Star Chamber (1608), attorney general (1613), privy counselor (1616), lord keeper of the seal (1617), and lord chancellor (1618). Whether or not the prematurely removed Nicholas Bacon remained an "idol which he [Francis] worshipped all the rest of his life,"[3] as Paul Kocher suggests, the son's four decades of public service reflected his father's pattern.

The son's public career ended abruptly in ignominy, but not his humanist's pride in public achievement. His enemies used his bribe-taking as a weapon to drive him permanently from office.

Bacon's conception of his public experience, as Markku Peltonen informs us, is telling: "Bacon himself thought his life akin to that of a Roman senator. He emphasized throughout his life the values of the *vita activa* and chose as his first title a Roman town — Verulam. At the moment of his impeachment he compared himself with Demosthenes, Cicero, and Seneca. And toward the end of his life he not only planned to erect by his will a lecture in both universities on 'natural Philosophy, and the sciences thereupon depending,' but also decided to imitate "Cicero, Demosthenes, Plinius Secundus, and others" by preserving his orations and "letters."[4] Like Cicero, Demosthenes, and Seneca, his public vocation had ended in disaster. A letter to Lancelot Andrewes affirms that their "examples confirmed me much in a resolution" to invest "that poor talent, or half talent, or what it is that God hath given" in writings that would serve "the general good of men" and "mine own country."[5] In their lengthened shadow, the part-time intellectual work of his left hand would become the full-time vocational work of his right hand.

Bacon's stance is consistent with his "standard humanist training."[6] The books purchased for the Bacon sons by their Cambridge tutor, John Whitgift, indicates a humanist reading regimen in philosophy, rhetoric, and history. Predictable authors included Aristotle, Plato, Cicero, Julius Caesar, Demosthenes, Sallust, and Xenophon.[7] The healthy number of rhetorical treatises and orations has a special pragmatism for sons of a high level public servant expected to trace the father's footsteps into public life. Nicholas Bacon's reputation for public eloquence and respect for the Latin rhetorical tradition add further resonance.[8]

However much the father inspirited his sons' educational and professional lives, their mother's complementary spirit may have been more important. Anne Bacon's presence is a suggestive conclusion to this study of the early modern self since the province of women in its formation invites our expanded attention. Anne Bacon played a crucial role in selecting John Walsall, a young cleric recently graduated from Christ Church, Oxford, as family chaplain and tutor of the humanist education of her only two children.[9] With her sisters, she had been educated by her distinguished humanist father, Anthony Cooke. Her impressive learning was undergirded by Reformed convictions at work in her translation of sermons by the Calvinist, Bernardino Ochino, and by her translation of John Jewell's *Apologia Ecclesia Anglicanae* (1564). Nicholas Bacon's premature death, when Francis was only 19, left the learned, activist Anne Bacon as the lone surviving parent. She continued to offer counsel to her sons well into their adult lives. The vocational sense galvanizing her intimate and forceful letters to her sons defines her presence.

That forceful vocational thrust creates its own ironies. Much indicates that she chafed against the containment of women in the private domain. Early modern vocational commentary stations the wife in the household along with the husband maintaining domestic discipline. The wife's latitude ranges from subordinate helpmeet to joint domestic governor with the husband. In contrast, the husband's vocation includes the more important public station closed to women. What Margot Todd calls the "spiritualized household" of the English Reformed tradition also enlisted the wife in the discipline and instruction of the young. English humanists of the early sixteenth century, in particular Erasmus, Thomas More, and the sometime resident Juan de Vives, also endorsed the importance of marriage and the educated family.[10] Both traditions lie behind Anthony Cooke's tutoring of his five daughters, and Anne Cooke Bacon's complementary role in her sons' early education follows naturally. However, her translation of the Ochino and Jewell texts complicates the matter.

Women's enclosure within the private world was by its very nature especially problematical for learned women. Lynne Magnusson, whose valuable analysis of Anne Bacon's letters joins the "current pursuit of neglected women writers,"[11] views Bacon in light of this problem. Magnusson notes the plausible claim that translations of Ochino's sermons and Bishop Jewell's *Apologia* kept Bacon's learning within "acceptable and unthreatening boundaries."[12] Equally plausible is that translating the *Apologia* represented a half step into the public realm. The treatise was a public document, no less political for being ecclesiastical. Her letters show her chafing against the constraints of the woman's vocational role while standing on ambiguous ground between private and public worlds. The letters comprise not only the widow's correspondence with her adult sons, but also with important public figures. One letter on behalf of nonconforming preachers is written to William Cecil, then Lord Treasurer (1584), another to the Earl of Essex admonishing his immoral behavior (1592). The extant letters to her sons fall within a mother's private vocational responsibility, although most were written in the 1590s while in her sixties. Even these later years reveal her to be strongly and forcefully convinced of her vocational responsibility to guide her sons' lives, even though both were mature adults in active public careers, not children under her domestic governance. Such conviction may be taken as intrusiveness or, contrarily, as a talented woman's attempt to maintain a role within narrow cultural constraints, or both. For example, a 1592 letter to Anthony Bacon on his return to England after several years in France expresses a mother's affection for both sons and dutiful encouragement for moral and spiritual well-being. The sons were in their thirties; both had served the public interest for many years, Anthony as a representative of the Crown in France, Francis as a member of Parliament. The letter ranges from the pragmatic to the spiritual: its intention is affectionate, blunt counsel about proper behavior and about other persons appropriate as sources of advice in her absence. Her religious convictions guide her forthright counsel: "This one chiefest counsel your Christian and natural mother doth give you even before the Lord, that above all worldly respects you carry yourself ever at your first coming as one that doth unfeignedly profess the true religion of Christ, and hath the love of the truth now by long continuance fast settled in your heart, and that with judgement, wisdom, and discretion, are not afraid or ashamed to testify the same by hearing and delighting in those religion exercises of the sincerer sort, be they French or English." Equally direct is her annoyance when sons turn a deaf ear to her advice: "Remember you have no father. And you have little enough, if not too little, regarded your kind and no simple mother's wholesome advice from time to time."[13] Her self-confidence tends to

muffle the irony, at least for a modern reader, that this is a
60-year-old's counsel for two successful, worldly sons. That irony
is muffled further if we note that Nicholas Bacon died when
Francis was 19, Anthony 22, leaving the legal management of complicated family financing and provision of parental support solely
in her hands. Her Protestant mother's strong vocational sense is
habitual.

A side glance at Elizabeth Jocelin's *The Mothers Legacy to her
Vnborn Childe* is especially informative here. This posthumous
work captures the dutiful maternal love inherent in early modern Protestantism that contributed to formation of self. Jocelin
(b.1595?) died young in 1622, nine days after giving birth to her
first child, a girl. Her letter of advice to her unborn child, with
its accompanying letter to her minister husband, was discovered
posthumously in her writing desk. The metaphoric conception
dutifully binds mother, father, and child together: the child's
letter is a "legacy," the child is the "executor" and the husband
is the "ouerseer" ("an individual appointed by a testator to super-
vise the executor of a will").[14] Generically, the *Legacy* is a mother's
advice book;[15] its broad assumption is that the husband and wife
share joint vocational responsibility for educating the child.
Jocelin's letter to her husband immediately addresses her duty to
the unborn child: "Mine owne deare loue, I no sooner conceiued
an hope, that I should bee made a mother by thee, but with it entred
the consideration of a mothers duty, and shortly after followed
the apprehension of danger that might preuent mee from execut-
ing that care I so exceedingly desired, I meane in religious training our Childe" (47). The "legacy" is conceived as spiritual and
moral instruction "overseen" by her husband in her absence.
That instruction speaks to interrelationships with God and other
humans, including the child's dutiful obedience to parents. A
detailed early regimen for training the child incorporates these
intentions.

Unlike Anne Bacon, Jocelin resists displaying her considerable learning. Thomas Goad, a Church of England minister, in his
introductory "The Approbation" to the 1624 *Legacy*, juxtaposes
her "education and eminent vertues." Goad's ambivalent logic is

that impressive learning validates her instruction, while modest humility appropriately suppresses a woman's self-display of that learning. Notably, her own education overseen by her distinguished grandfather, Bishop Lawrence Chaderton, further validates her "Manuell" (44) written for moral and spiritual instruction. In her "tender yeeres" her grandfather had "carefully nurtured her "in Languages, History, and Some Arts, so principally in studies of piety" (42). As a wife, she independently studied "morality and history, the better by the helpe of forraine languages, not without a taste and faculty in Poetry"; most recent were "no other studies than Diuinity" (43). In writing the *Legacy*, her habitual modesty, obedience, and humility keep pride in "secular learning" appropriately at bay. In Goad's "approbation" she emerges as a model wife recommended by the secular learning appropriately set aside in her final vocational act.

In that dutiful act she has her child's vocation in mind. Her advice to a possible son leaves no room for doubt about her preference: "If I had skill to write, I would write all I apprehend of the happy estate of true labouring Ministers: but I may plainly say that of all men they by their calling are the most truly happy" (59). The letter to her husband, the first intended reader of the *Legacy*, assumes his like mind: "I doubt not but thou wilt dedicate it to the Lord as his Minister" (49). Vocational intentions for her daughter are complicated by characteristic self-effacement ambiguously reflecting on her own experience when writing to her husband: "I desire her bringing vp may bee learning the Bible, as my sisters doe, good housewifery, writing, and good workes: other learning a woman needs not: though I admire it in those whom God hath blest with discretion, yet I desired not much in my owne, hauing seene that sometimes women have greater portions of learning, than wisdome . . . But where learning and wisdome meet in a vertuous disposed woman, she is the fittest closet for all goodnesse. Shee is like a well-ballanced ship that may beare all her saile. Shee is — Indeed, I should but shame my selfe, if I should goe about to praise her more" (49, 51). Self-effacement struggles with self-esteem, indirection with the strength of her own learning, a woman's cultural reticence with the "closet of all goodnesse."

She believes but only implies that, just as her son should copy his father's vocational model, her daughter should copy hers. The role of "writing," modestly couched between "good housewifery" and "good workes," reflects on the *Legacy* as her own vocational act. Her advice to her daughter, in contrast to explicit intentions for her son's vocation, is apologetic, indirect, and elusive: "And if thou beest a daughter, thou maist perhaps thinke I have lost my labour; but read on, and thou shalt see my love and care of thee and thy salvation is as great, as if thou were a sonne, and my feare greater." Besides the vocational limitation that a woman's domain is private, not public, a dead mother ceases to be an immediate exemplar, unavailable "euery day to praise or reproue it as it deserues." Yet even an absent mother has a continuing responsibility for her own daughter's salvation. Only she can guide her own daughter, "writing in this kinde," not relying on "so many excellent bookes" written generally for "the world" (59, 61). To obey the instructive written text is to obey her mother. Writing itself links mother and child; it is the mother's means to fulfill her own vocation as a pattern for her daughter, through the daughter's obedience to the written text. The child's obedience to the loving mother's instruction is the way to become like the mother and, the father knows, a "closet of all goodness."

Likenesses between Elizabeth Jocelin and Anne Bacon point to a learned woman's role in forming the early modern self. Familial love and vocational duty are inseparable in both women. And in Jocelin's maternal duty that reaches beyond death, we find a deeply rooted purpose like that guiding a 60-year-old widow's counsel to her adult sons. Both exemplars provide a telling perspective on an educated woman's contribution to early modern formation of self. In alliance with their husbands, both work to establish an instructive environment of humanist learning and Protestant vocation. Both women walked a razor's edge in a culture where women's learning was too readily regarded as transgressive. Thomas Goad's ambiguous, perhaps fully knowing praise of Jocelin's impulse "rather to hide, than to boast of" her impressive learning, prepares the reader for her warily negotiated, contradictory self-effacement, and confidence in writing to her husband.

The razor's edge looms larger in a "writing" where she implicitly offers herself as a pattern for the unborn daughter. Bacon's willingness to confront as well as walk the razor's edge does not erase
the likeness of maternal purpose between the two women.

Anne Bacon was a learned woman boldly seeking an expanded
vocational role as a "widow." That search goes hand-in-hand
with her extended maternal counsel as well as her longstanding
activism on behalf of Reformed preachers. Lynne Magnusson
points to her advocacy of a reformed "church organization in
England built upon the Word of God and the model of the Apostolic
Church" and advancing "a fully reformed English nation."[16] Some
Reformed thought, supported by a biblical distinction in 1 Timothy
between busybody young widows searching out replacement husbands and older widows devoted to good works, hewed out a
vocational place in the church for older widows. Magnusson suggests that this context explains the high valency of Bacon's sig-
nature in letters to important persons to which she appended
"widow" in Greek.[17] The learned Bacon, whose command of
Greek gave her more direct access to the Word, was advocating
her own vocational suitability as a widow to preach the Word.
Magnusson notes that the Calvinist leader, Theodore Beza, who
dedicated his *Chrestiennes Meditations* to Bacon, also developed
the commentary in the *Geneva Bible* underlining the distinction
between categories of widows. This thread in Magnusson's important analysis can be teased out further in terms of vocation.
About the "yonger widowes," who "are begone to waxe wanton
against Christ" (1 Tim. 5:11), the marginal commentary adds
"forgetting their vocation" and elaborates their damnable state
in the next verse with "they haue not onely donne dishonor to
Christ in leauing their vocation, but also have broken their
faith."[18] By inference, godly older widows of good works fulfill their
vocations. Whether or not Bacon is advocating a vocational role
for women as preachers of the Word, as Magnusson persuasively
argues, her actions can be interpreted to indicate a conviction of
the widow's justified vocational role in the church. Forthright
maternal advice to adult sons is consistent with this expanded
vocational role.

Anne Bacon's personal history yields a necessary perspective on the early modern self. Her instruction of her sons stands in line with Katharine Parr's Erasmian instruction in Henry VIII's court, including the Princess Elizabeth; and Anthony Cooke's instruction of Edward VI and, more important, his own daughters. Her vocational boldness in contrast to Elizabeth Jocelin's self-effacement, a difference owing in part to a higher social rank, paradoxically emphasizes how different women incorporate the same prevailing cultural continuities that set aside their differences. The Bacon family was exceptional, not that they were an abnormal departure from a cultural norm, but rather a remarkable fulfillment of its edifying coalescence of Christian humanist and Protestant values. Anne Bacon's history points more broadly to the early modern women's important role in transmitting these values. Her experience is especially instructive in the continuing debate about the early modern self, its alleged centrifugal energies, and its counterbalancing factors of coherence. In her experience we find an executor and overseer of an indelible legacy that weathered historical dislocations and resists modern claims of a fragmented early modern self.

Notes

Notes to Introduction

1. William Shakespeare, *King Lear: A Conflated Text*, in *The Norton Shakespeare*, ed. Stephen Greenblatt (New York: W. W. Norton & Company, 1997), 1.4.205. All citations from the play are from this edition, with act, scene, and line numbers hereafter given parenthetically within the text.

2. Jonathan Dollimore, *Radical Tragedy: Religion, Ideology, and Power in the Drama of Shakespeare and His Contemporaries* (Chicago: The University of Chicago Press, 1986). See chapters 12 and 16.

3. Katharine Eisaman Maus, *Inwardness and Theater in the English Renaissance* (Chicago: The University of Chicago Press, 1995), 2.

4. Ibid., 11.

5. Debora Kuller Shuger, *Habits of Thought in the English Renaissance: Religion, Politics and the Dominant Culture* (Berkeley: University of California Press, 1990), 6.

6. Judy Kronenfeld, *King Lear and the Naked Truth: Rethinking the Language of Religion and Resistance* (Durham: Duke University Press, 1998), 13.

7. Weaknesses in new historicist and cultural materialist interpretations of early modern subjectivity have contributed to continuing debate. See Hugh Grady, "On the Need for a Differentiated Theory of (Early) Modern Subjects," in *Philosophical Shakespeares*, ed. John Joughin (London: Routledge, 2000). Grady looks to the early Frankfurt School disposition to "supplement its Marxism with Freudian psychoanalysis," which created a promising, but "incomplete synthesis" (44). This synthesis can lead to a "theory of subjectivity," incorporating psychoanalytic theory and recognizing "the creative potential of subjectivity, as well as its embeddedness in the social" (45).

More detailed criticism of new historicist and cultural materialist interpretations of the early modern self can be found in John Lee, *Shakespeare's*

'Hamlet' and the Controversies of Self (Oxford: Oxford University Press, 2000). Lee's strong objections to the narrow, poststructuralist constrictions of subjectivity provide the backdrop for claims centered in Hamlet's sometime "Protean rhetorical sense of self" (226) expressed in images of liquidity, but qualified by a paradoxical sense of inner nutshell-confinement competing with infinite inner space.

8. Lee, *Shakespeare's 'Hamlet,'* 89.

9. Catherine Belsey, *The Subject of Tragedy: Identity and Difference in Renaissance Drama* (New York: Routledge, 1991), 5.

10. Stephen Greenblatt, *Renaissance Self-Fashioning: From More to Shakespeare* (Chicago: The University of Chicago Press, 1980), 256.

11. Alan Sinfield, *Faultlines: Cultural Materialism and the Politics of Dissident Reading* (Oxford: Clarendon Press, 1992), 155.

12. Maus, *Inwardness and Theater*, 11.

13. Ibid., 13.

14. Robert Ellrodt, *Seven Metaphysical Poets: A Structural Study of the Unchanging Self* (Oxford: Oxford University Press, 2000), 7 (quoting Cornelius Castioridis).

15. Ibid., 21, n. 70.

16. Ibid., 13.

17. For discussion of Bacon vs. Coke, see "Writing the Law," in Richard Helgerson, *Forms of Nationhood: The Elizabethan Writing of England* (Chicago: The University of Chicago Press, 1992), 63–104.

18. Sir Philip Sidney, *A Defence of Poetry*, in *Miscellaneous Prose*, ed. Katherine Duncan-Jones and Jan Van Dorsten (Oxford: Clarendon Press, 1973), 72.

19. For discussion of Sidney's education and early vocational pathway, see "Imitation and Identity," in Edward Berry, *The Making of Sir Philip Sidney* (Toronto: University of Toronto Press, 1998), 3–27.

20. William Perkins, *Treatise of the Vocations, or Callings of men, with the sorts and kinds of them and the right use thereof*, in *Workes* (London, 1612), 1:750. First published posthumously in 1602, this work was written much earlier in the 1590s. Hereafter cited parenthetically in the text with the appropriate page number as *Vocations*.

21. For one account of the longevity of Erasmian and other early humanist influences, see Margot Todd, "The Transmission of Christian Humanist Ideas," in *Christian Humanism and the Puritan Social Order* (Cambridge: Cambridge University Press, 1987), 53–95. Todd discusses how these influences affected "Elizabethan and early Stuart Englishmen in general" and "puritans in particular" (52). The influence was especially strong in the area of social thought.

22. Sinfield, *Faultlines*, 181–213.

23. See Todd, "The Transmission," 87. She notes that John Milton's contemporaries at Cambridge were still reading Erasmus, including the *Enchiridion*.

24. See Erasmus, *The Handbook of the Christian Soldier: Enchiridion, militis christiani,* trans. Charles Fantazzi, in *Collected Works,* 66 (Toronto: University of Toronto Press, 1974): "But lest you be deterred from the path of vitue by the fact that it is harsh and forbidding, or that you must renounce the comforts of the world or wage a constant battle with the three relentless enemies, the flesh, the world, and the devil, set this third rule before your eyes. You must ignore, after the example of Virgil's Aeneas, all those spectres and phantasms which spring up before you as if you were at the very gates of hell" (58). Hereafter called *Enchiridion,* with the appropriate page number given parenthetically within the text. Cf. Sidney, *Defence:* "Only let Aeneas be worn in the tablet of your memory, how he governeth himself in the ruin of his country; in the preserving his old father, and carrying away his religious ceremonies; in obeying God's commandment to leave Dido, though not only all passionate kindness, but even the human consideration of virtuous gratefulness, would have craved other of him, etc" (98).

25. For a brief discussion of the literary tradition behind Erasmus's handbook, see Anne M. O'Donnell's introduction to *Enchiridion Militis Christiani: An English Version,* ed. A. M. O'Donnell (Oxford: Oxford University Press for The Early English Text society, 1981), xviii–xix.

26. Todd, *Christian Humanism,* 47.

27. Cicero, *De Officiis,* trans. Walter Miller (Cambridge: Harvard University Press; Loeb Classical Library, 1990). All citations are from this edition, with book and section given parenthetically within the text.

28. See Margaret Atkins, "Notes on Translation," in Cicero, *On Duties,* ed. M. T. Griffin and E. M. Atkins (Cambridge: Cambridge University Press, 1991), xlv. Atkins indicates that *officium* and *beneficium* were closely allied in the Roman "network of social relationships" involving the "exchange of services" and mutual obligations. "The benefit given could be described as either *officium* or *beneficium.* Duties engendered by one's role were also called *officia:* sometimes the closest translation would be 'responsibilities'. Cicero chose the *officia* as the nearest Latin equivalent to the Stoic technical term *kathekon,* or 'appropriate action'. In doing so he enriched what he took from Stoic ethics with Roman associations; *De Officiis* interprets the virtues in terms of the obligations of role and relationships, obligations to other individuals or to the *res publica* as a whole."

29. See Cicero, *De Finibus,* 3:58–61, for a discussion of *officium* as an appropriate act. Also, for a discussion of Cicero and "appropriate acts" in the context of Greek and Roman Stoicism, see J. M. Rist, "Appropriate Acts," in *Stoic Philosophy* (Cambridge: Cambridge University Press, 1969), 97–111.

30. Cicero's assumption that there is a "sort of innate desire on the part of human beings to form communities" (*Republic and Laws,* trans. Niall Rudd [Oxford: Oxford University Press, 1998]), 1.39 is informed by

334   Notes to Pages 13–16

Greek social and political thought, including Aristotle, whose works were

334   Notes to Pages 13–16

Greek social and political thought, including Aristotle, whose works were available to early modern audiences both directly and indirectly through Cicero. Aristotle's *Politics* included the widely circulated claim encapsulating Cicero's thought in this regard "that the state is a creation of nature and that man is by nature a political animal" (*Politics*, 1. 36–37 in *Works, 2, trans.* B. Jowett [Princeton: Princeton University Press, 1985]). Paul MacKendrick has this aspect of Cicero's Greek influence in mind when he says that Cicero "thinks like a citizen of a city-state (a *polis*), an attitude long gone from Greece; he is a genuine Aristotelian *political* animal" (*The Philosophical Books of Cicero* [London: Duckworth, 1989]), 5.

31. See Quentin Skinner, *The Foundations of Modern Political Thought* (Cambridge: Cambridge University Press, 1978), 1: xxiii–xxiv: "*Studia humanitatis* . . . in its original Renaissance meaning" refers to "a particular group of disciplines centred around the study of grammar, rhetoric, history and moral philosophy."

32. One of several examples can be found in "An Exhortacion concernyng Good Ordre and Obedience to Rulers and Magistrates," in *Certain Sermons or Homilies (1547); and A Homily against Disobedience and Wilful Rebellion (1570): A Critical Edition*, ed. Ronald B. Bond (Toronto: University of Toronto Press, 1987): "Every degree of people in their vocacion, callyng and office, hath appoynted to them their duetie and ordre. Some are in high degree, some in lowe, some kynges and princes, some inferiors and subjectes, priestes and laimen, masters and servauntes, fathers and chyldren, husbandes and wifes, riche and poore, and every one have nede of other: so that in all thinges is to be lauded and praysed the goodly ordre of God, without the whiche, no house, no citie, no common wealth can continue and endure" (161).

33. Paul Marshall, *A Kind of Life Imposed on Man: Vocation and Social Order from Tyndale to Locke* (Toronto: University of Toronto Press, 1996), 32.

34. Skinner, *Modern Political Thought*, 1.225.

35. A. N. McLaren, *Political Culture in the Reign of Elizabeth I: Queen and Commonwealth 1558–1585* (Cambridge: Cambridge University Press, 1999), 81. McLaren's amplification follows: "In this framework, self-interest, whether narrowly economic or more broadly political, began to be perceived not exclusively as a declension from political virtue in the Aristotelian sense but equally as the means by which Antichrist attempted to subvert the True Church and simultaneously the English nation. Its antithesis was a breadth (or community) of vision allowed for by a spiritual capacity which transcended self-interest and caste identity by recognizing the claims of the 'commonweal' or 'commonwealth' — a term signaling bonds of brotherhood among the godly as well as, increasingly an English habitation" (ibid.).

36. Skinner, *Modern Political Thought*, 1.226.

37. For discussion of the attribution, see Mary Dewar's introduction to *A Discourse of the Commonweal of This Realm of England: Attributed to Sir Thomas Smith*, ed. M. Dewar (Charlottesville: The University Press of Virginia for The Folger Shakespeare Library, 1969), xviii–xxvi. All citations from the text are taken from this edition, hereafter cited in the text as *Discourse* with the appropriate page number.

38. Skinner, *Modern Political Thought*, 1.225.

39. Dewar, *Discourse*, unnumbered footnotes, 16.

40. Robert Crowley, *The Voyce of the laste trumpet, blowen by the seuenth Angel (as is mentioned in the eleuenth of the Apocalips) callyng al estats of men to the ryght path of theyr vocation, wherin are conteyned .xii, Lessons to twelue seueral estats of men, which if thei learne and folowe, al shall be wel, and nothing amis*, in *The Select Works*, ed. J. M. Cowper (London: Early English Text Society, 1872; reprint Millwood, N.Y.: Kraus Reprint Co., 1975), 9. All citations are from this text, with the line numbers given parenthetically within the text.

41. "If therefore, being prisoner in the Lord, pray you that ye walke worthie of the vocation whereunto ye are called" (Eph. 4:1). Translation is from the Geneva Bible.

42. Margot Todd, *Christian Humanism*, 123.

43. See John Calvin, *Institutes of the Christian Religion*, trans. Ford Lewis Battles (Philadelphia: The Westminster Press, 1972), 3.24.8: "there are two kinds of call. There is the general call, by which God invites all equally to himself through the outward preaching of the word — even those to whom he holds it out as a savor of death [cf. 2 Cor. 2:16], and as the occasion for severer condemnation. The other kind of call is special, which he deigns for the most part to give to the believers alone, while by the inward illumination of his Spirit he causes the preached Word to dwell in their hearts."

44. Perkins here appears to have conflated Eph. 4:1 (see n. 41 above) with 1 Cor. 7:20, his text for the work, which he translates as follows: "Let every man abide in that calling, where in he was called."

45. For a discussion of "fitness" and the Protestant calling, see my *Herbert's Prayerful Art* (Toronto: University of Toronto Press, 1989), 79–81.

46. William Perkins, *A Grain of Mustard Seed*, in *The Work*, ed. Ian Breward (Appleford, Abingdon, Berkshire: The Sutton Courtenay Press, 1970), 407.

47. John Donne, *Pseudo-Martyr*, ed. Anthony Raspa (Montreal: McGill-Queen's University Press, 1993), 165–66.

48. George Herbert, *Works*, ed. F. E. Hutchinson (Oxford: Clarendon Press, 1959), 29.

49. John Milton, *Complete Poems and Major Prose*, ed. Merritt Y. Hughes (Indianapolis: The Odyssey Press, 1957). All citations of poetry are from this edition, with title, book and line numbers given parenthetically within the text.

50. David Little, *Religion, Order and Law: A Study in Pre-Revolutionary England* (Chicago: The University of Chicago Press, 1984), 31–32, 107, 165–66.

51. Ibid., 137–38.

52. John Whitgift, *Works*, ed. John Ayre (Cambridge: Cambridge University Press for the Parker Society, 1853), 3.590.

53. Marshall, *A Kind of Life*, 54–66.

54. William Tyndale, *The Obedience of a Christian Man*, ed. David Daniel (London: Penguin Books, 2000), 49. All citations are from this modern spelling edition based on the first edition, published in Antwerp, 1528; hereafter cited as *Obedience* with page numbers given within the text.

55. John Ponet, *A Shorte Treatise of politike power, and of the true Obedience which subiectes owe to kynges and other ciuile Gouernours, with an Exhortacion to all true naturall Englishe men* (1556), a facsimile edition, in *John Ponet (1516?–1556): Advocate of Limited Monarchy*, ed. Winthrop S. Hudson (Chicago: The University of Chicago Press, 1942), 47. All citations are from this edition with page numbers given parenthetically within the text.

56. Skinner, *Modern Political Thought*, 2.234–35.

57. Christopher Goodman, *How superior powers oght to be obeyd of their subiects: and Wherin they may lawfully by Gods Worde be disobeyed and resisted* (Geneva, 1658; facsimile reprint New York: Da Capo Press, 1972), 9.

58. In his introduction to the play, Greenblatt notes that "scholars generally assign Shakespeare's composition of *King Lear* to 1604–5" (*The Norton Shakespeare*, 2308). Elizabeth died in 1603.

59. Jonas A. Barish and Marshall Waingrow, "'Service' in *King Lear*," *SQ* 9 (1958): 349.

60. Richard Strier, "Faithful Servants: Shakespeare's Praise of Disobedience," in *The Historical Renaissance*, ed. Heather Dubrow and Richard Strier (Chicago: The University of Chicago Press, 1988), 111. Hereafter page numbers are given within the text.

61. Ibid., 120.

62. Ibid., 104.

63. Shuger, *Habits of Thought*, 94.

64. Ibid., 257.

65. Cristina Malcolmson, *Heart-Work: George Herbert and the Protestant Ethic* (Stanford: Stanford University Press, 1999), 71–72.

66. Perkins, *An Instruction Touching Religious or Divine Worship*, in *The Work*, 324.

67. Sherwood, *Herbert's Prayerful Art*, 4, 30–31.

68. Izaak Walton, "The Life of Mr. George Herbert," in *The Lives of John Donne, Sir Henry Wotton, Richard Hooker, George Herbert and Robert Sanderson* (London: Oxford Unversity Press, 1966), 314.

69. For a discussion of Donne's theology based on created likeness

between the Trinity and the tripartite human soul, see my *Fulfilling the Circle: A Study of John Donne's Thought* (Toronto: University of Toronto Press, 1984), 7–10, 57. For more detail regarding Donne's Trinitarian theology, see Jeffrey Johnson, *The Theology of John Donne* (Cambridge: D. S. Brewer, 1999), 2–37.

70. See Sherwood, *Fulfilling the Circle*, 181–90.

71. Anthony H. Dawson and Paul Yachnin, *The Culture of Playgoing in Shakespeare's England* (Cambridge: Cambridge University Press, 2001), 11–37.

72. Reid Barbour, *Literature and Religious Culture in Seventeenth-Century England* (Cambridge: Cambridge University Press, 2002), 14.

73. Ibid., 163.

74. Ibid., 164.

75. Terry G. Sherwood, "'Ego videbo': Donne and the Vocational Self," *John Donne Journal* 16 (1997): 103.

76. Barbour, *Literature and Religious Culture*, 165. The context for this passage can be found in *The Sermons of John Donne*, ed. George R. Potter and Evelyn M. Simpson (Berkeley and Los Angeles: University of California Press, 1963), 8.178. Hereafter cited within the text as *Sermons*, with appropriate volume and page number.

77. Anne Ferry, *The "Inward" Language: Sonnets of Wyatt, Sidney, Shakespeare, Donne* (Chicago: University of Chicago Press, 1983), xi.

78. Ellrodt, *Seven Metaphysical Poets*, 7.

79. Ibid., 22.

80. Richard Helgerson, *Self-Crowned Laureates: Spenser, Jonson, Milton and the Literary System* (Chicago: The University of Chicago Press, 1980), 1–9.

81. John Milton, *Areopagitica*, ed. Ernest Sirluck, in *Complete Prose Works of John Milton*, ed. Don M. Wolfe et al. (New Haven: Yale University Press, 1959): "That vertue therefore which is but a youngling in the contemplation of evill, and knows not the utmost that vice promises to her followers, and rejects it, is but a blank vertue, not a pure; her whitenesse is but an excrementall whitenesse; Which was the reason why our sage and serious Poet *Spencer*, whom I dare be known to think a better teacher than *Scotus* or *Aquinas*, describing true temperance under the person of *Guion*, brings him in with his palmer through the cave of Mammon, and the bowr of earthly blisse, that he might see and know, and yet abstain" (2.515–16).

Notes to Chapter One

1. Edmund Spenser, *The Faerie Queene*, ed. A. C. Hamilton (Longman: London, 1977). All references to the poem are from this edition, with book, canto, stanza, and line numbers given parenthetically within the text.

Hereafter, this edition is referred to as Hamilton with the appropriate page number.

2. Edmund Spenser, "A letter of the Authors expounding his whole intention in the course of this worke: which for that it giueth great light to the Reader, for the better vnderstanding is hereunto annexed," in Hamilton, 737. Hereafter cited as "Letter" parenthetically within the text with the appropriate page number.

3. For a useful discussion of the letter, its content, and the attendant critical problems, see A. Leigh DeNeef, "Raleigh, Letter to," in *The Spenser Encyclopedia*, ed. A. C. Hamilton (Toronto: University of Toronto Press, 1990), 582–84.

4. For useful discussion of the flexible term "gentleman," see Louis Adrian Montrose, "Of Gentlemen and Shepherds: The Politics of Elizabethan Pastoral Form," *ELH* 50 (1983): 429, 433, 452.

5. The distinction between the mutually dependent adjectives, gentle and noble, honors social hierarchy and, ambiguously, applies these adjectives to both gentles and nobles. Spenser is not alone among early modern writers in taking advantage of this ambiguity.

For one perspective on these terms, see Sir Thomas Elyot, *The Boke Named the Gouernour*, ed. H. H. S. Croft (New York: Burt Franklin, 1967), 2, 27–29. (Hereafter cited as *Boke*, with volume and page given parenthetically within the text.) Here Elyot reflects on gentle behavior in light of true nobility. Only the king is a "superior" magistrate (or governor); all others are "inferior" magistrates. Like Spenser, Elyot addresses an audience that includes both gentlemen and nobles as members of the ruling class, "inferior" governors under the monarch. Morally, persons in both social strata can have "gentle" and "noble" moral qualities. In Elyot's historical account of true nobility ("very nobilitie"), goods held in common were awarded to persons of noteworthy virtue, whose "labour and industrie" created a "commune benefite." Readiness to confer that benefit was "in englisshe gentilnesse." The "state" of the superior, virtuous person was "after called nobilitie, and the persons noble, whiche signifieth excellent." These persons, readily and generously accorded "benefits" to others. The term "noble" is "more ample than gentill, for it containeth as well all that whiche is in gentilnesse, also the honour or dignities therefore received, which be so annexed the one to the other that they can nat be separate." The presumption is that inherited high place remains a figure for truly "noble" or "excellent character behavior," even if not in fact. A corollary is that truly excellent "noble" persons have a "gentle" disposition to benefit others. In terms of individual human capacity, Elyot erases the moral difference between these two social strata without disturbing the hierarchy, in fact. Morally, all inferior magistrates are expected to be both "noble" and "gentle" persons.

6. See DeNeef, "Raleigh, Letter to": "In Spenser's announced intention 'to fashion a gentleman or noble person in vertuous and gentle

discipline,' to *fashion* means not only 'to represent or delineate,' but also 'to train and educate,' even 'to create or make.' The term *discipline* carries a similar complex meaning, for it refers both to moral teaching generally and, more specifically, to instruction which has as its aim the reformation of the pupil to proper conduct" (583).

7. For discussions of contemporary theatrical "person" and "personation" see Andrew Gurr, *Playgoing in Shakespeare's London* (Cambridge: Cambridge University Press, 1989); Anthony Dawson and Paul Yachnin, *The Culture of Playgoing in Shakespeare's England: A Collaborative Debate* (Cambridge: Cambridge University Press, 2001). Gurr states that beginning in the 1590s the term "personation" applied to the "arrival of stage heroes" as "embodiments of Elizabethan emotions" through whom many of the spectators could identify themselves and their wants (136–37). Dawson underlines the pivotal importance of the "body" in "person." The bodily personation of the individual in theatrical production assumes the mainline Church of England eucharistic thought whereby the individual, bodily "person" participates in the collective communal body. See my introduction, pp. 46–48 above, for my application of Dawson's discussion.

8. For a discussion of early modern intention with reference to agency and action in a legal frame, as represented in the drama, see Luke Wilson, *Theaters of Intention: Drama and the Law in Early Modern England* (Stanford: Stanford University Press, 2000), 3–24.

9. Sir Philip Sidney, *A Defence of Poetry*, in *Miscellaneous Prose*, ed. Katherine Duncan-Jones and Jan Van Dorsten (Oxford: Clarendon Press, 1973), 86. Hereafter cited within the text as *Defence* with appropriate page numbers.

10. Baxter Hathaway, *The Age of Criticism: The Late Renaissance in Italy* (Ithaca, N.Y.: Cornell University Press, 1962), 142.

11. Ibid., 131.

12. Ibid., 144–58. For a broadly based discussion of exemplary heroic virtue in the poetic theory of the Italian Renaissance, the immediate background for both Sidney and Spenser, also see Bernard Weinberg, *A History of Literary Criticism in the Italian Renaissance*, 2 vols. (Chicago: University of Chicago Press, 1961).

13. Thomas Becon, *The Gouernaunce of virtue, teaching all faithfull Christians how they ought dayly to leade their life, and fruitefully to spend theyr tyme, unto the glory of God, and the healthe of their owne soules*, fol. ccxxv., hereafter cited within the text as *Gouernaunce*, with the abbreviation "fol." and Roman numbering.

The *Gouernaunce* was published in volume 1 (1564) of a three volume collected works. The latter two volumes, published respectively in 1560 and 1563, contained works written after the earlier works in volume 1. Written prior to Edward's 1547 accession, *Gouernaunce* was dedicated later to Jane Seymour, perhaps when Becon was associated with the household of the Lord Protector Edward Seymour during Edward's reign.

14. A. N. McLaren, *Political Culture in the Reign of Elizabeth I: Queen and Commonwealth 1558–1585* (Cambridge: Cambridge University Press, 1999), 70.

15. See Hamilton, 29. In his notes on 1.1.1–6, the editor points to medieval pictorial conventions underlying the account of Redcrosse with the maid and her lamb.

16. A. S. P. Woodhouse, "Nature and Grace in *The Faerie Queene*," *ELH* 16 (1949): 194–228.

17. For a discussion of transformation of sixteenth century English political culture caused by Elizabeth's presence, see McLaren, *Political Culture*, esp. 1–74.

18. Mary Ellen Lamb, "The Cooke Sisters: Attitudes toward Learned Women in the Renaissance" in *Silent But for the Word: Tudor Women as Patrons, Translators, and Writers of Religious Works*, ed. Margaret Patterson Hannay (Kent, Ohio: The Kent State University Press, 1985), 108.

19. Ibid., 111.

20. Ibid.

21. Ibid., 121.

22. John N. King, "Patronage and Piety: The Influence of Catherine Parr," in Hannay, *Silent But for the Word*, 53.

23. Ibid., 49–50.

24. Ibid., 52.

25. Pembroke Hall (later Pembroke College) and St. John's College were together distinguished by their contributions to Protestant culture, both as intellectual seedbeds and sources of governors later serving Elizabeth's Protestant regime. Spenser was preceded at Pembroke by the scholarly Edwin Grindal, later the archbishop of Canterbury under Elizabeth until removed from office. John Young, later bishop of Rochester when he hired Spenser as a secretary, was Master of Pembroke Hall during Spenser's matriculation there.

For discussion of Spenser's religious thought in light of Cambridge libraries, especially Pembroke as a site of advanced Protestant thought, see Carole Kaske, *Spenser and Biblical Poetics* (Ithaca: Cornell University Press, 1999). Other important recent discussions pointing to Spenser's breadth of reading and understanding of religious and theological matters include: Darryl Gless, *Interpretation and Theology in Spenser* (Cambridge: Cambridge University Press, 1994); John N. King, *Spenser's Poetry and the Reformation Tradition* (Princeton: Princeton University Press, 1990); Harold L. Weatherby, *Mirrors of Celestial Grace: Patristic Theology in Spenser's Allegory* (Toronto: University of Toronto Press, 1994).

26. Elizabeth removed Grindal from the office of archbishop for his refusal to quell the "prophesyings" by Protestant clerics and others.

These popular sessions devoted to interpretation of the Bible were viewed by Elizabeth as potential occasions for fostering singularity that threatened her attempt to secure uniformity and public order. Spenser's apparent sympathy with the moderate reform policies of Grindal is expressed in both the May and June eclogues of *The Shepeardes Calender.*

27. Recent scholarship dealing with the early modern period in England has incorporated the notion of the "imagined community" to capture the shared sense of national identity expressed in some literary texts. For the source of this notion, see Benedict Anderson, *Imagined Communities: Reflections on the Origin and Spread of Nationalism* (London: Verso, 1991).

28. For discussion of "visual epistemology" and its intellectual history, see Forrest G. Robinson, *The Shape of Things Known: Sidney's Apology in its Philosophical Tradition* (Cambridge: Harvard University Press, 1972).

29. The early modern conception of thought and knowledge in visual terms had a long Platonic and Neoplatonist history influencing both Sidney and Spenser. See Robinson, *The Shape of Things Known* for a usefully developed discussion of this history. Additional early modern influences affecting notions of the visual include Ramist diagrammatics, the emblem tradition, development of theory in the visual arts, and the print revolution. Poetry conceived as picture by Sidney and Spenser comes as no surprise in this context.

30. S. K. Heninger, *Sidney and Spenser: The Poet as Maker* (University Park: The Pennsylvania State University Press, 1989), 96–100. For the centrality of vision in *The Faerie Queene,* in relation to the inner and outer eye, see Kathleen Williams, "Spenser and the Metaphor of Sight," *Rice University Studies* 60 (1974): 153–69.

31. Ibid., 306–95.

32. Ibid., 272–74.

33. Blair Worden, *The Sound of Virtue: Philip Sidney's* Arcadia *and Elizabethan Politics* (New Haven: Yale University Press, 1996): "The *Arcadia* is, among other things, a political allegory" (6).

34. Kenneth Borris, *Allegory and Epic in English Renaissance Literature: Heroic Form in Sidney, Spenser and Milton* (Cambridge: Cambridge University Press, 2000). Borris meets head on the time-honored claims that Sidney was an enemy to allegory. He situates Sidney's two *Arcadias* in the long tradition running from Homer to Milton, especially in light of literary theory of the sixteenth and seventeenth centuries, to show the especial linkage of allegory with heroic poetry in critical discourse throughout the period. Borris's detailed discussion of Sidney can be found in two chapters on the *Arcadias* (109–44).

35. Kenneth Borris, *Spenser's Poetics of Prophecy in "The Faerie Queene V"* (Victoria, Canada: English Literary Series, University of Victoria, 1991), 175.

36. Joseph Wittreich, *Visionary Poetics: Milton's Tradition and His Legacy* (San Marino, Calif.: Huntington Library, 1979), 26.

37. Ibid., 24. Wittreich acknowledges debt for this term to John Bender, *Spenser and Literary Pictorialism* (Princeton: Princeton University Press, 1972), 154.

38. Ibid. Wittreich finds this useful epithet in George Stanley Faber, *The Sacred Calendar of Prophecy: or a Dissertation on the Prophecies* (London: C. and J. Rivington, 1828), 1.15.

39. Borris, *Spenser's Poetics*, 75.

40. For a useful discussion of Sidney's Protestant notion of vocation in relation to civic duty, see Edward I. Berry, *The Making of Sir Philip Sidney* (Toronto: University of Toronto Press, 1998): "The religious overtones in Sidney's allusion to poetry in *A Defence* as his 'unelected vocation' call attention to another dimension of his training for a career as a statesman. As his father's letter makes clear, Philip's 'profession of life' is defined within a Christian framework. The first action of every day is prayer, and God Himself is invoked to make the young man 'a good servant to [his] prince and country.' Philip's headmaster at Shrewsbury, Thomas Ashton, was well-known as a Calvinist. Although we do not know exactly how Ashton's Calvinism shaped the curriculum, there is no doubt that it did, and in ways that are likely to have complemented Sir Henry's fusion of Christianity and career. Sidney's later commitment to the Protestant cause in Europe, which he shared with his father and uncles, Leicester and Warwick, would have been anticipated at Shrewsbury by not only a humanistic but a Calvinistic conception of service to the state" (23–24).

41. Patrick Cheney, *Spenser's Famous Flight: A Renaissance Idea of a Literary Career* (Toronto: University of Toronto Press, 1993).

42. Richard Rambuss, *Spenser's Secret Career* (Cambridge: Cambridge University Press, 1993), 7.

43. The related vocabularies of vocation, career, and profession can be troublesome when discussing early modern literature. Rambuss's secularized notion of "career" as a field for sequential professional achievement did not develop until later. In the current study, vocation is not a synonym for profession, our modern secular notion of trained professional employment, even though the notions and the vocabularies gradually merge in this period. See William Prest, "Preface" in *The Professions in Early Modern England* (London: Croom Helm, 1987). He notes that by the mid-seventeenth century "profession" was "being used more generally as a synonym for calling, occupation or vocation" (ii). The original religious sense of vocation remained, though often adulterated as various economic sectors expanded and became more self-conscious. But "calling" or "vocation" used throughout this study assumes a personal relationship or covenant with an external power whether God or a divinized corporate identity. That "personal" notion

differs substantially from the secular "profession" that we know as specialized, contractual employment performed by members of a self-protective body that defines terms of training and certification. Gradual blurring of boundaries accompanied increasing secularization and development in public economic sectors. It is that emergent, secularized notion of "profession" that is the more delimited subject in the recent *John Donne's Professional Lives,* ed. David Colclough (Cambridge: D. S. Brewer, 2003).

But "profession" remained colored by its own religious history, in Donne and others. Its received meanings included a vow on entering a religious order, a religious order itself, or the declaration of one's belief in a religious system (*OED*). Accordingly, we can find a given writer interconnecting vocation and profession when examining a religious calling. For example, in recommending that each person select a model to follow in vocation, Donne says, "Be sombody, be like sombody, propose some good example in thy calling and profession to imitate" (180), in *Sermons,* vol. 8, ed. Evelyn M. Simpson and George R. Potter (Berkeley: University of California Press, 1962).

44. For a useful capsule account of Spenser's civil service in Ireland, see Rambuss, *Spenser's Secret Career,* 7–9.

45. See Andrew Hadfield, *Spenser's Irish Experience: Wilde Fruit and Salvage Soyl* (Oxford: Clarendon Press, 1997). Hadfield's argument is that Spenser increasingly doubted that English standards of civil order could be applied in unruly Ireland, given Elizabeth's indecisive reluctance to conduct a sufficiently strong-willed interventionist regime. The failure of British colonial rule in Ireland specifically accounts for the discoloration of Spenser's vision later in *The Faerie Queene.*

46. Lodowick Bryskett, *A Discovrse of Civill Life: Containing the Ethike part of Morall Philosophie. Fit for the instructing of a Gentleman in the course of a vertuous life* (London, 1606). Hereafter cited within the text as *Discovrse* with the appropriate page number.

Notes to Chapter Two

1. All references are to *The Norton Shakespeare,* ed. Stephen Greenblatt (New York: W. W. Norton & Company, 1997). Act, scene, and line numbers are given parenthetically within the text.

2. All biblical quotations are from the Geneva Bible.

3. Philip S. Watson, "Luther's Doctrine of Vocation," *Scottish Journal of Theology* 2 (1949): 369.

4. Ibid., 369–70. For another useful characterization of Luther's notion of the multiple stations within a vocation, see Paul Althaus, *The Ethics of Martin Luther,* trans. Robert C. Schultz (Philadelphia: Fortress Press, 1965): "Luther's enumeration of the stations clearly indicates that

each person belongs to a variety of stations simultaneously: a prince or lord can also be a husband and father, and hold an ecclesiastical office as well. Every man stands in several relationships to other people. Each one, however, has the duty of serving God and man in his stations and fulfilling the law of his station" (38).

5. Watson, "Luther's Doctrine of Vocation," 370.

6. Ibid., 364.

7. Gustav Wingren, *Luther on Vocation*, trans. Carl C. Rasmussen (Philadelphia: Muhlenberg Press, 1957), 137.

8. John Calvin, *Institutes of the Christian Religion*, trans. Ford Lewis Battles (Philadelphia: The Westminster Press, 1973), 3.10.6.

9. William Perkins, *Treatise of the Vocations*, in *Works* (London, 1612–13; first published posthumously in 1602), 750.

10. Ibid., 757.

11. Ian Breward, ed., introduction and notes to *The Work of William Perkins* (Appleford, Abingdon, Berkshire, England: The Sutton Courtenay Press, 1970), 444.

12. Lawrence Stone, *The Crisis of the Aristocracy 1558–1641* (Oxford: Clarendon Press, 1965), 7–15.

13. Richard M. Douglas, "Talent and Vocation in Humanist and Protestant Thought," in *Action and Conviction in Early Modern Europe*, ed. Theodore K. Rabb and Jerrold E. Seigel (Princeton: Princeton University Press, 1969), 296.

14. Perkins, *Treatise of the Vocations*, 776.

15. Ibid., 776–77.

16. Ibid., 760.

17. Ibid., 758.

18. For a discussion of "fitness," see my chapter four, "Fit Framing," *Herbert's Prayerful Art* (Toronto: University of Toronto Press, 1989), 77–99.

19. Perkins, *Treatise of the Vocations*, 778.

20. M. C. Bradbrook, "Role-Playing in *Henry IV*," in Harold Bloom, ed. *William Shakespeare's "Henry IV, Part 2"* (New York: Chelsea House, 1982), 80.

21. Jesus compares ten virgins to the kingdom of heaven. Five foolish virgins took no lamp oil to meet the bridegroom, who was unexpectedly delayed at night. By contrast, five wise virgins were prepared for the delay, hence remained in waiting, their lamps in readiness. On return from purchasing oil, the unprepared, foolish virgins were denied entry and recognition by the bridegroom: "Verily, I say unto you, I knowe you not" (Matthew 25:12).

22. G.R. Elton, *The Tudor Constitution: Documents and Commentary*, 2nd ed. (Cambridge: Cambridge University Press, 1982), 12.

23. Ibid., 150, n. 14.

24. Ibid., 148.

25. Charles Gray, "Parliament, Liberty and the Law," in *Parliament*

and History from the Reign of Elizabeth to the Civil War, ed. Jack H. Hexter (Stanford: Stanford University Press, 1992), 158.

26. Elton, *The Tudor Constitution,* 150.

27. Ibid., 17–18.

28. Gray, "Parliament, Liberty and the Law," 162.

29. Elton, *The Tudor Constitution,* 150.

30. David Lindsay Keir, *The Constitutional History of Modern Britain since 1485,* 9th ed. (London: Adam & Charles Black, 1969), 29.

31. On the role of the chief justices in the Star Chamber, see Elton, *The Tudor Constitution,* 165 and J. R. Tanner, *Tudor Constitutional Documents: A.D. 1485–1603 with an historical commentary* (Cambridge: Cambridge University Press, 1951), 254.

32. Keir, *Constitutional History,* 29.

33. Charles Howard McIlwain, *The High Court of Parliament and Its Supremacy: An Historical Essay on the Boundaries between Legislation and Adjudication in England* (New Haven: Yale University, 1910), 42–100.

34. W. S. Holdsworth, *A History of English Law* (London: Methuen, 1909), 3:360.

35. Holdsworth, *English Law* (1903), 1:73.

36. Elton, *The Tudor Constitution,* 17–18.

37. Ibid., 234.

38. Ibid., 234–35.

39. See Tanner, *Constitutional Documents:* "It is true that the chief business of a Tudor Parliament had come to be what we should call legislation, but the change in its position was not perceived by Tudor statesmen, who continued to think and speak of it in the old way as a Court. In 1589 the Speaker reminded the Commons 'that every member of this House is a Judge of this Court, being the highest Court of all other courts, and the Great Council also of this realm,' and urged upon them a sobriety of demeanour such as became the office of a judge. In 1591 Lambarde called it 'our chief and highest court,' and wrote of the making of new law there almost as if it were 'the decision of a new case,' or 'the reversal of an error of a preceding Parliament'" (511).

40. Elton, *The Tudor Constitution,* 246.

41. Ibid., 14.

42. Cf. Lorna Hutson, "Not the King's Two Bodies: Reading the 'Body Politic' in Shakespeare's *Henry IV,* Parts 1 and 2," in *Rhetoric and Law in Early Modern Europe,* ed. Victoria Kahn and Lorna Hutson (New Haven: Yale University Press, 2001), 166–98. Hutson argues that *Richard II* and the two *Henry IV* plays express an emergent civic consciousness of a "body politic" different from the mystical notion of the king's two bodies. That earlier notion embodied the public weal mystically in the king and encouraged royal prerogative. Hutson's discussion points to the developmental reformation in Hal whereby he submits to the authority

of the lord chief justice. "The techniques of probability or verisimilitude that Shakespeare employs to make the timing of Hal's reformation seem credible are . . . self-consciously related to the techniques of proof characteristic of the equitable development of the common law in this period" (182). In Elizabethan legal considerations, a practice of equity increasingly emphasized the intention of the law, not the arbitrary application of the letter. The deference of the newly crowned Hal/Henry to the lord chief justice at the expense of his own royal prerogative is consistent with that practice.

43. Watson, *Luther's Doctrine of Vocation*, 376.

44. E.g., Bradbrook, "Role-Playing in *Henry IV*," 71–83; David Boyd, "The Player Prince: Hal in *Henry IV Part 1*," *Sydney Studies in English* 6 (1980–81): 3–16: Anthony Miller, "Roles and Players in *Henry IV, Part I*," *Sydney Studies in English* 7 (1981–82): 32–48; Thomas F. Van Laan, *Role-playing in Shakespeare* (Toronto: University of Toronto Press, 1978), 147–51.

45. Harold C. Goddard, "*Henry IV*," in *Henry IV, Pt. 1*, ed. Harold Bloom (New York: Chelsea House, 1987), 22.

46. Leonard Tennenhouse, *Power on Display: The Politics of Shakespeare's Genres* (New York: Methuen, 1986).

47. Coppelia Kahn, *Man's Estate: Masculine Identity in Shakespeare* (Berkeley: University of California Press, 1981), 71.

48. Tennenhouse, *Power on Display*, 84.

49. John Cox, "The Elizabethan Hal," in *Shakespeare and the Dramaturgy of Power* (Princeton: Princeton University Press, 1989), 111.

50. Sherman H. Hawkins, "Virtue and Kingship in Shakespeare's *Henry IV*," *ELR* 5 (1975): 313–43.

51. Tennenhouse, *Power on Display*, 82.

52. Kahn, *Man's Estate*, 71.

53. Perkins, *Treatise of the Vocations*, 762.

54. See D. J. Palmer, "Casting off the Old Man: History and St. Paul, in 'Henry IV,'" *Critical Inquiry* 12 (1970): 267–83.

55. Norman Rabkin, "Rabbits, Ducks, and *Henry V*," *SQ* 28 (1977): 279.

56. Tennenhouse, *Power on Display*, 82.

57. Hawkins, "Virtue and Kingship," 342.

58. Maynard Mack, introduction to *The History of Henry the Fourth [Part One]*, in *The Complete Signet Classic Shakespeare*, ed. Sylvan Barnet (San Diego: Harcourt Brace Jovanovich, 1972), 640.

59. Stephen Greenblatt, "Invisible Bullets: Renaissance Authority and Its Subversion, *Henry IV* and *Henry V*," in *Political Shakespeare: New Essays in Cultural Materialism*, ed. J. Dollimore and A. Sinfield (Manchester: Manchester University Press, 1985), 37–39.

60. Perkins, *Treatise of the Vocations*, 750. For a useful discussion of Perkins in relation to the development of vocational notions, see

Paul Marshall, *A Kind of Life Imposed on Man: Vocation and Social Order from Tyndale to Locke* (Toronto: University of Toronto Press, 1996).

61. The multivalency of *impose* is suggestive. Contemporary meanings include: "to lay on hands in blessing; or in ordination, confirmation"; "to place authoritatively"; "to lay on, as something to be borne, endured, or submitted to"; "to inflict (something) *on* or *upon*; to levy or enforce authoritatively or arbitrarily"; "to put or levy (a tax, price, etc.) *on* or *upon* (goods, etc.)"; "to put or subject (a person, etc.) *to* a penalty, observance"; "to put oneself *upon*; in various senses *on* [To impose itself forcibly, authoritatively, or strikingly; to exert an influence *on*; to be of imposing character or appearance]; To encroach *upon* to 'put' *upon*" (*OED*).

62. Louis Montrose, *The Purpose of Playing: Shakespeare and the Cultural Politics of Elizabethan Theater* (Chicago: The University of Chicago Press, 1996), 208.

63. Ibid., 20.

64. Marie Acton, *The Queen's Two Bodies: Drama and the Elizabethan Succession* (London: Royal Historical Society, 1977).

65. Claire McEachern, "*Henry V* and the Paradox of the Body Politic," *SQ* 45 (1994): 56.

Notes to Chapter Three

1. *The Sermons of John Donne*, ed. George R. Potter and Evelyn M. Simpson, 10 vols. (Berkeley: University of California Press, 1953–62), 3:109–10. All references to the sermons are to this edition, hereafter referred to as *Sermons*, with volume and page numbers given parenthetically within the text.

2. R. C. Bald, *John Donne: A Life* (Oxford: Clarendon Press, 1970), 320. Biographical information on Donne is drawn from this work, unless otherwise noted; hereafter cited as *A Life*.

3. Reid Barbour, *Literature and Religious Culture in Seventeenth-Century England* (Cambridge: Cambridge University Press, 2002), 163.

4. See my introduction, 46–48.

5. Thomas Docherty, *John Donne, Undone* (London: Methuen, 1986), 26–29.

6. Ibid., 123–44.

7. John Carey, *John Donne: Life, Mind and Art* (London: Faber and Faber, 1981). See chapters 1–4.

8. David Aers and Gunter Kress, "'Darke Texts Needs Notes': Versions of Self in Donne's Verse Letters," in *Literature, Language and Society in England: 1580–1680*, ed. D. Aers, B. Hodge, and G. Kress (Totowa, NJ: Barnes and Noble Books, 1981), 30.

9. Annabel Patterson, "All Donne," in *Soliciting Interpretation: Literary Theory and Seventeenth-Century English Poetry*, ed. Elizabeth D. Harvey and Katharine Eisaman Maus (Chicago: The University of Chicago Press, 1990), 51.

10. Ibid., 25.

11. Ibid., 51.

12. David Norbrook, "The Monarch of Wit and the Republic of Letters: Donne's Politics," in *Soliciting Interpretation*, 21.

13. Ibid., 25.

14. Carey, *John Donne*, 220–21, 253, 276–77.

15. Introduction to John Donne, *The Divine Poems*, ed. Helen Gardner (Oxford: Clarendon Press, 1978), xxxi. All references to Donne's divine poems are to this edition, hereafter cited as *Divine Poems*, with the line numbers given parenthetically in the text.

16. John Donne, *Essays in Divinity*, ed. Evelyn M. Simpson (Oxford: Clarendon Press, 1967), title page.

17. A language of dropsy expresses a core relationship between Donne's consuming, lifelong encyclopedic erudition and his amorous desire. In a 1608 lament to Henry Goodyere, he acknowledged the danger of learning separated from vocational responsibilities. Earlier, he "was diverted by the worst voluptuousness, which is an Hydroptique immoderate desire of humane learning and languages"; but this "desire . . . needed an occupation, and a course." The same letter connects the God-given "thirst and inhiation after the next life" in humane nature and his own constant "desire of the next life: always present despite diversions" ("To Sir H. Goodere," in *Letters to Severall Persons of Honour*, ed. C. E. Merrill [New York: Sturgis & Walton Co., 1910], 18.42–45). Unless indicated otherwise, all references to Donne's prose letters are from this edition, cited as *Letters*, with letter and page numbers given parenthetically within the text.

His sonnet on Ann Donne interconnects human and divine love: from "she whome I loved" followed that "admyring her my mind did whett / To seeke thee God" (1,5). Spirituall dropsy follows: "But though I have found thee, and thou my thirst has fed, A holy, thirsty dropsy melts me yett" (6–7). Dropsy's paradox captures both the headlong greed of "inhiation" and fullness beyond measure, both the lover's and the scholar's desire. A scholar's lifelong "ordinary diet, which is reading" feeds the thirst of learning. ("To the Earl of Dorset" [?] in *The Life and Letters of John Donne*, ed. Edmund Gosse [New York: Dodd, Mead and Company, 1899; reprint Gloucester, Mass.: Peter Smith, 1959], 2:208; hereafter cited as *Life and Letters*, given with volume and page number parenthetically). In a prayer written during his intense study of theological literature prior to ordination, he once again confesses learning's power to divert him: "Thou hast given mee a desire of knowledg, and some meanes to it, and some possession of it; and I have arm'd myself with thy weapons against thee" (*Essays in Divinity*, 97). The scholar's thirst, like the lover's thirst for "prophane mistresses" in "What if this present were the world's last night?" — 10), had known various diversions; but the headlong, hydropsical desire in Donne's nature remained constant.

18. Patterson, "All Donne," 58.

19. Dennis Flynn, *John Donne and the Ancient Catholic Nobility* (Bloomington: Indiana University Press, 1995). See 134–46 for discussion of Donne's experience in France and Belgium, and 170–72 for his presence later in the Stanley household.

20. For a discussion of Donne's touching efforts to assuage his mother's grief at Anne Lyly's death, see Bald, *A Life,* 316. Bald sets Anne's death "about 1616" (239).

21. See *John Donne's "desire of more": The Subject of Anne More in His Poetry,* ed. M. Thomas Hester (Newark: University of Delaware Press, 1996). This useful volume addresses the longstanding need in Donne criticism to provide a systematic assessment of Anne Donne as a subject in his life and works. Her shadow presence will necessarily remain elusive in spite of these substantial efforts.

22. Arthur Marotti, *John Donne, Coterie Poet* (Madison: University of Wisconsin Press, 1986), xi.

23. All citations from the verse letters are taken from John Donne, *The Satires, Epigrams and Verse Letters,* ed. W. Milgate (Oxford: Clarendon Press, 1978).

24. In addition to the more obvious "nausea," the *OED* points to other dimensions in "queasie." These include: "an unsettled condition, even the times; unhealthiness or an inclination to sickness; a delicacy or fastidiousness of sensibility; scrupulous conscience." The verb "disuse" assumes a habitual practice to be broken.

25. Elegy 16. "On His Mistress," (4). All quotations from the secular love poetry are from *The Elegies and The Songs and Sonnets,* ed. Helen Gardner (Oxford: Clarendon Press, 1965), with line numbers given parenthetically in the text.

26. Achsah Guibbory, "'Oh, let mee not serve so': The Politics of Love in Donne's *Elegies,*" *ELH* 57: 811–33.

27. David Blair, "Inferring Gender in Donne's *Songs and Sonnets,*" *Essays in Criticism* 45 (1995): 241, 243.

28. "To the Most Honourable and my most honoured Lord, the Marquess of Buckingham" in *Life and Letters,* 1:176; see n. 17 above for full bibliographical information.

29. *A Life,* 75.

30. See H. L. Meakin, "Donne's Domestic Muse: Engendering Poetry in the Early Verse Letters," in *John Donne's Articulation of the Feminine.* (Oxford: Clarendon Press, 1998), 24–84. Meakin addresses in detail the feminine muse in Donne's early verse letters, a subject that has received only modest attention in the scholarship on Donne. The letters were written for a male, primarily Inns of Court readership. Despite this masculinist project, Donne's "phallic 'phansie' is never able to banish entirely the

feminine Muse from his masculine exchanges" (84). Meakin's productive insights into the feminine presence in Donne's imagination do not lead her to ponder the necessary connections among the muse, the feminine soul, and the feminine characterization of virtue.

31. Ted-Larry Pebworth and Claude J. Summers, "'Thus Friends Absent Speake': The Exchange of Verse Letters between John Donne and Henry Wotton," *MP* 81 (1984): 361–77.

32. See Milgate's discussion of Woodward's request and the date in *The Satires, Epigrams and Verse Letters*, 223.

33. Ibid., xxxv–xxxix.

34. Ben Jonson, "Conversations with William Drummond of Hawthornden," in *Ben Jonson*, ed. Ian Donaldson (Oxford: Oxford University Press, 1985), 3.34–5.598.

35. Barbara Kiefer Lewalski, *Donne's 'Anniversaries' and the Poetry of Praise: The Creation of a Symbolic Mode* (Princeton: Princeton University Press, 1973), 108–41.

36. "20. Prayer," in John Donne, *Devotions upon Emergent Occasions*, ed. Anthony Raspa (Montreal: McGill-Queen's University Press, 1975), 109.

37. Jonson, "Conversations with William Drummond," 3.32–35. (596).

38. Maureen Sabine, *Feminine Engendered Faith: The Poetry of John Donne and Richard Crashaw* (Basingstoke: The MacMillan Press Ltd., 1992), 90.

39. Elizabeth Harvey, *Ventriloquized Voices: Feminist Theory and English Renaissance Texts* (London: Routledge, 1992), 10.

40. Ibid., 107.

41. Ibid., 112.

42. "The Second Anniversary," in *John Donne: The Anniversaries*, ed. Frank Manley (Baltimore: The Johns Hopkins Press, 1963), 92.

43. The related notions are idea, generation, conception, and birth. The Father's mind contains Ideas, which are preconceptions that inform or generate or cause conceptions in the divine being. The Ideas, which are associated with the Son or Word, are eternally generated in the Father's mind; these ideas or preconceptions generate or induce conception, the fruitful reception of ideas in other media. In turn, the overshadowing Holy Spirit (who proceeds eternally from Father and Son, but who enters time) generates the eternal Son in Mary's temporal womb; Mary's womb conceives the eternal Son in human form. For a thumbnail discussion of the received theology of Donne in this matter, see my *Fulfilling the Circle: A Study of John Donne's Thought* (Toronto: University of Toronto Press, 1984), 6–9.

44. See ibid., 7–10 for a discussion of (1) the Spirit's role externally in Creation, internally in re-creation, and (2) conformity with Christ as the linchpin of Donne's mature thought.

45. "So the Lord, which was with thee in the first conception of any good purpose, Returnes to thee againe, to give thee a quickning of that blessed childe of his, and againe, and againe, to bring it forth, and to bring it up, to accomplish and perfect those good intentions, which his Spirit by over-shadowing thy soule, hath formerly begotten in it" (*Sermons* 5: 371).

46. Anna K. Nardo, *The Ludic Self in Seventeenth-Century English Literature* (Albany: State University of New York Press, 1991), 50.

47. Ibid., 53.

48. Melanie Klein argues that the human being is congenitally an anxious creature desiring gratification. Fear of separation caused by birth trauma, fear of annihilation, and fear of unsatisfied bodily needs all comprise a destructive primary anxiety that opposes the desire for gratification. The mother is the natural object of this congenital opposition of forces. She has the power either to increase persecutory anxiety or to satisfy desire. Congenital anxiety if not relieved creates frustration, anger, aggression, distrust, and hatred; contrarily, satisfaction of need and desire creates love, enjoyment, and gratitude. The particular mother, as the external object whose responses shape these opposing energies, is also the external model on which the child projects and, hence, objectifies its negative and positive energies. This model provides the basis for relationships to other human objects later. The elements of this model are also internalized as aspects that make up the growing self. If the conflicting destructive and productive energies have not been integrated, patterns of splitting, disintegration, and fragmentation develop in the self. These patterns can be carried into adult life. For one encapsulation of these ideas see Melanie Klein, "Notes on Some Schizoid Mechanism" (1946) in *Envy and Gratitude and Other Works 1946–1963* (London: Hogarth Press, 1975; reprint, London: Virago Press, 1990), 1–24.

49. See Gerald Aylmer, "Conditions of Entry and Service," "Payment of Officers; Sale and Value of Offices," and "Who the King's Servants Were: A Chapter of Social History," in *The King's Servants: The Civil Service of Charles I, 1625–1642* (London: Routledge & Kegan Paul, 1961), 69–336.

50. A. J. Smith, *John Donne, Complete English Poems* (London: Penguin Books, 1986), 516.

51. For a discussion of Donne's letters to Ann, see Ilona Bell, "'Under Ye Rage of a Hott Sonn &Yr Eyes': John Donne's Love Letters to Ann More," in *The Eagle and the Dove: Reassessing John Donne,* ed. C. J. Summers and T.-L. Pebworth (Columbia: University of Missouri Press, 1986), 25–52.

52. See n. 17 above for bibliographical information on the prose letters.

53. See n. 31 above.

54. *Life and Letters,* 1:165. See n. 17 above for complete bibliographical information.

55. Sherwood, *Fulfilling the Circle,* 4, 134–37.

56. See n. 17 above.

57. Louis Adrian Montrose, "Of Gentlemen and Shepherds: The Politics of Elizabethan Pastoral Form," *ELH* 50 (1983): 429, 433, 452.

58. Lawrence Stone, *The Crisis of the Aristocracy, 1558–1641,* abridged ed. (London: Oxford University Press, 1967), 8.

59. The low survival rate of Donne's letters prevents accurate estimates of how many he wrote. His correspondence with Magdalene Herbert illustrates the problem. Early in their friendship, he promises in a 1607 letter from Mitcham that an "entire colony of letters, of hundreds and fifties must follow"; less than two weeks later he speaks of "my resolution of writing almost daily to you" (*Life and Letters,* 1:164–55). Only her death and Donne's 1627 funeral sermon concluded their long-lived friendship. Bald tells us that "Walton claimed to possess a considerable number of the letters they exchanged, but he printed only four [in *Life of George Herbert*], all of which belong to the early stages of the friendship" (*A Life,* 181). Earlier, Gosse had observed that all the originals in Walton's possession "doubtless perished among Lady Cook's collection of MSS. When Higham House was burned by the Roundheads" (162). In short, the number of letters written to Lady Danvers remains anybody's guess.

60. For useful discussion of issues in epistolarity, including the artifice of presence in absence, see Janet Gurkin Altman, *Epistolarity: Approaches to a Form* (Columbus: Ohio State University Press, 1982), esp. 118–40.

61. On Donne's paradoxical joy in suffering, see Sherwood, *Fulfilling the Circle,* 117–18, 127–29.

62. A cohort of affections appears with frequency in the sermons: amorousness sublimated as devotion, or misdirected as wantonness or licentiousness; ambition veering in one direction toward secular honor and preferment or in another toward divine glory; covetousness seeking to possess wealth or a spiritual realm. Although coexistent, the three members of the cohort are sometimes identified respectively by Donne with youth, middle years, and age. The cohort has flexible boundaries for him: amorousness emerges as gross lust and ambition as competition for place; covetousness modulates into envy, a competitive desire to have what others possess. One succinct statement of the cohort can be found in the retrospectively confessional *Devotions upon Emergent Occasions:* "the fuell of *Lust,* and *Envie,* and *Ambition,* hath inflamed mine" [i.e., heart] (59).

But Donne had identified this cohort much earlier in his works. His 1590s letter to Henry Wotton ("Sir, more then kisses") locates "pride, lust, covetize" in "all three places," countries, courts and towns (31–32). Defensive scorn in "The Sunne Rising" and "The Canonization" opposes spiritualized love competitively to the base world of ambition and covetousness. But to be "all States, and all Princes" (21) in "The Sunne Rising" confesses ambition, just as "the'India's of spice and Myne" that "lie here with mee" (17–18) sublimate covetousness and envy. In "The Canonization" love's explosive aggression overcompensates for ambition's path to "a course" or "a place" (5) now blocked and for desired preferment from "his Honour, or his grace" (6) or the King now compromised. This commemorative poem that competes with "a well wrought urne" (33) struggles to reform covetous envy of place, wealth, and power.

63. Joan Webber, *The Eloquent 'I': Style and Self in Seventeenth-Century Prose* (Madison: University of Wisconsin Press, 1968), 34ff.

64. See Erasmus, *The Handbook of the Christian Soldier: Enchiridion, militis christiani*, trans. Charles Fantazzi *in Collected Works*, 66 (Toronto: University of Toronto Press, 1974), 33–34. Donne may have this passage in mind, with its reference to Jerome's "beloved female captive in mind." Fantazzi tells us that in a letter "Jerome refers allegorically to *Deuteronomy* 21:10–13, where the Israelites are permitted to take female captives if they shave their heads and pare their nails" (277–78, n. 34).

65. William Kerrigan, "The Fearful Accommodations of John Donne," *ELR* 4 (1974): 354–55.

66. Surgical circumcision applies more generally, but not exclusively to males; in both cases purification is the issue. The drama of Donne's ambiguity plays on the maleness of the Judaic-Christian practice.

67. Sherwood, *Fulfilling the Circle*, 104.

68. "But by my death can not be satisfied
My sinnes, which passe the Jewes impiety:
They kill'd once an inglorious man, but I
Crucifie him daily, being now glorified."
(*Divine Poems*, "Spit in my face yee Jewes," 5–8)

69. Donne's theology of conformity bears a heavy debt to Augustinian conformity of divine and human wills, but the affective likeness to Christ is Pauline. "For whom he did foreknow, he also did predestinate to be conformed to the image of his son, that he might be the firstborn among many brethren" (Rom. 8:29): "That I may know him, and the power of his resurrection, and the fellowship of his sufferings, being made conformable unto his death" (Phil. 3:10).

70. Sherwood, *Fulfilling the Circle*, 5–13, 44–50, 53–60.

71. For an obvious application of this commonplace notion, see William Perkins, *A Treatise of the Vocations*. Written in the late 1590s and first published posthumously in 1602, Perkins's treatise is the most developed discussion of "calling" in the English Reformation. Perkins establishes 1 Corinthians 5:20 as its keynote, and the principle of labor or work in a lawful calling is everywhere explicit.

72. Dave Gray and Jeanne Shami, "Political Advice in Donne's *Devotions:* No Man Is An Island," *MLQ* 50 (1989): 337–56. Cf. Richard Strier, "Donne and the Politics of Devotion" in *Religion, Literature, and*

Politics in Post-Reformation England. 1540–1688 (Cambridge: Cambridge University Press, 1996). Strier rejects the Gray/Shami claim that "there are two main political themes in the *Devotions,* the vulnerability and the public responsibilities of the King" (98). Instead, the work's primary concern is not governmental but "ecclesiastical politics" (104). The polemical *Devotions* joins "the attack of the Arminian wing of the Church of England on those who would further reform the liturgy and practice of that church" (101). More broadly, Strier targets those including Shami, Annabel Patterson, and David Norbrook who are "searching for oppositionality [i.e., to the Crown] in Donne's sermons" (94).

73. For discussion of Donne's role in the *Directions for Preachers,* see Shami's "'Faire Interpretation': The *Directions* and the Crisis of Censorship," in *John Donne and Conformity in Crisis in the Late Jacobean Pulpit* (Cambridge: D. S. Brewer, 2003), 102–38.

74. Jeanne Shami, "The Absolutist Politics of Quotation," in *John Donne's Religious Imagination: Essays in Honor of John T.* Shawcross, ed. Raymond-Jean Frontain and Frances M. Malpezzi (Conway, Arkansas: University of Central Arkansas Press, 1995), 403.

75. Paul Harland, "Donne's Political Intervention in the Parliament of 1629," *JDJ* 11 (1992): 21–37.

76. Barbour, *Literature and Religious Culture,* 162. Also, see my introduction in this book for discussion of some relationships between the pulpit and the theater.

77. Shami, *John Donne and Conformity in Crisis,* 141.

78. Ibid., 274.

79. Ibid., 140.

Notes to Chapter Four

References to Jonson's poetry, *Timber or Discoveries,* and *Conversations with William Drummond of Hawthornden* are from *Ben Jonson,* ed. Ian Donaldson (Oxford: Oxford University Press, 1985). This edition is hereafter referred to as Donaldson. Individual works and line references from this edition will be given parenthetically within the text using the following abbreviations: *Epigrams = Epig; The Forest = For; Discoveries = Disc; The Underwood = Und; Ungathered Verse = UV; Conversations = Conv.* Also used occasionally is *Ben Jonson,* 11 vols., ed. C. H. Herford, Percy and Evelyn Simpson (Oxford: Clarendon Press, 1925–51), referred to as H & S with the appropriate volume number, page, and line numbers.

1. John Dryden, *A Discourse Concerning the Original and Progress of Satire* in *Essays,* ed. W. P. Ker (New York: Russell & Russell, 1961), 2:18.

2. Alexander Pope, "The Preface of the Editor to *The Works of*

Shakespear," in *The Prose Works of Alexander Pope,* vol. 2, ed. Rosemary Cowler (Oxford: Archon Books, 1986), 19.

3. Thomas M. Greene, "Ben Jonson and the Centered Self," *SEL* 10 (1970): 326. Also see Richard Helgerson, *Self-Crowned Laureates: Spenser, Jonson, Milton and the Literary System* (Berkeley: University of California Press, 1983), 40: "the something of great constancy at the center of the laureate's work is easily defined. It is the poet himself. His deliberately serious poetic is grounded on a serious, centered self." Helgerson's acknowledged debt to Greene includes Jonson in a wider application to other poets.

For a more skeptical treatment of Jonson's habitual emphasis upon centeredness, see Ian Donaldson, "Gathering and Losing the Self: Jonson and Biography," in *Jonson's Magic Houses: Essays in Interpretation* (Oxford: Clarendon Press, 1997), 26–46. Donaldson argues that "his imagination was simultaneously drawn to the idea of a self that was not fast but loose, duplicitous, mercurial" (44).

4. Greene, "Jonson and the Centered Self," 330.

5. Richard S. Peterson, *Imitation and Praise in the Poems of Ben Jonson* (New Haven: Yale University Press, 1981), 25.

6. Cf. John Donne, "A Valediction: forbidding Mourning," in *The Elegies and The Songs and Sonnets,* ed. Helen Gardner (Oxford: Clarendon Press, 1965), 63. The lovers' "two soules" (21) are "stiffe twin compasses" (26); hers is the stable "fixt foot" (27) at the center, growing "erect" (32) on his return, its centered, spiritual rectitude or "firmnes" justifying his "circle" (35–36).

7. Peterson, *Imitation and Praise,* 24–29.

8. For a discussion of Herbert and Donne's friendship, see R. C. Bald, *John Donne: A Life* (Oxford: Clarendon Press, 1970), 164–70.

9. Also see my "Reason, Faith, and Just Augustinian Lamentation in Donne's Elegy on Prince Henry," *SEL* 13 (1973): 55–59.

10. John Selden, *Titles of Honor* (London: William Stansby, 1614), a2.

11. Also included between Selden's dedication to Hayward and Jonson's poem are two very brief poems in Greek. The first is a short four-line poem by Selden, honoring William Camden, with an English title: "To that singular Glory of our Nature and Light of *Britaine, M.Camden Clarenceulx.*"

12. Who shall doubt, Donne, whe'er I a poet be,
     When I dare send my epigrams to thee?
   That so alone canst judge, so alone dost make;
     And in thy censures, evenly dost take
   As free simplicity to disavow
     As thou hast best authority to allow.   (*Epig* 96.1–6)

13. See chapter 3, 170–71, for a discussion of this notion of friendship in Donne's letters.

14. "It is an act of tyranny, not love, / In course of friendship wholly to reprove, / And flattery, with friends' humours still to move." (*UV* 49.18–20)

15. Edward Fry, "John Selden, 1584–1654," in *Dictionary of National Biography*, ed. Leslie Stephen and Sidney Lee (London: Oxford University Press, reprint 1937–38), 18:1152.

16. David Sandler Berkowitz, *John Selden's Formative Years: Politics and Society in Early Seventeenth-Century England* (Washington, DC: The Folger Shakespeare Library, 1988), 22.

17. Selden, "To my most beloued Friend and *Chamberfellow, M. Edward Heyward*," in *Titles of Honor* [1614], a2–a3.

18. John Selden, "To my most beloued Friend, *Edward Heyward* of *Cardeston* in *Norfolk*, Esquire," in *Titles of Honor: The Second Edition* (London: William Stansby, 1631), 1 [my numbering].

19. Ibid., 3.

20. Ibid., 4.

21. Modernized spelling and line numbering are taken from Donaldson. Jonson's verse letter was included in both the 1614 and 1631 editions of *Titles of Honour* as well as *Underwoods*, which was published posthumously in 1640 as part of the expanded folio edition prepared by Kenelm Digby.

22. Selden, *Titles of Honor*, 4.

23. Ibid., 5.

24. Ibid., 6.

25. Edward Heyward commendatory poem in Jonson's first Folio.

26. Katharine Eisaman Maus, *Ben Jonson and the Roman Frame of Mind* (Princeton: Princeton University Press, 1984), 111–50.

27. For one discussion of these dislocations and uncertainties, see Lawrence Stone, *The Crisis of the Aristocracy 1558–1641*, abridged ed. (Oxford: Oxford University Press, 1966), 11–13.

28. David Riggs, *Ben Jonson: A Life* (Cambridge: Harvard University Press, 1989), 353.

29. Robert C. Evans, *Ben Jonson and the Poetics of Patronage* (Lewisburg, PA: Bucknell University Press, 1989), esp. 23–30.

30. For an informative discussion of Jonson and his immediate context in relation to the epideictic tradition, see Michael McCanles, "'Vera Nobilitas' as a Theory of Epideictic Rhetoric," in *Jonsonian Discriminations: The Humanist Poet and the Praise of True Nobility* (Toronto: University of Toronto Press, 1992), 139–80. McCanles epitomizes Jonson's notion of praise as follows: "True praise of those whose true nobility merits it by a poet whose authority establishes the credibility of both: this describes not only the purpose of much of Jonson's poetry but its central subject as well" (139).

31. See chapter 3, 172–75.

32. Jonson's varied legion of patrons during his career attests not only to his importance and wide appeal, but also to the alliances neces-

sary for adequate support. Royal patrons included Kings James and Charles, Queens Ann and Henrietta, and the short-lived Prince Henry; titled patrons included Lucy Bedford, Lucius Carey, Robert Carr, William Cavendish, Robert Cecil, Thomas Egerton, Lucy Harrington, Philip and William Herbert, Thomas Howard, Edward Sackville, Robert Sidney, Esmé Stuart, and Richard Weston; other patrons included Robert Cotton and Kenelm Digby.

33. Richard Helgerson, "Ben Jonson," in *The Cambridge Companion to English Poetry: Donne to Marvell*, ed. Thomas N. Corns (Cambridge: Cambridge University Press, 1993), 149.

34. See especially chapter 2, "Jonson and 'Vera Nobilitas,'" in McCanles, *Jonsonian Discriminations*, 46–101.

35. Hang all your rooms with one large pedigree:
     'Tis virtue alone is true nobility.
   Which virtue from your father, ripe, will fall;
     Study illustrious him, and you have all.
   ("To Kenelm, John, George" in "Eupheme" [untitled], *Und* 84:8.19–22)

Cf. "tota licet veteres exornent undique cerae / atria, nobilitas sola est atque unica virtus" [even if you decorate your hall from one end to the other with wax images, Virtue remains the one and only real nobility]. Juvenal, *Satires*, 8.19–20.

36. Blair Worden, "Ben Jonson among the Historians," in *Culture and Politics in Early Stuart England* (Stanford: Stanford University Press, 1993), 87.

37. McCanles, *Jonsonian Discriminations*, 201–06.

38. Ibid., 186.

39. Seneca, *De Beneficiis*, 1.1.8, in *Moral Essays*, vol. 3, trans. John W. Basore (Cambridge: Harvard University Press, 1989).

40. See Riggs, *Ben Jonson*, 283–84, for discussion of Jonson and friendship.

41. See Donaldson, 646, on dating the *Epigrams*.

42. Ben Jonson, "To The Great Example of Honor and Virtue, The Most Noble William, Earl of Pembroke, Lord Chamberlain," in *Cataline*, ed. W. F. Bolton and Jane F. Gardner (Lincoln: University of Nebraska Press, 1973), 3. Hereafter referred to as *Cataline*, with page and line number given parenthetically with the text.

43. See Cicero, *De Oratore*, ed. E. W. Sutton and H. Rackham (Cambridge, MA: Harvard University Press, 1996), 2.15.62–65. Here Cicero discusses the criteria for historical writing, with special emphasis upon the criterion of truth. Also see n. 51 below.

44. For a discussion of Jonson's genealogical intentions as a poet in relation to Philip Sidney and the Sidney family, in particular to Sidney's daughter, the Countess of Rutland, see Raphael Falco, *Conceived Presences: Literary Genealogy in Renaissance England* (Amherst:

University of Massachusetts Press, 1994): "Thus his [Sidney's] fatherhood is revealed to be twofold: he is at once the Countess of Rutland's biological father and also a father figure to the poets who follow him, not least among them the aspiring Jonson himself . . . . Both his own poetry and the countess are Sidney's progeny. But his writing, 'that most masculine issue of his braine' (6), though the zenith of English literary achievement, pales in value before the glorious attributes of his child" (130).

45. Donaldson (741) notes that lines 540–45 in *Discoveries* borrow from Justus Lipsius (*Politica*, 1.1), in turn indebted to Tacitus (*Historia*, 4.17) and Seneca (*Epistulae Morales*, 98).

46. Francis Bacon, *The Advancement of Learning*, ed. W. A. Wright (Oxford: Clarendon Press, 1963), 1.6.1.

47. For a brief, useful capture of the "sister arts tradition," see Christopher Braider, "The Paradoxical Sisterhood: 'Ut pictura poesis,'" in *The Cambridge History of Literary Criticism*, vol. 3, *The Renaissance*, ed. Glyn P. Norton (Cambridge: Cambridge University Press, 1999), 168–75. Braider notes that "The doctrine *ut pictura poesis* ('as is' or 'as in painting, so is' or 'so in poetry') lies at the heart of Renaissance aesthetics, the central theme and presiding dogma of the theory and practice of painting and poetry alike" (168). Jonson's discussion of "Pictura et poesis" in *Discoveries* (1502–1600) borrows explicitly and implicitly from the obvious traditional sources such as Pliny, Plutarch, Horace, and Quintilian cited throughout Renaissance discussions of aesthetics. Braider notes that "Horace's defining tag (*Ars Poetica* 361) appears virtually in every treatise on art or poetry in the early Renaissance to the close of the Enlightenment" (168). Jonson's poetic translation of Horace in *Ars Poetica* fixes him in that tradition.

48. Donaldson glosses Jonson's marginal *ingenium* as "talent" (754, n. 2434). Jonson's discussion is more specific about inspiration as a component in the poet's gift: "For whereas all other arts consist of doctrine and precepts, the poet must be able by nature and instinct to pour out the treasure of his mind" (*Disc* 2434–36). The notion of ascent through "poetical rapture" (2439) is consistent with "My own true Fire" by which "my thought takes wing" in "And must I sing?" (*For* 10.29–30). The gift of "natural wit" includes the poet's full powers of imagination and rational intuition.

49. "A poem, as I have told you, is the work of the poet; the end and the fruit of his labour and study. Poesy is his skill or craft of making; the very fiction itself, the reason, or form of the work. And these three voices differ, as the thing done, the doing, and the doer; the thing feigned, the feigning, and the feigner; so the poem, the poesy, and the poet" (*Disc* 2398–2403).

50. Cf. Jonson's 1610 masque *Hymenai*, in *Ben Jonson: The Complete Masques*, ed. Stephen Orgel (New Haven: Yale University Press, 1969).

Jonson's explanatory notes describe "two ladies, the one representing Truth, the other Opinion, but both so alike attired as they could by no note be distinguished. . . . These, after the mist was vanished, began to examine each other curiously with their eyes, and approaching the state, the one expostulated the other in this manner" (98.620–26). Truth's expostulation rigorously scores her insubstantial look-alike:

> It is confirmed. With what an equal brow
> To Truth Opinion's confident! And how
> Like Truth her habit shows to sensual eyes!
> But whosoe'er thou be in this disguise,
> Clear Truth anon shall strip thee to the heart,
> And show how mere fantastical thou art.   (99.645–50)

51. Jonson's commendatory poem on Walter Raleigh's *The History of the World* (1614) was included in the book's prefatory materials. The poem comments on the book's elaborate frontispiece (repr. in Donaldson 345) including four pillars upholding a temple-like structure labeled "The History of the World." The four pillars are respectively labeled "Testis Temporum," "Nuncia Vetustatis," "Lux Veritatis," and "Vita Memoriae." Standing within the left alcove formed by the first two pillars is a fully clothed female figure labeled "Experientia"; standing within the right alcove formed by the latter two pillars is a naked female labeled "Veritas." Jonson's poem addresses these and other specific details in the frontispiece:

> Of truth that searcheth the most [hidden] springs
> And guided by experience, whose straight wand
>   Doth mete, whose line doth sound the depth of things,
> She cheerfully supporteth what she rears,
>   Assisted by no strengths but are her own;
> Some note of which each varied pillar bears;
>   By which, as proper titles, she is known
> Time's witness, herald of antiquity,
>   The light of truth, and life of memory.   (*Und* 24.10–18)

The concluding couplet translates the four pillars, including the "light of truth," a commonplace widely accepted by Raleigh, Jonson, and others.

For Cicero's characterization of history see *De Oratore*, 2.9.36: "Historia vero testis temporum, lux veritatis, vita memoriae, magistra vitae, nuntia vetustatis, qua voce alia, nisi oratoris, immortalitati commendatur." [And as History, which bears witness to the passing of the ages, sheds light upon reality, gives life to recollection and guidance to human existence, and brings tidings of ancient days, whose voice, but the orator's, can entrust her to immortality?] For an extended discussion of the commonplace Ciceronian "light of truth" notion in early modern historical discourse, see D. R. Woolf, *The Idea of History in Early Stuart England: Erudition, Ideology, and 'The Light of Truth' from the Accession of James I to the Civil War* (Toronto: University of Toronto Press, 1990).

Jonson shared this Ciceronian ground knowing that other studious intellectuals like Camden, Selden, Hayward, and Cotton likewise viewed historical writing as the "light of truth." *Sejanus* assumes this illumination.

52. "To the Readers" in Ben Jonson, *Sejanus: His Fall*, ed. Philip J. Ayres (Manchester: Manchester University Press, 1990), 50. All references are to this edition of Jonson's 1605 publication, hereafter referred to as *Sejanus*. Act and line numbers are given parenthetically within the text. For an interpretation of Jonson's "truth of argument," see Joseph Allen Bryant Jr., "The Significance of Ben Jonson's First Requirement in Tragedy: 'Truth of Argument,'" *SP* 49 (1952): 195–213.

53. For a discussion of Jonson's use of Roman history and whether or not he should be viewed as a historian in *Sejanus*, see Ayres's introduction to *Sejanus*, 28–37.

54. Ben Jonson, *Every Man Out of His Humour*, ed. Helen Ostovich (Manchester: Manchester University Press, 2001), 3.1.526–27. All citations are from this edition, cited as *Every Man Out*, with act, scene, and line numbers given parenthetically in the text; also cited as Ostovich.

55. Ben Jonson, *Epicoene*, ed. Edward Partridge (New Haven: Yale University Press, 1971), 23–25. All citations are from this edition, hereafter cited as *Epicoene*, with act, scene, and line numbers given parenthetically within the text. Partridge notes that Jonson's principled claim to "content the people" ("Prologue," 2) owes to Terrence's *Andria* (174, n. 2).

56. Partridge, introduction to *Epicoene*, 18.

57. Ibid., 18.

58. Partridge, notes to prologue in *Epicoene*, 174.

59. Jonas Barish, *Ben Jonson and the Language of Prose Comedy* (Cambridge, MA: Harvard University Press, 1960).

60. For a discussion of this influence on Jonson, see Adrian McCrea, *Constant Minds: Political Virtue and the Lipsian Paradigm in England, 1584–1650* (Toronto: University of Toronto Press, 1997), 138–70.

61. In 1597 Jonson was imprisoned along with the actors Gabriell Spencer and Robert Shaa for his part in the probably subversive *The Isle of Dogs*. The play was largely the work of Thomas Nashe. After the 1603 performance of *Sejanus His Fall*, the Privy Council questioned him for alleged treasonous allusions. See Ayers's introduction to *Sejanus*, 16–22, for the role of Jonson's implacable enemy, Lord Henry Howard, in these events. (The performance version included some work of a collaborator, probably George Chapman, but the highly annotated 1605 Quarto version was Jonson's own.) He was imprisoned again in 1605 for *Eastward Ho*, written in collaboration with George Chapman and John Marston. This play targeted the Scottish King James I's sale of ready-made

knighthoods, particularly to Scots. Riggs captures Jonson's legal troubles as follows: "This man appears to have spent the better part of his adult life courting disaster" (*Ben Jonson*, 141).

62. See Roma B. Gill, "The Renaissance Conventions of Envy," *M & H*, n.s., 9 (1979): 215–30. Also helpful in understanding the conventions readily available to Jonson in the late sixteenth century is Ronald Bond, "Envy" in *The Spenser Encyclopedia* (Toronto: University of Toronto Press, 1990), 248–49. Spenser's most immediate influence on Jonson is expressed in the characterization of a detractor as "a blatant beast" ("To My Detractor," *UV* 37.9), referring to the rapacious allegorical beast representing malicious slander and detraction in *The Faerie Queene*, book 6.

Reference to Ovid's allegorization of Envy lies behind most early modern characterizations. See Ovid, *Metamorphoses*, trans. Rolfe Humphries (Bloomington: Indiana University Press, 1955), 2.758–833.

> She [Minerva] came to Envy's house, a black abode,
> Ill-kept, stained with dark gore, a hidden home
> In a deep valley, where no sunshine comes,
> Where no wind blows, gloomy, and full of cold,
> Where no bright fire burns ever, where the smoke
> Is the grey fog of everlasting mist. (759–64)
>   there was Envy
> Eating the flesh of snakes, the proper food
> To nourish venom with. Minerva turned,
> As Envy rose, torpid and slow, the snakes
> Half-eaten on the ground, and she came forward,
> Torpid and slow, and as she saw the goddess,
> All bright and beautiful in all her armor,
> She groaned aloud and sighed for that bright presence.
> Pale, skinny, squint-eyed, mean, her teeth are red
> With rust, her breast is green with gall, her tongue
> Suffused with poison, and she never laughs
> Except when watching pain; she never sleeps,
> Too troubled by anxiety; if men
> Succeed, she fails; consumes, and is consumed,
> Herself her punishment.
>   . . . .
> And Envy watched her, sidelong, out of sight,
> Mumbling and muttering, sorry to be helpful
> In any victory, picked up her staff
> All wound with thorns, but on the cloudy mantle
> In which she travels and wherever she goes
> The grasses wither, the tall trees are blighted,
> And towns and houses and their people tainted.

At last she looked on Athens, that fine city
Shining with art and wealth and peace and pleasure,
And weeps almost, since she sees nothing there
That anyone could weep at.   (768–82, 787–97)

63. For the role of *Poetaster* in these hostilities, see Matthew Steggle, *Wars of the Theatres: The Poetics of Personation in the Age of Jonson* (Victoria, BC: English Literary Series, University of Victoria, 1998), 21–61.

64. Ben Jonson, *Poetaster*, ed. Tom Cain (Manchester: Manchester University Press, 1995), 71. All citations are from this edition, with act, scene, and line numbers, plus other elements, given parenthetically within the text.

65. For Lucian's influence on Jonson, see Christopher Robinson, *Lucian and His Influence in Europe* (London: Duckworth, 1979), 103–09, especially 105–06 regarding the emetic pill; Douglas Duncan, *Ben Jonson and the Lucianic Tradition* (Cambridge: Cambridge University Press, 1979), esp. 130–38 for discussion of *Every Man Out* and *Poetaster*. Also see Riggs, *Ben Jonson*, 134–35.

66. Lucian, "Slander: on not being quick to put faith in it," in *Works*, trans. A. M. Harmon. (Cambridge: Harvard University Press, 1953), 1:359–93.

67. Thomas Elyot, *The Boke of the Gouernour*, ed. H. H. S. Croft (New York: Bert Franklin, 1967), 417. Elyot was an English "wit," along with others, singled out by Jonson as worthy of the English nation (*Disc* 911).

68. David Cast, *The Calumny of Appelles: A Study in the Humanist Tradition* (New Haven: Yale University Press, 1981), 32.

69. Ibid., 77. "In 1531, Sir Thomas Elyot included the description of Apelles' allegory in his book, *The Gouernour*. Doubtless it was this citation that suggested to the artist Antonio Toto that he might give a painting of this subject to Henry VIII some mere seven years later, recognizing that the theme was one now known and thus readable in England. The visual models of Raphael and Mantegna were powerful enough to lay the foundations for what we might think of as a self-generating tradition. But behind them — in fact or theory — was a text, or the kind of explanation that a text, and only a text, could provide."

For extended discussion of Thomas Elyot's chapter in relation to Antonio Toto's painting, see David Cast, "Sir Thomas Elyot's Description of Detraction and a Lost painting by Antonio Toto," *In Memoriam Otto J. Brendel: Essays in Archaeology and the Humanities*, ed. L. Bonfante and H. von Heintze (Mainz, Germany: Verlag Philipp von Zabern, 1976), 215–25.

70. Cast, *The Calumny of Appelles*, 87.

71. Jonson viewed poetry and painting as closely related, imitative arts: "Poetry and picture are arts of a like nature, and both are busy about

imitation" (*Disc* 1523–24). His discussion includes the differing cognitive responses to the two arts as well as techniques in the visual arts. He also discusses important European visual artists, many of whose works he could have known only through reports of others (1524–1600). His personal conflict with Inigo Jones does not obscure his respect for visual art, even though he privileged poetry over painting given its essential appeal to the understanding. See n. 47, above on poetry and painting as "sister arts."

72. Gill, "Renaissance Conventions," 216.

73. "CORDATUS: The author's friend; a man inly acquainted with the scope and drift of his plot: of a discreet and understanding judgement; and has the place of a moderator" (Jonson, *Every Man Out*, 110).

74. Plutarch, *On Envy and Hate*, trans. Philip H. De Lacy and Benedict Einarson, in *Moralia* (London: William Heinemann, 1959), 8:95.

75. Ibid., 107.

76. Aristotle, *Rhetoric*, trans. W. Rhys Roberts, in *Works*, ed. Jonathan Barnes (Princeton: Princeton University Press, 1985), 2:1387a9.

77. Ibid., 1387b35–1388a2.

78. Ibid., 1388a31–32.

79. Ibid., 1388a34–35.

80. "ASPER his Character: He is of an ingenious and free spirit, eager and constant in reproof, without fear controlling the world's abuses; One whom no servile hope of gain or frosty apprehension of danger can make to be a parasite either to time, place or opinion" (Jonson, *Every Man Out*, 101).

81. John Davies, "To my well accomplish'd friend Mr Ben. Iohnson. Epi. 156" in H & S, 11.379–80.

82. Jonson's self-scrutiny of envy as a destabilizing personal threat to truth also expresses a satirist's broad cultural concern about its threat to society. At the same time, Jonson knew only too well that satirical attack pretending to serve the common good could be mere detraction based on selfish envy and malice.

Jonson's continuing interest in the relationships between envy and truth can be seen, in part, as a product of the satirical climate in his competitive environment. It is notable that the opposition between truth and envy (often delimited as "detraction") was a given in the formal satire of the 1590s. In the "Prologue" to "LIB. I." of *Virigidemiarum* (1597), Joseph Hall states the obvious:

> I First aduenture, with fool-hardie might
> To tread the steps of perilous despight:
> I first aduenture: follow me who list,
> And be the second English Satyrist.
> Enuie waits on my backe, Truth on my side:
> Enuie will be my Page, and truth my Guide.

> Enuie the margent holds, and Truth the line:
> Truth doth approue, but Enuy doth repine. (1–8)

(Joseph Hall, *Collected Poems*, ed. A. Davenport [Liverpool: University Press, 1949], 11). This poem was immediately preceded by "His Defiance to *Envie*" (7), about which Davenport notes (160): "This prefatory poem seems to have set a fashion. To his *Scourge of Villanie* (1598), Marston prefixed a poem entitled 'To Detraction.' His 'Defiance to Enuy' is prefixed to T. M.'s *Micro-Cynicon* (1599), and John Weever imitates Hall in the prefatory verses to his *Epigrammes* (1599)" (160). The rivalrous Marston was no less ready to take up Hall's challenge to become the second English Juvenalian satirist than he was to enter the lists against Jonson in the War of the Theatres.

The normative place of "truth" in sixteenth century formal English satire is categorically set forth in Thomas Drant's 1566 definition of formal satire: "The Satyrist loves truthe, none more then he, / An utter foe to fraude in eache degree." See Mary Claire Randolph, "Thomas Drant's Definition of Satire, 1566," *N&Q* 180 (1941): 417. Jonson wrote no formal Roman satire, although his comical satires and epigrams address the same standard opposition between truth and envy asserted by Hall.

83. Cf. Ian Donaldson, "Looking Sideways: Jonson, Shakespeare, and the Myths of Envy," *Ben Jonson Journal* 8 (2001): 1–22. Donaldson addresses the entrenched critical habit, beginning in the eighteenth century, of unfairly whipping Jonson with Shakespeare's strengths, in spite of Jonson's productive influence in their collaborative friendship. Donaldson also finds generosity in Jonson's retrospective assessment of Shakespeare's achievement in "To the Memory of My Beloved, The Author, Mr William Shakespeare, etc."

Notes to Chapter Five

All citations from Milton's prose are from *Complete Prose Works of John Milton*, gen. ed. Don M. Wolfe et al., 8 vols. (New Haven: Yale University Press, 1953–82), hereafter cited as *CPW*. Citations are given by volume and page numbers parenthetically within the text.

All citations of Milton's poetry are from *John Milton: Complete Poetry and Major Prose*, ed. Merritt Y. Hughes (Indianapolis: The Odyssey Press, 1957), hereafter cited as *Complete Poetry and Prose*. Book and line numbers are given parenthetically within the text.

1. *A Second Defence of the English People [Pro Populo Anglicano Defensio Secunda]*, *CPW*, 4.1.554, 557. Hereafter referred to as *A Second Defence*.

2. *[Pro Populo Anglicano Defensio]*. *CPW*, 4:1. Hereafter referred to as *First Defence*.

3. *The Reason of Church-Government, CPW,* 1:808: "Lastly, I should not chuse this manner of writing wherin knowing my self inferior to my self, led by the genial power of nature to another task, I have the use, as I may account it, but of my left hand." Milton's memorable distinction between the respective works of his left and right hands has left an indelible imprint on Milton commentary, even though the ambidexterity becomes less precise as Milton's practice as a prose writer developed. See David Loewenstein, "Milton and the Poetics of Defense" in *Politics, Poetics, and Hermeneutics in Milton's Prose,* ed. D. Loewenstein and J. G. Turner (Cambridge: Cambridge University Press, 1990), 171–92. Loewenstein demonstrates persuasively how Milton increasingly invested his polemical prose with his poetics, whereby the prose can be seen converging with the poetry. His primary example is *A Second Defence.*

4. Eph. 6:10–17.

5. Christopher Hill, *Antichrist in Seventeenth-Century England* (London: Oxford University Press, 1971): "So the second Beast in Revelation 13 and the Man of Sin in 2 Thessalonians 2 were traditionally identified with the Antichrist of John's Epistles, and all three with the Pope" (4). "Antichrist, the Beast, was not merely the Pope as a person, however, but the papacy as an institution which subsumed within itself all the evil, coercive, repressive aspects of the secular Empire" (5). "Milton, who had taken pains to associate Charles I with Antichrist in *The Tenure of Kings and Magistrates,* has a similar call to a crusade against antichristian monarchy all over Europe in *Eikonoklastes.* 'The present interest of the saints,' declared a pamphlet of 1649, is to 'combine together against the antichristian powers of the world.' 'Kings, yea Parliaments also and magistrates' must be put down before Christ's kingdom can be erected" (105).

6. *A Second Defence, CPW,* 4:1.622–27.

7. Milton's aggression and intemperate overreaction as a polemicist have set modern teeth on edge. For example, see Frederick Lovett Tafts, preface to *An Apology for Smectymnuus:* "What is revealed . . . is not always pleasant: sharp sarcasm, bitter wrangling, unreasoning and even indecent vituperation, pettiness . . . dealing in personalities, his anger, his plain bad manners" (*CPW,* 1:662). Also see William Kerrigan, *The Sacred Complex: On the Psychogenesis of "Paradise Lost"* (Cambridge: Harvard University Press, 1983): "His violence as a controversialist, after allowances are made for the rude rancor conventional in public disputes of the time, remains astonishing" (63).

Milton was especially abusive in his self-defensive *ad hominem* counterattack on Claudius Salmasius in the *First Defence.* See William Riley Parker, *Milton's Contemporary Reputation* (Columbus: The Ohio State University Press, 1940): Salmasius was one of the "leading scholars of Christendom (and a man whom he was proud to meet in argument)." But in Milton's hands he becomes a "fool, monster, pimp, parasite, Judas, mongrel, slave, buffoon, scarecrow, liar, turncoat, midget, madman, coward, slave-dealer, pander, pursesnatcher, scoundrel, and a variety of birds and beasts including cuckoo, dunghill cock, and filthy swine" (61).

8. [*Pro se defensio contra Alexandrum Morum*]. *CPW*, 4:2. Hereafter cited as *A Defence of Himself.*

9. [*Defensio Regia, Pro Carolo I*]. CPW, 4.2.983–1035.

10. [*Regii Sanguinis Clamor ad Coelum Adversus Parricidas Anglicanos*]. *CPW*, 4.2.1036–81. Hereafter referred to as *Cry to Heaven.*

11. The legal and judicial consequences of this dalliance are treated in compelling detail in two articles by Paul Sellin: "Alexander Morus Before the Hof van Holland: Some Insight into Seventeenth Century Polemics with John Milton," *PAANS* 7 (1994–95): 1–11; "Alexander Morus and John Milton II: Milton, Morus, and Infanticide," *PAAN* 9 (1995–96): 277–85. For the broader context involving the three formal defenses, as well as the Elisabeth Guerret events, see chapter 9, "'Tireless . . . for the Sake of Liberty' 1652–1654," in Barbara Lewalski, *The Life of John Milton* (Oxford: Blackwell Publishers, 2000), 278–318.

12. [*Fides Publica, Contra Calumnia Ioannis Miltoni*] *CPW*, 4.2. 1082–1128.

13. "There are two crimes of which I accused you: one is insult and outrage; the other, debauchery. The insult is that you stand forth as the author of that most clamorous lampoon against us; for that you should think that you could not sufficiently damage the people of England unless you damaged me exceedingly beyond all others — this I consider as an honor to me rather than an injury. But to recount your debaucheries, as they deserved, I regarded as no burden, for that reason which I would make plain: that he who published that *Cry* must be considered its author, and certainly no one but yourself has yet appeared from whose chaste lips that outcry should have burst forth. What do you say to this? You deny that you are the author of this pasquinade; and so sedulously, so prolixly do you deny it — though yet that little book does not at all displease you — that to me you seem more afraid of being discovered as the author of that libel than of confessing to those many infamous acts charged against you" (*CPW*, 4.2.701).

14. There are two major psychological interpretations of Milton and his works: Kerrigan, *The Sacred Complex*; John T. Shawcross, *John Milton: The Self and the World* (Lexington: The University Press of Kentucky, 1993). Neither interpretation foregrounds the implications of Milton's excessive defensiveness against blame, although both interpretations are compatible with this emphasis. The central claim by Shawcross is that Milton is an anal retentive: "Perspective on Milton always points to an anal retentive personality, one not only who is self-disciplined, acquisitive, and obstinate, but one who is not given to airing his accomplishments or being fully satisfied with them once they have been aired. Note, for example, the alteration of the text of *Comus*

in 1645 after its first publication in 1637, of the 'Nativity Ode' in 1673, and so significantly of *Paradise Lost* in its second edition. But the prose, too, is revised: the second edition of *The Doctrine and Disciplines of Divorce* (1644) is almost double the length of the first (1643); *Eikonoklastes* and *The Tenure of Kings and Magistrates* have additions, for the most part unimportant, however, in 1650 printings; and *The Ready and Easy Way*, within a month's time in March/April 1660, almost becomes two different books" (249). Defensiveness against criticism and blame is a natural corollary of such a nature. Kerrigan's Freudian interpretation agrees in principle that Milton has an "anal retentive character: thrift, orderliness, and stubborness" (44). The virgin Lady Alice of *Comus* embodies Milton's own "defensive ethics epitomized by the anal child" (46). Her virginity is symptom of an Oedipal conflict informing Milton's character and works, which was resolved by the time of the late works. Virginity protects against both unsatisfied desire for maternal love and suppressed anger against the father's law, thereby slowing development of the mature superego that would eventually fulfill both. Milton's own progress toward Oedipal resolution is expressed through a mythology of inner and outer temptations in his works, and a vocabulary of defense frequently surfaces in Kerrigan's discussion of that mythology.

Also, see Michael Lieb, *Milton and the Culture of Violence* (Ithaca: Cornell University Press, 1994). Although not a biography per se, Lieb's study of Milton's penchant for violent polemics is informed by a chronological perspective on Milton's psychology. Milton's deep-seated fear of bodily mutilation and dismemberment, generalized into fear of any attack upon the self, transformed into virulent counterattack on his enemies. Lieb's analysis of Milton's psychology of violence, like Kerrigan's discussion, includes a vocabulary relating to self-defense.

15. See n. 7 above.

16. Fornicating, adulterous clergymen are targets difficult to miss, and Milton was a skilled and experienced satirical marksman. The sexual history and paltry morality of the well-named Morus had been publicized internationally. For one catalog of his sexual activities that suggests their geographical scope, see CPW, 4.2.777, n. 199.

17. Admittedly, Milton as an abusive polemicist was in good company; by no means was he the worst offender. Moreover, there were both biblical and classical justifications for the "rougher accent" (CPW, 1:662) used first to attack his prelatical opponents, then others like Salmasius and More later. No "spot, or blemish" (CPW, 1.871) could be left on his reputation without besmirching the truth in which he participates with the fullness of his person. He regards himself as a prophetic voice elected by God; and he is fighting Christian warfare armed with weapons issued by God.

For a more recent contextualization of Milton as a polemical, combative satirist, see John N. King, *Milton and Religious Controversy: Satire and Polemic in* Paradise Lost (Cambridge: Cambridge University

Press, 2000). King finds the pervasiveness of Milton's "pugnaciously sar-
donic side" even in *Paradise Lost*, where "invective, mockery, surly
insult, parody, and satire, even at some of its most sublime moments,
demonstrate how thoroughly the text is embedded in contemporary
affairs during an age of revolution and reaction" (2). The "broad framework of Reformation cultural and polemical practice" (18) in which
King places Milton is intended to explain, not to excuse Milton's characteristic behavior. Such a cleansing could be convincing if everyone else
in this polemical arena found it impossible to defend themselves without similar aggression, vengeance, and satirical abuse. But the contrary
is true.

    William Walwyn is a case in point. He was mightily abused in Thomas
Edwards's *Gangraena: or A Catalogue and Discovery of Many of the
Errours, Heresies, Blasphemies, and Pernicious Practices of the Sectaries
of This Time* (644). Walwyn defended himself in five separate responses
(1645–46) to the virulent *Gangraena* and its frontal attack upon religious
toleration and the sectaries. Walwyn's modern editor characterizes these
five tracts as follows: "Walwyn's five responses to *Gangraena* stand
out among the many responses and are among Walwyn's most attractive
pieces. The contrast to Edwards' relentless censure is highlighted by
Walwyn's steady appeal to reason, frequent flashes of humor and irony,
and ultimate reliance on love." See Barbara Taft's introduction to *The
Writings of William* Walwyn, ed. J. McMichael and B. Taft (Athens:
University of Georgia Press, 1989), 17. In his *Walwyn's Just Defense* (1649),
also significant in the mid-century literature of self-defense, he demonstrated the same qualities of reason, patience, and refusal to fan the fires
of abusive polemicism. The comparison and contrast with Milton are
instructive.

    18. See n. 13 above.

    19. Lieb, *Milton and the Culture of Violence*, 29. For a theoretical dis-
cussion of *sparagmos*, the destructive mutilation and dismemberment
of the body, plus its transformation as a generative force, see chapter 1,
"The Slaughter of the Saints," 13–37. For discussion of Milton's satiric
destruction of Alexander More and its sparagmatic importance in Milton's
works, especially see chapter nine, "The Humiliation of Priapus," 202–25.
I agree that the attack on More is a central text in our attempts to understand Milton's thought, although my emphases differ.

    20. Milton's irresolution in sexual matters clearly entered into the
subject matter of his works. For the claim that homoeroticism and
homosexuality contributed to this irresolution, see chapter 3 in Shawcross,
John Milton: The Self and the World. Chapters 11–13 contain a useful
discussion of sexuality and gender. Kerrigan is dubious about Shawcross's
claims of Milton's homosexuality. See *The Sacred Complex*, 49: "he was
not a homosexual. Although his friendship with Diodati has some traces
of homoerotic feeling . . . Shawcross's belief in a real sexual adventure

runs contrary to the regularities of his character manifested by the bulk of his writings." Michael Lieb finds in Milton an uncertainty about gender expressed as androgyny or bisexuality throughout his works. This uncertainty was less an issue of sexual behavior than his self-conscious defensiveness about the body, its identity, and its integrity. Especially see, "The Pursuit of the Lady," in *Milton and the Culture of Violence*, 83–114.

21. On Milton's conception of himself as a prophet, see William Kerrigan, *The Prophetic Milton* (Charlottesville: University Press of Virginia, 1974); Joseph Wittreich, "'A Poet Amongst Poets': Milton and the Tradition of Prophecy," in *Milton and the Line of Vision*, ed. Joseph Wittreich (Madison: University of Wisconsin Press, 1975); Joseph Wittreich, *Milton's Visionary Poetics: Milton's Tradition and his Legacy* (San Marino, CA: Huntington Library, 1979); Louis Martz, "Milton's Prophetic Voice: Moving Toward Paradise," in *Of Poetry and Politics: New Essays on Milton and His World*, ed. P. G. Stanwood (Binghamton, NY: Medieval and Renaissance Texts & Studies, 1995).

22. For the Lutheran background to the notion of multiple vocations or stations within a vocation, see my discussion in chapter 2 above. Also see Philip S. Watson, "Luther's Doctrine of Vocation," *Scottish Journal of Theology* 2 (1949): 364–77; and Gustav Wingren, *Luther on Vocation*, trans. Carl C. Rasmussen (Philadelphia: Muhlenberg Press, 1957), 4–5.

For a detailed discussion of Milton's notion of vocation in its Reformed context, see John Spencer Hill, *John Milton: Poet, Priest and Prophet: A Study of Divine Vocation in Milton's Poetry and Prose* (London: MacMillan, 1979).

23. For the influence of classical oratory in Milton, see Joseph Wittreich, "'The Crown of Eloquence': The Figure of the Orator in Milton's Prose Works," in *Achievements of the Left Hand: Essays on the Prose of John Milton*, ed. Michael Lieb and John Shawcross (Amherst: The University of Massachusetts Press, 1974), 3–54; for the classical background to Milton's satire, see Joel Morkan, "Wrath and Laughter: Milton's Ideas on Satire," *SP* 69 (1972): 475–95.

24. See James Holly Hanford, "Milton and the Art of War," *SP* 18 (1921): 232–66.

25. For one example, see *An Apology for Smectymnuus in CPW*, 1.883–86.

26. Arthur E. Barker, *Milton and the Puritan Dilemma, 1641–1660* (Toronto: University of Toronto Press, 1942), 234.

27. See Charles H. McIlwain, *The High Court of Parliament and Its Supremacy: An Historical Essay on the Boundaries Beween Legislation and Adjudication in England* (New Haven: Yale University Press, 1910). According to McIlwain, the notion of parliament as the highest court in the judiciary dates from Norman times, with many vestiges remaining even in the twentieth century. The crucial change from a judicial to a

legislative conception of parliamentary functions began with the Long Parliament in reaction to the Stuart monarchy. But this is a matter of a developing emphasis on Parliament as a sovereign legislative assembly, while continuing to assume that it is still the highest court in the judiciary. McIlwain notes Milton's strong support of this changed emphasis on parliament's legislative sovereignty (94).

28. Robert Thomas Fallon, *Milton in Government* (University Park: The Pennsylvania State University Press, 1993), 15–16.

29. Jonathan Goldberg, "Dating Milton," in *Soliciting Interpretation: Literary Theory and Seventeenth-Century English Poetry,* ed. E. Harvey and K. Maus (Chicago: The University of Chicago Press), 200.

30. Ibid., 201.

31. Ibid., 200. Also see: "From the position of any of the historicisms, new or old, that I have outlined here, the dating of the sonnet that I have suggested would be unacceptable, since the temporality it claims has eschewed the a priori truth of teleological chronology or the possibility that the historic moment is present-to-itself, that it is outside of subsequent narrativization. (The temporality sketched here could be called, after Freud, Nachtraglichkeit, and would insist that what is retrospectively constructed is not necessarily, is necessarily *not* what was; rather, in Derrida's elegant phrase, it would be 'a past that has never been present,' nor would it be present in its rewriting.)" (205).

32. Ibid., 219.

33. Loewenstein, "Milton and the Poetics of Defense," 183.

34. See n. 14 above.

35. The phrase is borrowed from Dayton Haskin, *Milton's Burden of Interpretation* (Philadelphia: University of Pennsylvania Press, 1994). See nn. 50 and 51 below.

36. For a useful and persuasive discussion of the biographical criticism of Milton's works, see Ashraf H. A. Rushdy, *The Empty Garden: The Subject of Late Milton* (Pittsburgh: University of Pittsburgh Press, 1992), 364–78. More generally, see the rest of Rushdy's discussion in his chapter 5, "Confronting the Author: The Art of Politics," 345–437.

37. Marshall Grossman, *"Authors to Themselves": Milton and the Revelation of History* (Cambridge: Cambridge University Press, 1987), 2. Grossman continues suggestively: "They have the authority of authors, that is, of writers, and they will augment or magnify the life histories they write as they accumulate experiences. As progenitors of the human race, they will similarly magnify human history by augmenting, magnifying, authoring a 'race of worshippers'" (7.630).

38. Anthony Paul Kerby, *Narrative and the Self* (Bloomington: Indiana University Press, 1991), 41.

39. Ibid., 8.

40. Paul Ricoeur, *Oneself as Another,* trans. Kathleen Blamey (Chicago: The University of Chicago Press, 1992), 179.

41. Ibid., 141.

42. Paul Ricoeur, *Time and Narrative*, trans. K. McLaughlin and D. Pellauer (Chicago: The University of Chicago Press, 1984), 1:198–200.

43. William G. Riggs, "The Poet and Satan in *Paradise Lost*," in *Milton Studies*, vol. 2, ed. James D. Simmonds (Pittsburgh: University of Pittsburgh Press, 1970), 80.

44. Ibid., 63.

45. Milton's use of Satan, as complex perspective on his own experience, does not disengage Satan as a vehicle for Milton's satirical religious polemic. See King, *Milton and Religious Controversy*, esp. chapter 3, "Satan and the Demonic Conclave," 44–68.

46. See the facsimile title page of this edition in *Complete Poetry and Prose*, 470.

47. See Stephen B. Dobranski, "Text and Context for *Paradise Regain'd* and *Samson Agonistes*," in *Altering Eyes: New Perspectives on* Samson Agonistes, ed. Mark R. Kelley and Joseph Wittreich (Newark: University of Delaware Press, 2002), 30–53. Dobranski discusses Milton's explicit actions taken to publish the two poems together, encouraging readers "to experience the two works as a unified structure" (31).

48. Lewalski, *The Life of John Milton*, 523.

49. Joseph Wittreich, *Interpreting* Samson Agonistes (Princeton: Princeton University Press, 1986).

50. Joseph Wittreich, *Shifting Contexts: Reinterpreting* Samson Agonistes (Pittsburgh: Duquesne University Press, 2002), 196:

> But in *Samson Agonistes* Milton allows for our measuring not only himself but Cromwell against Samson, his Englishmen against the Israelites, and those other Englishmen against the Philistines. In doing so, he discovers that distinctions blur, that there is too much of Samson on both sides — and too much of the Philistine; that there is not enough of the spiritual Israel on his own side to win the revolution, let alone sustain its ideals.

51. David Loewenstein, "The Kingdom Within: Radical Religious Culture and the Politics of *Paradise Regained*," *Literature and History* 3 (1994): 63–89. For Loewenstein's expanded discussion of Milton's radical activism and iconoclasm related to *Samson Agonistes*, see chapter 6, "Spectacle of Power: *Samson Agonistes* and the Drama of History," in *Milton and the Drama of History* (Cambridge: Cambridge University Press, 1990), 126–51.

52. Lieb, *Milton and the Culture of Violence*, 235–36. For Lieb's justification of Samson's violence, see the concluding chapter, "The Politics of Violence," 226–63.

53. "Even the heroic Samson, though his countrymen reproached him saying, Judges 15, 'Knowest thou not that the Philistines are rulers over us?' still made war single-handed on his masters, and, whether prompted by God or by his own valor, slew at one stroke not one but a host of his

country's tyrants, having first made prayer to God for his aid. Samson therefore thought it not impious but pious to kill those masters who were tyrants over his country, even though most of her citizens did not balk at slavery" (4.1.402).

54. John Guillory, "The Father's House: *Samson Agonistes* in Its Historical Moment," in *Re-Membering Milton: Essays on the Texts and Traditions*, ed. M. Nyquist and M. Ferguson (New York: Methuen, 1988), 171.

55. Helen Gardner, introduction to John Donne, *The Divine Poems* (Oxford: Clarendon Press, 1964), xxxi.

56. For a discussion of dating Sonnet 19, see Shawcross, *John Milton: The Self and the World*, 168–69.

57. John Shawcross, *The Uncertain World of* Samson Agonistes (Cambridge: D.S. Brewer, 2001), 4.

58. Stanley Fish, *How Milton Works* (Cambridge, MA: The Belknap Press of Harvard University Press, 2001), 478.

59. Mary Ann Radzinowicz, "*Paradise Regained* as Hermeneutic Combat," *University of Hartford Studies in Literature* 15 (1983): 99–103.

60. Haskin, *Milton's Burden of Interpretation*, chapters 4 and 5.

61. Stanley E. Fish, "Spectacle and Evidence in *Samson Agonistes*," *Critical Inquiry* 15 (1989), 567.

62. For a useful discussion of Samson's alleged spiritual regeneration, see Rushdy, *The Empty Garden*, 292–306.

63. Ibid., 306–21.

Notes to Postscript

1. Brian Vickers, introduction to *Francis Bacon*, ed. Brian Vickers (Oxford: Oxford University Press, 1966), xxviii.

2. Ibid., i.

3. Paul H. Kocher, "Francis Bacon and His Father," *HLQ* 21 (1958): 157.

4. Markku Peltonen, "Introduction," in *The Cambridge Companion to Bacon*, ed. M. Peltonen (Cambridge: Cambridge University Press, 1996), 14. Hereafter cited as *Cambridge Bacon*.

5. Francis Bacon, "To the Right Reverend Father in God, Lancelot Andrewes" in *Works*, ed. James Spedding (London: Longmans, Green, Reader and Dyer, 1874; reprint Stuttgart-Bad Cannstatt: Friedrich Frommann Verlag Gunther Holzboog, 1963), 14:372–73.

6. Vickers, *Francis Bacon*, xxxvii.

7. Ibid., xxxviii.

8. See Brian Vickers, "Bacon and Rhetoric," in *Cambridge Bacon*: "Bacon must have been introduced to rhetoric at an early age, born as he was into one of the leading humanist families in England. George

Puttenham, author of one of the most humane Renaissance works in rhetoric and poetics, arguing that 'our writing and speaches publike ought to be figurative,' instanced as examples of public speakers who had mastered 'the use of rhetorical figures' and could therefore speak 'cunningly and eloquently' both Bacon's father '*Sir Nicholas Bacon* Lord Keeper of the great Seale' and his uncle (Lord Burghley) 'the now Lord Treasurer of England . . . From whose lippes I have seen to proceede more grave and naturall eloquence, than from all the Oratours of Oxford and Cambridge . . .' Puttenham records that 'I have come to the Lord Keeper Sir *Nicholas Bacon* & found him sitting in his gallery alone with the works of *Quintilian* before him, in deede he was a most eloquent man, and rare learning and wisedome as even I knew England to breed . . .' The precision of Puttenham's testimony as to the book being read, coupled with its vagueness about the time and place of occurrence, may put this anecdote in the category of the mythical rather than the historical, but its collocation of rhetoric and Tudor humanism is undoubtedly accurate" (204–05).

9. Ibid., 205.

10. Margot Todd, "The Spiritualized Household," in *Christian Humanism and the Puritan Social Order* (Cambridge: Cambridge University Press, 1987), 96–117.

11. Lynne Magnusson, "Widowhood and Linguistic Capital: The Rhetoric and Reception of Anne Bacon's Epistolary Advice," *ELH* 31 (2001): 5.

12. Ibid., 3.

13. Anne Bacon quoted in Francis Bacon, *Works*, 8:112–13.

14. Elizabeth Jocelin, *The Mothers Legacy to her Vnborn Childe*, ed. Jean LeDrew Metcalfe (Toronto: University of Toronto Press, 2000), 43, n. 1. Hereafter cited as *Legacy* with page numbers given parenthetically within the text.

15. Notably, a facsimile edition Jocelin's *Legacy* is included in the *Mother's Advice Books*, selected and introduced by Betty S. Travitsky (Aldershot, Hants, England: Ashgate, 2001). This is Goad's 1624 "Manuell," a portable edition.

16. Magnusson, "Widowhood and Linguistics Capital," 30–31.

17. Ibid., 28.

18 1 Tim. 5 in *The Geneva Bible: A Facsimile of the 1560 Edition*, ed. Lloyd Berry (Madison: The University of Wisconsin, 1969), 99.

Index

Achilles, 91
Adam (in *Paradise Lost*), 288–90, 299–301
adventures, 53–54, 86–90
Aeneas (fictional character), 69
Aers, David, 147
Ajax, 273
Albany (fictional character), 41
allegory, 89, 92–94, 341n34
Alma (fictional character), 78–79
ambition. *See* patronage system
Amoret (fictional character), 59–60
Amoretti (Spenser), 97
"Anagram, The" (Donne), 154
Analecton Anglobritannicon (Selden), 199
androgyny, 80, 86, 154–55, 180–83
Animadversions Upon the "Remonstrants" Defence, against Smectymnuus (Milton), 284
Anniversaries (Donne), 159–62
Antichrist, the pope as, 31–32, 260, 365n5
anti-papalism, 31–32
Antiquity of Faerie (fictional book in *The Fairie Queene*), 79
anxiety, 351n48
Apelles, 245–46, 362n69
apocalyptic elements, 92–93
Apologica Ecclesia Anglicanae (Jewell), 324
Archimago (fictional character), 61–63
Areopagitica (Milton), 290

Argante (fictional character), 58–59
Aristotle, 13, 251–52, 333–34n30
Arruntius (fictional character), 232–34, 240
Artegall (fictional character), 57–58, 65–66, 68, 88–89, 92–93
Arthur (fictional character), 52–53, 56–60, 64, 67–68, 77–81, 88, 92–97
artistic rivalry, 247–48, 255–56
Asper (fictional character), 250, 252, 363n80
Augustine, 181
Augustus (fictional character), 242, 244, 246–47

Bacon, Anne Cooke, 81–83, 323–25, 328–29
Bacon, Anthony, 322, 325
Bacon, Francis, 8, 225, 321–29
Bacon, Nicholas, 82, 321–22
Bald, R. C., 146, 156, 166–67
Barbour, Reid, 46–47
Barish, Jonas, 38, 240
Barker, Arthur, 290
"Batter my heart, three person'd God" (Donne), 159
Becon, Thomas, 16, 70–71, 83
Bedford, Lucy, 147–48, 157–58, 173, 222
Belphoebe (fictional character), 61
Belsey, Catherine, 2–4
Bible, 28–29, 33, 70. *See also* Christ; Jesus; John (Apostle); Paul; Peter (Apostle)

Poetaster (Jonson), 242–44, 246–48
poetry and poets: and the common
  good, 207, 239, 243–44, 248;
  Donne's love poetry, 152–56;
  and the self, 48; in service to
  monarchy, 95–96; and truth, 247;
  and virtue, 68–69, 90–92; and
  vocation, 94–95
Poins, Ned (in *Henry IV*), 104–05
Ponet, John, 35–36
Pontia. *See* Guerret, Elizabeth
Pope, Alexander, 193, 258
pope, as Antichrist, 31–32, 260,
  365n5
professions. *See* vocation
prophetic vision, 92–94
Protestantism. *See* Reformed
  Protestantism
Psalms, 262–63
Pseudo Martyr (Donne), 24
The Public Faith of Alexander More
  (More), 262, 276
public service, 12, 14, 39, 322
"publike weale." *See* common good
Puttenham, George, 372–73n8

Rabkin, Norman, 136
Radigund (fictional character), 60–61
Radzinowicz, Mary Ann, 316
Raleigh, Walter, 50–55, 87, 359n51
Rambus, Richard, 98–99
Ratcliffe, Margaret, 218, 224
reason, 11, 66–67, 271–72
Reason of Church Government
  (Milton), 281, 287, 293
reciprocal actions, 211–13
reciprocal duties. *See* hierarchical
  order
Redcrosse (fictional character), 57,
  61–63, 77–79, 86–89, 92–94
Reformation, 9–10
Reformed Protestantism: and the
  Cooke sisters, 81–83, 323–25;
  and learning, 70; and public
  service, 322; Spenser and, 84; and
  vocation, 3, 8–10, 15–16, 50–51,
  105–12; women and, 83–85,
  324–29
regicide, 25, 126, 261
religion: and the English Renaissance,
  2–3, 43; of friendship, 169–71
Renaissance: and civic humanism, 3;

views on envy, 251–52,
  363–64n82; views on slander,
  245–46, 286
Renaissance Self-Fashioning
  (Greenblatt), 4
repentance, 162–63
resistance theory, 35–38
resurrection, bodily, 144–45, 149–50
Revelation (John), 92–93
Richard II, 126
Ricoeur, Paul, 294
Riggs, David, 208, 256
Riggs, William, 296
rivalry, artistic, 247–48, 255–56
Roe, Thomas, 195–97, 218
role-playing, 122–24, 128, 141
Rushdy, Ashraf, 317

Sabine, Maureen, 159–60
Sabinus (fictional character), 231–33
Sackville, Edward, 209, 211–13, 216
"The Sacrifice" (Herbert), 25
Saint George, 77
Salmasius, Claudius, 261, 268–69,
  274, 365–66n7
Samson Agonistes (Milton), 301,
  306–19
Samson (in *Samson Agonistes*),
  306–19
Satan, 283
Satan (in *Paradise Lost*), 296–307
Satyrene (fictional character), 63
Savile, Henry, 219
"Scandal" (Lucian), 245
*A Second Defence of the People of
  England* (Milton), 260–62, 268–71,
  278–80, 293
Sejanus (Jonson), 230–34
Selden, John, 199–201, 204–06, 216,
  237
self: bifurcated, 44–45; centered,
  195–215, 355n3; and continuities,
  7; decentered, 1–8; definition of,
  3–5, 43, 48–49; in *The Fairie
  Queene*, 4; inner and outer,
  43–46; integrated body and soul,
  149–50; Jonson on true self,
  195–215, 355n3; and narrative
  interpretation, 295; physical,
  278–79; and poetry, 48; public
  and private, 123–27, 141–42; in
  Shakespeare's Henriad, 138–45;

and vocation, 43–47; women's role in forming, 328
self-defensiveness and Milton, 259–75, 280, 282–91, 297–301, 311–19, 365–66n7
self-esteem, 279–91
self-knowledge, 255–57
Seneca, 211, 213
senses, 226–27
Sermons (Donne), 145, 180
Seymour, Anne, 83–84
Seymour, Edward, 83
Shakespeare, William: Christ imagery in Henriad, 130–31; and Jonson, 192–94, 241; and vocation, 37–43, 49, 103–13; works by: *Henry IV* and *Henry V*, 103–05, 112–43; *King Lear*, 1, 37–43
Shami, Jeanne, 189–90
Shawcross, John, 313, 366n13
The Shepheardes Calender (Spenser), 84–85, 95–98
"A Shorte Treatise of Politike Power" (Ponet), 35–36
Shuger, Debora, 2, 43–45
Sidney, Philip: and allegory, 341n34; and civic humanism, 93–98; compared with Spenser, 91–92, 97–98; and Elizabeth I, 9; and vocation, 8–10, 93–98, 342n40; works by: *A Defence of Poesy*, 68–69, 90–92
Sidney, William, 223–24
Silus (fictional character), 231–33
sin, 180–81, 352–53n62
Sinfield, Alan, 2, 5, 10
Skinner, Quentin, 16, 36
slander, 245–46, 286. *See also* false witness
Smectymnuans, 260, 284
Smith, Thomas, 16–17
social responsibility. *See* common good
Son, the. *See* Jesus
Songs and Sonnets (Donne), 164
Sordido (fictional character), 251
soul, human, 158–59
Spenser, Edmund: and civic humanism, 93–98; as colonial secretary, 99; compared with Sidney, 91–92, 97–98; and Elizabeth I, 81, 85–88, 96; and

female readers, 52, 81–86; in Ireland, 343n45; letter to Raleigh, 50–55, 87; and the person, 77–81; and Reformed Protestantism, 84; roots in British national culture, 77–81; Virgil's influence on, 95–98; and vocation, 49–51, 93–98; works by: *Amoretti*, 97; *Epithalamium*, 97; *The Fairie Queene*, 4, 50–71, 77–81, 85–102, 341n29; *Fowre Hymnes*, 97; *The Shepheardes Calender*, 84–85, 95–98; *A View of the Present State of Ireland*, 99
Squire of Dames (fictional character), 58
Strier, Richard, 39
Stuart, Esmé, 199, 209
subjection, 32–34
subjectivity, 2–8
The Subject of Tragedy (Belsey), 2
succession, 125–30, 133–34, 142
surrogacy, 131–32
Syminges, John, 150–51

Tacitus, 219
Tasso, Torquato, 69
Taylor, Charles, 295
The Temple (Herbert), 45
temptation, 305–07, 313–14
Tennenhouse, Leonard, 136
The Tenure of Kings and Magistrates (Milton), 261, 283
textual revisions, 292–94, 366–67n14
theater. *See* drama
Tiberius (fictional character), 231–33
Timber of Discoveries (Jonson), 216
Timon (fictional character), 68
Titles of Honor (Selden), 199–201, 204–06, 216
Todd, Margot, 21, 324
"to his Mistris Going to Bed" (Donne), 154
"To my well'accomplish'd friend Mr. Ben Johnson" (Davies), 253
"To the Countesse of Bedford" (Donne), 158
"To Penshurst" (Jonson), 241
A Treatise of the Vocations (Perkins), 16, 108–12
Trinitarian theology, 45–47
Truewit (fictional character), 236–40